THE BEST
AMERICAN
MAGAZINE
WRITING

2003

THE BEST AMERICAN MAGAZINE WRITING 2003

American Society of Magazine Editors

Perennial

An Imprint of HarperCollins*Publishers*

FIRST EDITION

Designed by Nancy Singer Olaguera

Library of Congress Cataloging-in-Publication Data is available.

ISBN 0-06-056775-9

03 04 05 06 07 ❖/RRD 10 9 8 7 6 5 4 3 2 1

In memory of Art Cooper and Mike Kelly,
masters of the craft of magazine journalism

Contents

Introduction

I grew up over a dentist's office. In certain rooms of the house we could hear the soft gurgle of the spit sink downstairs, the supersonic howl of the drill, the relieved see-you-next-time murmurs of the numb and the cured as they headed for the waiting room and the shady street outside. This was suburban New Jersey in the sixties and seventies. The practice was modest: one dentist, one receptionist-hygienist, two chairs, a few drawers filled with silvery treasures for the children, rings that flashed Batman when turned to the right, Robin when turned to the left. To the occasional horror of the patients—middle-class Irish and Italian Catholics, a few Jews, one ex-first baseman for the Yankees—the "dentist's office music" in this dentist's office was not Muzak, as was the custom in those pre–"soft rock" days, but Muddy Waters, Howlin' Wolf, Bessie Smith. The dentist was my father.

Sometimes, after school or on Saturday mornings when my father was seeing patients, I would hang out in his waiting room, and, slumped in one of the scoop-shaped yellow plastic chairs, read through piles of the magazines that he subscribed to and kept in clear plastic folders, the better to keep them crisp and nicely stacked. It was a small, cool room, and I read there for hours, my own periodical reading room, making my way through the pictorial puzzles in *Boys' Life* ("Find the scissors, lawn clippers, and stapler in this landscape. Win prizes!"), exploring the human body in *Reader's Digest* ("I am Joe's pancreas!"), surveying page after page of the war in Vietnam in *Life,* and laughing at the cartoons of James Stevenson and George Booth in *The New Yorker.* For the practice he kept, my father could probably have been accused of oversubscribing. He had stacks of magazines. There was *Esquire, Highlights, Look, Time* or *Newsweek* depending on obscure annual caprice, some outdoor and fishing magazines (my brother's preserve), some fashion magazines, especially *Vogue.* There was nothing ultra-hip (*Rolling Stone, Crawdaddy, Creem*) or ultra-highbrow (readers of *Telos* would have to find another dentist), nor had the consuming magazines of celebritydom and gossip arrived—the *People* leviathan had not yet awoken. And my father, while no snob, was not any more ready for *The National Enquirer* in his waiting room and office than he was for Percy Faith.

As time went by, and the now dated magazines were allowed to make their journey up the basement stairs to where we lived, I spent even more time with them and began to read, it seemed to me, the most exciting journalism imaginable. Gay Talese on Frank Sinatra. Hunter Thompson on the 1972 Presidential campaign. Pauline Kael on the movies. Michael Herr on Vietnam. Roger Angell on Bob Gibson. Sara Davidson on the scene around Venice, California. Frances FitzGerald. Joan Didion. Frank Deford. It is hard to explain the strange thrill of reading something of lasting value when it comes out in a form of ephemeral pretensions: a magazine. Perhaps it's like hearing a great song on the radio, immediately, unexpectedly, long before the song is on the charts and you've bought the album. Even now I love going to the library and spending time with the bound volumes of old magazines: the jumbo-formatted *Fortune,* the short-lived *Flair,* the soigné *Vanity Fair,* Mays- and Mantle-dominated copies of *Sports Illustrated. Collier's. The Saturday Evening Post. Harper's.* "The old custom of binding up magazines and periodicals in book form," George Orwell wrote in one of his "As I Please" columns, "seems to have gone out almost entirely, which is a pity, for a year's issue of even a very stupid magazine is more readable after a lapse of time than the majority of books. . . . A good six-pennyworth was a year's issue of the *Cornhill* when either Trollope or Thackeray, I forget which, was editing it. . . . The great fascination of these old magazines is the completeness with which they 'date.' Absorbed in the affairs of the moment, they tell one about political fashions and tendencies which are hardly mentioned in the more general history books."

As in much else, Orwell was right. There are "very stupid" magazines. There are routine magazines, dull magazines, serviceable magazines. But what's interesting, even subversive, about the American magazine is the degree to which the form is utterly open-ended in its possibilities. Magazines can be the pile in the corner you haven't got around to throwing out, but the magazine is also a form that is elastic in its ambitions and in its aesthetics, capable of almost anything. When I made the change from writing to editing at *The New Yorker,* my friend, Henry Finder, the magazine's editorial director, gave me a bunch of old magazines: literary magazines, sports magazines, fashion magazines, humor magazines, novelty magazines. There was something deeply moving about that heap of print that went well beyond my own memories of the titles; every magazine there, each in its own way, suggested a possibility of form, of vibrancy. If Henry meant his gift to be one of suggestion, editor to editor, well, I hope I got the message.

Of the many realms of expression—humor, photography, poetry, painting, cartoons, fiction—that have been essential elements of the American magazine, journalism is foremost. And journalism is, mainly, what is celebrated each year by the American Society of Magazine Editors. Not long ago, New York University called on a group of writers, editors, and academics to nominate a list of the leading works of journalism in the twentieth century. Much of the list consists of magazine work, beginning with landmark journalism such as Lincoln Steffens's "Shame of the Cities," first published in *McClure's* between 1902 and 1904; Max Eastman's articles about the 1913 Ludlow Massacre in *The Masses*; Dorothy Thompson's reports on Hitler's rise in *Cosmopolitan* and *Harper's*; Robert Capa's and Margaret Bourke-White's war photographs in *Life*; Joseph Mitchell's stories of city life and A. J. Liebling's reports from the European front in *The New Yorker*; James Agee writing in *Time* and John Hersey in *The New Yorker* about Hiroshima; Murray Kempton in *The New Republic* and *The New York Review of Books*.

It is hard to tell which, if any, of the pieces here will be read in ten or fifty years' time. What they surely represent, though, is exemplary ambition and much of the best of what the moment had to offer. That is, in part, the enterprise of magazines, whether you discover them first on a newsstand or in a mailbox or, as it sometimes happens, in a quiet dentist's office, happily distracted, waiting for the drill.

—*David Remnick*

Acknowledgments

"The most essential gift for a good writer," said Ernest Hemingway, "is a built-in, shock-proof shit detector. This is the writer's radar, and all great writers have had it."

Mr. Hemingway—who contributed to magazines from *Life* and *Look* to *Esquire, Collier's,* and *Holiday*—would no doubt be intrigued, amused and inspired by this year's edition of *The Best American Magazine Writing.* The nineteen pieces in this volume were among the finalists and winners at the thirty-eighth annual National Magazine Awards held in New York this spring. The Academy Award–like celebration is run by the American Society of Magazine Editors (ASME), in association with the Columbia University Graduate School of Journalism. After reviewing some 1,300 entries in 20 categories, the judges—160 top editors—narrowed the list to just over 100 finalists and then chose 20 winners for our industry's top honor, the Ellie, named for the Alexander Calder stabile *Elephant.*

This compendium would not have been possible without the exceptional Marlene Kahan, ASME's executive director, who in addition to deftly orchestrating the awards program itself, selected this marvelous collection of prose and reportage, with the help of Mark Bryant, our editor at HarperCollins. We are also grateful to Columbia's associate dean, Evan Cornog, and

Columbia's National Magazine Awards director, Robin Blackburn, both of whom worked closely with our judges and provided expert advice.

This fourth-annual volume of *The Best American Magazine Writing* features both long-established writers and some newcomers, but I dare say that all of them owe a debt to at least one strong editor who worked to bring out their finest efforts. So a special thanks to all the editors who stand proudly behind their writers' bylines. If you enjoy this collection, go out and buy more of your favorite magazines, and perhaps try one you've never read before. You may even find yourself reading one of next year's award winners.

—*Susan Ungaro*
Editor-in-Chief, *Family Circle*
President, ASME (2002–2004)

THE BEST
AMERICAN
MAGAZINE
WRITING
2003

GQ

FINALIST, FEATURE WRITING

The Most Dangerous Beauty

The breathtaking illustrations of the human body in Pernkopf's Anatomy *came from a very dark place. The models used were the cadavers of more than 1,000 Austrians executed by the Third Reich. Michael Paterniti's "The Most Dangerous Beauty" is an exquisitely written tale of the ethical, aesthetic and moral dimensions of this medical atlas, which was ultimately banned, and of the American professor who was ostracized because of his love for the book.*

Michael Paterniti

The Most Dangerous Beauty

You are not supposed to look at <u>Pernkopf's Anatomy</u>. It is a thing of wonder, a breathtaking book that maps the human body in elaborate detail and vivid brushstrokes. But it was born of nightmare science, marred by the stamp of swastikas, and now the world has banned it. Still, one man couldn't stop looking.

Beneath this black roof, on a well-clipped block, in a small midwestern town on the Wabash River, a professor wakes in the dark, confused at first by an outline under the sheets, this limp figure beside him in bed. From some primordial haze slowly comes recognition, then language: *bed, sheets, wife . . . Andrea.* He kisses her and rises. He is 58 years old, and he wakes every morning at this ungodly hour, in his finely appointed brick house with exploding beds of lilies, phlox and begonias. After three heart attacks, he goes now to cardiac rehab. Wearing shiny blue Adidas sweats, he drives off in the family's Nissan. Once at the medical center, he walks briskly on the treadmill, works the cross-trainer machine and then does some light lifting. It's a standing joke that if he's not there at 6 A.M. sharp, the staff should just put on ties and go straight to the funeral home. After his workout, as he drives to his house, the town glows in a flood of new light; the river bubbles in its brown banks as the flies rise; the lawns are almost too bright, green with beauty and rancor.

He feels better for this visit, more alive, as if it's a daily penance ensuring him another day on earth, another chance to breathe in the smell of cut grass before a spasm of summer lightning. He takes Lopressor, Altace and aspirin to thin his thick blood. Even now fragments accumulate, arteries begin to clog, his cardiac muscle weakens, slows, speeds again to make up time. There is so little time.

He wears his silvered hair neatly parted. A creature of habit, he's worn the same style of round tortoiseshell glasses for thirty years. He drinks a cup of chai every afternoon of his well-plotted life at a café near his office at Purdue University, where he teaches medical illustration. He is a humble, somewhat conservative man, a Roman Catholic whose joy for the most simple things can be overwhelming, inexplicable. After his third heart attack, when they jammed tubes into him and he was pretty sure it was over, he became insistent. "Just tell me I'm going to mow the lawn again!" he said to his doctor. "Tell me I'm going to mow the lawn!"

These were nearly his last words.

If this man can be oversensitive and a bit obsessive, if he has an exact recall of the little injustices that have been done unto him—he keeps old hurtful letters on file—he knows he must unburden himself now, make peace with those in his life: wife, children, friends, colleagues. And with the vanished ghosts that roam the rooms of his memory: mother, father, brother.

And what of Pernkopf? What of Batke?

He can't fathom where to begin with the Book, now forever out of print, effectively banned. When considering it, he often conjures the language of some illicit affair: rapture, consumption, shame. And if he was betrayed by that lover, does it lessen all those days he spent in love? Ah, the Book, the nearly unbearable perfection of its paintings, and then, weltering behind it, armies clashing across the face of Europe, 6 million spectral Jews. Under pressure, history splits in two: the winners and the losers, the righteous and the evil.

It is not like this man to act impulsively, to yield control, to risk missing cardiac rehab, to wander 7,000 miles from his dear doctor, but he does. He packs a bag with some old journals, drives from West Lafayette to Indianapolis and gets on a plane. He travels eight hours in coach, through spasms of lightning, wearing his Adidas jumpsuit, hair neatly parted. Fragments accumulate; arteries begin to clog. He drinks some wine; he pores through his journals, these copiously recorded memories of a sabbatical he took twenty-three years ago, when he went on a pilgrimage to find the Book's greatest artist, when he still worshiped—yes, really, that's the word—the Book's achievement. He naps, wakes, reads his decades-old handwriting again. If he were to die on this plane, in a hotel lobby in Vienna, in the echoing halls of the Institute searching for some truth, will he have been cleansed? After all, he didn't do the killing or throw the bodies from the window. He didn't spew the hate that incited a hemicycle of fanatics.

No, his sin, if that indeed is what it is, was more quotidian: He found beauty in something dangerous. There are days when he can't remember how it began, and nights when he can't sleep, remembering.

.   .   .

A cloudy afternoon, Vienna, 1957. A man sits and smokes, a body laid before him. A creature of habit, he wears a white lab coat and a white polyester turtleneck, no matter what the weather. He is small, with a crooked nose and skewed chin that give him the appearance of a beat-up bantamweight. He has a lot of nervous energy, except when he sits like this. When he sits like this, he seems almost dead, a snake in the heat of day. Before him lies a nameless cadaver that was brought up from the basement of the Institute, from the formaldehyde pools of torsos and limbs, then perfectly prepared like this: an incision, a saw to the breastbone, the rib cage drawn open, the heart removed. He stares at this open body, looks down at the floor, stares some more.

In his right hand, he holds a Habico-Kolinsky, one with long sable hairs, his brush of choice. On the rag paper before him, he has sketched some rough lines, has plotted his colors. And now, after this prolonged stillness, he bursts from his chair. He paints across the entire canvas, maniacally, almost chaotically. He lays in washes of color, gradually building the glazes. His hand darts back and forth. He goes at the bronchus and then the thoracic duct. With his tongue, he licks the brush and lifts off pigment to show phantasmic light on this internal landscape. He flicks turquoise here and there to make the fascia appear real. What he does is highly intricate, but at this speed it's like running on a tightrope. He is in deep space, underwater, gravityless. He works in a fever, shaking and levitating. Weeks pass, and still he stands before this painting, this body.

What is his desire? To be a rich man, to paint what he chooses, to hang in museums, to make love to beautiful women, but he is on the wrong side of history. And yet he isn't a demagogue or a war criminal. He is merely a trained fine artist who must paint dead bodies for the money—and that's what he will do, for nearly five decades of his life: brains, veins, viscera, vaginas. Perhaps his sin is quotidian, too: In 1933 he says yes to a job because he's hungry, and so sells his soul, joining Pernkopf's army of artists, which soon becomes part of Hitler's army. Now a silver light pours thickly through the tall glass windows. He lifts pigment, then swabs his brush over the *Aquarellfarben* cake. He expertly paints in the ascending aorta and pulmonary trunk, giving them ocher and purple colors. He creates this astral penumbra of arteries and air pipes, galaxies within the body. For one moment, he does it so well he vanquishes memory. It has always been just him and the canvas. And as certain as he will be forgotten, with each painting he believes he won't. He is the righteous one, the butcher's son made king.

The dead have no color. His power is that he gives them color.

·   ·   ·

They don't know now to treat him, this unusual specimen, this volcanic event. He shakes and levitates in his temporary palsy. It is the summer between seventh and eighth grades, 1957. Far away, in another world, an unknown man named Franz Batke paints in Vienna while this unknown boy, David Williams, has some sort of infection. His body has burst with huge open sores on his face, back and chest. The shots put him into a high fever that brings on convulsions. He is a supernova; he could be cursed.

Outside, the Michigan sun burns, it rains lugubriously, and then there is bright light on the panes again. The floor shines menacingly. There is no explanation for this suffering. No treatment that the doctors can find. Inside him a cell has split in two. He is a boy who, by some internal chemical flood of testosterone and disease, is fast becoming something else, a different animal.

In the fall, he is released from his hospital cell. He lifts weights and runs the sand dunes by the lake to build his body back. He dreams of being the middleweight champion of the world, the kid from Muskegon, Michigan, hitting someone so hard that he separates the guy from his body. If only he could convert his rage to power and skill, it might happen. After school he takes a football and runs through the cornstalks in the backyard, pretending each stalk is a tackler. It is twilight now, and the boy has been running through these cornstalks for hours, for days. His shirt is streaked with blood from where he's been stabbed by the stalks, the scabs broken open, releasing pustulants from the body. When he heals, his skin will be runneled and pocked. He will always live a word away from that good-looking upperclassman, the one in the locker room who, before everyone, called him Frankenstein. It will take him decades to understand these scars and what has happened to him. What has happened to him?

Years later, after crossing an ocean in search of something he can't put a name to, he finds himself in a room with the old man, who smokes so many cigarettes it seems he is on fire. They talk about the thing they both loved most: art. Sitting in that studio in Innsbruck, David Williams, the would-be middleweight champion of the world from Muskegon, Michigan, who speaks in faltering German, feels immediately at home with this Austrian, Franz Batke, who speaks no English and who, unbeknownst to him, is a former Nazi. How has this happened? Because they speak only of art. Williams will write in his journal, "I am truly beginning to see this man as a genius." After all, among the scarred carapaces of lost civilizations, among the ugly ruins and tormented dreams of history's fanatics, some beauty must rise, mustn't it?

Mustn't it?

.   .   .

The cell has split in two. There is no diagnosis, no explanation. Clouds cover the city, hyena shaped, turning on themselves. The tanks are rolling, and the people come out of their houses, clutching bouquets to pledge allegiance to their invaders, without fully understanding. They throw flowers and sing. They are thin already, engraved by rib cages and dark rings beneath their eyes. It is not easy to understand. Their euphoria is blinding.

On this morning, Eduard Pernkopf rises at 4 A.M. He is a short, stout man with gray-blue eyes, dour and phlegmatic, though not entirely humorless. He wears round glasses and diligently reads his well-thumbed Schopenhauer. He has a scar on his left cheek from a duel he once fought. It is hard to imagine this particular fellow in a duel. And it is equally hard to imagine what moves inside him—ambition, zealotry, some canted idealism? Or is it just sickness? He has thyroid problems and crippling headaches. A blood clot is moving slowly toward his brain. When his first wife dies of tuberculosis at 27, he pens a symphony dedicated to her titled *The Pleasure and Pain of Man*. He marries her sister. He smokes exactly fifteen cigarettes a day. He comes to care about only two things: the Book and the Party.

The Book begins as a lab manual while Pernkopf is teaching at the Anatomy Institute in Vienna. He needs a dissection guide to help students better identify the organs and vessels of the body, but he finds other anatomy texts outdated or unsatisfactory, and he is a maniacal perfectionist. He soon has what seems like an impractical dream: to map the entire human body. And this dream is what leads to his life's work: an epic eponymous four-volume, seven-book anatomical atlas, an unrelenting performance spanning thirty years of eighteen-hour workdays. Here our mortality is delivered in Technicolor, in 800 paintings that illuminate the gooey, viscous innards of our own machine, organized by regions: the Chest and Pectoral Limb; the Abdomen,

Pelvis and Pelvic Limb; the Neck; and the Topographical and Stratigraphical Anatomy of the Head.

The group he recruits to paint comprises fine artists, some of whom have trained for years and are known as *akademische Maler*. At this time—the early 1930s—there is no work in Vienna. People scrounge for crumbs. Beggars line the streets. On Fridays shopkeepers leave small plates of pennies out for the poor. A rich person is someone who owns a bicycle, and the artists take their jobs willingly, thankfully. Perhaps in another place and time, they'd be famous for their watercolors of Viennese parks or Austrian landscapes. But here they draw the cold interiors of the human body.

Pernkopf oversees these men and women: four, seven, nine, then eleven artists in all. Perhaps he is dimly aware that this moment may never repeat itself. Never again will social conditions warrant that so many talented fine artists gather together to detail the body, and never again will the art of medical illustration veer so close to that of fine art itself. The book will coincide with the discovery and refinement of four-color separation: All anatomical works before it will seem to be from Kansas, while *Pernkopf's Anatomy* will seem to hail from Oz.

For his part, Pernkopf directs the dissections and preparations of the cadavers for painting. These preparations can be exacting, hour upon hour spent pinning back skin on a forearm, scraping fascia from a bone, sawing skulls open to reveal a fine minutiae of arteries, the skein of veins beneath the dura. But he learns quickly: The better the preparation—the more fresh and vivid the viscera—the better the painting.

He is driven by ideas of accuracy and clarity. He stresses again and again: The paintings must look like living tissue, even *more* alive than living tissue, if such a thing is possible. He strikes a deal with a publisher named Urban & Schwarzenberg, which after seeing the early work is convinced that Pernkopf's book may one day be mentioned in the same breath as da Vinci's sketches of the body, Vesalius's *Fabrica* or Sobotta's *Atlas der Anatomie des Menschen*.

Meanwhile, the cell has split. The Jewish diaspora of the late nineteenth century—one bringing thousands from southern Poland and western Ukraine to Vienna—has also now projected Jews into the highest reaches of society, causing deep-seated rancor. Anti-Semitism becomes commonplace. Even at the Institute, competing anatomical schools rise under one roof to segregate the Jews from their Austrian detractors, a student army of National Socialists. Passing in the halls, students come to blows.

For Pernkopf this violence is as it should be. From the moment he enrolls as a student at the University of Vienna, in 1907, at 18, he joins a nationalistic German fraternity, which becomes the foundation for his later fervency as a National Socialist, including his belief that Jews have corrupted German culture. Shortly after secretly joining the Nazi Party in 1933—which is against the law in Austria at the time—he joins the Sturmabteilung, or Brown Shirts, the underground uniformed army of Nazis. And then he waits.

Months, then years, pass. Life worsens. The Institute is only a microcosm of Vienna itself, of Austria as a whole, of this entrenched hatred pushing up through the dirt of society. On March 12, 1938, Hitler enters the country uncontested, in an open limousine. He speaks from the balcony of the town hall in Linz to crazed flower-throwing crowds and claims his beloved birthplace, Austria, as his own—a blank-check Nazi annexation known as the Anschluss. In Vienna, where Hitler once made watercolors of Gothic buildings, flags bearing swastikas are unfurled. Some feel a rush of hope; others, like Sigmund Freud, who lives only four blocks from the Institute, pack to leave.

And so, on this morning, Pernkopf readies himself for the most important speech of his life. It is 4 A.M., the time he usually reserves for writing the words that accompany the paintings in his atlas. He writes in shorthand, striving to find the right intonations and arpeggios, giving words to some echo he hears in his head. Later his wife will type the loose pages, and then he will stand in the hemicycle at the Institute before a room packed with medical-school staff, pledging allegiance to Adolf Hitler, in his storm trooper's uniform, a swastika on his left elbow. He will call for "racial hygiene" and the "eliminating of the unfit and defective." He will call for the "discouragement of breeding by individuals who do not belong together properly, whose races clash." He will call for sterilization and "the control of marriage." And finally he will praise Hitler for being a man who has found "a new way of looking at the world," as someone "in whom the legend of history has blossomed."

The speech becomes an overt declaration of war within the university. Jewish students will soon be thrown from the third floor of the Anatomy Institute to a courtyard below, and 153 Jewish faculty members will be purged—some will eventually be sent to concentration camps; others will flee. In this milieu of bloodlust, the bodies of those tried and guillotined after the Anschluss—more than 1,000 in all, mostly political opponents, patriots, Communists and petty criminals, among them eight Jews—will be stacked like cordwood behind the Institute, to be used as preparations for Pernkopf's sacred atlas. From the legend of these human limbs, his temple rises.

· · ·

His favorite gift as a kid is a chemistry set with which he relentlessly experiments. And the boy obsessively draws. He draws humans and animals. He does crude landscapes in watercolor. When he holds a brush in his hand, when he puts that brush to paper, he becomes invisible. He cannot be seen. He has no history, no scars.

He becomes the first in the Williams family to graduate from high school, then goes to community college. In his freshman biology class, he sketches a frog, the insides of a frog, with amazing accuracy and clarity. When his instructor sees it, she tells him about universities where one can learn to draw the insides of frogs—and other animals, including humans.

David, the artist, may be an enigma to his factory-working parents, but his younger brother, Greg, is an aberration. While David is short, stocky and a loner, Greg is tall, angular and outgoing. As David has his art and science, Greg toys with the idea of becoming a priest.

If the brothers dwell in alternative realities, they unconsciously remain each other's lodestars, each other's partial reason for hope. For they have the same goal: to escape the blue-collar drudgery of gray Muskegon and a house that has slowly gone from Norman Rockwell portrait to Ingmar Bergman film, mother listing into alcoholism and mental illness, father burdened by some deeply hidden guilt from his own unspoken past. Each son is searching for some kind of euphoria to obliterate the pain of growing up in this house. At the age of 20, David abruptly moves to Hamburg to live with a woman he met when she was visiting the States and who loves him, his scarred self, something he once thought impossible. Greg finds theater and opera, then men and drugs.

Years pass. Greg moves to Detroit, New York City. David splits with the woman in Hamburg, returns home, is accepted into the University of Cincinnati's medical-illustration program, meets his wife, a schoolteacher, after being set up in a Muskegon bar. Shortly after they marry, he encounters the Book for the first time.

He remembers the exact particle reality of that moment. At the university, he lives in an almost obsessive world in which people spend a hundred hours drawing a horse hock or the tendons of a human arm, in thrall to brush on paper. One of his professors has purchased *Pernkopf's Anatomy*, a mythic work Williams has heard defined as pure genius, and he goes to the professor's office to see it.

The books are enormous, with blank green cloth covers. Inside could be almost anything—Monet's water lilies, pornography, the detailed mechanics of a car—but when he opens it, when the binding cracks and the dry-cleaned scent of new pages and ink wafts up to his nostrils, there appear before him thousands of thick, glossy sheets; these wild colors, these glowing human bodies!

It is an electric moment, a pinnacle, of which a life may contain not more than a handful. But it is more than just the bright frisson of discovery, the wordless awe before some greater fluency. If this is a book with emanations, with a life of its own, then perhaps what startles him most is the glint of self-recognition that he finds in its pages: While he sees the timeless past in the trenches and deep spaces of the body, he also, oddly—and he can't yet put words to this—sees his own future.

What he doesn't know yet, flipping through these pages, is that twelve years from now, as an associate professor, he will take a sabbatical and go in search of the Book, that he will find its last living artist, Franz Batke, who will take him under his wing, impart his lost techniques. He doesn't yet know that he will return again to Batke just before the old man dies—and learn what he'd rather not know about him. That he will write an academic paper about the Book for an obscure journal of medical illustration, in which he'll praise *Pernkopf's Anatomy* as "the standard by which all other illustrated anatomic works are measured." It will briefly help his academic career and bring him a measure of fame. But with it comes a backlash. He will lose friends, question himself and be judged guilty of Pernkopf's crimes by mere association; he will refuse to talk about the Book, curse the day he first saw it.

If this is indeed a Book with emanations, as he will come to believe, perhaps even his heart attacks can be blamed on it—Pernkopf, in white lab coat, reaching from the grave for one last cadaver.

.   .   .

The book is blindingly beautiful, an exaltation, a paean and a eulogy all at once. Page after page, the human body unfolds itself, and with each page the invisible becomes visible, some deeper secret reveals itself. What is it?

Here is an eardrum, whole, detached from the vestibulo-cochlear organ and floating in space. It appears as a strange wafered planet. Here is a seemingly glass liver through which appears a glass stomach and then glass kidneys, all in a glass body, an utterly transparent figure, us, glittering. Here is a skull wrapped in red arterial yarn, and here a cranium packaged in the bright colors of the holiday season. There are eyes that look out, irises in bottomless depth, a disembodied gaze that is the gaze of poetry itself. There is an unpeeled penis, a pulsating liver the color of a blood orange, a brigade of soulful brains, levitating.

And then there are the drawings of dead people—cadavers, faces half intact, half dissected, skin drawn back in folds from the thoracic cavity, heads half shelled, showing brain. Consider Erich Lepier's watercolor of the neck. In nearly black-and-white-photographic detail, the dead man seems to be sleeping; the intact skin of his neck is supple, his lips are parted, his eyes half closed. His head is shaved, and he has a mustache. Even the fine hairs of his nose are visible. Inside him a superficial layer of the neck's fascia comes in two strange shades of color: a bluish pearlescent and a translucent olive green. The acoustic meatus, pathway to the inner ear, is visible, as is the mastoid process. Every changing texture is felt, every wrinkle recorded. Half of this dead man is in exact decay and half of him seems alive. The painting is its own kind of pornography, half violation and half wonder.

Or consider Batke's watercolor of the thoracic cavity after the removal of the heart. It is like gazing on a psychedelic tree of life: arteries, veins, bronchus, extending like complex branches inside their bizarre terrarium. Batke employs all the colors of the rainbow, these interwoven lines of yellow, blue, orange, purple, but invented and mixed by him, all these appear as new colors. The bronchus, which rises in the background, is striped and Seusslike in white and umber. Although the painting's concern is the minute sorting and scoring of these air and blood tunnels, it still captures an undulating energy, fireworks, the finely rendered thrum of the body. The painting nearly takes wing from the page.

Page by page, *Pernkopf's Anatomy* is stunning, bombastic, surreal, the bone-and-muscle evidence, the animal reality of who we are beneath the skin. And yet, as incomprehensible and terrifying as these landscapes can be, as deep as our denial that life is first and finally a biological process, hinging even now on an unknown blood clot orbiting toward the brain, on a weak heart, on the give of a vein wall, the Book brings its own reassurance. Lepier's detached eyes, like spectacular submersibles, Batke's precisely wrought otherworldly vaginas, Schrott's abstract, almost miraculous muscles/ducts/lymph nodes, Karl Endtresser's bizarre spinal configurations—all of these slavishly striving for the thing itself while being regarded, through Pernkopf's eyes and those of the artists, as beautiful, nearly spiritual objects.

So what can be said about this Book? That its intentions are good? That it is a masterpiece? That each painting contains its own genius? And what if a number of these paintings have been signed with swastikas, what then? Is it possible that only Nazis and their myriad obsessions with the body could have yielded such a surprising text?

And what of the dead stacked like cordwood at the Institute, their body parts pulled down by pitchfork? Do the secrets revealed in the Book count less than the secrets kept by it? Does its beauty diminish with these facts or the political beliefs of its general and foot soldiers? In a righteous world, perhaps it should, but does it?

•   •   •

Shortly after the Anschluss, after thousands of Austrians have been conscripted for the front lines of a war against the world, after more and more Austrians have died of starvation, the euphoria fades, the master race begins to devour itself. And yet Eduard Pernkopf ascends, his name a *Hakenkreuz* and a haunted house.

He is first and foremost a scientist, believing, mimicking, the racial politics of the Third Reich. Well received by the powers in Berlin, he is first named dean of the medical school, then *Rektor Magnificus,* or president, of the University of Vienna. Shortly after the Anschluss—March 12, 1938—he issues a letter to all university staff: "To clarify whether you are of Aryan or non-Aryan descent, you are asked to bring your parents' and grandparents' birth certificates to the dean's office. . . . Married individuals must also bring the documents of their wives."

Under his presidency, medical experiments are conducted on the unfit and retarded; children are euthanized. Somewhere in his building is the severed head of the Austrian general, the patriot Wilhelm Zehner who, in the first days of the Anschluss, either committed suicide in political protest against the Nazis or was murdered by the Gestapo. Among the more than 1,000 guillotined bodies Pernkopf claims for himself from the district court, he searches for the best, the youngest, the finest specimens of muscle and skin. He opens the bodies like walnuts, discards what won't serve him. Those he decides to keep go to the formaldehyde pools in the Institute's basement, a kind of Brueghelian hell.

So who is Pernkopf? If he's taciturn with his painters, it is because he maintains the utmost professionalism. A dreamer, an intellect, a lover of music, he is in the workshop early in the morning and late at night: He is simply an overwhelming presence. The Book becomes both his great unwritten symphony and, slowly, his madness. Whether or not he encourages them, some of his artists now sign their work to show their Nazi allegiance: Lepier follows his name with a swastika, Endtresser fashions the double S of his name as an SS lightning bolt, and Batke seems to do the same with the number 44 when he dates his paintings from 1944.

But even before the American bombs fall on the Institute— mistaking it for a factory, leveling half the building—even before the lot of these men are left scattered on the wrong side of history, half anesthetized by the past and half consumed by it, there is this one last moment in which they believe they are the righteous ones. These paintings of the human body belong to the highest expression of their Nazi idealism, but they exceed even that classification. If they save human lives—which they do every time a surgeon uses them to heal the body—each one is an act of salvation.

•   •   •

There was no note, but nonetheless he knows. He knows from a conversation they had the last time his brother, Greg, came from New York City to West Lafayette, when they sat on the front stoop drinking beers. They talked about everything, and Greg mentioned how he believed hedonism was the highest possible expression of self and that to die in an act of euphoria was the only way to really live. In context it was not alarming, nor really surprising. In retrospect it explained everything.

When he learned of his brother's suicide, David Williams drove four hours to Muskegon, straight to his parents' house. His mother was sitting in the living room shaking her head, and his father refused to believe the body was Greg's, since there hadn't been a positive identification. Someone had to go to New York to identify the body. "You work with dead bodies all the time," his father said, maybe a little cruelly. "You can do this."

The next morning, the elder son flew to La Guardia, then took a bus and walked to the morgue at Bellevue to see the younger son. The waiting room was crowded with people there to identify family members who had been shot, knifed, beaten or killed by gang members. A very large black man in a uniform, an officer of some sort, brought him into a room with a curtained window. He asked twice if David Williams was ready, and the second time Williams feebly answered, "Yes." When the curtain parted, there was his brother, still tall and angular, lying on a metal dissecting table, in severe rigor mortis, with the back of his head resting on a wooden block, exactly like a cadaver in a gross-anatomy lab. But this was his brother—and there was no longer anything beautiful about him, only a pallid mask where his face had been, a lifeless slab in place of his animated body.

If his brother's death left no mark on the greater world, the rest of those dark days in 1978 are part of David Williams's personal history: how he fell into the arms of the large black man who carried him from the room; how he refused to sign a piece of paper that said his brother was found with needle marks on his arm; how he went to the YMCA to pick up his brother's belongings; and how, when he arrived back in Muskegon, his parents were in denial about their son's sexuality and about his suicide, an act that meant he could not be buried, according to Catholic rite, with the other generations of Williamses at St. Mary's Cemetery.

And it's part of history, too, that his brother, the person whose life most closely tracked his own, ended in the cold, unconsecrated ground of Muskegon, among the graves of factory workers, back in this place they both tried so hard to escape.

•   •   •

Not long after, on sabbatical, David Williams goes to see Franz Batke. He is nervous; he doesn't know what to expect. He leaves his family behind in Munich and drives to Innsbruck. He thinks it is no coincidence that shortly after falling in love with his wife, he first saw the Book, and now, shortly after his brother's death, he arrives in Innsbruck to visit the dying old man who is the last living vestige of the Book itself. But what is it that draws him here? He is looking for answers, yes, or perhaps merely reasons to live. And even if Batke's paintings hadn't changed his life—as they have—it is not so strange that a young man suffering loss might seek counsel from an old man who knows a great deal about loss.

What he finds is that Batke is a hermit living in a cell in self-imposed exile. Batke has come to Innsbruck from Vienna, leaving behind his wife, because Vienna represents the past to him, haunting him even now, defeating him, and after more than fifty years with his wife, he is not sure whether or not he still loves her. And he has come here because he has been offered work by Werner Platzer, the man who after the war and Pernkopf's death brought the last books of the atlas to fruition. Platzer, who is hard driving with frantic dashes of intellect and craziness, has promised his friend Batke pay and living quarters in return for paintings to fill a new book on vaginal surgery.

So Batke lives in two rooms at Innsbruck's Institute of Anatomy, where Platzer is the new director. The old man never leaves, never goes out to take the air. Students bring him his food and sundries. Usually, he drinks ice water all day while he works. At night he has trouble sleeping, due to a bad cough, ominous and deep, which worries even him. Against his doctor's orders, he continues to smoke cigarettes. If he is smoking himself to death, the cigarettes may also be what keeps him alive for two more years.

At first he is mistrustful of David Williams, thinking the American scholar has been sent to spy by the publisher or by someone else looking to profit from him. But slowly Batke realizes that the professor is here for seemingly no reason other than to watch him paint—and to be taught. It dawns on him that, even if he has been remembered by only this one American, he has still achieved a certain kind of immortality. Though they can barely communicate, they become closer and closer. They don't discuss politics, only art. And at the end of each day, Williams records another entry in his journal.

"Herr Batke fixes lunch—scrambled eggs and small pieces of pork and wurst. I continue to work on the vein—he says to paint the middle valve first and then add the dark and light *dichweiß*. He wants me to stop using such small choppy strokes."

And "Even in German, I understand him: 'Loosen up. It's no big deal.' I feel it finally beginning to happen. . . . I actually enjoy it physically—the way the paint floats around. I really think this way of painting can suit me. He also demonstrates a vein. He can still do it at 77 years old. He works for two and a half hours on a very small section."

Under Batke's eye, the body becomes beautiful again for David Williams. After the shock of seeing his brother as a cadaver, he perhaps retrieves some small part of Greg with each new painting. And yet, for all of the gemütlichkeit, for all the warmth David Williams feels toward the master, Batke himself seems broken. He has been stranded on the wrong side of history, and now he never leaves the Institute.

Night after night, they sit up talking. Batke shows so many little kindnesses, serves food, cakes, wine. One day when David Williams's family comes to visit, he has presents for the children, charms the American's wife.

So how does one quantify the joy he feels when Batke speaks to him as a friend and mentor—as a father really—when Batke tells him that he, David Williams, might be the only artist with the ability to paint like the old man himself, someone to carry on the mythic tradition handed down by Pernkopf? Or how does one share what it meant that last day in Innsbruck, to see Batke come downstairs and step outside for the first time in years, to stand in a downpour of sunlight, just to say good-bye?

Isn't there something to be said for these moments? Aren't they a part of this man and this Book's history, too?

. . .

The tanks are rolling, and the people come out of their houses, clutching bouquets to pledge allegiance to their liberators. They throw flowers and sing. After landing at Omaha Beach, the Allied Army sweeps across France, liberating Paris, and breaches the Siegfried Line near Aachen. Hitler flees to his underground bunker and commits suicide with his mistress, Eva Braun, and the Third Reich implodes.

When American troops arrive in Vienna, they arrest Eduard Pernkopf and Franz Batke. Both are removed to prison camps, where they are placed in what is called a de-Nazification program, one in which prisoners are subjected to hard labor and a history lesson in the truth: movies showing the reality of the concentration camps, among other horrors of the war. Pernkopf, who is 57 now, who has lived with visions of grandeur, is lost and broken. Still, he has visitors sneak in his work, at which he continues to toil during his three-year stay.

Meanwhile, at the university, the members of the old regime have been imprisoned or removed, and the school issues a letter to those still-living former Jewish faculty members now scattered about the world, inviting them back. Of hundreds, only one returns, a man named Hans Hoff, whose wartime travels have taken him from New York City to Baghdad. Well regarded before the Anschluss, he is put in charge of the Neurological Institute. When released from prison, Pernkopf is barred from teaching at his own beloved Anatomical Institute but somehow finagles two light-filled rooms under Hoff's roof to finish his Book. The atlas is all he has left—and all that keeps him alive.

In these tattered postwar times, with jobs scarce again, he is able to regather his former artists and then add two more. He works his eighteen-hour days, remaining wholly unsympathetic to those who can't keep up. Among his painters, disillusionment and internecine squabbles are now pandemic. Batke and Lepier represent opposite extremes, the improvisational versus the mathematical, and both work to fill the Book with their own work in order to bring more glory to it.

In 1952, Pernkopf publishes *Der Hals (The Neck)*, but time is short. A blood clot in his brain causes a stroke, and he dies on April 17, 1955, before the completion of his last two books. Werner Platzer, who is regarded by many as Pernkopf's scientific son, finishes those.

Despite Pernkopf's long fall from grace, his burial turns out the entire faculty. He is celebrated by fellow professors as a perfectionist, a stirring teacher and the impresario of what many increasingly regard as the world's greatest anatomy book. Some of those present are former Nazis and some are not, but all who have lived through the war now seem to bear their own burdens, secrets and sins, and clearly they regard Pernkopf as one of their own. So they commend him to Heaven.

The Jew, Hans Hoff, is there, too, in a black suit. But what passes through his mind, what he says to himself as Pernkopf is lowered to the grave, is lost now in the ash of all unspoken things. Perhaps to stand there in the first place, on Viennese soil again, he has already begun the difficulty of forgetting. Or perhaps he marks the moment indelibly, unapologetically. Creator, destroyer—let him lie beneath the burnt grass and dying blossoms of his own history now.

•   •   •

One day, during the height of the debate over *Pernkopf's Anatomy*, a close acquaintance, a kind Jewish woman, approaches David Williams and says sharply, "Why would you want to be remembered for your association with this book, of all books?"

He has no answer. Another time, in England, while giving a lecture at Cambridge on the atlas, he is confused when a Jewish woman breaks down in tears and is helped from the room, pained by how this man, this American, has found beauty in the ugliest of books. What sickness moves inside of him?

And there is more. He receives a letter from a distinguished academic, challenging his paper for its whitewash of history. "Have you not been struck by the fact, Mr. Williams, when visiting cemeteries in small Austrian towns, how many innocent young men lost their lives on the eastern or western front, but these originators of the Nazi mentality survived?" he writes. "As convenient as it seems to be, one cannot separate a man's professional work from his spiritual being."

Meanwhile, an oral surgeon at Columbia Presbyterian Medical Center in New York City, Howard Israel, has referred to *Pernkopf's Anatomy* before every new surgery of his career. When he finds out about its past, he feels deeply betrayed. He researches the Book with another Jewish doctor, William Seidelman, asserting in a medical journal that cadavers from concentration camps may have been used in the making of the atlas. Their evidence: the appearance of roughly shaved heads and circumcised penises. When Williams is asked about this by a reporter from *The Jerusalem Report*, he disputes the fact, saying that when he asked Batke if death-camp cadavers were used in the Book, the old man became enraged and denied it vehemently. Even famed Nazi hunter Simon Wiesenthal examined the records, and his conclusions seem to bolster Williams's side. The two doctors, however, take a dimmer view of Williams as one of the Book's greatest defenders.

Williams is not alone in his view of the Book. Following the publication of his paper, the two most prestigious American medical journals review *Pernkopf's Anatomy* and declare it in "a class of its own" and "a classic among atlases," with illustrations that "are truly works of art." Nonetheless, Williams increasingly feels isolated, doubtful. How could beauty have made him half blind? Is he, as it appears to some, a Nazi apologist? On public radio, he is asked how it feels to be the one benefiting from a Nazi text, and he fumbles for an answer.

He loses friends; he loses sleep; his heart begins to hurt. He meets several times with the local rabbi, who tells him that his sin may be one of perspective. He must imagine the unimaginable when it comes to the Holocaust, must feel the grief of that woman at Cambridge, assuming she may be like so many who lost mothers and fathers, sisters and brothers, children and spouses, in the ovens and dark chambers of places like Dachau, Auschwitz and Buchenwald. How hard could it be to see that, for some, the Book is not a metaphor for beauty or salvation or transfiguration, that it's not the highest expression of what saves David Williams from Muskegon, Michigan, or, in some complicated way, brings Greg back? No, for that woman at Cambridge, the Book is nothing but a dirty crime scene, violated bodies that might include her brethren. The artists are no better than vultures over their carrion. What affliction or hubris has kept that from him?

Three heart attacks and several angioplasties later, he is a different man, one who still lies awake at night thinking about the Book, but thinking about it from the point of view of that woman who broke down at Cambridge. He doesn't speak about *Pernkopf's Anatomy* for years, though he follows developments from afar. Under pressure, the University of Vienna launches and concludes an investigation into *Pernkopf's Anatomy*, claiming, in November 1998, that circumstantial evidence suggests Jewish cadavers were probably not used in the making of the atlas. Reviewing the hundreds of pages of findings, Williams is left unconvinced, believes the university administration has obscured the results to protect its reputation.

From some primordial haze slowly comes recognition. It is the spring of 2002, and in West Lafayette he now prepares to return to Vienna, to Munich. He packs his bags, and when he is briefly overcome with doubt, his wife says, "You are *Pernkopf's Anatomy*. A big part of that Book is who you are." So he travels eight hours in coach, through spasms of lightning. But this time he arrives aggrieved, angry, skeptical, confused, searching for truth—more, perhaps, as a Jew would. He has come to avenge the naïveté of his younger self and to make his final good-byes to the paintings, for he is sure he will never see them again in this lifetime, nor perhaps ever have the desire.

·   ·   ·

In bright sun, beneath a heavy roof, the Institute occupies half a city block along the trolley routes and shops of Ringstrasse. The first time he came to Vienna, the weather was bad—rain, thick clouds rolling over themselves—and somehow the city seemed cold, less receiving, left him empty and alone. This time he feels more resolute. Somewhere in the locked rooms and forgotten closets, among the thousand cadavers used by a new generation of anatomy students, he hopes, is a more clear answer to the past.

He meets with professor after professor. He is unfailingly polite, phrases sensitive declarations of fact as questions in his midwestern lilt. A few he meets are defensive; most, quite the opposite. A gentle old man, a former president of the university who knew Pernkopf, serves him tea and cakes. Later, he finds out that the old man was an SS officer. Many records, including those of the identities of a number of cadavers, were destroyed by those American bombs that brought down half the Institute. Others were tampered with by those looking to obscure their crimes, so exactness is elusive. Rather than thinking there's a cover-up here, David Williams begins to feel pity for these people, relentlessly driven back to an increasingly untraceable past.

One professor leads him through the Institute on a tour: They stand on the spot where guillotined bodies once were piled in ten-foot-high drifts and taken down for Eduard Pernkopf's use by pitchfork. They stand in the hemicycle, where Pernkopf headily praised Hitler and called on his colleagues to lead a new age of medical experimentation, a period that would come to include the sterilization of the retarded and the euthanasia of nearly 800 defective children. They go to the basement of the Institute, a dark, dank, spooky place, to look upon the formaldehyde pools that once held Pernkopf's cadavers. An attendant opens the lid on one of the pools, activates a hydraulic lift, and suddenly several bodies, bloated and pale, each one donated for use in the school today, appear from the depths on metal trays.

Somehow, on his last visit he failed to mark all these spots, or perhaps unconsciously didn't entirely want to or feel he needed to. Now he does, shaking his head, grimacing.

Finally, he dines with a young historian, Daniela Angetter, the woman charged with investigating much of the University of Vienna's Nazi legacy. Her world is one of chilling medical experiments and severed heads, and she wears her work with a gaunt hauntedness and weary eyes. Allergic to protein and lactose, she eats potato chips at dinner while her husband, a plumber, eats blood sausage. "This has been horrible for me, to see dead bodies," she says. "I'm a historian, and to think that people were executed because they were starving and stole a pig and ate it. Would I have been strong enough to stand up? If you didn't conform to the party, you were executed. I've stayed awake many nights thinking about these things."

Sitting there, moved by this young woman, believing her, David Williams comes to realize this: All these people are run down by ghosts, too. He is not alone in his confusion. After illustrious postwar careers, former SS officers serve afternoon tea; a new generation born thirty years after the war pores over the past, making amends for its grandparents. Even now, on a sunny spring day in 2002, on the eve of the anniversary marking fifty-seven years since the fall of Nazi Germany, students carry urns bearing the last discovered remains of victims at the university during Pernkopf's reign; the government calls for calm in the streets of Austria's capital, deploying 1,500 police officers to ensure that neo-Nazi demonstrators don't rampage in the Heldenplatz, the square where Hitler addressed hundreds of thousands of euphoric Austrians in 1938.

Here is an entire country living the events of the war over and over and over again. Later, in Munich, Williams spends an afternoon with his friend Michael Urban, the erudite 63-year-old grandson of Eduard Urban, the man who first struck a deal in 1933 with Pernkopf to publish his atlas. Having inherited his grandfather's company, Urban sold it to a company that decided to cease publication of the Book. He believes it to be a troubled masterpiece, one that should continue in print with a foreword detailing the most harrowing events of its creation. Now, while the German quietly listens, the American attempts to put into words something that has troubled him, continues to trouble him on this trip: He wonders if, by being friends with Franz Batke, by seeing the magnificence in *Pernkopf's Anatomy*, he is doomed. And yet he feels that to reject both fully is a sin of its own: betrayal.

"David, there's nothing wrong with you," says Urban. "We are moving on two planes: the principal, everyday plane and then one made up of these overwhelming feelings and emotions. When we try to talk about this, we move into a wordless dimension." Here he pauses, runs a tapered finger over his furrowed brow, smiles weakly. "My father was at one of these mass rallies, the Goebbels speech at the Sports Palace in 1943, and he said his arm was up in a Nazi salute before he knew what he was doing. It was hysteria. It's inconceivable what people did to one another during the war. But you must remember: People endure."

• • •

The next day, he goes to see the original paintings. He is wary, excited and nervous. Urban has arranged for the paintings to be delivered to the downtown offices of the publishing house. And he has also arranged for Werner Platzer, the man who finished the atlas after Pernkopf's death, to come to Munich to lead Williams through nineteen oversize black binders stuffed with 800 original pieces of art.

Platzer operates three cups of coffee ahead of the world. He doesn't eat; he doesn't pee. He just sits with the paintings, providing long discourses on each. And Williams sits with him, a student again, savoring every moment, but this time questioning too. He asks Platzer why he thinks the Book is out of print, and Platzer shakes his head, incensed. "It's too good," he says. "The Book is too good." When Williams points to a painting that many feel is that of a Jewish cadaver with a shaved head, Platzer explodes. "What does a Jew look like?" he says. "Tell me. It is absurd. I wish you Americans ate what we ate then: nothing. Three days a week, I might not eat. I looked like this man here. Absolute nonsense."

Williams sits before him, unblinking, and presses his concerns. He believes the swastikas and SS symbols have been removed from some of the originals, as they were removed from subsequent printings of the Book, so a laborious hour is spent trying to locate the paintings in question. In the end, he discovers the symbols have been erased, and he seems troubled, angry.

And yet, when he comes upon a Batke painting of the inner ear, he holds it up and stares for a long time. "It's just so alive," he says softly, passing a hand lightly over it. When he sees another, of the chest, he says, "I'd give anything to have that hanging on my wall." The two men look at the Lepiers and Dietzes, Endtressers and Schrotts. They marvel at the near psychedelic colors and intricate brushwork. With each painting—with each proliferation of arteries, with each gravityless organ—the body becomes that exalted place again.

The viewing takes seven hours, and in the end he feels it all over and over: joy, curiosity, shame, awe. In person, in full color, the paintings still shimmer and mesmerize. They still emanate.

But this time in their presence, he is not exactly euphoric. If he feels a deep sense of fulfillment in seeing these paintings one last time, he also feels a strange sadness. When it is over, when the sun dips below a building and a streetlight blinks on in the window, he is almost trembling. He pulls out a handkerchief, removes his glasses and wipes his face. His hair is slightly disheveled. He exhales, looks once at the oversize binders against the wall, presses his lips tightly together and then turns his back and leaves the room.

· · ·

The old man sits and smokes, a bottle of beer set before him. He has a crooked nose and a skewed chin. Night pours through the windows of his cell. Sitting across from him is the American, fellow exile and good friend now, who has remembered him, who has made a pilgrimage to record a way of painting that will be forever lost with his death. It is 1980, and they have spent months together now, eating, drinking, laughing. There is so little time. Though they don't speak fluently to each other, they have formed a bond through painting. And now they are a little drunk, and their conversation veers from art to the war.

The old man suddenly rises and disappears for a moment, then returns with a small cardboard box that makes a jingling sound. It is dust covered and full of medals, including an Iron Cross he won for valor on the Russian front, where he was shot in the groin. He passes the medal to the American, who feels its weight in his hand, turns it in the light, admires it. The old man, who trusts the young man now, who is being a little vain and showy, sad and funny, mentions that he is still proud to have worn his Brown Shirt uniform. He says the Americans blew it, joining the war on the wrong side, and accuses the Jews of forcing the Americans to enter the war against the Germans rather than with them. He chides his guest for this. He describes his imprisonment and his days being de-Nazified. And David Williams, the American professor, listens, nods and later writes in his journal, "The evening seems like a dream to me . . . perhaps it's the beer. This man who I have admired for so long—I should say his work—there is no doubt in my mind that as a painter he is a <u>genius</u>!!—this man reveals himself as a common Nazi, a Jew hater, a Brown Shirt. . . . Is it possible that all makers of great works of art are ultimately exposed as thus?"

And ever after, he will wonder: Who is this old man, this last living vestige of the Book? And what secret has he found after his life as a vulture at the side of carrion? It appears there is no secret. The Nazis have lost, and he is dying on the wrong side of history. The mouth is made for food, the penis for the vagina, the heart made to beat. Until it simply ceases. Death is no salvation. The only thing left is to paint.

On the wall above David Williams's desk at home today in Indiana hangs a painting by Franz Batke, near an old portrait of Eduard Pernkopf. Sometimes, at the end of the day, after mowing the lawn, he spends a minute gazing at them. But if asked why the pictures are there, David Williams shakes his head; he can't say why. But he doesn't take them down.

Harper's

Horseman, Pass By

"Horseman, Pass By" combines elements of memoir, history and journalism into a seamless whole. His story of Secretariat, told within the larger framework of the racing world and its continuing quest to breed successors to one exceptional horse, parallels a recollection of author John Jeremiah Sullivan's own sportswriter father that goes beyond anecdote to suggest an approach to writing (and life) that becomes a legacy worth the inheriting.

John Jeremiah Sullivan

Horseman, Pass By

Glory, grief, and the race for the Triple Crown

Far back, far back in our dark soul
the horse prances.
—D. H. Lawrence

In the Month of May

My only real awareness of the Kentucky Derby, growing up across the river from Louisville, lay in noticing the new commemorative glass that appeared in the cupboard each May, to be dropped and broken, as often as not by me, before the next one arrived. Although my father attended the race every year for more than a decade, occasionally taking my older brother along, he never said anything to me about it apart from to ask, when I got old enough, which horse I would like him to bet on with my allotted two dollars. His position, in general, was that to talk about work was the same as being at work, and there was already plenty of that.

A sportswriter gets used to people coming up to him in restaurants or at PTA meetings and taking issue with something he said in a column or on some call-in show. And my father was sensitive to the slightest criticism—really the slightest mention—of his writing, almost to the point of wincing, which may have stemmed from his having come to the job somewhat backward. As opposed to the typical sportswriter, who has a passion for the subject and can put together a sentence, my father's ambition had been to Write (poetry, no less), and sports were what he knew, so he sort of stumbled onto making his living that way. When the alternative weekly paper in Columbus, Ohio—where we moved when I was twelve so he could take a job writing for the *Columbus Dispatch*—started running a regular column entitled "The Sully," in which they would select and expand upon what they felt to be my father's most bizarre sentence from the previous week (e.g., " 'Second base is still an undefined area that we haven't wrapped our arms around,' Tribe general manager John Hart said, sounding very much like a man about to have his face savagely bitten"), we were amazed by his pained reaction. The compliment behind the teasing would have been plain to anyone else, but he would not have the thing in the house.

Two years ago, in May, I sat with him in his hospital room at Riverside Methodist, in Columbus. He was in recovery from what was supposed to have been a quintuple bypass operation but became, on the surgeon's actually seeing the heart, a sextuple bypass. There had, in the preceding year, already been the aneurysm surgery, then the surgery (unsuccessful) to repair the hernia caused by the aneurysm surgery. "My succession of infirmities," as he put it to me in a letter, "has tended finally to confront me with blunt intimations of mortality." Otherwise it was not a morbid scene. The last operation had gone well, and he seemed to be feeling better than he had any right to. The waning sedative and, I suppose, twenty-four hours without cigarettes had left him edgy, but he was happy to talk, which we did in whispers, because the old man with whom he was sharing a room that night had already gone to sleep.

I asked him to tell me what he remembered from all those years of writing about sports, for he had seen some things in his time: Michael Jordan at North Carolina, a teenage John McEnroe, Bear Bryant, the Big Red Machine in Cincinnati. This is what he told me:

I was at Secretariat's Derby, in '73, the year before you were born—I don't guess you were even conceived yet. That was . . . just beauty, you know? He started in last place, which he tended to do. I was covering the second-place horse, which wound up being Sham. It looked like Sham's race going into the last turn, I think. The thing you have to understand is that Sham was fast, a beautiful horse. *He* would have had the Triple Crown in another year. And it just didn't seem like there could *be* anything faster than that. Everybody was watching him. It was over, more or less. And all of a sudden there was this . . . like, just a disruption in the corner of your eye, in your peripheral vision. And then before you could make out what it was, here Secretariat came. And then Secretariat had passed him. No one had ever seen anything run like that—a lot of the old guys said the same thing. It was like he was some other animal out there . . .

I wrote that down when I got back to my father's apartment, where my younger sister and I were staying the night. He lived two more months, but that was the last time I saw him alive.

A year later I went to the New York Public Library and looked up the pieces he had written for the *Courier-Journal* (then the

Courier-Journal & Times) on that first Saturday in May 1973. There were two by "Mike Sullivan, Staff Writer": the procedural one, about Sham; and another, stranger piece, buried well into the section, which may be of interest to scholars of the newspaper business someday, if only because it shows how far into the provinces the New Journalism had penetrated by the early seventies. In it my father describes floating around Churchill Downs on the morning of the Derby, looking for something to write about. Midway through the story "The Kid" appears, "loose-limbed . . . fitted out in old jeans and sneakers . . . he looked very much like a groom or stable boy." My father always wore a white linen suit to the Derby, à la his great hero, Mark Twain (though his colleague and friend the noted horsewriter Billy Reed once wrote that he looked more like "a deranged Colonel Sanders," a look that I imagine would have made him quite approachable to a confused hippie).

The Kid confesses to my father that he has snuck in without a ticket, and says that he is trying to get the jockey Laffit Pincay's autograph for his "buddy" back in Michigan. Some weird post-sixties dialogue ensues. My father advises him not to go forward with his plan of impersonating a groom (*they* might catch him) but instead to "wedge against the runway fence after the race" and try for the autograph there. The Kid is then given a meeting place for after the Derby. "At that time, he would tell whether he'd gotten the autograph . . ."

It was the next and last sentence that, for some reason, struck me as odd and oddly affecting, coming across it there in the hum and the mortuary light of the microfilm machine. It is: "If The Kid failed in his mission, this story will end here."

Among the Yearlings

All horses turn one on the first of January following their birth, New Year's Day being roughly when the new crop starts to appear. Given that the breeding season runs from February to June, and that a mare carries her foal for eleven months, a horse can be anywhere from seven to twelve months old when it becomes a yearling, which means that the animals for sale last September at Keeneland, in Lexington, Kentucky, were between sixteen and twenty-one months old. This may be when thoroughbreds are at their most beautiful. They have just outgrown the awkward stiffness and knobby knees of the foal, and their muscles have begun to develop, subtly rippling under their coats like waves seen from a height.

A two-day sale was scheduled for September 10 and 11. I got there on the morning of the tenth, a day of exquisite weather, the low, overcast skies so often seen in central Kentucky replaced with brilliant blue and small clouds. At the door I was given my "hip book," the catalogue that lists all the as yet nameless colts and fillies (each of which has a lot number affixed to its hip), with the names of their consignors or owners. The book also includes elaborate, page-long pedigrees that note the amount of prize money won by each horse's sire and dam. At the top of each page is a crow's-foot family tree going back three generations. Most of the people here have the book in hand, consulting it, scribbling in the margins. It is a kind of libretto for one of the most unusual pieces of theater in America.

The process by which the individual horses are brought to the gavel begins in the week before the sale, when the trainers, owners, and others with serious intent to buy gather at the Keeneland stables, where the yearlings are kept on view. Each animal gets a thorough veterinary exam, the results of which will be broadcast on closed circuit just before it enters the bidding. Prospective buyers are informed if the horse is a "cribber" (one that likes to chew on fences, which can lead to gastrointestinal problems) or a "ridgling" (a condition that comprises both the "monorchids" and the "cryptorchids," colts with either one or both testicles undescended, respectively). The trainers check the animals all over, do even deeper research into their pedigrees (there is a library on-site for this purpose), and watch them run around a bit. Most of the hard decisions, about which horses a prospective buyer wants to bid on and how high he or she might be willing to go, are made before the public sale even begins.

The sale itself is about nerves, for those who plan to part with a lot of money, and spectacle, for those who have come only to watch. The horses are led, one after another, on a circuitous route from the stables to the stage, beginning outside, moving slowly (always slowly) into the paddock, then through an oblong, covered corral, stopping at various points along the way so that the stressed-out trainers, about to gamble with millions of someone else's dollars, can get a last look. The grooms are brushing them the whole time, combing their hair, whispering to calm their nerves, doing everything possible to make them look gorgeous and even-tempered. The amount of money that can be lost by a sudden, unexpected move, which can cause the horse to act up and look too high-strung in front of the bidders, is ridiculously large. People hang over the railings, watching them pass. Most conspicuous in the crowd are the Arabs, who move about with entourages of unsmiling bodyguards and assistants. Some of the horses notice the attention and tug against their bridles, as if it annoys them. The higher-profile trainers will sometimes walk into the corral with a horse that has caught their attention. They stand with arms folded, chewing their lips, their eyes moving deliberately over the animal's body, taking in every angle and sinew as they try to gauge the worth of a racehorse that has never run competitively in its life.

From the corral the horses arrive at a sort of backstage area, the last stop before they go up for sale. At this point people intending to bid on an animal whose approach they have followed move into the amphitheater, where the auctioneer sits. As each hip number is called, a twenty-five-foot-high wooden door, like the entrance to a medieval castle, is pushed open, and a different groom, in a fancy green jacket and black pants, takes the bridle and brings the yearling onto the wooden stage. Then the door is pushed closed again.

Dawn

Among our first conscious signs of ourselves, in the prehistoric caves of Spain and France, they are already there, prancing, stampeding, and evidence suggests that we had already begun to see them as something more than themselves. Writers on Ice Age art mention the paradoxical fact that horses make up a sizable percentage of the painted images in caves where they are hardly to be found among the discarded bones. There is even what looks like an altar to the horse, in a cave in the south of France, dating back 15,000 years, a "kneeling sandstone figure" of what looks to be a mare amid skulls and horsehead jewelry. Our awe in their presence—who has not felt it, just standing across the fence from one?—is as old as anything we can call ours.

They began 50 million years ago, in North America, on what is now the Great Plains. They were *Eohippus*, "dawn horse," the size of a small dog, with multiple clawed toes on their feet. At some point during the Miocene, when the Alps were forming and the primates were starting to diversify, they found their way down into South America and across the land bridge over the Bering Strait—opposite to the way we came—and colonized Europe and Asia: herds of wild horses, alpha stallions with their harems of mares, "bachelor bands" of subdominant males, moving across the steppe and the plains. They had become ungulates, mono-toed. They had developed those enormous eyes that seem always to see you no matter where you stand, like the eyes in old family portraits, which allowed them to watch the grass they were eating and the predators lurking in it at the same time. And they had become fast, faster than anything on the solid earth apart from the cats, and the cats could maintain their speed for only a few hundred yards or so, whereas this creature could run from morning to night. The entire genius of evolution had gone into crafting *asva*, as it was called in Sanskrit, this verb made flesh, this thing whose every atom wanted to run, from the giant nostrils, drawing huge drafts of air into the cavernous heart and lungs, to its long, powerful hindquarters. The horse essentially leaps when it gallops, like a tremendous hare.

Among the Yearlings II

The seats in the amphitheater itself are reserved for high rollers, but at any given time enough of them are out looking at upcoming lots that you can slip into one of their seats and watch the action. The auctioneer sits atop an enormous podium, fifteen feet above the stage. The horses themselves are so tall that he has to be up that high to see over them, and these absurd proportions make him seem like an indifferent judge in a Kafka story. He uses the frenetic, twanging banter of the country fair rather than the somber drone of the art auction. (There is wonderful unnecessity to this style; surely no horse would sell for a dollar less if he were simply to say, "I have a bid for five hundred thousand dollars. Would anyone like to bid seven hundred and fifty?") The banter runs ceaselessly, from morning till evening, as the hip numbers are called in unbroken succession: when one auctioneer gets tired another slides into his place, and when one horse exits stage left another is poised to enter stage right, a carousel of every admixture of black, brown, white, red, and gray.

The auctioneer is flanked at the podium by two relay men. His calls are based not on what he sees but on what they whisper to him. They are watching the spotters, men who stand at the feet of the aisles and scan the crowd for that raised eyebrow or click of the pen that signals a higher bid. This conspicuous anonymity on the part of the wealthiest bidders has its uses, since for an unknown buyer there is cachet to be had in going head-to-head with one of the "names" on the floor, a sort of gamesmanship that can quickly turn expensive for all concerned. As an experiment, I take a seat in the front row and turn around to face the crowd, curious to see if I can spot the bids: I do not catch one. When the spotter registers someone willing to rise to the auctioneer's bait ("I'mlookingforfourhundredmillionnow-fourhundredmillion . . ."), he spins on his heels with a "Hyah!" or a "Hey!" Each has his own yell. The relay man writes down the new bid and repeats it, sotto voce, to the auctioneer, and suddenly—mysteriously, because the first event in the chain is almost totally imperceptible—the price goes up.

The yearlings themselves pace back and forth, occasionally rearing, their hooves clacking on the hard wood of the stage, their dark eyes roving crazily in their sockets, swallowing the crowd like that panther in the Rilke poem. Somehow it is much, much stranger and more unsettling to be in the presence of a thoroughbred than in the presence of, say, a giraffe, or some other novelty animal whose defining characteristic is its weirdness. These horses are mystical in their beauty; I cannot help noticing how much, despite their tails, they resemble enormous deer. Every motion of their limbs is a kind of flickering, so that one blinks and expects them to vanish. Many of them snort while they are being sold. Others are silent. One in ten will whinny, as if to protest being stared at so insolently, and the sound will scissor through the room above the auctioneer's breathless tally. They shit prodigiously, and there is with them on the stage, apart from the groom, a uniformed sweep, who brushes the pile into a pan as soon as it hits the floor.

These two men are the only black people I see at the sale, which I am embarrassed to say I have to remind myself to notice, having spent too much time down South to find it remarkable. It is appalling, if not entirely fair, to note that if you were to trace backward through time the job of the man sitting atop the

podium—the Keeneland auctioneer—you would eventually
make your way to a man named Jerry Delph, said to be a model
for the slave dealer in *Uncle Tom's Cabin*. Delph sold both human
beings and horses off the same auction block in the Cheapside
district of Lexington, a neighborhood that "is still tainted,"
according to the unofficial state historian, Thomas D. Clark, "by
the indignities committed there against humanity."

It is something to see these animals looking back at all that
Arab royalty and Irish aristocracy, the Japanese billionaires and
the old Southern money and the New Economy arrivistes
searching for some new hobby to fight off the boredom, and at
you. There is an innocence to these creatures; they are children,
after all. Yet their pride is undeniable, too: they seem to know
that the whole affair, the hundreds of millions changing hands
every year, the roaring crowds, the pageantry, the tears, are about
them, and are nothing without their power. Yet their power is
ambiguous, for they have already accepted the bit and the bridle.
And just as they are the reason for this display, so all this money
in the crowd, all this arrogance, is the reason for their existence.

On my way out of the pavilion, I spot Bob Baffert and Prince
Ahmed bin Salman bin Abdul Aziz of Saudi Arabia in the back
row, surrounded by local news anchors and fans. They are the
owner-trainer team behind the Thoroughbred Corporation,
which in a fairly short time has become one of the most successful breeding and racing concerns in the world. Baffert has solid
white hair just long enough to call floppy, and he is wearing, here
inside, his trademark dark glasses (he is allergic to hay and keeps
the shades on to hide the redness of his eyes). Bin Salman has a
chubby, friendly face, with hair he keeps oiled and a black mustache. Baffert is the most recognizable human face in the game,
and Bin Salman is arguably its most powerful player, yet they are
the antithesis of the old Kentucky horseman (Baffert lives in California and got his start as a jockey on déclassé quarter horses,
and there is the matter of his hay allergy), so Lexingtonians tend

to love and hate them even more strongly than everyone else loves and hates them. On Baffert's advice, Bin Salman has just bid something close to $5 million on hip number 203, a chestnut great-grandson of Secretariat. Just for fun I try to count how many of the 573 horses for sale have Secretariat's blood in them but get bored at a hundred: the great champions sire armies of offspring.

Amazingly, the bid is not high enough. Sheikh Mohammed bin Rashid al Maktoum, the defense minister of the United Arab Emirates, wins the auction at five and a half. I later ask Rogers Beasley, the director of sales, whether the sheikh and the prince ever get competitive on the floor, going higher just to outdo the other. "Used to," he says. "They got a little smarter on us." He is not complaining: on this day alone, more than $60 million worth of horseflesh is sold. Bin Salman, smiling and giving the palms-up "What can you do?" sign for the cameras, seems philosophical about having lost out, but Baffert is visibly disappointed. He was looking forward to training that horse.

A Cold Eye

My trip to the September yearling sale was only the second time I had been back to Lexington since we had buried my father there a year before. On the evening of the twelfth, after the last hip number had been called and most of the buyers had been driven to the airport, I pulled away from Keeneland under an almost radioactive violet sky that had the first tinge of fall in it, passing a skinny, bald-headed man who was walking shirtless along the side of the road, listlessly waving an American flag. The car was pointed toward my grandmother's house, where I was staying, but I veered at the last minute toward the cemetery.

His grave is at Calvary, a Catholic cemetery that lies directly across the road from Lexington Cemetery, site, as it happens, of the first racetrack in town and the place where all of my Episcopalian family on my mother's side are buried. The two graveyards, starkly separated from each other by the road and the traffic and the fences, seemed at the time to sum up rather neatly how opposite my parents were in almost every way: he Catholic, she Protestant; she Old Lexington, he a grandson of Irish immigrants, brought up in White Plains, New York, who moved to Lexington only as a teenager when his father, a construction supervisor, got a job overseeing the building of an IBM plant outside of town; she a former boarding-school cheerleader, he a former Memphis hippie (the freakiest of the hippies, as any survivor can tell you); and the list is long. It is a riddle how they stayed together for twenty years.

The headstone was not on the grave yet, the grass had not come in. No one else was around. I had no flowers or anything else to leave and felt slightly awkward, as if I were trespassing.

One of the most difficult things in dealing with my father's death—for many of the people he left behind, I think—is how totally inappropriate grief and mourning seem beside any memory of the man himself. He was a deeply funny person, a collector and disseminator of bawdy jokes and carefully clipped page 10 stories about insane trailer-park crimes. He had inherited some variant of that dark and antic strain of Irish humor that runs through Synge and Flann O'Brien, by which the worst imaginable scenarios, the worst outbursts of temper, would flower in a joke that made everything bearable. It was a quality not without its regrettable side, for he used it to keep our concern over his health at bay. I have a letter from him, written less than a month before he died, in response to my having asked him about an exercise regimen that his doctor had him on. In typically epithetic style (it was his weakness), he wrote, "Three days ago didst I most stylishly drive these plucky limbs once around the 1.2-mile girth of Antrim Lake—and wasn't it a lark watching the repellently 'buff' exercise cultists scatter and cower in fear as I gunned the Toyota around the tight turns!"

For all the joking, his disappointments and sadnesses never quit him. His own father had died when he was only nineteen, dropping dead in harness, as it were, on the job at a construction site. "Four men came up to my mother at the funeral," my father told me once, "and claimed to be the one who caught him, which is how she knew that no one did." He was devastated; he had worshiped the man. He dropped out of college, utterly lost for a while. I see now that he was always, in some sense, a son. In one of his journals are plans for a book that would tell his father's story, the story of "a great and unknown man." But he never wrote it. His temperament was not suited for the long commitment, for the artist's obliviousness to competing responsibilities, which necessitates a certain cruelty, let us admit. So he accepted his defeat, with dignity, and with a total lack of self-pity. He wrote his newspaper stories, and wrote them well, downstairs at his vast green-leather-topped desk, on his creaking chair, in a haze of smoke. The desk was accidentally lost during the settlement of his estate. It is in a Salvation Army somewhere in Louisville, or at the dump.

The night he died I went back to his bachelor apartment in the dismal complex and sat down at the old desk, among his few things. In the drawers were his "quitting journals," as he called them, special notebooks, set apart from the others, filled with his rapid, loopy script. He would start a clean one with each new attempt to kick cigarettes. I had glanced at them once or twice, without permission, when he was alive. Now they belonged to me, along with all of his "creative work," under the terms of the will. They were largely self-excoriations, full of dark thoughts, efforts to locate and take hold of his own willpower. How *badly* he wanted to change. Worse than any of us could want that for him. I remember a notecard on the table by the bed, written during a brief period when he was attending a support group: "Reasons to quit: 1) It worries my children."

Icon

We have never been certain whether the horse meant death or life, peace or war; it depends what culture you consult, and down through time it wavers, like a compass at the pole. Symbols become more polysemous as they grow in familiarity: jade will always signify purity, but the apple can stand for anything. And nothing, until, say, 1913, when Henry Ford began using interchangeable parts—or until now, on some parts of the planet— has been more familiar to us than the horse. It is not too much to say that a person today who knows horses, really *knows* them, understands more about what it meant in the past to be human than the most knowledgeable historian.

In many places—pretty much everywhere in the industrialized world—the horse has passed out of our common life. It is a pet, or a police horse; at most it carries an unregenerate cowboy. But thousands of years of symbiosis leave a trace. It shows up most clearly in the language, this deep familiarity, in all the excellent words. You can go mad noticing them. Beyond all the metaphors that have passed into our speech—all the ponytails and tantivies, the horsebeans, horseleeches, and horselaughs, beyond all the junkies shooting white horse and all the cutpurses hung from the mare foaled of an acorn—beyond that there is, most excellent of all, the terminology, the words we have evolved in order to live in such close association with these beings for such a long time, to be able to talk about them and what they do: piebald and roan, withers and farrier, crupper and martingale. A Martian, equipped only with time and a dictionary, could reconstruct the history of the human race by looking for these proliferation-points of vocabulary, where the language suddenly explodes, signaling long intimacy, necessity. And yet, in an irony both strange and somehow perfect, when our Martian got to the word "horse" itself, he would find that white flag of lexicography: "origin unknown."

There is a theory that our language itself—our real language, Indo-European—is before all else the language of horsemen. Historical linguists have long wondered why we speak a derivative of an obscure tongue that is thought to have developed 6,000 years ago on the Central Asian steppes rather than one of the many languages once dominant in Eurasia, of which today Basque is the only survival. An archaeologist named David Anthony, at the Institute for Ancient Equestrian Studies in New York, put this enigma together with the fact that the steppes are where he and other excavators have unearthed 5,000-year-old horse skulls showing the world's earliest known signs of bit-wear, a discovery that pushes the advent of riding back a full millennium.

One afternoon, the theory goes, a group of people belonging to one of these steppe societies were probably standing around looking at the horses in a pen, and someone (Anthony speculates that it may have been a child) decided to try to climb on top. It was a notion that could have occurred in regard to only a few animals, camels and elephants being the other two. Although *Equus* can be quite threatening when it needs to, it is alone among hooved quadrupeds in having no horns or antlers to hurt us, and its back is long and sturdy enough to accommodate our bodies, a biological affinity that Darwin noticed when he wrote, in *The Voyage of the Beagle*, "A naked man on a naked horse is a fine spectacle; I had no idea how well the two animals suited each other."

The species—both species—never looked back; what had been separate destinies were woven together in a double helix. The horse was saved from the extinction it had been headed inexorably toward, and the people became riders. These riders, it may be, speaking their harsh proto-Indo-European, having climbed atop and learned to guide the beasts that everyone else was still using for meat or milk—or simply watching with admiration—were able not only to spread their culture at formerly unimaginable speeds but also to put the fear of God (literally, perhaps) into whomever they met. Before long everyone spoke their tongue, worshiped their horse-headed gods, and rode horses.

First Saturday in May

I know that some old Lexington friends have seats just above track level, in front of the wire, so I vacate my seat in the press box at Churchill Downs and head down the white metal staircase to the grandstand. Shadowy men in vests and sunglasses, carrying sniper rifles and binoculars, are ranged along the edges of the roof. Security is said to be extra tight this year, owing partly to the presence of Prince bin Salman, a member of the Saudi royal family and as such one of the only people on earth the Arab fundamentalists hate more than us and the Israelis. In order to get through the checkpoints, all of your food has to be in clear plastic.

My friends, Chris and Becky, and Chris's brothers, have clear plastic bags full of ham biscuits, a Kentucky delicacy, which they feed me. There is a blimp hovering overhead and two propeller planes towing banners: "Merrill Lynch discriminates against women" and "Dèja Vù: Totally Nude Gentlemen's Club. SHOW-GIRLS." The sun is getting bright. A guy in a Panama hat is smoking a joint right next to a female army private in camouflage, and people are taking their picture.

Chris and his brothers, John and Patrick, run a flower business together, and they tell me a story about last year's Derby, when they decided they would have a close-up look at the traditional Derby wreath, a horseshoe-shaped mantle of roses that is placed around the neck of the winning horse. When they found it, a woman was standing there, entrusted with keeping it safe.

"Hey, where do those roses come from?" John asked her.

"Why, these are *special* roses," the woman said, "grown right here in Kentucky."

"Bullshit," he said, "those are Ecuadoran."

"Yeah, you're right," she said, "but don't tell anybody, okay?"

The "undercard," the term used to refer to all the non-televised races run before the "big one," which, when there is a big one, always comes near the end of a meet, is under way. My friends are arguing over their bets, but I have decided to wager all my money on the Derby.

For the past eight months, ever since the yearling sale, I have been following the crop of two-year-olds, and now three-year-olds (the age of the horses that run in the Triple Crown), hoping to get lucky and to end up accidentally having followed a contender. I have won a lot of money on a sublime black colt named Mayakovsky, who placed, as I had bet he would, in the Hopeful at Saratoga, and I have lost even more money watching an Irish horse, Johannesburg, sprint across the wire in the Breeder's Cup at Belmont Park. I have worked to educate myself about the sport. In the process I have become a devoted reader of the *Daily Racing Form*, only dimly aware of world events beyond the two apologetic headlines printed in each day's issue, on the fourth page, under the title "News Briefs."

Back at the paddock—the circular staging area where horses are held, saddled, and mounted before each race—people are crushed against the railing, not so much to see the horses as to see the celebrities, who are not there to see the horses, either, but to see one another, and to make sure that *USA Today* gets their good side. Sean "Puffy" Combs is here, in a white suit, along with 'N Sync's Joey Fatone, the one with the shoe-polish goatee; so is the Backstreet Boys' Kevin Richardson, the thin-faced one with the costume-shop goatee. Richardson is a Lexingtonian: I heard him sing "The Star-Spangled Banner" before a Wildcats game, which he did with real pizzazz. Someone says, "Hey, is that Britney Spears?" But no, it is Jessica Simpson, another blonde pop singer. Ivana Trump is here, too, in a tasteful feathered hat.

A heavyset frat-looking guy in a white T-shirt and a white cap is screaming at Ivana, and people actually quiet down to enable him. "Ivana!" he bellows. She goes on chatting. "I-V-A-N-A! We love you, Ivana!" She keeps her back turned to him, but it is clear to all that she is now consciously keeping her back to him, which is fun to see. He has pierced the veil. Emboldened, he switches to Puffy, who now goes by P. Diddy. "P. Daddy! P. Daddy!" he cries. A woman walks up and starts giving him a good slap on the back every time he lets loose with one of his wild namings. I hear her refer to him, in conversation with another bystander, as "my son."

The behavior of this lunatic and his dam raises a question about the people inside the paddock, which is, What kind of person would voluntarily endure what is essentially a foodless outdoor cocktail party of strangers in heavy sun, in a concentration-camp-style enclosure, wearing outlandish clothes and trying to appear relaxed while being gawked at and openly insulted by hundreds if not thousands of drunken hill people? It is sad to be reminded, once again, that all this horse-racing business is about the rich, for the rich are hideous. There is nothing they cannot ruin. And, of course, if there is one other thing that horse racing is all about, it is people who do not have money to lose—the bettors—losing it.

So it is beautiful when the horses themselves appear, in their ignorance and their majesty, and assert their presence amid all this crappiness. "Oh Horse, Horse, Horse," wrote D. H. Lawrence in a letter, "when you kick your heels you shatter an enclosure every time," and now I know just what he means. Only those with souls most thoroughly hollowed out by fame fail to turn and watch the three-year-olds when they take their slow lap around the paddock. And the jockeys! Who could not love a sport with its own paid battalion of wee men, their bright, gay silks, their young faces, their ambiguous quasi-midgetry. We have had to evolve a special race of human beings, when you think about it, so that the thoroughbreds may have riders.

The blimp passes just overhead, causing a momentary eclipse of the sun, and I make up my mind to get inside the paddock itself, given that I have gone to the trouble of getting a press pass. But it is too close to Derby time. Although I get past the first security guard, another guy, in a newer uniform, puts his hand on my chest and says, "Only if you are with NBC." Why I do not simply call this man my buddy and tell him that if Mr. Costas is not drinking this bottle of water in thirty seconds we can both start looking for another job, I do not know. As I am escorted out, I see Bob Baffert, shaking hands with one hand and patting his horse with the other. As of last night, he and Bin Salman had two horses entered in the Derby, but one of them, Danthebluegrassman, has been scratched from the race this morning, and he is left now with just one horse, a black colt with a white star between its eyes, War Emblem, which is tossing its head nervously. I had never heard of the horse until this morning. Baffert looks confident, despite having already received a beating in the press for having entered Danthebluegrassman late, which kept another, Kentucky-based trainer out of the race altogether.

I have a cousin somewhere in the fabled "infield," so I go in search of her, thinking that I am sure to see some sights. But this, too, is a disappointment. The infield crowd is incredibly *well behaved* (all the papers will report on this the next morning—fewest crimes ever). The rifles and the plastic-bag dictum seem to have done the trick. I expect at least to see titties and knife fights, but this is more like Slip N' Slide and keg stands, men kissing women's bellies, that sort of thing, though the infield remains a wonderful place to see a certain kind of Kentucky face, a face made obsolete in other parts of the world by dentistry and nutritional guidelines. One Southern stereotype that is not in the least exaggerated, and that lends some support, perhaps, to the old canard about Appalachian people having held onto an English cultural inheritance squandered by the rest of the country, is the extraordinary state of many Kentuckians' teeth, which seem to fall or get knocked out in groups, rather than singly, lending a rather shocking aspect to their smiles.

I get to the seat that my friends have saved for me just in time to see the horses being led to post, their jockeys floating atop them, their coats shimmering in the perfect sun as if they were covered in oil. Each is accompanied by a gentle pony whose nerves are not so tweaked as those of the thoroughbred, and each hides its face in the pony's neck as they near the gate. A voice comes over the loudspeaker announcing that we will now sing "My Old Kentucky Home." Here and there, a hanky is unfurled, as some native son or daughter cannot suppress a tear. In the box directly in front of us, there is a group of men in their late twenties with the look of well-heeled WASPs who have not yet woken up to their homosexuality, a type found everywhere in the South. They are wearing bespoke poplin suits that sort of match, and shirts of the softest, softest pastels, and their arms are around one another. Each looks to the others' faces as they sing and sway, as if for confirmation of the feeling they are feeling. When we get to the second line of the song—which was changed in the program notes only in 1972 from Stephen Foster's " 'Tis summer, the darkies are gay" to the line I learned in school, " 'Tis summer, the people are gay"—the boys smile broadly and emphasize the original word.

The singing of this line is a somewhat charged moment in the history of the Derby. Whites fought hard against the change even at that late date, and one must bear in mind that the track was segregated well into the 1950s: separate entrances, separate grandstand, separate rest rooms, this for a sport with a history not only of devoted and skillful black grooms—which fit easily enough into the old white Southern vision of "their place"—but of great black jockeys as well. In the first Derby, held in 1875, thirteen of the fifteen jockeys, including the winning jockey, were black. (Ask any Southerner why lawn jockeys are black. They have no idea.) The only black faces I have seen today were in the paddock, and belonged to rappers.

Darkness

It is worth reading the complete lyrics of the song itself, "My Old Kentucky Home," one of Foster's most famous. They are not at all what you think. The "darkies" are not really "gay"—not even in the song, I mean. Foster is toying with you there, seeing if he can get you to take out your hanky. Legend has it that he composed the song during a party, a "gay ball" at an old country home, amid dancing belles and beaus. We must picture him there, jotting down the last verse on the back of some sheet music while he pretends to listen to some drunken son of a landowner talk about how *his* family's darkies have no complaints:

> The head must bow and the back will have to bend;
> Wherever the darkey may go:
> A few more days, and the trouble all will end
> In the field where the sugar-canes grow.
> A few more days for to tote the weary load,
> No matter 'twill never be light,
> A few more days till we totter on the road,
> Then my old Kentucky Home, good-night!

"No matter 'twill never be light." Few lyrics, outside the early blues and British heavy metal, could match that one for hopelessness. The Derby commissioners should make the crowd sing the whole thing, rather than bowdlerizing one line.

Several of Foster's songs were hits in his lifetime, and he was able to negotiate a royalties deal with a New York music publisher. But he was an alcoholic of cosmic dimensions and drank himself into such chronic debt that he started selling off the rights to his compositions for a few dollars apiece, then spending those dollars on beer.

He died in a Bowery hotel in January of 1864, while the Civil

War raged. He had been in bed for days with a fever, his wife and child having long since left him. In the early morning he rose to call a chambermaid for help, but he swooned, gouging his head on the washbasin next to the bed as he fell. He was found hours later by George Cooper, one of the only friends he had left. Cooper described the scene:

> Steve never wore any night-clothes and he lay there on the floor, naked, and suffering horribly. He had wonderful big brown eyes and they looked up at me with an appeal I can never forget. He whispered, "I'm done for", and begged for a drink. . . . We put his clothes on him and took him to the hospital.

Foster died three days later. History has recorded his possessions at time of death: In his tattered leather purse were thirty-eight cents and a scrap of paper on which he had written, in pencil, "Dear friends and gentle hearts."

Down the Stretch

Your experience of a horse race is strongly colored by where you choose to sit. Here, at the wire, I will see the field pass twice—once just out of the gate, and once as they hit the finish—but I will see nothing of the rest of the race. I cannot even see the gigantic electronic screens posted at each of the turns. From the press box (the opposite extreme), I could look through binoculars and watch the entire thing develop, see the moves, the jostling for position, who is using the whip and when. But you never know when you will be back to the Kentucky Derby, and I want to taste the track off their hooves, to see their eyes.

When the gates fly open the horses are like a freak storm moving over the track together, their legs attended by a cloud of dust that they trail behind them, their colors flashing kaleidoscopically in the sunlight. The loudness of their pounding takes me by surprise. It overwhelms even the crowd. I am so stunned by the sight of them that by the time I collect my mind, they have disappeared around the turn. We who are sitting close to the wire stand listening to the call, waiting for them to return.

As the race unfolds through the track announcer's sharp, metallic call, I notice that it is dominated by unfamiliar names, and one name in particular: War Emblem. He leads from the break. Our eyes strain in the sun to catch the field emerging around the final turn, and when it does War Emblem is still in front. He comes across the wire having never lost the lead, the green-and-white silks of the Thoroughbred Corporation—of the Saudi flag—rustling on the jockey's back.

The crowd is strangely quiet. There is more clapping than cheering. There has been virtually no talk about this horse, and the great majority of bettors base their decisions on talk, which is why racetracks make money.

In the post-race interviews Baffert and Bin Salman are genuinely ecstatic. "That last hundred yards," Baffert says, "you wish it would last forever." The reporters are understandably gentle on the subject of the prince's being the first Arab owner ever to win the Derby, in this of all years, and not just an Arab but a Saudi, and not just a Saudi but a man with a "bin" in his name. The prince broaches the topic himself by saying that he has won this one not for himself but "for the Saudis, the great friends of the Americans," but when one brave scribe ventures something along the lines of "Don't you think this is a bit weird?" Bin Salman is quick to brush him off. "I am a businessman, not a politician," he says—a strange remark for a prince to make, but an accurate one. "I'll leave [these questions] to your politicians and my politicians."

More interesting to the daily reporters is the question of

whether Bin Salman and Baffert have "bought the race." The story of their association with War Emblem is both totally lacking in romance and deeply American. Three weeks before the Derby, they realized that they had no contenders. This was not an acceptable place to be for Bob Baffert, who had already won the Derby twice. So one day, back in Riyadh, the prince was watching the Illinois Derby via satellite and saw something in the winning horse, which led from the wire and took it going away. He called Baffert, who promptly acquired the colt from its original owner, a Chicago steel magnate named Russell Reineman, for $900,000 (said Reineman later, of the decision to sell, "The steel business has been terrible lately"). Baffert liked War Emblem, despite the horse's being something of a head case (before what would have been his first race, in September of 2001, War Emblem threw his jockey and ran out of the paddock into a parking lot), and the trainer immediately started pointing him toward the Triple Crown. All in all, the story could not be more at odds with what horse-racing fans and the people who write for them like to hear, the favorite story being, "We raised this colt from a yearling on our beautiful farm down South, saw its promise, always believed in it, and now here we are."

Bin Salman does not go for what I would consider the obvious response to this challenge, which would be to point out that Reineman and his trainer, Frank Springer, had not been planning to enter War Emblem in the Derby at all (the horse has bone chips and other "soundness" issues), meaning that none of us would have had the joy of seeing this animal run. Instead he goes for a more direct answer, and also probably a truer one. What he says makes me like him: "Everybody buys the Derby, because you have to buy a horse or raise a horse in order to win. If you tell me who is going to win [next year], I'll buy him again."

The next morning, the paperboy brings the *Courier-Journal*, post–Derby Day edition. None of my beautiful colts of the year gone by, I reflect, has warranted even a mention. Most of them did not even make it to the race, not Mayakovsky (never entered) or Buddha (scratched), not Officer, which I heard Bin Salman describe on television as the best two-year-old he had ever seen. The copydesk boys at the *Courier* go for a bit of ye olde historical echo: in tall bold letters the headline reads, IT's WAR EMBLEM.

Beauty

For the last couple of years I have had on my computer screen three grainy little video clips that I got off the Internet. I click on them at the end of the day, when the blood sugar dips and aphasia sets in. They were bootlegged from some late-seventies TV sports documentary about Secretariat, and each of them shows him winning one of the legs of the '73 Triple Crown. The quality is so poor that you hardly see anything beyond a bunch of pixelated brown masses, but the audio track includes the calls by the three announcers, which are for the ages. One of these—Chick Anderson's, from Belmont Park, which ends with Anderson holding back tears of disbelief as he shouts, "It looks like he's opening ... The lead is increasing! Secretariat is *widening* now! He is moving like a TREE-MENDOUS MA-SHEEN!"—is up there with Herb Morrison's Hindenburg broadcast for sheer power of description and spontaneous verbal majesty. Secretariat had a habit, especially early in his career, of starting races in last place; in fact, in the Derby call, you do not hear him mentioned (except in the obligatory early rundown of the field) until the pack has almost reached the final turn, so that when the sound of his name bursts into the call, you can close your eyes and see him breaking through.

That afternoon he ran each of the last three quarters faster than the preceding one, after having spent the entire first quarter dead last. His official time, 1:59 and ⅖ seconds, is still the Kentucky Derby record, going on the thirtieth anniversary of his race. Sham also broke the previous Derby record that day, which should give you a sense of the field.

Secretariat has a Boswell, or it might be truer to say a Homer, whose name is William Nack, the author of *Secretariat: The Making of a Champion* (1975). It is a masterpiece of the genre, possibly the only masterpiece of the genre. Writing a good horse book is no easy thing if you are writing for adults. Beasts do not make good protagonists, for the simple reason that unless you have money riding on their success or failure it is impossible for anyone older than ten to identify with them fully. The books that succeed, such as last year's *Seabiscuit*, by Laura Hillenbrand, do so by spending most of their time with the human beings whose fates run more or less parallel to the track. There is plenty of that in Nack's book, too, but he somehow came across a technique that allowed him to make his horse the central character without personifying it, without even indulging, more than once or twice, in pathetic fallacy. The style is akin to art criticism, and appropriately so.

Nack's description of Secretariat's Hopeful, a race for two-year-olds held every September at Saratoga Racetrack in New York, perfectly captures a certain mystical quality that Secretariat's races possessed, one that you notice when you watch the tapes: not that he was above the field—not a bully or a tedious dominator, in other words—but that he was *outside* of it:

> Secretariat moved to the field with a rush, accelerating outside as they made the bend, without urging from Turcotte, bounding along as if independent of whatever momentum the race possessed, independent of its pace and tempo, independent of the shifting, slow-motion struggles unfolding within it, the small battles for position and advantage. [He] was not responding to any force the race was generating, but rather moving as though he'd evolved his own kinetic field beyond it, and Turcotte would later recall sitting quietly and feeling awed.

Secretariat was "by," as horsepeople say, Bold Ruler, his sire; he was "out of" a mare named Somethingroyal, his dam—her fourteenth foal, Nack tells us. He was a chestnut colt, his coat "like a new penny," with stockings of white on three of his feet and a white star between his eyes. For most of his life he would be called Big Red, his "stable name." He was given his racing name some months after his birth, as is the custom with thoroughbreds. The rulebook stipulates, among other criteria, that the name of a racehorse must be no more than eighteen characters—spaces included—and that it can be neither obscene nor already taken, whether by another horse or by a "notorious" person. Elizabeth Ham, an employee at Meadow Stables in Virginia, where the horse was foaled, had before that been the personal secretary of Norman H. Davis, American delegate to the 1933 disarmament conference in Geneva, "the home of the League of Nations' secretariat." She put forward the name.

He is best described not as the greatest horse, nor as the greatest runner, nor even as the greatest athlete of the twentieth century, but as the greatest creature. The sight of him in motion is of the things that we can present to the aliens when they come in judgment asking why they should spare our world.

A few contrarians maintain that Man o' War was greater, but the majority of the people who saw both horses run with their own eyes hold with Secretariat, and there is the fact that Man o' War, whose career took place at a time when "doping" with opiates was unregulated, has also been described as the "greatest hophead horse of all time." When Man o' War died, in 1947, he was embalmed—the first horse for which this was done—and lay in state for three days. Two thousand people filed past his coffin. He had died with an enormous erection, which somehow remained tumescent after the embalming process. Someone thoughtfully covered it with a blanket before the parade of mourners began.

Off Track

After the Kentucky Derby, I become one of a large group of people who subscribe to the theory that War Emblem—and/or Victor Espinoza, his jockey—"stole" the race. A horse is said to "steal" a race when it comes out fast and sets a false pace. The other, stronger horses, stalking the lead horse, mistake its speed for the limit of its abilities, and so wait just off pace for it to tire out. But the horse is holding something back. And when the stalking horses begin to make their move, it unleashes its reserves, capitalizing on its lead to take the race. It is a legitimate tactic not entirely deserving of its pejorative name, but it is a ruse, one that often does not indicate which is actually the fastest horse in a field. It is my opinion, one I share with many people, that War Emblem will be a no-show in the Preakness and the Belmont Stakes—the two remaining legs of the Triple Crown— because the jockeys will have seen his tricks and will be sure to burn him out before he makes the homestretch.

I watch the Preakness at an Off Track Betting shop in China-town, just a couple of blocks from the hotel where Stephen Foster met his end, as it happens. Inside every OTB is a fully functioning self-contained culture, a yin and yang of cautious hope and stoical depression that swirls inside each head and circulates through the room itself. Such a *serious* atmosphere. I get the feeling that many of these men have been here since the shop opened, and will leave only in the evening when it closes, and have done this every day for years. The men (no women) are Chinese and Hispanic, mostly. The atmosphere is devoid of festivity. Everyone is intent on his betting sheet, or on one of the TV monitors, or on one of the automated machines at which you can enter in your picks. Here and there I see a "stooper," a man who does not have the money, or is too cheap, to bet, but who walks around picking up discarded tickets, hoping some greenhorn has failed to realize that when a horse he has bet to show ends up placing instead, for instance, he still wins money.

At the track, you can usually tell the difference between a hard-core gambler and a horse fan by whether or not a person yells the horse's name or its number during the race. Here it is all, "Six! Six! Six!" and some of the sheets used by the bettors to calculate odds, I notice, do not even include the names of the horses. What these men are doing is calculating elaborate mathematical equations, over and over, trying to convert their paychecks into something a little fatter. The bets tend to be small. When a race is done, one rarely hears a groan or a whoop. They turn away and go back to one of the counters.

I approach a machine and consult with the *Daily Racing Form* for the numbers. A Chinese man with incredibly thick spectacles is behind me the entire time, saying, "Okay, sir. Please, sir. Okay, sir." A race he wants to put money on is coming up. I finally figure out the machine, which spits out my slips with a whir and a *thunk*.

Moments later the race begins. I cannot hear the call for all the chatter, but I see clearly enough what is happening. Unusually for War Emblem, he is not first out of the gate. Instead, the lead is shared by a horse called Menacing Dennis and one called Booklet, trained by John T. Ward. I have money on the latter. But by the first turn, Booklet has dropped away, and it is War Emblem who shares the lead with Menacing Dennis. Then it is War Emblem alone. I am shaking my head. As they head down the stretch (the Preakness is the shortest of the Triple Crown races—it happens almost comically fast, given how much anticipation it generates), I watch Proud Citizen, trained by the Kentuckian D. Wayne Lukas, come within a length of War Emblem. And I think, this is it. They're calling his bluff. But then something goes wrong. Victor Espinoza gives his horse the whip, and instead of the nothing that is supposed to happen War Emblem surges. He is the real thing, goddammit. He pulls *away* from Proud Citizen. Then in the final yards he gets *another* challenge, this time from a horse called Magic Weisner. But War Emblem is running even faster, pulling away from this one too. Suddenly he has won. Suddenly he has positioned himself to win the first Triple Crown in twenty-four years. And this time there is no question of "stealing." They came after him, but he was too good.

In the OTB no one cares. They are already scanning the sheets for the next race, already lining up at the machines. Of course, I am forced again to admit: This is what racing is all about. These men. The upturned proud and lonely faces of these men, cathode horses shining in their eyes, numbers dancing in their heads. I wad up my tickets and leave them in the trash can by the door.

Blood

In *Stud* (2002), *The New Yorker* writer Kevin Conley's book about horse breeding, Conley makes the intriguing point that James Weatherby's *General Stud Book,* which first appeared in 1791, preceded the first edition of *Burke's Peerage* by thirty-five years. There was, in other words, an official registry of equine aristocracy before there was one for human beings. We could follow this trend—of looking to horse breeding as a model on which to pattern human reproductive affairs—both forward and backward in time. It begins with Theognis, a Greek poet of the sixth century B.C., who wrote to a friend that in "horses . . . we seek the thoroughbred, and a man is concerned therein to get him offspring of good stock; yet in marriage a good man thinketh not twice of wedding the bad daughter of a bad sire if the father give him many possessions."

Two and a half thousand years later, this idea was picked up by Sir Francis Galton, a cousin of Charles Darwin. Galton is known as the father of eugenics. In *Inquiries into Human Faculty and Its Development* (1883), he argued that governments of the future could take a page from horse trainers, who recognized that "it is better economy, in the long run, to use the best mares as breeders than as workers." Galton's work was greeted with great enthusiasm all over Europe and America.

In the twentieth century, that work was carried forward primarily by two men. One was an American, Charles Davenport, a promising biologist turned quack social engineer who wrote in *Heredity in Relation to Eugenics* (1911), "Man is an organism—an animal; and the laws of improvement of corn and race horses hold true for him also. Unless people accept this simple truth and let it influence marriage selection . . . progress will cease." Davenport inculcated the wife of the railroad tycoon E. H. Harriman with his ideas, and with her money (Rockefeller pitched in, too) he was able to establish the Cold Spring Harbor labs on Long Island, where researchers gathered to prove the necessity of eliminating the "feeble-minded" and other undesirables (read, Negroes) from the population. Hideous experiments were carried out, and the data were misrepresented effectively enough that several states adopted the policy of sterilizing "mental incompetents." Laboratory archives show that Davenport spent $75,000 (this was in the 1930s) acquiring "research in genetics of the Thoroughbred horse."

The other torchbearer of eugenics in our time was Adolf Hitler, who compares horses to Jews in *Mein Kampf*. The Jewish "will to self-sacrifice," he wrote, "does not go beyond the individual's naked instinct of self-preservation. . . . The same is true of horses which try to defend themselves against an assailant in a body, but scatter again as soon as the danger is past," indicating that, in addition to his violent stupidity on all matters having to do with human affairs, Hitler knew little about the behavior of *Equus* in the wild (he was not a good rider). Nonetheless, he found something to admire in the thoroughbred, looking forward to the day when the "folkish philosophy of life" would "succeed in bringing about that nobler age in which men no longer are concerned with breeding dogs, horses, and cats, but in elevating man himself."

Once More unto the Breach

[DEPUTY SECRETARY OF DEFENSE] PAUL WOLFOWITZ: If you would indulge me for a minute, actually, I have with me a dispatch that came with from one of our Special Forces guys who is literally riding horseback with a sword with one of the Northern Alliance.

[CBS NEWS ANCHOR] BOB SCHIEFFER: With a sword?

WOLFOWITZ: With a sword, with the Northern Alliance group of several hundred people [who] had nothing but horses and rifles. And he said, "I'm advising a man . . . how best to employ light infantry and horse cavalry in the attack against Taliban tanks, mortars, artillery and machine guns," a tactic which I think became outdated with the invention of the Gatling gun. . . . It's, in a sense, the return of the horse cavalry, you might say, but no horse cavalry in history before this could call in airstrikes from long-range bombers.

SCHIEFFER: Do these people—do the people in the Special Forces know how to ride horses? I mean, there is a difference in jumping on a horse and hanging on and being able to ride. Are they trained to ride horses?

WOLFOWITZ: I can't say for sure, but apparently these guys were. They're trained in an extraordinary range of survival skills and local customs and language, and they're quite an amazing group.

—*Face the Nation*, November 18, 2001

Tracker

My only real "personal" experience with a flesh-and-blood horse came in the summer I turned eleven. At that age I was spending all of my time in the woods across the street from our house in Indiana, dressed in camouflage, practicing fighting off the Russian invasion that television had convinced me was pending. I must have gotten a reputation in the neighborhood for knowing my way around back there—or, more accurately, as the weird chubby boy who knew his way around back there. Not only was I going through a fat phase that year but I had convinced myself that if I slicked my hair back flat to my head with water, it would make me look thinner, which meant that I had constantly to sneak into the rest room at school; on top of that, both of my top front teeth had fallen out, but only one had come back in, and that one was snaggled on the end. My smile was more easily conceived than described, and on top of it I was given to wearing a camouflage beret. My father, until the end of his life, carried my school photo from this period in his wallet. He said it cheered him up.

The daughter of one of my father's colleagues had lost her pony, Flicka, and her mother called my mother and asked if I could look for it. I accepted the mission with pride and solemnity, perhaps even applying a little extra paint to my face that afternoon. I tramped around in the woods for hours, ridiculously, looking in the leaves for signs. At one point, coming down a path that I often took, I looked up to see a red fox coming toward me. It was the only wild animal I ever saw in those woods, which did not even deserve the name of "woods"—they were scrublands between two subdivisions. Eventually, when I was hungry and ready to cry, I found a bleached deer skull in a creek bed. Seizing it triumphantly, I ran with it all the way to the house of the bereaved girl, formulating the account of my discovery.

By the time I got there, they had already found the horse. It was twenty yards beyond the edge of their back yard. Somehow it had gotten free and gone running into the trees, but the rope that was still hanging from its harness became entangled. The pony pulled and pulled till it broke its own neck, they said. It was half-decomposed in a horrible way, the tissue showing through the skin in patches. I walked back to the woods, slowly, and threw the skull into a thicket.

Dead Horses

There are more than 100,000 people at Belmont on the day of the race, a record crowd by thousands, at a time when Americans are supposed to be scared of large gatherings. There is a chance to see a horse win the Triple Crown, something you can tell your grandchildren about, and people want to be there, even if War Emblem *is* owned by a Middle Eastern dude.

Thousands are picnicking out back on the grass. Another day of perfect weather. The atmosphere is straight out of the nineteenth century—it feels as though a four-hour-long program of religious speakers could begin at any moment—though the people here, apart from the famous, are not as dressed up as they were at the Derby.

Only reporters who write for dailies are allowed in the press box today, so I borrow someone else's seat in the grandstand, high enough up that I can see the whole track through binoculars. I am just in time to hear the gates shoot open for the fourth race. About twenty seconds into it, as the field approaches the first turn, I see a horse go down on the track, and then another horse. A sickened groan goes up from the crowd. Immediately the accident begins to be replayed on the huge electronic screens, the same groan going up each time, with diminishing volume. A filly named Imadeed trips—it looks as if her front legs have simply given way—and another horse, Pleasant County, trips on her.

Over and over they crash hideously in slow motion. One can see, in the replay, that Pleasant County is already dead. She falls on her head, and by the time her great body settles onto the track her legs are already stiff. Imadeed staggers to her feet and begins to limp around. The jockeys weirdly mimic this scene: one hops up, but Pleasant County's rider stays down. The one who is able to stand runs over and helps the other jockey to his feet. A horse ambulance pulls up, and a couple of men bring out the folding gray screen that signifies: dead horse. This screen comes in especially handy when a horse has to be euthanized on the track. Nothing makes a crowd feel less like betting money on horse races than watching an animal be shot between the eyes. Imadeed is led, hobbling but alive, into another ambulance, and both vehicles tear away.

It is with a morbid desire to find out what will happen to the body of the dead filly that I head for the stable area, through a long, dim tunnel that smells wonderfully of hay and horseshit. At the end of the tunnel I step into the light and see the wooden stables ranging away from me in rows, lined up along quiet streets. It is *so* quiet back here, so pastoral. I can still hear the loudspeaker back at the track, but it already seems to emanate from another world. I have no idea where I am going, and like a fool I have forgotten to bring my *Racing Form*, which would have told me the name of the horse's trainer. The stables go back for a mile.

Two Hispanic guys pass me in a golf cart. I wave them down and tell that I am "*buscando el caballo muerto.*" They exchange glances, and the one on the passenger side tells me that they have not heard about the accident. He says that they can take me to the information booth and moves over so I can hop in. I ask them where they are from: Puerto Rico and Panama. What do they do, work with the horses? "No, man, we clean the shit and carry the water. The dirty work."

A huge majority of the grooms and stable boys working at

American tracks and farms are Hispanic, and the reason for this—apart from the obvious reason: their willingness to work hard and cheap—is the same reason that so many of those early jockeys were black. Rich white (and now Japanese and Arab) people own horses, but they tend not to know much about them. They need people around with expertise and knowledge. And who really *knows* horses? The people who work with them— workers. In 1875, the year of the first Derby, those workers were former slaves, the men who had been entrusted with the horses' care back on the plantation, who had lived with the animals, in some cases even slept under one roof with them, as Secretariat's black groom, Eddie Sweat, slept with his horse the night before the Preakness in 1973. Today, in the United States, it is getting harder to find people of any color who know horses in this way—that is, other than as pets—so the owners and trainers have taken to importing their barn workers.

Our golf cart arrives through shady paths at the information booth, but the security guards there, all of whom are in their forties or fifties and are already exhausted from what is for them the busiest day of the year, do not want to hear that I am looking for a dead horse. They look down at my shiny blue-and-orange press badge and shake their heads wordlessly. "I just want to find out what happened to her," I say through the window. "Can you tell me which barn her trainer is in?"

One of them leans way back in his office chair and says to a guy in the far corner, "Do you know who trained that dead horse?"

"It's already gone," the other guy says.

"Really?" I say. "They already took her away?"

"You can see the other horse," the guy says, by which he means Imadeed, the one who lived. "She's one of Steve Young's."

The grooms at Young's barn eye me suspiciously, which I understand: their boss does not need bad press about how his extremely expensive horse went down and caused the death of someone else's extremely expensive horse. I try to make it clear that I am only curious. If I knew the Spanish, I would say, "Look, I'm just a hack!" But instead I ask, with barely intelligible grammar, about "*el caballo que se calle.*" They nod toward the one they are feeding. "*¿Es ella?*"

"Who are you?" one of them says, very pointedly in English.

"A journalist," I say. "*Por una revista.*"

"Talk to Mr. Young," he says, and points me toward the other end of the barn.

I find Young, the trainer, in his office. He is kicked back in his chair, a remote control in his hand, watching television—live feed from the track. He jumps up when he sees me, looking very displeased. His eyes are bright red and his speech is choked with saliva—he has either been drinking or crying. I suspect the latter.

The first thing he says, before I even ask a question, is, "We don't know yet."

"How bad is it?" I ask.

"As bad as it gets."

"She looks so good."

"She's content. But there's a contusion. We worry about infection."

Initial reports are that Imadeed might be saved as a broodmare, but circulation never fully returns to her right leg, and she will be put down back in Kentucky on June 20.

I start to walk deeper into the stable area, away from the track, and it only gets quieter and more bucolic as I go. Roosters, barn cats, pigeons roosting on bales of hay. And the horses, standing in the shadows of their stalls, having already raced or about to do so, now and then looking up from their chewing to watch you pass, their bored eyes taking you in and then letting you go.

Larger

On the way back to Bin Salman's barn I take a slight detour and loiter for a minute in front of Barn 5, where Secretariat was stabled before his Belmont. There is little activity now, but in '73 every person who had access or could get through security was here, wanting just to see him. From this barn, Stall 7, he was led to the most remarkable horse race ever run. "Perfect achievements," Kafka wrote in "The Aeroplanes at Brescia," "cannot be appreciated." This one could.

Sham led the field going into the first turn. He was flying. Everyone watching the race knew that he was going too fast. The strategy for Secretariat, for *any* horse, would have been to hang back and let Sham destroy himself, but Ronnie Turcotte decided to contest the pace. It was, to all appearances, an insane strategy. William Nack writes that up in the press box, turfwriters were hollering, "*They're going too fast!*"

Secretariat caught him just after the first turn, and for the first half of the race it was a duel between the two rivals. Then, around the sixth furlong, Sham began to fall apart. Laffit Pincay pulled him off in distress, and Secretariat was alone. Turcotte had done nothing but cluck to the horse.

This is when it happened, the thing, the *unbelievable thing*. Secretariat started going faster. At the first mile, he had shattered the record for the Belmont Stakes, and at a mile and an eighth he had tied the world record (remember that he was only three years old; horses get faster as they age, up to a point). Everyone— in the crowd, in the press box, in the box where the colt's owner and trainer were sitting—was waiting for something to go wrong, because this was madness. Yet he kept opening lengths on the nearest horses, Twice a Prince and My Gallant.

Turcotte, turning around, could hardly see the rest of the field. At a mile and three eighths, Secretariat had beaten Man o' War's world record. He was, at that moment, almost certainly the fastest three-year-old that ever existed. And still he kept opening lengths. Twenty-nine, thirty. If he was not lapping them, as my father remembered, it would not have taken him long, at that clip, to do so.

He finished thirty-one lengths ahead of Twice a Prince. His time: 2:24. He had clobbered the world-record time—for a horse of any age—at twelve furlongs, beating it by two and two-fifths seconds. Unprecedented. Unreal. People were crying uncontrollably. Reporters wanted to know what Turcotte had done, why had he so pressured Secretariat, when the race was clearly over? But Turcotte had never showed his whip. He had hardly even touched the horse.

There is a passage on the tape from the '73 Belmont that I noticed only after watching it dozens of times. It occurs near the end of the race. The cameraman has zoomed up pretty close on Secretariat, leaving the lens just wide enough to capture the horse and a few feet of track. Then, about half a furlong before the wire (it is hard to tell), the camera inexplicably stops tracking the leader and holds still. Secretariat rockets out of the frame, leaving the screen blank, or rather filled with empty track. I timed this emptiness—the space between Secretariat exiting and Twice a Prince entering the image—with my watch. It lasts seven seconds. And somehow each of these seconds says more about what made Secretariat great than any shot of him in motion could. In the history of profound absences—the gaps between Sappho's fragments, Christ's tomb, Rothko's black canvases—this is among the most beautiful.

Secretariat ran a few more races after the Belmont, winning all but one. His value as a stud was too great for his owners to risk having him injured on the track, so he was retired to Claiborne Farm, in Lexington. He stood there for many years, siring countless progeny, but in 1989 he developed laminitis, a cruelly painful condition that affects the hooves, and he had to be euthanized. William Nack was in Lexington when it happened and wrote a piece about the experience for *Sports Illustrated*. He interviewed Dr. Thomas Swerczek, the vet who performed the autopsy on Secretariat. This is what Swerczek told him:

I've seen and done thousands of autopsies on horses, and nothing I'd ever seen compared to it. The heart of the average horse weighs about nine pounds. This was almost twice the average size, and a third larger than any equine heart I'd ever seen. And it wasn't pathologically enlarged. All the chambers and the valves were normal. It was just larger.

Last Leg

At Prince bin Salman's barn there is a crowd, but not a large one—turfwriters, mostly. Bin Salman himself is not in attendance, citing business affairs back home, though rumors of death threats have been flying since this morning. (Sadly, today is his last chance to see War Emblem run. The prince will die of a heart attack on July 22 back in Saudi Arabia, at the age of forty-three.) It is getting extremely close to race time, and a sportscaster standing a few feet away from me says, for the rolling camera, "Baffert says he's not in *any* hurry. He'll be there on time." Baffert himself is standing just inside the barn, his arms draped over his young son's shoulders, looking back at us, inscrutable behind his dark glasses.

Just across the road, behind us, is the barn of D. Wayne Lukas, one of Baffert's rivals. Tension between the two trainers increased when Lukas made a point of saying to the *New York Times* that his horse, Proud Citizen, would wear a blanket reading "FDNY" before and after the race. (No Arab owners here!) It seems that neither man wants to lead his horse out first.

Suddenly Lukas defers and decides to go ahead. We all turn to watch Proud Citizen being led toward the tunnel that connects to the paddock, his entourage flowing around him. Almost immediately Baffert starts out, too, having proved his point. He has War Emblem by the bridle, then passes it to a groom. This truly is a beautiful horse—not black in the way that Mayakovsky was black, not inky, but very dark brown, with a long proud face, and the white star.

We all fall into step, careful to keep a few feet between us and the horse. It is weirdly silent. The only sound is the soft crunching of gravel. The thickness of history in the air is like the pressure of your own blood in your ears. Each of us is wondering if we are participating, however tangentially, in a Triple Crown. War Emblem is looking around, noticing the commotion. All his life, since he was sold as a yearling, it has been like this, strangers staring at him. *Why are they here?*

It is wonderful to walk through the tunnel behind him, to try to keep our eyes on his dark head as it disappears and unexpectedly pops up again in the shadows, to see the dust swirling in the sunlight at the paddock end of the tunnel, where we are headed, and to hear the crowd around the paddock start to roar, to see the faces when he first steps forth, prancing now, into the light. This, too, we have to concede in fairness—it is also about this. About glory.

I did not expect to be back in the stable area for so long, and I have yet to place my bets, though I more or less emptied out my bank account this morning for that purpose. I rush out of the paddock and back up to the second level, where, ever faithful, I bet the Sullivan System, a decent amount on every horse between ten-to-one and twenty-to-one to place. I run outside to my seat, binoculars swinging. I have already missed the elaborate 9/11 mourning rite.

This race does not feel like any of the races I have been to in the past year. There is something circulating through the crowd. I want to say that it is like goodwill. We are all waiting to see something beautiful, something that almost never happens, that almost never has a *chance* to happen, but which might happen today. In all the conversations I have had and overheard since this morning, no one has expressed the slightest concern about the fact that War Emblem's owner is Saudi. They know that a horse has to be owned by *somebody*. Bob Costas is talking about it, but nobody else is. It is just like the Clinton scandals. This total indifference to the counterfeit reality that pundits and op-ed writers work daily to force down our throats seems to me very American, and, for the moment, I love my country.

People are shouting before the race even begins, waving their programs in the air. But War Emblem stumbles at the very start (later, watching the replay, I see that he almost goes to the ground), and although he rallies, he never regains the lead. The race is won by *another* horse that nobody has ever heard of, one with a beautiful name: Sarava. A colt called Medaglia d'Oro places, at ten-to-one.

As at the Derby, the crowd is strangely muted. First War Emblem shocked them into silence, now he has disappointed them into silence.

Funny, I did not think that I wanted this horse to win all that badly. His story was so *crass*. But when I finally drop the binoculars, my eyes are full of tears. It takes me a full beat to realize that I have just won $500 on Medaglia d'Oro.

Coda

Back home in Manhattan it is morning, and the sun floats between buildings like a bubble of molten steel, though here in the Village there is only a glow, a brightening behind the blinds that feels tenuous, like a false dawn, as if any moment the light could think twice and just slip back, tidelike, into the sea, and all would be darkness and waiting again. This is that single silent hour between the last cokehead finally kicked out of the bar, braying, not having been laid, and the first of the rumbling yawns of the shop-front gates being rolled up, over, and out of sight. It is fearfully still.

Once more I put on my headphones and click on the sorry little clips, and in my ears I hear the calls. Once more I close my eyes and watch him run: the Derby, the Preakness, the Belmont Stakes, 1973. I listen to Chick Anderson as he struggles and fails, in the human way, to describe perfection, to describe what no one had ever seen, and what no one there would ever see again.

And still the old question hangs over it all: Why? Why did he run as he did, with no one forcing him, or even urging him, with no one or thing to defeat anymore, with no punishment waiting for him if he slowed? For this morning, at least, at last, the answer is clear. It requires no faith. He ran that way, I know, because he could, and we cannot.

One does not, if one is beauty, have to know what beauty is.

The New Yorker

WINNER, REPORTING

In the Party of God

Penetrating the closed world of radical Middle Eastern politics, reporter Jeffrey Goldberg constructs a brilliant and chilling portrait of Hezbollah, the Iranian-sponsored organization that's seen as terrorism's "A-Team." Wide-ranging, yet told with an economy born of effective detail, Goldberg's story vividly illuminates an organization whose reach is growing beyond the Mideast to South America and the United States.

Jeffrey Goldberg

In the Party of God

Are terrorists in Lebanon preparing for a larger war?

I—The Meeting

The village of Ras al-Ein, which is situated in the Bekaa Valley of Lebanon, falls under the overlapping control of the Syrian Army, the Iranian Revolutionary Guard Corps, and the Shiite terrorist group Hezbollah, or Party of God. The village is seedy and brown, and is decorated with posters of martyrs and potentates—Ayatollah Khomeini is especially popular—and with billboards that celebrate bloodshed and sacrifice.

I visited Ras al-Ein this summer to interview the leader of a Hezbollah faction, a man named Hussayn al-Mussawi, who, twenty years ago, was involved in kidnapping Americans. Many of those kidnapped were held in Ras al-Ein; they were kept blindfolded, and chained to beds and radiators. It is thought that

Ras al-Ein is where William Buckley, the Beirut station chief of the Central Intelligence Agency, was held for a time before he was killed by Hezbollah, in 1985.

When I arrived, it was midday; the air was still and the heat smothering, and the streets were mostly empty. A man was selling ice cream in a park at the center of town. Slides and swing sets, their paint peeling, dot the park; in the middle is a pond covered by a skin of algae. Several women and children were there. The women wore gray chadors, and their heads were covered by scarves, pinned high and tight under the left ear, so that no strand of hair could escape.

Like the rest of the town, the park was crowded with ferocious Hezbollah art. One poster showed an American flag whose field of stars had been replaced by a single Star of David. Another portrayed the Dome of the Rock, the Muslim shrine in Jerusalem, cupped in the bony hand of a figure with a grotesquely hooked nose. A third poster, extolling the bravery of Shiite martyrs, showed a Muslim fighter standing on a pile of dead soldiers whose uniforms were marked with Stars of David. The yellow flag of Hezbollah could be seen everywhere; across the top is a quotation from the Koran, from which Hezbollah took its name—"Verily the party of God shall be victorious"— and at the center is an AK-47 in silhouette, in the hand of the Shiite martyr Husayn, a cousin of the Prophet Muhammad. In the background is a depiction of the globe, suggesting Hezbollah's role in the worldwide *umma*, or community of Muslims. Along the bottom of the Hezbollah flag is written "The Islamic Revolution in Lebanon." I did not see the red-green-and-white flag of Lebanon anywhere in Ras al-Ein.

I had taken a taxi from Ashrafieh, the prosperous Christian neighborhood in Beirut, to Ras al-Ein, a two-hour trip over pot-holed roads and through a modest number of roadblocks. The soft Mediterranean air soon gave way to the dry-bones heat of the Bekaa. The taxi-driver, an elderly Christian, had been hesitant about the trip (Lebanon's Christian minority is fearful of Shiite gunmen), but he smoothly negotiated the passage through two Syrian Army checkpoints. At one, a sergeant of about thirty, who carried a side arm and wore a round helmet covered in black mesh, inspected my American passport, handed it back to me, and said, enigmatically, "Osama bin Laden."

We had by then reached the outskirts of Baalbek, the main Bekaa town. Baalbek is famous for three well-preserved Roman temples, of Jupiter, Venus, and Bacchus. (A statue of Hafez al-Assad, the late dictator of Syria and the father of the current dictator, stands at the entrance to the town.) The temples, which are enormous— the two main temples are larger than the Parthenon— are the site of an annual international cultural festival that draws the élite of Beirut, and Lebanese officials like to point to it as proof of Lebanon's normalcy. This year, the festival featured a performance of Michael Flatley's "Lord of the Dance." Ras al-Ein is a couple of miles from the temples, and we soon arrived at the Nawras Restaurant, next to the park, where I was to meet Mussawi. I sat at a table outside, with a view of the street. Two men nearby were smoking hookahs. I ordered a Pepsi and waited.

● ● ●

Shiism arose as a protest movement, whose followers believed that Islam should be ruled by descendants of the Prophet Muhammad's cousin Ali, and not by the caliphs who seized control after the Prophet's death. The roots of Shiite anger lie in the martyrdom of Ali's son Husayn, who died in battle against the Caliph Yezid in what is today southern Iraq. (I have heard both Shiites from southern Iraq and Iranian Shiites refer to their enemy Saddam Hussein as a modern-day Yezid.) At times, Shiism has been a quietist movement; Shiites built houses of mourning and study, called Husaynias, where they recalled the glory of Husayn's martyrdom.

In Lebanon in the nineteen-sixties, the Shiites began to be drawn to the outside world. Some joined revolutionary Palestinian movements; others fell into the orbit of a populist cleric, Musa Sadr, who founded a group called the Movement of the Deprived and, later, the Shiite Amal militia. Hezbollah was formed, in 1982, by a group of young, dispossessed Shiites who coalesced around a cleric and poet named Muhammad Hussayn Fadlallah. They were impelled by a number of disparate forces, including the oppression of their community in Lebanon by the country's Sunni and Christian élites, and the rapture they felt in 1979 as Iran came under the power of "pure" Islam. A crucial event, though, was Israel's invasion of Lebanon in June of 1982.

Fatah, which is part of the Palestine Liberation Organization, had been firing Katyusha rockets into northern Israel from Lebanon, where it had its main base, and Prime Minister Menachem Begin, on the advice of his defense minister, Ariel Sharon, ordered Israeli forces into Lebanon. The stated purpose was to conquer what had come to be known as Fatahland, the strip of South Lebanon under Yasir Arafat's control, and to evict the P.L.O.'s forces. Sharon, though, had grander designs: to secure a friendly Christian government in Beirut and to destroy the P.L.O. It was not so much the invasion that inspired the Shiites, who were happy to see the South free of Arafat and Fatah. The Shiites took up arms when they realized that Sharon, like Arafat, had no intention of leaving Lebanon.

Hezbollah, with bases in the Bekaa and in Beirut's southern suburbs, quickly became the most successful terrorist organization in modern history. It has served as a role model for terror groups around the world; Magnus Ranstorp, the director of the Centre for the Study of Terrorism and Political Violence, at the University of St. Andrews, in Scotland, says that Al Qaeda learned the value of choreographed violence from Hezbollah. The organization virtually invented the multipronged terror attack when, early on the morning of October 23, 1983, it synchronized the suicide bomb-

ings, in Beirut, of the United States Marine barracks and an apartment building housing a contingent of French peacekeepers. Those
attacks occurred just twenty seconds apart; a third part of the plan,
to destroy the compound of the Italian peacekeeping contingent, is
said to have been jettisoned when the planners learned that the
Italians were sleeping in tents, not in a high-rise building.

·   ·   ·

Until September 11th of last year, Hezbollah had murdered
more Americans than any other terrorist group—two hundred
and forty-one in the Marine-barracks attack alone. Through terror tactics, Hezbollah forced the American and French governments to withdraw their peacekeeping forces from Lebanon.
And, two years ago, it became the first military force, guerrilla or
otherwise, to drive Israel out of Arab territory when Prime Minister Ehud Barak withdrew his forces from South Lebanon.

Using various names, including the Islamic Jihad Organization and the Organization of the Oppressed on Earth, Hezbollah
remained underground until 1985, when it published a manifesto condemning the West, and proclaiming, "Every one of us is
a fighting soldier when a call for jihad arises and each one of us
carries out his mission in battle on the basis of his legal obligations. For Allah is behind us supporting and protecting us while
instilling fear in the hearts of our enemies."

Another phase began in earnest in 1991, when, at the close of
Lebanon's sixteen-year civil war, the country's many militias
agreed to disarm. Nominally, Lebanon is governed from Beirut
by an administration whose senior portfolios have been carefully
divided among the country's various religious factions—
Maronite and Greek Orthodox Christians, Sunnis and Shiites
and Druze. But in fact Lebanon is under the control of Syria; and
the Syrians, with encouragement from Iran, have allowed

Hezbollah to maintain its arsenal, and even to expand it, in the interest of fighting Israel as Syria's proxy. The Syrians also allowed Hezbollah to control the Shiite ghettos of southern Beirut, much of the Bekaa Valley, and most of South Lebanon, along the border with Israel.

Hezbollah's current leader, Sayyid Hassan Nasrallah, is as important a figure in Lebanon as the country's ruling politicians and the Syrian President, Bashar al-Assad. Hezbollah officials run for office in Lebanon and win—the group now holds eleven seats in the hundred-and-twenty-eight-seat Lebanese parliament. But within Hezbollah there is little pretense of fealty to the President of Lebanon, Émile Lahoud, who is a Christian, and certainly none to the Prime Minister, Rafiq Hariri, who is a Sunni Muslim. The only portraits one sees in Hezbollah offices are of Khomeini and of Ayatollah Khamenei, the current ruler of Iran.

Hezbollah has an annual budget of more than a hundred million dollars, which is supplied by the Iranian government directly and by a complex system of finance cells scattered around the world, from Bangkok and Paraguay to Michigan and North Carolina. Like Hamas in Gaza, Hezbollah operates successfully in public spheres that are closed off to most terrorist groups. It runs a vast and effective social-services network. It publishes newspapers and magazines and owns a satellite television station that is said to be watched by ten million people a day in the Middle East and Europe. The station, called Al Manar, or the Lighthouse, broadcasts anti-American programming, but its main purpose is to encourage Palestinians to become suicide bombers.

· · ·

Along with this public work, Hezbollah continues to increase its terrorist and guerrilla capabilities. Magnus Ranstorp says that

Hezbollah can be active on four tracks simultaneously—the political, the social, the guerrilla, and the terrorist—because its leaders are "masters of long-term strategic subversion." The organization's Special Security Apparatus operates in Europe, North and South America, and East Asia. According to both American and Israeli intelligence officials, the group maintains floating "day camps" for terrorist training throughout the Bekaa Valley; many of the camps are said to be just outside Baalbek. In some of them, the instructors are supplied by the Iranian Revolutionary Guard Corps and Iran's Ministry of Intelligence. In the past twenty years, terrorists from such disparate organizations as the Basque separatist group ETA, the Red Brigades, the Kurdistan Workers' Party, and the Irish Republican Army have been trained in these camps.

A main focus today appears to be the training of specifically anti-Israel militants in the science of constructing so-called "mega-bombs," devices that can bring down office towers and other large structures. The explosion of a mega-bomb is the sort of event that could lead to a major Middle East war. In fact, such attacks have been tried: in April, a plot to bomb the Azrieli Towers, two of Tel Aviv's tallest buildings, was foiled by Israeli security services; in May, a bomb exploded beneath a tanker truck at a fuel depot near Tel Aviv, but did not set off a larger explosion, as planned. Had these operations been successful, hundreds, if not thousands, of Israelis would have died. Salah Shehada, a Hamas leader in Gaza, is said by Israel to have been planning a coordinated attack on five buildings in Tel Aviv. (In July, an Israeli warplane dropped a one-ton bomb on the building where Shehada lived; he was killed, along with at least fourteen others, including nine children.)

Gal Luft, an Israeli reserve lieutenant colonel and an expert on counterterrorism, told me that Hezbollah's role in these plans is unknown. "Hezbollah has experience with bulk explosives," Luft said. "You can make the case that the Hezbollah provides inspiration and advice and technical support, but I wouldn't rule out its own cells trying this." Luft said that it is only a matter of time before a "mega-attack" succeeds.

Hezbollah agents have infiltrated the West Bank and Gaza, and Arab communities inside Israel, helping Hamas and Islamic Jihad and attempting to set up their own cells; many Palestinians revere Hezbollah for achieving in South Lebanon what the Palestinians have failed to achieve in the occupied territories. In the past year, Hezbollah has also been stockpiling rockets for potential use against Israel. These rockets, most of which are from Iran, are said to be moved by truck from Syria, through the Bekaa Valley, and then on to Hezbollah forces in South Lebanon.

Hezbollah has not been suspected of overt anti-American actions since 1996, when the Khobar Towers, in Saudi Arabia, were attacked, but, according to intelligence officials, its operatives, with the help and cover of Iranian diplomats, have been making surveillance tapes of American diplomatic installations in South America, Southeast Asia, and Europe. These tapes, along with maps and other tools, are said to be kept in well-organized clandestine libraries.

In recent days, top American officials have suggested that Hezbollah—and its state sponsors—may soon find themselves targeted in the Bush Administration's war on terror. Deputy Secretary of State Richard Armitage recently called Hezbollah the "A-team" of terrorism and Al Qaeda the "B-team." The C.I.A. has lost at least seven officers to Hezbollah terrorism, including William Buckley. Sam Wyman, a retired C.I.A. official, who recommended Buckley for the job in Beirut, told me that "those who work the terrorism problem writ large, and those who are working the Hezbollah problem writ small, know that this is an account that has not been closed." The chairman of the Senate intelligence committee, Bob Graham, of Florida, says he wants the Administration's war on terrorism to focus not on Iraq but on Hezbollah, its Bekaa Valley camps, and its state sponsors in

Iran and Syria. "We should tell the Syrians that we expect them to shut down the Bekaa Valley camps within x number of days, and, if they don't, we are reserving the right to shut them down ourselves," Graham said last month.

•   •   •

After drinking a third Pepsi, I watched a Land Cruiser pull up to the restaurant and deliver a stiff and unhappy-looking man with a well-kept beard. The man sat down silently across from me. Three men, one of whom wore a leather jacket, despite the terrific heat, stood quietly by the Land Cruiser.

The bearded man was not Hussayn al-Mussawi, whom I had hoped to meet. He said that his name was Muhammad, that he was an aide to Mussawi, and that he had been sent to assess my intentions. I was here, I said, to examine the claim that Hezbollah had transformed itself into a mainstream Lebanese political party.

I said that I also wanted to gauge the group's feelings about America, and look for any sign that its implacable opposition to the existence of Israel had changed.

"Are you going to ask about past events?" Muhammad asked. I indicated that I would.

When he pressed me further, I admitted that I was curious about one person in particular, a Hezbollah security operative named Imad Mugniyah. Mugniyah, who began his career in the nineteen-seventies in Arafat's bodyguard unit, is the man whom the United States holds responsible for most of Hezbollah's anti-American attacks, including the Marine-barracks bombing and the 1985 hijacking of a T.W.A. flight, during which a U.S. Navy diver was executed. He is also suspected of involvement in the attack on the Khobar Towers, in which nineteen American servicemen were killed.

Last year, the U.S. government placed Mugniyah on the list of its twenty-two most wanted terrorists, along with two of his colleagues, Ali Atwa and Hassan Izz-al-Din. (Atwa and Izz-al-Din are wanted specifically in connection with the hijacking of the T.W.A. flight in 1985.) The very mention of Mugniyah's name is a sensitive issue in Lebanon and Syria, which have refused to carry out repeated American requests—one was delivered recently by Senator Graham—to shut down Hezbollah's security apparatus, and assist in the capture of Mugniyah. Lebanon's Prime Minister Hariri became agitated when, in a conversation this summer, I asked why his government has refused to help find Mugniyah and his accomplices. "They're not here! They're not here!" Hariri said. "I've told the Americans a hundred times, they're not here!"

Seated in the Nawras Restaurant in Ras al-Ein, across from a man who called himself Muhammad, I said yes, Imad Mugniyah would figure in my story. At that, Muhammad rose, looked at me dismissively, and left the restaurant without a word.

II—The Goal

The chief spokesman for Hezbollah is a narrow-shouldered, self-contained man of about forty named Hassan Ezzeddin, who dresses in the style of an Iranian diplomat: trim beard, dark jacket, white shirt, no tie. His office is on a low floor of an apartment building in the southern suburbs of Beirut, which are called the Dahiya. Hezbollah has five main offices there, and all are in apartment buildings, which helps to create a shield between the bureaucracy and Israeli fighter jets and bombers that periodically fly overhead. The shabby offices are sparsely furnished; apparently, the idea is to be able to dismantle them in half an hour or less, in case of an Israeli attack.

The eight members of Hezbollah's ruling council are said to meet in the Dahiya once a week. Lebanese police officers are stationed at a handful of intersections, but they don't stray from their posts. The buildings housing Hezbollah's offices are protected by gunmen dressed in black, and plainclothes Hezbollah agents patrol the streets. Once, while walking to an appointment, I took out a disposable camera and began to take pictures of posters celebrating the deaths of Hezbollah "martyrs." Within thirty seconds, two Hezbollah men confronted me. They ordered me to put my camera away and then followed me to my meeting.

The Shiite stronghold in the southern suburbs of the city is only a twenty-minute drive from the Virgin Megastore in downtown Beirut, but it might as well be part of Tehran. Ayatollah Khomeini and Ayatollah Khamenei stare down from the walls, and the Western fashions ubiquitous in East Beirut are forbidden; many women wear the full chador. The suburbs are the most densely packed of Beirut's neighborhoods, with seven- and eight-story apartment buildings, many of them jerry-built, jammed against one another along congested streets and narrow alleys. The main businesses in the Dahiya are believed to be chop shops, where stolen automobiles and computers are taken apart and sold.

I was introduced to Ezzeddin by Hussain Naboulsi, and he translated our conversation. Naboulsi is in charge of Hezbollah's Web site. He spent some time in America, and incorporates American slang unself-consciously into his speech. He is young and gregarious, but he grew evasive when the subject of his background came up. "We lived in Brooklyn, and I was going to go to the University of Texas, but then we moved to Canada. . . ." He trailed off.

Ezzeddin said that anti-Americanism is no longer the focus of his party's actions. Hezbollah, he said, holds no brief against the American people; it is opposed only to the policies of the American government, principally its "unlimited" support for Israel. Like all Hezbollah's public figures, Ezzeddin is proud of the victory over Israel in South Lebanon, two years ago, and he spoke at length about the reasons for Hezbollah's success. He quoted a statement of Hezbollah's leader, Sayyid Hassan Nasrallah, made shortly after the Israeli withdrawal: "I tell you: this 'Israel' that owns nuclear weapons and the strongest air force in this region is more fragile than a spiderweb." Ezzeddin explained that Ehud Barak pulled out his troops because the soldiers—and their mothers—feared death. This isn't true for Muslims, he said. "Life doesn't end when you die. To us, there is real life after death. Reaching the afterlife is the goal of life. Once you have in mind the goal of dying, you stop fearing the Jews."

.   .   .

After Israel withdrew from southern Lebanon, many experts on the Middle East assumed that Hezbollah would focus on social services and on domestic politics, in order to bring about a peaceful transformation of Lebanon into an Islamic republic. Even before the Israeli pullout, a leading scholar of Hezbollah, Augustus Richard Norton, of Boston University, wrote a paper entitled "Hezbollah: From Radicalism to Pragmatism?" In his paper, Norton said that in discussions with Hezbollah officials he had got the impression that the group "has no appetite to launch a military campaign across the Israeli border, should Israel withdraw from the South."

But Hezbollah is, at its core, a jihadist organization, and its leaders have never tried to disguise their ultimate goal: building an Islamic republic in Lebanon and liberating Jerusalem from the Jews. Immediately after the withdrawal, Hezbollah announced that Israel was still occupying a tiny slice of Lebanese land called Shebaa Farms. The United Nations ruled that Shebaa Farms was not part of Lebanon but belonged to the Israeli-occupied Golan Heights, and thus was a matter for Israeli-Syrian negotiations. Hezbollah disagreed, and, with Syria's acquiescence, has continued to launch frequent attacks on Israeli outposts in Shebaa.

Ezzeddin seemed to concede that the Hezbollah campaign to

rid Shebaa of Israeli troops is a pretext for something larger. "If they go from Shebaa, we will not stop fighting them," he told me. "Our goal is to liberate the 1948 borders of Palestine," he added, referring to the year of Israel's founding. The Jews who survive this war of liberation, Ezzeddin said, "can go back to Germany, or wherever they came from." He added, however, that the Jews who lived in Palestine before 1948 will be "allowed to live as a minority and they will be cared for by the Muslim majority." Sayyid Nasrallah himself told a conference held in Tehran last year that "we all have an extraordinary historic opportunity to finish off the entire cancerous Zionist project."

The balance of forces on Israel's northern border suggests that Hezbollah's ambitions are unrealizable. Its fighters number in the low thousands, at most; the Israeli Air Force is among the most powerful in the world. But the pullout from Lebanon heightened Hezbollah's self-regard, its contempt for Jews, and its desire for total victory. "Everyone told us, 'You're crazy, what are you doing, you can't defeat Israel,'" Ezzeddin said. "But we have shown that the Jews are not invincible. We dealt the Jews a serious blow, and we will continue to deal the Jews serious blows."

•　　•　　•

The withdrawal of Israeli forces from southern Lebanon, after eighteen years, closed a disastrous chapter in Israeli military history. The conflict destroyed the government of Menachem Begin, and Begin himself; he lived out his final days as a recluse. An Israeli commission held Ariel Sharon, his defense minister, "indirectly responsible" for the massacre by pro-Israeli Christian militiamen of approximately eight hundred Palestinians at the Sabra and Shatila refugee camps, in Beirut, in 1982. The Lebanon invasion seemed to have ended Sharon's career. By the time the troops left, more than nine hundred Israeli soldiers had been killed in

Lebanon. The withdrawal was badly managed and chaotic. The Army abandoned equipment, and also deserted its Christian allies, a militia called the South Lebanon Army.

In one of the Israeli Army's final acts, sappers tried to bring down the twelfth-century Beaufort Castle, a fortress that sits high over the upper Galilee. The castle had served as a platform for P.L.O. rocket attacks on Israeli towns and farms before Sharon's invasion, and, in the final days of the occupation, the Army was hoping to deny the Palestinians the shelter of its battlements. The Israelis succeeded only in part. The walls did not crumble, and the Hezbollah flag now flies from the highest tower.

I visited Beaufort on a brilliantly hot day this summer, and the only people around were a handful of Hezbollah fighters, a group of Beirutis on a day-long excursion through the South, and two Iranian tourists, with cheap cameras hanging from their necks. One of the Hezbollah guerrillas, a pimply man in his early twenties named Na'im, showed me around. We picked our way across half-collapsed battlements, among thorn bushes and patches of purple and yellow wildflowers, to the remains of the outer rampart, which overlooks a steep drop to the floor of the Litani River valley. Na'im wore bluejeans and a red-and-green plaid shirt. He carried a rifle, which he used as a walking stick. He told me that the castle dated back to the Islamic conquest of the Holy Land. In fact, Beaufort was built by the Crusaders, but in Na'im's version the castle began as a Muslim fortress. "Saladin used this to defeat the Crusaders," he said, in a rehearsed manner. "Hezbollah will use it to defeat the Jews."

From where we stood, we had a clear view into the Israeli town of Metulla, with its red-roofed, whitewashed houses, small hotels, and orchards. "The Jews are sons of pigs and apes," Na'im said. We walked down the crumbling rampart, past a dry cistern, and up a ridge to the high tower, where the Hezbollah flag waved in the wind.

From Beaufort, I headed to the village of Kfar Kila, and the border, where the Fatima Gate is situated. During the occupation, Israel called it the Good Fence; it was the entrance to Metulla for Lebanese workers. The Good Fence has been sealed, and is now famous as the place where Palestinians and Lebanese throw rocks at Israeli soldiers.

I saw, on my drive down, the digging of what appeared to be anti-tank trenches, but, though the South may be a future battlefield, it is also a museum of past glory. Of the four or five main Islamic fundamentalist terror organizations in the Middle East, Hezbollah has by far the most sophisticated public-relations operation, and it has turned the South into an open-air celebration of its success against Israel. The experience of driving there is similar in some ways to driving through Gettysburg, or Antietam; roadside signs and billboards describe in great detail the battles and unit formations associated with a particular place. One multicolored sign, in both Arabic and English, reads:

> On Oct. 19, 1988 at 1:25 p.m. a martyr car that was body trapped with 500 kilogram of highly exploding materials transformed two Israeli troops into masses of fire and limbs, in one of the severe kicks that the Israeli army had received in Lebanon.

Most of the signs place the word "Israel" in quotation marks, to underscore the country's illegitimacy, and every sign includes a fact box: the number of "Israelis" killed and wounded at the location, and the "Date of Ignominious Departure" of "Israeli" forces. The historical markers also carry quotations from Israeli leaders praising the fighting abilities of Hezbollah's martyrs. One sign reads, "Zionists comments: 'Hezbollah's secret weapon is their self-innovation and their ability to produce bombs that are simple but effective.' " The attribution beneath the quote is "Former 'Israeli' Prime Minister Ihud Barak."

According to Israeli security sources, the Israelis have never been able to infiltrate Hezbollah as they have the P.L.O. One intelligence official told me that Hezbollah leaders have so far been immune to the three inducements that often lure Palestinians to the Israeli side. In Hebrew, they are called the three "K"s: *kesef*, or money; *kavod*, respect; and *kussit*, a crude sexual term for a woman.

The centerpiece of Hezbollah's propaganda effort in the South is the former Al-Khiam prison, a rambling stone-and-concrete complex of interconnected buildings, a few miles from the border, where I stopped on the way to Kfar Kila. For fifteen years, the prison was run by Israel's proxy force in Lebanon, the South Lebanon Army, with the assistance of the Shabak, the Israeli equivalent of the F.B.I. Prisoners in Al-Khiam—which held almost two hundred at any given time—were allegedly subjected to electric-shock torture and a variety of deprivations. The jail has been preserved just as it was on the day the Israelis left. There are still Israeli Army–issue sleeping bags in the cells. Hezbollah has added a gift shop, which sells Hezbollah key chains and flags and cassettes of martial Hezbollah music; a cafeteria; and signs on the walls of various rooms that describe, in Hezbollah's terms, the use of the rooms. "A Room for Investigation and Torturing by Electricity," reads one. "A Room for the Boss of Whippers." "A Room for Investigation with the Help of the Traitors." And "The Hall of Torturing-Burying-Kicking-Beating-Applying Electricity-Pouring Hot Water-Placing a Dog Beside." A busload of tourists, residents of a Palestinian refugee camp outside Beirut, were clearly in awe of the place, treating the cells as if they were reliquaries and congratulating the Hezbollah employees.

Like me, the tourists were headed for the border at Kfar Kila, where one can walk right up to the electrified fence, and where Israeli cameras feed real-time pictures to a series of fortified observation stations just south of the line. An Israeli bunker sits about fifty feet in from the fence—one man told me that the Israeli soldiers never show their faces—and the Palestinians took turns taking pictures and yelling curses. I drove a short distance to a Hezbollah position that faces a massive concrete Israeli fortress called Tziporen. The tour bus, headed for the same place, stopped on the way at an overlook, and the Palestinians got out. On the Israeli side, on a track that ran parallel to the Lebanese road, was a Humvee and three Israeli soldiers. They were protecting a group of workers who were repairing a section of the road. The Israelis were no more than forty feet away, on the lower part of the slope. The experience for the Palestinians—and for a group of Kuwaitis who arrived by car—was something like a grizzly sighting in a national park. "*Yahud!*" one Kuwaiti said, dumbfounded. "Jews!" His friends produced video cameras and began filming. The Israeli soldiers waved; the Arabs did not. A few began cursing the soldiers and, once it was decided that the workers were Israeli Arabs, cursed them, too. "*Ana bidi'ani kak!*" one Palestinian yelled at the soldiers—"I want to fuck you up." "*Jasus*"—"spy"—another called out. An argument broke out on the ridge, and the Palestinians decided that it was not right to curse the Arab workers, who were only earning a living in oppressive circumstances. Apologies were offered, and what was by now a cavalcade moved forward, to the Hezbollah position opposite the Israeli fortress.

Tziporen, the fortress, overlooks the mausoleum of a Jewish sage named Rav Ashi, who was the redactor of the Babylonian Talmud, and who died in 427. The modest mausoleum sits half in Lebanon and half in Israel. Barbed wire runs atop it, and, with the help of a southerly breeze, the Hezbollah flag planted on the Lebanese side of the mausoleum flapped into Israel. The fighters at the Hezbollah position warned us not to get too close to the fence; the Israelis might fire. Rock throwing from a comfortable distance was encouraged, and the Palestinians aimed for the roof of the fort. On weekends, when the crowds are thicker, villagers drive in tractors full of rocks to supply the tourists.

Because it was too risky to approach the fence, it was impossible to read a large billboard planted three feet north of the line. It faced south into Israel, carrying what was obviously a message for the Israelis alone. The border is, of course, sealed, so it was a month before I got a clear look at the billboard. It read, in Hebrew, "Sharon—Don't Forget Your Soldiers Are Still in Lebanon." The message was written under a photograph of a Hezbollah guerrilla holding, by the hair, the severed head of an Israeli commando.

III—The Suicide Channel

The true propaganda engine of Hezbollah is the Al Manar satellite television station. Unlike most of Hezbollah's public offices, the studios of Al Manar are not shoddily built or cheaply decorated. The station's five-story headquarters building in the Dahiya, at the end of a short side street, is surrounded by taller apartment buildings. Guards carrying rifles patrol its perimeter, but, inside, Al Manar has a corporate atmosphere. The lobby is glass and marble, and behind the reception desk a pleasant young man answers the telephone. He sits beneath a portrait of Abbas al-Mussawi, the previous Hezbollah leader, who was assassinated ten years ago by Israel. At the reception desk, women whose dress is deemed immodest can borrow a chador.

Al Manar's news director is Hassan Fadlallah, who is in his early thirties and is a member of the same clan as Muhammad Hussayn Fadlallah, the Hezbollah spiritual leader. Fadlallah, a studious-looking man who had several days' stubble on his face, is working on a Ph.D. in education. He apologized for his poor English. A waiter brought us orange juice and tea.

I began by asking him to compare Al Manar and the most famous Arabic satellite channel, Al Jazeera. "Neutrality like that of Al Jazeera is out of the question for us," Fadlallah said. "We cover only the victim, not the aggressor. CNN is the Zionist news network, Al Jazeera is neutral, and Al Manar takes the side of the Palestinians."

Fadlallah paused for a moment, and said he would like to amend his comment on CNN. "We were very happy with Ted Turner," he said. "We were so happy that he was getting closer to the truth." He was referring to recent comments by Turner, the founder of CNN, who talked about suicide bombers and the Israeli Army and then said, "So who are the terrorists? I would make a case that both sides are involved in terrorism." Turner was criticized harshly in the American press and by supporters of Israel, and later said that he regretted "any implication that I believe the actions taken by Israel to protect its people are equal to terrorism." Fadlallah claimed that Turner revised his statement because "the Jews threatened his life." He said Al Manar's opposition to neutrality means that, unlike Al Jazeera, his station would never feature interviews or comments by Israeli officials. "We're not looking to interview Sharon," Fadlallah said. "We want to get close to him in order to kill him."

Al Manar would not rule out broadcasting comments from non-Israeli Jews. "There would be one or two we would put on our shows. For example, we would like to have Noam Chomsky." Fadlallah suggested, half jokingly, that I appear on a question-and-answer show. (Later, another Al Manar official suggested that I answer questions about what he termed "the true meaning of the Talmud.")

Fadlallah said that one of Al Manar's goals is to set in context the role of Jews in world affairs. Anti-Semitism, he said, was banned from the station, but he was considering a program on "scholars who dissent on the issue of the Holocaust," which would include the work of the French Holocaust denier Roger Garaudy. "There are contradictions," Fadlallah said. "Many Europeans believe that the Holocaust was a myth invented so that the Jews could get compensation. Everyone knows how the Jews punish people who seek the truth about the Holocaust."

It would be a mistake, Fadlallah went on, to focus solely on Al Manar's anti-Israel programs. "We have news programming, kids' shows, game shows, political news, and culture." At the same time, he said, Al Manar is "trying to keep the people in the mood of suffering," and most of the station's daily schedule, including its game shows and children's programming, tends to center on Israel. A program called "The Spider's House" explores what Hezbollah sees as Israel's weaknesses; "In Spite of the Wounds" portrays as heroes men who were wounded fighting Israel in South Lebanon. On a game show entitled "The Viewer Is the Witness," contestants guess the names of prominent Israeli politicians and military figures, who are played by Lebanese actors. Al Manar also has a weekly program called "Terrorists."

Avi Jorisch, a fellow at the Washington Institute for Near East Policy, a pro-Israel think tank, who is writing a book about Al Manar, has visited the station and watched several hundred hours of its programming. The show "Terrorists," he told me, airs vintage footage of what it terms "Zionist crimes," which include, by Hezbollah's definition, any Israeli action, offensive or defensive. According to Jorisch, Al Manar, with its estimated ten million viewers, is not as popular in the Arab world as Al Jazeera, although he noted that Arab viewership is not audited. He said that his Lebanese sources credit Al Manar as the second most popular station among Palestinians in the West Bank and Gaza. (Al Manar can be received in the United States via satellite.)

Al Manar regularly airs raw footage of violence in the occupied territories, and it will break into its programming with what one Al Manar official called "patriotic music videos" to announce Palestinian attacks and applaud the killing of Israelis. When I visited the station, the videos were being produced in a basement editing room by a young man named Firas Mansour. Al Manar has modern equipment, and the day I was there Mansour, who was in charge of mixing the videos, was working on a Windows-based editing suite. Mansour is in his late twenties, and he was dressed in hip-hop style. His hair was gelled, and he wore a gold chain, a heavy silver bracelet, and a goatee. He spoke colloquial American English. I asked him where he learned it. "Boston," he said.

Mansour showed me some recent footage from the West Bank, of Israeli soldiers firing on Palestinians. Accompanying the video was a Hezbollah fighting song. "What I'm doing is synchronizing the gunshots to form the downbeat of the song," he told me. "This is my technique. I thought of it." He had come up with a title: "I'm going to call it 'Death to Israel.' " Mansour said that he can produce two or three videos on a good day. "What I do is, first, I try to feel the music. Then I find the pictures to go along with it." He pulled up another video, this one almost ready to air. "Try and see if you could figure out the theme of this one," he said.

The video began with Israeli soldiers firing on Palestinians. Then the screen filled with pictures of Palestinians carrying the wounded to ambulances, followed by an angry funeral scene. Suddenly, the scene shifted to Israelis under fire. An Israeli soldier was on the ground, rocking back and forth, next to a burning jeep; this was followed by scenes of Jewish funerals, with coffins draped in the Israeli flag being lowered into graves.

Mansour pressed a button, and the images disappeared from the screen. "The idea is that even if the Jews are killing us we can still kill them. That we derive our power from blood. It's saying, 'Get ready to blow yourselves up, because this is the only way to liberate Palestine.' " The video, he said, would be shown after the next attack in Israel. He said he was thinking of calling it "We Will Kill All the Jews." I suggested that these videos would encourage the recruitment of suicide bombers among the Palestinians. "Exactly," he replied.

●   ●   ●

The anti-Semitism of the Middle East groups that oppose Israel's right to exist often seems instrumental—anti-Jewish ste-

reotypes are another weapon in the anti-Israeli armamentarium.
The rhetoric is repellent, but in the past it did not quite touch
the malignancy of genocidal anti-Semitism. The language has
changed, however. In April, in a sermon delivered in the Gaza
Strip, Sheikh Ibrahim Madhi, a Palestinian Authority imam,
said, "Oh, Allah, accept our martyrs in the highest Heaven. Oh,
Allah, show the Jews a black day. Oh, Allah, annihilate the Jews
and their supporters." (The translation was made by the Middle
East Media Research Institute.) In Saudi Arabia, where anti-
Semitism permeates the newspapers and the mosques, the imam
of the Al Harram mosque in Mecca, Sheikh Abd al-Rahman al-
Sudais, recently declared, "Read history and you will understand
that the Jews of yesterday are the evil forefathers of the even
more evil Jews of today: infidels, falsifiers of words, calf worship-
pers, prophet murderers, deniers of prophecies . . . the scum of
the human race, accursed by Allah." Hezbollah has been at the
vanguard of this shift toward frank anti-Semitism, and its leaders
frequently resort to epidemiological metaphors in describing the
role of Jews in world affairs. Ibrahim Mussawi, the urbane and
scholarly-seeming director of English-language news at Al
Manar, called Jews "a lesion on the forehead of history." A biochemist named Hussein Haj Hassan, a Hezbollah official who
represents Baalbek in the Lebanese parliament, told me that he is
not anti-Semitic, but he has noticed that the Jews are a pan-
national group "that functions in a way that lets them act as par-
asites in the nations that have given them shelter."

The Middle East scholar Martin Kramer, a biographer of Sayyid
Muhammad Fadlallah, told me that he has sensed a shift in hard-
line Shiite thinking in the past twenty years. In the first burst of revolution in Iran, the United States was cast by Ayatollah Khomeini
and his allies as the "Great Satan." Israel occupied the role of "Little
Satan." This has been reversed, Kramer said. Today, Shiite authorities in Lebanon view America as one more tool of the Jews, who
have achieved covert world domination. President Mohammad

Khatami of Iran, who is often described as a reformer, last year called Israel "a parasite in the heart of the Muslim world."

There are bitter feelings, to be sure, about Israel's invasion of Lebanon, about Israel's treatment of Palestinians in the occupied territories, about the Israeli Air Force's not infrequent patrols in the skies over Beirut. But even some cosmopolitan Beirutis I met, Christians as well as Muslims, seemed surprisingly open to anti-Jewish propaganda—for instance, that the World Trade Center was destroyed by Jews.

•   •   •

A young Shiite scholar named Amal Saad-Ghorayeb has advanced what in Lebanon is a controversial argument: that Hezbollah is not merely anti-Israel but deeply, *theologically* anti-Jewish. Her new book, "Hezbollah: Politics & Religion," dissects the anti-Jewish roots of Hezbollah ideology. Hezbollah, she argues, believes that Jews, by the nature of Judaism, possess fatal character flaws.

I met Saad-Ghorayeb one afternoon in a café near the Lebanese American University, where she is an assistant professor. She was wearing an orange spaghetti-strap tank top, a knee-length skirt, and silver hoop earrings. She is thirty years old and married, and has a four-year-old daughter. Her father, Abdo Saad, is a prominent Shiite pollster; her mother is Christian.

Saad-Ghorayeb calls Israel "an aberration, a colonialist state that embraces its victimhood in order to displace another people." Yet her opposition to anti-Semitism seemed sincere, as when she described the anti-Jewish feeling that underlies Hezbollah's ideology. "There is a real antipathy to Jews as Jews," she said. "It is exacerbated by Zionism, but it existed before Zionism." She observed that Hezbollah, like many other Arab groups, is in the thrall of a belief system that she called "moral utilitarianism." Hezbollah, in other words, will find the religious justification for an act as long as the act is useful. "For the Arabs, the end often justifies the means, even if the means are dubious," she said. "If it works, it's moral."

In her book, she argues that Hezbollah's Koranic reading of Jewish history has led its leaders to believe that Jewish theology is evil. She criticizes the scholar Bernard Lewis for downplaying the depth of traditional Islamic anti-Judaism, especially when compared with Christian anti-Semitism. "Lewis commits the . . . grave error of depicting traditional Islam as more tolerant of Jews . . . thereby implying that Zionism was the cause of Arab-Islamic anti-Semitism," she writes.

Saad-Ghorayeb is hesitant to label Hezbollah's outlook anti-Semitism, however. She prefers the term "anti-Judaism," since in her terms anti-Semitism is a race-based hatred, while anti-Judaism is religion-based. Hezbollah, she says, tries to mask its anti-Judaism for "public-relations reasons," but she argues that a study of its language, spoken and written, reveals an underlying truth. She quoted from a speech delivered by Hassan Nasrallah, in which he said, "If we searched the entire world for a person more cowardly, despicable, weak and feeble in psyche, mind, ideology and religion, we would not find anyone like the Jew. Notice, I do not say the Israeli." To Saad-Ghorayeb, this statement "provides moral justification and ideological justification for dehumanizing the Jews." In this view, she went on, "the Israeli Jew becomes a legitimate target for extermination. And it also legitimizes attacks on non-Israeli Jews."

Larry Johnson, a former counterterrorism official in the Clinton State Department, once told me, "There's a fundamental view here of the Jew as subhuman. Hezbollah is the direct ideological heir of the Nazis." Saad-Ghorayeb disagrees. Nasrallah may skirt the line between racialist anti-Semitism and theological anti-Judaism, she said, but she argued that mainstream Hezbollah ideology provides the Jews with an obvious way to repair themselves in God's eyes: by converting to Islam.

IV—"The Logic of War"

One day near the end of my stay in Lebanon, I visited Sayyid Fadlallah, Hezbollah's spiritual leader, at his home in the Dahiya. Fadlallah, who is sixty-seven, is a surpassingly important figure in Shiism, inside and outside Lebanon. As many as twenty thousand people pray with him each Friday at a cavernous mosque near his home. He is a squat man with a white beard, and wears the black turban of the sayyid, a descendant of the Prophet Muhammad. Fadlallah has long denied any official role in Hezbollah. Some experts take him at his word; others believe that he is dissembling. However, intellectually Fadlallah has taken an independent course, and people close to him told me that he privately scorns Hezbollah's most important patron, Ayatollah Khamenei, as a mediocre thinker and cleric.

Several attempts have been made to assassinate Fadlallah. He believes that the C.I.A., working with Saudi Arabia, tried to kill him by setting off a bomb near his apartment building in 1985, an event cited in Bob Woodward's book "Veil: The Secret Wars of the C.I.A. 1981–1987," which, Fadlallah told me, he has read carefully and repeatedly. His offices are well guarded by men who have apparently been assigned to him by Hezbollah. My briefcase was taken from me for ten minutes and thoroughly searched by the guards. A man carrying a pistol sat in on our interview, along with three translators: Fadlallah's; mine (a Christian woman from East Beirut, who had been required to wear a chador for the occasion); and Abdo Saad, Amal Saad-Ghorayeb's father, who had arranged the interview.

Fadlallah entered the meeting room slowly and deliberately. He sat in a plush chair, the rest of us on couches near him. The room was lit with fluorescent light; as always, a picture of Khomeini stared down from the wall.

Fadlallah framed the core issues in political, not religious, terms. "The Israelis believe that after three thousand years they came back to Palestine," he said. "But can the American Indian come back to America after all this time? Can the Celts go back to Britain?" He said that he has no objection to Jewish statehood, but not at the expense of Palestinians. "The problem between Muslims and Jews has to do with security issues."

Like many Muslim clerics, he holds romantic, condescending, and contradictory views of the historic relationship between Jews and Muslims. He is aware that for hundreds of years, while Jews were persecuted and ostracized in Christian Europe, they were granted the status of protected inferiors by the caliphs, and subjected only to infrequent pogroms. Yet, despite his assertion that the dispute between Jews and Muslims was political, he made the theological observation that the Jews "never recognized Islam as a true religion." I asked him if he agreed with this passage from the Koran: "Strongest among men in enmity to the believers wilt thou find the Jews and Pagans." Yes, he said. "The Jews don't consider Islam to be a religion."

I tried to turn the conversation to Islamic beliefs—in particular, the rationale for suicide attacks. In the early nineteen-eighties, Fadlallah was accused of blessing the suicide bomber who destroyed the U.S. Marine barracks in Beirut in 1983, a charge that he heatedly denied to me. He pointed out that he was among the first Islamic clerics to condemn the September 11th attacks, though he blamed American foreign policy for creating the atmosphere that led to them. He has, however, endorsed attacks on Israeli civilians. Suicide, he said, is not an absolute value. It is an option left to a people who are without options, and so the act is no longer considered suicide but martyrdom in the name of self-defense. "This is part of the logic of war," he said.

On the killing of Israeli civilians, Fadlallah said, "In a state of war, it is permissible for Palestinians to kill Jews. When there is peace, this is not permissible." He does not believe in a peaceful settlement between two states, one Palestinian, the other Israeli; rather, he favors the disappearance of Israel.

I thought about Saad-Ghorayeb's argument that many in Hezbollah consider all Jews guilty of conspiring against Islam, and I asked Fadlallah if it was permissible to kill Jews beyond the borders of Israel, the West Bank, and Gaza. Hezbollah and its Iranian sponsors are considered by the governments of Israel, the United States, and Argentina to be responsible for the single deadliest anti-Semitic attack since the end of the Second World War: the suicide truck-bombing of the Jewish community center in Buenos Aires, in 1994, which left more than a hundred people dead. As in the case of other accusations of terrorism, Hezbollah and Iran say that they were not involved in the attack. "We are against the killing of Jews outside Palestine," Fadlallah said. "Unless they transfer the war outside Palestine." When I asked if they had, Fadlallah raised an eyebrow, and let the question go unanswered.

．　　　．　　　．

Major General Benny Gantz is the chief of the Israeli Army's Northern Command, which is responsible for defending Israel from Hezbollah and Syria and any other threats from the north. Until recently, Gantz was the commander of Israeli forces in the West Bank.

When we met this summer, at an airbase outside Tel Aviv, he seemed pleased to have left behind the moral and strategic ambiguities of service in the West Bank. Gantz is forty-three, tall, lean, and cynical. Much of his career has been spent dealing with the Lebanon question. Before serving in the West Bank, he was the top Israeli officer in Lebanon in the days leading up to the withdrawal. A helicopter was waiting to carry him north to the border after our meeting. Gantz is almost certain that he will soon wage war against Hezbollah and Syria. "I'll be surprised if we don't see this fight," he said.

The Israelis believe that in South Lebanon Hezbollah has more than eight thousand rockets, weapons that are far more sophisticated than any previously seen in the group's arsenal.

They include the Iranian-made Fajr-5 rocket, which has a range of up to forty-five miles, meaning that Israel's industrial heartland, in the area south of Haifa, falls within Hezbollah's reach. One intelligence official put it this way: "It's not tenable for us to have a jihadist organization on our border with the capability of destroying Israel's main oil refinery."

Hezbollah officials told me that they possessed no rockets whatsoever. But one reporter who has covered Hezbollah and the South for several years said he believes that Hezbollah has established a "balance of terror" along the border. The reporter, Nicholas Blanford, of the Beirut English-language newspaper the *Daily Star*, said that he is "pretty certain" that Hezbollah has "extensive weaponry down there, stashed away." He added, "Their refrain is, we're ready for all eventualities."

Blanford, who has good sources in the Hezbollah leadership, said, "They seem to be convinced that sooner or later there's going to be an Israeli-Arab conflict. In the long term, Israel cannot put up with this threat from Hezbollah." It seems clear that in ordinary times Israel would already have moved against Hezbollah. But these are not ordinary times. Intelligence officials told me that Israel cannot act preemptively against Hezbollah while America is trying to shore up Arab support for, or acquiescence in, a campaign to overthrow Saddam Hussein. To do otherwise would be to risk angering the Bush Administration, which needs Israel to show restraint. One Israeli Army officer I spoke to put it bluntly: "The day after the American attack, we can move."

Both Israel and the United States believe that, at the outset of an American campaign against Saddam, Iraq will fire missiles at Israel—perhaps with chemical or biological payloads—in order to provoke an Israeli conventional, or even nuclear, response. But Hezbollah, which is better situated than Iraq to do damage to Israel, might do Saddam's work itself, forcing Israel to retaliate, and crippling the American effort against an Arab state. Hezbollah is not known to possess unconventional payloads for its missiles, though its state sponsors, Iran and Syria, maintain extensive biological- and chemical-weapons programs.

If Hezbollah wants to provoke Israel, it has other options. Early this year, it tried to smuggle fifty tons of heavy Iranian weapons—including mines, mortars, and missiles—to the Palestinian Authority aboard a ship called the Karine A. The Israeli Navy seized the ship in the Red Sea. Intelligence officials believe that the operation was under the control of a deputy of Imad Mugniyah, the Hezbollah security operative. According to a story in the London-based Arabic newspaper *Al-Sharq al-Awsat*, King Abdullah of Jordan told American officials that Iran was behind attempts to launch at least seventeen rockets at Israeli targets from Jordanian territory. Hezbollah, meanwhile, is working with Palestinian groups, including Islamic Jihad, which, like Hezbollah, is sponsored by Iran, and which, like Hezbollah, is searching for the means to deliver a serious blow to Israel.

•   •   •

There is no affection for Saddam Hussein among the ruling mullahs in Iran, which lost a vicious war to Iraq in the nineteen-eighties, with hundreds of thousands of Iranians dead; or in the office of President Bashar al-Assad, in Syria. But some American analysts think that both regimes are alarmed by the prospect of Saddam's overthrow. Dennis Ross, the Clinton Administration's Middle East envoy, told me that American success against Iraq would legitimatize American-led "regime change" in the Middle East. It would also leave Iran surrounded by pro-American governments, in Kabul, Baghdad, and Istanbul. "They see encirclement," Ross said. "This explains the incredible flow of weaponry to Hezbollah after Israel left Lebanon."

Ross said that Bashar al-Assad's interest in forestalling an American attack on Iraq by igniting an Arab-Israeli war is more subtle, but still present. "Bashar realizes that if we go ahead and do this in Iraq he runs an enormous risk" by continuing to support terrorist organizations. The State Department lists Syria as a sponsor of terror. Ross also believes that Bashar, unlike his late father, is not thoughtful enough to grasp the cost of a war with Israel. "He still thinks that Israel will stay within certain boundaries," Ross said. "He needs to hear from us that, if he provokes a war, don't expect us to come to your rescue. He's playing with fire." Indeed, in April this year the Bush Administration had to intervene with Syria to halt Hezbollah rocket attacks on Israel.

General Gantz told me that if Hezbollah uses rockets against Israel his forces will be hunting Syrians as well as Lebanese Shiites. Lebanon may be the battlefield, he said, but the twenty thousand Syrian soldiers in Lebanon will be fair targets. "Israel doesn't have to deal with Hezbollah as Hezbollah," he continued. "This is the Hezbollah tail wagging the Syrian dog. As far as I'm concerned, Hezbollah is part of the Lebanese and Syrian forces. Syria will pay the price. I'm not saying when or where. But it will be severe."

The Syrian Army, which used to have the Soviet Union as its patron, is no match for Israel, Gantz said. "I think the Syrians can create a few problems for us. But it's very hard to see in what way they're better than us. I just don't know how Bashar is going to rebuild his army after this. Assad, the father, was a smart guy. He knew how to walk a tightrope. His son is trying to dance on it."

• • •

In conversations with people in Beirut, and especially in the Christian areas to the city's north, I found great anxiety about an Israeli counterstrike against Lebanon. Hezbollah understands that the Lebanese have grown used to peace, and that they fear an Israeli attack; many Lebanese would hold Hezbollah responsible for the devastation caused by an Israeli attack. Among some of Lebanon's religious groups, particularly the Maronite Christians and the Druze, there is a feeling that the Syrians have overstayed their welcome in the country. These groups fear Hezbollah, too, but they do not express it; after all, Hezbollah is the only militia that is still armed, long after the end of the civil war.

Israel's foreign minister, Shimon Peres, mentioned these constraints when I spoke to him recently. "Hezbollah must not appear to be the destroyer of Lebanon," he said. Peres noted, however, that Hezbollah is an organization devoted to jihad, not to logic. "These are religious people. With the religious you can hardly negotiate. They think they have supreme permission to kill people and go to war. This is their nature."

When I met with Prime Minister Hariri, he alluded to some of these worries. Hariri, a Sunni, is a billionaire builder who made most of his money in Saudi Arabia. We spoke in a building that he constructed in Beirut, with his own money, to serve as his "palace"; it seems to be modelled on a Ritz-Carlton hotel. Hariri has tense relations with Hezbollah, which has accused him of trying to thwart development in poor Shiite areas. Hariri understands that Israel will make the Lebanese people suffer for any attacks that are launched from Lebanese territory. He loathes and fears Ariel Sharon, and said to me that Sharon was "no different" from Hitler in his belief "in racial purity." The people of southern Lebanon do not want the Israelis provoked, Hariri said. "Look around the South," he said. "Look at all the building."

In recent weeks, the borderland has become even more unstable. An Israeli soldier was killed last month when Hezbollah fired on an Israeli outpost in Shebaa; and the Lebanese government, with the endorsement of Hezbollah, announced plans to divert water that would otherwise be carried by the Hatsbani River into Israel. Israel has said that it will not allow Lebanon to curtail its water supply. General Gantz assumes that internal political considerations will not trump its desire for jihad. As he prepared to board his helicopter and fly to the border, he said, "I was the last officer to leave Lebanon, and maybe I'll be the first one to return."

National Geographic Adventure

Wild in the Parks:

The Moonbow Chronicles

Tim Cahill's rollicking narrative of discovery takes readers through the unseen parts of Yellowstone National Park, one of the greatest natural playgrounds on Earth.

Tim Cahill

Wild in the Parks: The Moonbow Chronicles

Even after 130 years, Yellowstone has new tales to tell. Join an expedition into the secret heart of the park in search of vaporous wonders, goblin rocks and one of those 240 recently "discovered" waterfalls that have everybody all riled up.

I was sitting in what amounted to a wilderness hot tub under a 150-foot-high waterfall near the southwest corner of Yellowstone Park. It was late at night, and the moon was just about to clear the canyon. Its light would illuminate the falls, especially in that place where water exploded off the rocks below in an ephemeral mist that drifted on the evening breeze. I believed that there would be a certain very specific bending of light: a silver luminescence trembling in the vapor; the experience of a lifetime. Or the phenomenon might be entirely mythical, an incandescence out of the imagination, a goblin of the light, something all shivery to contemplate in theory but a complete no-show in the reality department.

There are a lot of strange and wondrous things happening in the largely unknown backcountry of Yellowstone. The park is big, bigger, in fact, than some states: about two and a quarter million acres, with 94 trailheads and at least a thousand miles of trail, as well as great expanses of land that aren't served by any trails at all. A man might spend a lifetime walking the backcountry and never know it all. This means there is always something to discover, and I was coming to the end of a summer of doing just that. Over the previous three months, I had trudged several hundred miles through the hidden country, propelled, in part, by a book I didn't much like.

In *The Guide to Yellowstone Waterfalls and Their Discovery*, by Paul Rubinstein, Lee Whittlesey, and Mike Stevens, published in 2000, the authors report that they "discovered" 240 unknown, unmapped, or unphotographed waterfalls. No kidding? In this day and age, new discoveries! Well, not precisely. A foreword, by Dr. Judith Meyer, a geography professor at Southwest Missouri State University, puts the matter in perspective: "The title of 'discoverer' is not necessarily bestowed on someone who sees something for the first time. A discoverer discloses information to others," in the manner, for instance, that Christopher Columbus discovered America.

This is not an evil, or even a fraudulent, book. The authors may have truly found some unseen water. Maybe. But they themselves acknowledge that a few "privileged" individuals "did see some" of the waterfalls before they did. "Most of them failed, however, to write reports . . . or photograph them, or even map them" and therefore "missed their chance at credit for their discoveries."

Some of those privileged individuals, it must be said, missed their chance in the name of what I can describe only as the preservation of wonder. Certain rangers, guides, and knowledge-able hikers find the concept of credit for discovery disagreeable. The authors themselves note that "some wilderness advocates hate the idea of official names in wilderness areas and love the idea of large spaces on the maps where there are no names."

. . .

And that was the gist of the argument swirling about the book on the fringes of Yellowstone Park, where I live. It was a low-level dispute: No one doubted the authors' honesty or good intentions, only the wisdom of their catalog approach to wilderness. Others, generally outside the area, just read the headlines. Friends and colleagues called from New York, curious about the 240 new waterfalls.

Which, the authors said, was part of the plan. "We hope the revelation of these beautiful natural features will spur city dwellers, who need these places for mental health and restoration more than anyone else"—nutcases!—"to use every wherewithal to protect them—by voting for environmental candidates rather than the developers, by yelling loudly whenever there are threats to these places. . . ." And so on, in admirable openhanded altruism.

It occurred to me that if these three guys could spend seven summers searching for waterfalls on behalf of the sanity of city dwellers everywhere, the least I could do for the pitiable urban-ites was to spend a single summer selflessly hiking the backcountry with my friends. I'd let the water fall where it may, and later we could all go out and yell at some developers together.

Hiking Yellowstone, out of sight of any road, seems to be on everyone's unfulfilled wish list. It is often said that 99 percent of the visitors to Yellowstone never see the backcountry. Out of curiosity, I checked this out and found that the statistic is somewhat understated. In 2001, according to Yellowstone Visitors Services, the park had 2,758,526 recreational visitors, of which 19,239 applied for backcountry camping permits. That means—rounding the numbers off a bit—that, in 2001 anyway, 99.3 percent of park visitors didn't overnight in the backcountry.

I am, myself, an example. I have lived just 60 miles north of the park for 25 years and can count my overnight backcountry trips on the fingers of one hand, a shameful statistic in itself. Just another reason to get out on the trail.

As it happens, my neighbor, photographer Tom Murphy, has been a guide in Yellowstone for the past 17 years and knows it as well as anyone of my acquaintance. Together we planned three forays into the park. All of our destinations involved several days' worth of walking, an activity that both Tom and I knew buys solitude in Yellowstone.

Our first trip started at the Pacific Creek trailhead, just outside Grand Teton National Park. It led generally northeast up over the mountains of the Bridger-Teton National Forest, then into Yellowstone Park, where we passed by the Thorofare Patrol Cabin, 32 miles from the nearest road, the most remote occupied dwelling in the contiguous United States. The second trip took us to the Goblin Labyrinths, and the last was a visit to the River of Reliable Rainbows.

Chapter One: Land of the Ghost Trees

And so, on that first trip in late July, five of us found ourselves walking north toward the top of the world, the Continental Divide, at a place called Two Ocean Pass, just outside the southeast corner of the park. The divide itself runs through a marshy bog about three miles long. Pacific Creek flows out of the bog south and west. At the north end of the bog, the watercourse flowing north and east is called Atlantic Creek. As the names suggest, these two streams, separated by only three miles, empty into entirely disparate oceans.

"So," Tom explained to me, "a fish could conceivably swim up Pacific Creek, muddle through the bog, and end up swimming down Atlantic Creek." That's why Tom wanted to walk 32 miles, enduring 3,000 feet or more of elevation change, carrying his 90-pound backpack full mostly of camera gear. He wanted to see a place where a fish could swim across the Continental Divide. Tom, I should explain, grew up on a cattle ranch in South Dakota, 60 miles from the nearest town, and is prone to become excited about concepts like fish swimming over the Rocky Mountains.

We slogged northeast along the Pacific Creek Trail for several days but eventually stumbled into the bog at the top of the world. The map said we were 8,200 feet above sea level.

The bog was about half a mile across. Willows were thick but seldom more than waist high. Where the ground rose slightly, there were profusions of purple monkshood, a flower that looks pretty much like its name. Underfoot, slow-running copper-colored water made countless narrow furrows in the marshy ground, and these small streams—some of them no more than a foot wide—ran in long, roundabout, curving courses or in shorter, dithering meanders. Tom and I, along with another friend, Dr. David Long, a biochemist turned fine printmaker, postholed through the mud out into the marsh, looking for the exact place where black-spotted west-slope trout might slip over the divide and into the waters of the Atlantic.

Presently, Tom found a tiny ridgeline, about two or three feet higher than the surrounding land, and he stood there, in an area of rusty burned grasses about the size of a football field. Water to the west seemed to flow west; eastern waters east. We stood for a strangely triumphant moment on the exact instant of the Continental Divide and discussed transcontinental trout.

The narrow streams were a labyrinthine tangle—many of them hidden under willows—and none of us could say that there wasn't a connection somewhere. On the other hand, in June, during the season of snowmelt, the bog was probably more like a lake, and that, we decided sagely, is how and when fish swim over the Rocky Mountains.

Later in the day, we pushed off north and east, walking beside the outflow from the bog. Atlantic Creek dropped down through forests of burned trees, great limbless lodgepole pines, whole forests of standing dead, all of the trees weathered a ghostly silver-white. Sometimes the trail took us through meadows alive with every manner of wildflower—sego lilies, for instance, which look a bit like white tulips with round red spots on the inner petals. Eileen Ralicke, Dave's wife, who is a nurse practitioner, declared the sego lily "the most beautiful thing I've ever seen." Kara Krietlow, an emergency room nurse—Tom and Dave and I weren't taking any chances with our health, you see—agreed.

The land had risen from the west slope in a series of stair-step meadows, and now it was floating down to the north and east in meadows several miles wide where flowers grew in patchwork brilliance. This route, beyond Two Ocean Pass, is a corridor through the mountains so agreeable to travel that old-time trappers—the Jim Bridgers and Osborne Russells—called it the Thorofare.

•   •   •

We camped under the mountain called Hawks Rest, just outside the border of the park. I went off by myself, bathed in the Yellowstone River, then took a shortcut back to camp, which was a mistake, because the ground was the consistency of Jell-O, and it swallowed my legs to mid-calf. I was sweating profusely and pretty much entirely filthy when I got back to camp, which required a second trip, this one on a trail, back to the river for another bath.

So I was amazed early the next morning when I saw a huge bull moose trotting on his big pie-plate hooves through the same marsh that had eaten me alive the day before. Low clouds scattered the newly risen sun in slanting pillars, an effect that is locally called God light. The moose, a deep auburn color in the God light, moved effortlessly through the mud and the flowers, great muscles rolling in his immense shoulders. Beauty finds you where it will, and I was, at the time, squatting in the bushes performing my morning necessity.

We passed Hawks Rest, crossed the Yellowstone River on a wooden bridge, walked past Bridger Lake, and entered the park where a sign had fallen from a single ghost tree standing sentinel at the trail. From here it was a two-mile walk to the Thorofare Patrol Cabin, which meant we were halfway done with the trip. It seemed ironic that it had been necessary (and, I suppose, polite) to contact the Park Service, an agency of the United States government, to secure permission to speak with the person living in the most remote cabin in the contiguous United States. A sign on the door said, "The ranger on duty has departed." So much for calling ahead.

No matter. We moved on around the three-lobed mountain called the Trident and found our assigned campsites—yes, you have to make backcountry campsite reservations—in a thick forest of unburned lodgepole pine and Douglas fir. The lodgepole gave way to a vast expanse of meadow, and that is where we set up our tents: on the very edge of the Thorofare, the Mother of all Meadows. I could see for 20 miles in one direction, at a guess, and 15 in another. A fierce wind arose, and the grasses and the sedges and the forbs and the flowers danced a brief mad fandango; then all at once everything went calm, and dusk settled over the land. The moon rose, Mars scowled down, the Milky

Way spread across the known universe, and everywhere, in any direction I looked, there was not a single light.

I was still thinking about the privilege of solitude the next morning. In six days, we'd seen two hikers and two horsepacking parties, all back in the Bridger-Teton. Nobody in the Thorofare.

Suddenly, a sound like gunfire echoed off the walls of the mountains on either side of the rocky corridor that enfolded the meadow. It was a bright, windy day, and we'd been hearing these thunderclaps reverberating all about us every few hours. Tom said they were ghost trees falling in the distance, and indeed, this time we could see it. Across a narrow part of the meadow, in a fringing ghost forest on the flank of the mountain opposite, a huge lodgepole had toppled, caught on a neighboring tree for a moment, then fallen to the earth with a series of tremendous crashing echoes.

The ghost forests date mostly from the fires of 1988. New timber is growing in the midst of the ghost forests, living lodgepoles now eight and ten feet high and growing at the rate of about ten inches a year. Soon, as the older trees crash about them, the new growth will accelerate, each tree growing straight and fast, racing the others to the sun. In ten more years, the forest will be 16 to 18 feet high, and a hundred years from now the trees will be full grown, and there will be another fire. People are more than willing to argue this point—fire should be stopped, or it shouldn't be stopped, or it ought to be purposely set—but this is my reading of the history and natural history of the land: I believe we are privileged to see the forest regenerate itself in our lifetimes. We're at that point in the cycle: about a dozen years into a turnaround of a century or more.

We camped under Colter Peak and high-stepped across the marshy meadow of the Thorofare to the Yellowstone River. There was evidence on the muddy banks that this immense meadow was a Thorofare for life in general, with no particular nod to the human variety. All the tracks were fresh, but one tended to notice the grizzly first. His front foot was 12 inches across, by actual measurement. Nearby, there was a cylinder of scat with a little bit of hair in it. The wolf tracks leading away were bigger than those of a coyote that seemed to have come by later. A raven had strutted about the bank, and the beaver's track was plain enough as well: an endearing, pigeon-toed gait, with the flat rake of the tail dragging behind.

•   •   •

The next morning, we woke to the deep, aching, eerie howling of wolves in the near distance. It is a sound that sends a shimmer of gooseflesh down the arms and up the back.

Tom had a special mission that day. He was going to take us to a waterfall he'd found a while ago: one that wasn't in the *Waterfalls* book. The authors of that controversial work wrote, "We would be fools to believe we have found every waterfall in Yellowstone." Once again, they were right, and we had proof of that only 10 or 12 miles out of our way. Tom, who is one of those people who would rather not clutter up wilderness maps with a lot of names, said, "You can't give the location."

"What about all the people who live in the city and have mental problems," I argued. "Giving the location and naming the falls might help them."

But he didn't care about city dwellers' sanity, not even a little bit.

It was, let us say, a goodly walk, and it took us up on top of a low plateau, where the fires of 1988 had been particularly fierce and the ghost forest stretched on forever, on all sides. A brutal wind shrieked through the bones of the forest, and we could hear the trees creaking, creaking, creaking with their craving to finally and irrevocably fall.

And, coming through the forest, moving toward us along the trail, was a man on horseback who turned out to be backcountry ranger Bob Jackson. He had a bunch of work to do and not much time to chat. He lived in the Thorofare cabin, he said, from June 1 to the end of October and had since 1978. Used to be he caught a lot of poachers coming into the park during hunting season, looking for prize animals: elk and bighorn sheep mostly. There is less poaching going on today, but there are still bad guys out there. Bob's seen their tracks, and he plans to get them. "You know," he said, "almost every poacher, when I finally caught him, he cried." Bob Jackson liked that: catching crybaby poachers.

He asked us where we were going, and Tom described the waterfall. "One of the prettiest ones in the park," Bob said.

"You mean," I asked, "you know about this waterfall? Why don't you name it and take credit for its discovery?" Bob Jackson looked at me in the manner I imagine he looks at poachers. I didn't immediately burst into tears—though, on sober reflection, I believe that would have been the proper response. "It was a joke, Bob," I wanted to call after him as he rode off through the ghost forest.

Hours later, we reached the shores of Yellowstone Lake, which stretched out blue-gray as far as the eye could see, 14 miles wide, 20 miles long, with 110 miles of shoreline. So I can say that the unnamed waterfall was only about half a mile from the lake. That doesn't narrow it down too much.

Tom found it one day when he was "dinking around," looking for a spring, actually, because Tom will fill his canteen from a spring in preference to pumping and purifying water. He'd seen a lush hillside covered over in cow parsnip and mossy rock—good signs of water—and about 150 feet above, there was water gushing out of the side of the hill. It fell 18 to 20 feet and then cascaded down some rocks for another 35 to 40 feet. I thought it was all the more appealing because it was a waterfall that started as a spring. We filled our canteens, drank greedily, and then sat suffering ice cream headaches for ten minutes or so.

And now, since we'd gone 12 miles out of our way and were

moving at something less than three miles an hour, we were going to be late getting into camp. It is not usually a good idea to walk at night in the park. It's not even a good idea to walk at twilight, because, as Tom explained, bears are crepuscular, which means that they tend to feed in the half-light of dawn and dusk. I was thinking about that as we crossed a creek, and there, on the trail, was the track of a large grizzly. It was new: I could see the ridges like fingerprints on the pads of its toes. "About two minutes ahead of us," Tom said.

"You think so?"

"Look." There, beside the track, were several drops of water in the dusty soil, and they were moving forward, along with the tracks, so that it looked as if someone had been walking along carrying a wet rug, except that this was a grizzly track, and the wet rug had been a wet bear skin attached to the grizzly. We'd just crossed a creek, and so had the bear. The water drops were drying up even as I looked at them. The griz was about two minutes ahead of us.

And then the sun set, and we were walking in the dark, with headlamps, along the north side of the Southeast Arm of Yellowstone Lake, until we found our reserved campsite at about 11:30 at night. The sky was perfectly clear, the moon almost full, and waves lapped gently on the beach, so that, visually anyway, it felt as if there ought to be a palm tree silhouetted against the sky. But on this last day of July, the temperature stood somewhere to the south of 20 degrees. It was damn cold.

I left that morning, as planned. Tom stayed for another week.

Chapter Two: The Hard-Rock Circus

Three weeks later, Tom and I took our second trip into the backcountry. There were just the two of us making our way through the sagebrush-littered flats of the Lamar Valley, at the northeast end of the park, moving due south, toward Hoodoo

Basin, an area that P. W. Norris, the second superintendent of the park, called the Goblin Labyrinths.

Tom and I were taking big loops around bison weighing in the neighborhood of one ton. "Two days after you left the lake, I saw something that I thought only existed in folklore," he told me. "An evening rainsquall passed across the lake, and the last of the rain hung in the air. There was a light then, and I turned to see the full moon, which was just rising, on the horizon. When I turned back and looked into what was left of the rain, I thought I could see a faint, silvery sort of line, and then it grew bigger and bent around until I was looking at a kind of rainbow in negative. A moonbow."

"Any colors?" I asked, envious.

"It was all bluish white."

I'd missed the vaporous display by 48 hours. Experience of a lifetime going on up at Yellowstone Lake, and I was down in town having a drink at The Owl.

As if to put a certain emphasis on my regret, it began to rain intermittently. Tom, as it turned out, doesn't carry rain gear. If he has to, he says, he walks wet. If it's a cold rain, he walks fast. "But . . . ," I stammered, "you're a guide. You work search-and-rescue."

"I'm not saying it's right," Tom said. "When you grow up on a cattle ranch in South Dakota, you just don't have a lot of experience with rain." He thought a bit. "Rain was good."

•   •   •

Two days and 20 miles in, we arrived at the Upper Miller Creek Patrol Station and ran into ranger Mike Ross. He is tall and blond and handsome and is one of the few men I've ever met who didn't look like a complete dork in a ranger uniform.

Mike was one of the Park Service personnel who didn't agree with the concept of the *Waterfalls* book. "I grew up in the park," he said. "I know it pretty well, and those guys did some real exploration. But I had problems with the naming. I wrote Lee Whittlesey an e-mail and told him that the thrill he got naming and locating these falls was one he stole from every subsequent visitor." We stayed the night near the cabin and chatted with Mike until long after dark. "I don't get a lot of company here," he said. "And the people I do see usually turn back at this point."

"Why?" I asked. The Hoodoo Basin, with its weird formations, was just over the hill, about eight miles away and 2,500 feet above.

"Well, sometimes they've overestimated what they can do," Mike said. "And then it's a long, boring walk. I mean, there aren't a lot of sweeping views, and it's mostly burned. And finally, they don't want to make the 2,500-foot climb." He pointed to the forested wall behind the cabin. "We call that Parachute Hill," Mike said.

"How many people actually get to the Hoodoo Basin?" I asked.

Mike pulled out some kind of PalmPilot, scratched on it with a stylus, and said: "I downloaded this at the backcountry office a few days ago. So, as of August 26, there were three permits for the year. You guys are one of them. I doubt if 25 sets of eyes see the hoodoos in any given year."

Parachute Hill was a bastard, there's no doubt about it, a cruel set of switchbacks that took two long hours of trudging. We topped out on a grassy hillside of long, sloping meadows that gave way to cool, unburned forest at 9,500 feet. All about, lying on the ground near the trail, were obsidian chips: arrowheads and spear points and scrapers. These were tools chipped out of rock with rock by men who had found a pleasant and militarily advantageous place to work.

Tom and I walked up to the summit of Parker Peak, 10,203 feet in elevation, according to the map, and I could see the high peaks that fringed the park, which is actually the caldera of an immense and ancient volcano that last erupted 600,000 years ago. Most of the highest peaks in the Yellowstone area stand at the edge of the park, on what would have been the rim of all that molten fury.

Tom strolled down a short ridge running south off the summit. Where it dead-ended in cliffs, someone had built a small enclosure by setting rocks on edge and fitting them together with other, smaller rocks wedged into the interstices. The whole affair was about nine by six feet, an oval enclosure protected from the wind and overlooking the Lamar River to the southwest and the Beartooth Plateau to the northeast. It was a place where men came to discover what was sacred. A vision-quest site, and not on any map I know of.

·   ·   ·

We came down Parker Peak and made for the Hoodoo Basin. Superintendent Norris, in his 1880 report, noted that some prospectors working the head of the Upper Lamar River in 1870 had stumbled on "a region of countless remnants of erosion, so wild, weird and spectral that they named it the 'Hoodoo' or 'Goblin Land.' "

The trail led to a basin under the rounded, grassy summit of Hoodoo Peak. It appeared that 500 feet of vertical slope had eroded away from the mountain, leaving a haphazard labyrinth of oddly shaped reddish gray columns. There was one pillar, a hundred feet high, upon which a large rock was balanced precariously. It looked like nothing so much as a small car resting on its front bumper with its back wheels in the air. This formation was very much like one Norris sketched in the 1880 report. Could that top rock have held its position for more than 120 years? It occurred to me that I had arrived at an unfamiliar intersection between geology and acrobatics.

I moved below the permanently precarious hard-rock circus and walked around a high, flat blade of standing stone. It was growing late, and the sky above was still blue, but in the basin, where we were, shadows fell all about. I looked up at the flat rock rising 60 or 70 feet above me, and it resolved itself into a face, with a central protrusion of nose and a large pyramidal hat above, of the sort that might be worn by shamans or priests of some alien religion. But what made me stumble, startled in the silence, was the perfectly animate pair of eyes staring down at me. They were a cool, luminescent, living blue. I believe I may have said something clever, like "Whoa," as I wheeled backward, then stood still, pinned motionless under the intense blue gaze of the rock. I lived through five very odd seconds until the eyes resolved themselves into two round holes in the flattish rock: Now I was looking directly into the blue of the western sky.

Tom and I spent two days in the Goblin Labyrinths. The nights were deliciously creepy. The moon, half full behind us, illuminated the various figures in a pale light broken by irregular shadows. The stars, cold and bright, glittered through holes in the rock. They wheeled overhead as we sat for hours watching the shadows shift so that the rock figures assumed alternate shapes: a horse's head, a fierce crouching lion, a failed saguaro cactus, a sorcerer's apprentice.

The next day, we climbed Hoodoo Peak, which, at 10,563 feet, is a thousand feet and an hour's climb above the basin. There were more goblins set higher on the mountain, and they were not as eroded as the ones in the basin, so that from a distance they looked rather like the heads on Easter Island, only bunched closely together, as if conspiring in the wind. There were some fanciful columns and balancing acts. I rather liked the one that looked like a pig on a stilt.

Still, it was the basin that drew me back at dusk the next night. I went around the front side of the flat rock and stood in its shadow in order to stare it directly in the eyes. And the damn thing winked at me. "Whoa," I said.

"What?" Tom asked.

"The rock is winking at me."

I climbed up on a scree slope to get a better view. Aha! Some small bird, probably an owl, was moving in and out of one of the eyes, perching there for some moments as it scanned the ground for rodents. The owl blocked the sky and caused the rock face to wink.

When I dragged Tom to that vantage point to explain myself, the owl, of course, was gone.

Chapter Three: River of Reliable Rainbows

At the very southwest corner of the park is an area called the Bechler, named for the region's main river course. If the Bechler ever ran a personal ad seeking companionship, it would be a pretty sappy one: "If you like hot tubs and rainbows and water-falls, you'll like me. I'm the Bechler."

On this third trip, the party consisted of Tom, Dave, me, our medical crew from the first trip—Eileen and Kara—as well as Elizabeth Schultz, a friend and local interior decorator who was in charge of camp decor. We drove to Ashton, Idaho, then down the gravel road that leads to the Bechler's entrance. "We're doing this," I reminded everyone, "in the name of city dwellers' sanity." Just in case anyone thought we were only having fun.

And maybe it wouldn't be all that enjoyable. We were certainly pushing the weather. It was late September, and though it can snow on you any month of the year in Yellowstone, September and October are famous for days of mild summer temperatures followed by heavy, wet snows accumulating sometimes several feet in a matter of 24 hours. Roads are often closed in late August due to heavy snowfall. And in 2001, it snowed pretty hard in June.

"It won't snow on us," I told my hiking companions, "because I lead a good and virtuous life."

"We're dead," Dave said.

The trail was essentially flat and took us through the autumnal grasses of the immense Bechler Meadows. It was the season of rut for the elk, and we could hear various males bugling in the distance. This is a high-pitched noise, almost like the shriek air makes escaping from a balloon when the opening is stretched flat. It moderates down in tone to a kind of pained whine, as if the animal is saying, "Mate with me, mate with me, all of you, mate with me."

Elk were mating now, the males were fighting, and they had to chase the females, which depleted the fat that animals of both sexes had accumulated over the summer and thereby diminished their chances of surviving the winter. "It would be better for the elk," Dave said as we prepared dinner, "if the females just gave it up."

All three women stared at him. A silence ensued. Dave said, "Or I could be wrong."

Coyotes yipped and howled, harmonizing with the elk, and their vocalizations sounded nothing at all like the deep, eerie sounds made by wolves. In the morning, the grasses were frosted over, glittering in the sun, and we could see the snow-covered ridge of the Tetons in the southern distance. A bull moose was trotting along on the side of the meadow, near a fringe of trees. Moving out ahead, a female was running rapidly away, and not about to just give it up at all. The male animal was making a series of revolting sounds: It started with a kind of *eh-eh-eh*, followed by a tormented swallowing, and then a repulsive noise that sounded like someone seriously vomiting. ("Mate with me! Oh, God, I'm sick. Mate with me!")

The weather held—it's my good and virtuous life—and it was actually hot at noon. We moved up Bechler Canyon, which is famous for its waterfalls. The topography is this: Centrally located in the Bechler region is the Pitchstone Plateau, which is nearly 9,000 feet high. It drops off to the southwest, and water flows down a rocky slope that terminates in a number of sheer cliffs. This is Cascade Corner. The waterfalls of Cascade Corner pitch into the Bechler Meadows or the Falls River Basin.

Ouzel Falls is north of the main trail, dropping off a rock ridge at the entrance to the Bechler Canyon. From our first vantage point, there was no sense of water moving. The falls looked like a distant mirror glittering in the sun. There seemed to be no trail to the falls—none we could find—and we bushwhacked over animal trails and down timber, then moved up a deeply wooded canyon and stood at the foot of the falls, which drops 230 feet and is one of Yellowstone's tallest. It was now three in the afternoon, and the sun had cleared the trees on both sides of the narrow canyon. Rainbows danced in the spray.

Eileen scrambled up some talus to shower in the shifting shards of color. To see a rainbow, you need a light source behind you and water vapor floating on air in front. I moved this way and that, in order to position the sun and spray to enhance the colors hanging and shifting at the base of the falls. The map suggested that a great many of the falls in and around the Bechler region face generally south, which meant the sun would shine directly on them at least part of the day. And that meant that every day in which there was sun, there'd be a rainbow or two as well. You could count on them: I thought of the Bechler as the River of Reliable Rainbows.

Over the next several days, we moved up the Bechler and courageously endured the sight of many waterfalls generating many rainbows. Colonnade Falls, for instance, just off the trail, is a two-step affair, with a 35-foot plunge above, a pool, and a 67-foot drop below. The lower falls is enfolded in a curving basalt wall. The gray rock had formed itself into consecutive columns in the Doric tradition. It has a certain wild nobility, Yellowstone's own Parthenon, with falls and a fountain.

●　　　●　　　●

Some hours later, the canyon widened, and the trail moved through a meadow where vaguely oval hot pools 10 and 20 and

30 feet across steamed in the sun. In some of the pools, there were bits and shards of what appeared to be rusted sheet metal, as if someone had driven a Model T into the water 80 years ago. In fact, the shards were living colonies of microbes.

"If you cut into them," said Dave, the biochemist, "you see that the top layer uses the longest visible light, the second layer uses less long light, and so on, until all the light is used." I stared at the cooperative colony, and it still looked like chunks of old cars to me.

We branched off the main trail and followed the Ferris Fork of the Bechler. This little-used path drops down into another narrow meadow where there are a number of hot springs and pools. Steam rose off the boiling pools in strange, curvilinear patterns. There was a spectacular terrace of precipitated material on the opposite bank of the river. Hot water from the pool above ran down the bank of the terrace, which was striated in several colors: wet brown and garish pumpkin and overachieving moss, all interspersed with running channels of steaming water and lined in creamy beige. Just at river level, the green rock formed a pool perhaps ten feet in diameter, and its surface was the color of cream.

We followed the Ferris Fork up the drainage that led to the Pitchstone Plateau. There were five waterfalls in the space of a couple hours' walk. The top falls was unnamed—another one not in the *Waterfalls* book—but the bottom four were all on the map: Wahhi, Sluiceway, Gwinna, and Tendoy. They were all shadowed in foliage and faced vaguely north, so they were not good rainbow falls.

We came back down to the meadow near the steaming terrace and sat in the river, just where one of the bigger hot streams poured into the cold water of the Ferris Fork. It is illegal—not to say suicidal—to bathe in any of the thermal features of the park. But when these features empty into a river, at what is called a hot pot, swimming and soaking are perfectly acceptable. So we were soaking off our long walk, talking about our favorite waterfalls, and discussing rainbows when it occurred to us that the moon was full. There wasn't a hint of foul weather. And if you had a clear sky and a waterfall facing in just the right direction . . .

·   ·   ·

Over the course of a couple of days, we hiked back down the canyon to the Boundary Creek Trail and followed it to Dunanda Falls, which is only about eight miles from the entrance to the park. Dunanda is a 150-foot-high plunge facing generally south, so that, in the afternoons, reliable rainbows dance over the rocks at its base. It is the archetype of all western waterfalls. Water rolls over the lip at the top and catches in a series of notched pools just below, and these pools empty intermittently. Eileen, always one to test the shower, said that it felt like a pulsing showerhead, except that the pulse alternated between a gentle spray and a ten-gallon bucketload.

It was necessary to walk three miles back toward the ranger station and our assigned campsite. We planned to set up our tents, eat, hang our food, and walk back to the falls in the dark, using headlamps. We could be there by 10 or 11. At that time, the full moon would clear the east ridge of the downriver canyon and would be shining directly on the falls.

This evening stroll involved five stream crossings, and took us a lot longer than we'd anticipated. Still, we beat the moon to the falls.

Most of us took up residence in one or the other of the hot pots. Presently, the moon, like a floodlight, rose over the canyon rim. The falling water took on a silver tinge, and the rock wall, which had looked gold under the sun, was now a slick black, so the contrast of water and rock was incomparably stark. The pools below the lip of the falls were glowing, as from within, with a pale blue light. And then it started at the base of the falls: just a diagonal line in the spray.

"It's going to happen," I told Kara, who was sitting beside me in one of the hot pots.

Where falling water hit the rock at the base of the falls and exploded upward in vapor, the light was very bright. It concentrated itself in a shining ball. The diagonal line was above, and it slowly began to bend until, in the fullness of time (ten minutes, maybe), it formed a perfectly symmetrical bow, shining silver-blue under the moon.

Kara said she could see colors in the moonbow, and when I looked very hard, I thought I could make out a faint line of reddish orange above and some deep violet at the bottom. Both colors were very pale. In any case, it was exhilarating, the experience of a lifetime: an entirely perfect moonbow, silver and iridescent, all shining and spectral there at the base of Dunanda Falls. The hot pot itself was a luxury, and I considered myself a pretty swell fellow, doing all this for the sanity of city dwellers, who need such things more than anyone else. I even thought of naming the moonbow. Cahill's Luminescence. Something like that. Otherwise, someone else might take credit for it.

Sports Illustrated

WINNER, PROFILE WRITING

Lying in Wait

Thanks to profoundly deep reporting and riveting prose, the reader spirals downward right along with George O'Leary in his fall from grace as Notre Dame's head coach. In "Lying in Wait," Gary Smith renders his subject as the King Lear of the sports world with such pathos that even a reader with no interest in sports can feel his anguish. This is Smith, a master profiler, at the top of his game.

Gary Smith

Lying in Wait

As George O'Leary climbed the coaching ladder to his dream job at Notre Dame, a dirty secret was lurking in his résumé. But did he pay too high a price for a few lies?

W here, then, to start the story of the Notre Dame football coach's flaming fall from grace? Upon George O'Leary's hotel bed *that night*, as his hand keeps rubbing his face and his lips whisper, "Oh, Jesus . . . oh, Jesus . . . what will my mother say?" Or at the Minnesota Vikings office of George's old high school quarterback, who quietly shuts the door so no one will hear him sob?

No. They're both too close.

Perhaps on the laptop screen of the columnist in Chicago as the words "low-rent fraud" flash to life in his third sentence? Or on the sketch pad of *The Orange County Register* cartoonist as he draws George with a Pinocchio nose at a job interview, saying, "I can fly if I concentrate really hard."

No. They're both too far away.

How about in the kitchen of a white Cape Cod in Liverpool, N.Y.? Yes, that's it, the kitchen where an old Italian has just come to a halt, electrocuted by the radio news of the lies on George O'Leary's résumé and of his resignation on Dec. 14, five days after taking his dream job at Notre Dame. Luke LaPorta sags into a chair. His eyes close, and 23 years collapse: He's sitting in his office as athletic director at Liverpool High in the summer of 1978, asking his young Irish Catholic football coach a question so loaded, so personal, that he can barely squeeze it from his throat: "George . . . are there any inconsistencies in how you've represented yourself?"

Luke knows the answer. The school superintendent, Virgil Tompkins, has called him aside and informed him of inaccuracies in George's claims about his playing career and postgraduate credits, and now the heat's on Luke, who hired George over 84 other applicants the year before. But Luke still hopes against hope that it's all a misunderstanding, because if this man's a liar, then the world's flat and the moon's square and eagles are no better than cockroaches.

George flushes red. "A lot of people do that," he replies.

Maybe some other language has a word for what runs through Luke. It's something close to nausea and not far from deep, deep sorrow. "Yeah," Luca finally says. "I've got a long résumé, but . . . it all checks out." Luca—that's what his father, born in southern Italy, named him—comes from a Long Island neighborhood teeming with ethnic groups. So does George. Both know the dictionary of meanings contained in small gestures and flickers of eyes. George's shoulders shrug, his lips purse, and his eyes cut to one side. *The look,* Luca calls it. The look means:

That's all I'm going to say.

That's the way of the world.

You and I, we understand each other.

There's no need to do anything.

We'll just let it lie.

Right?

Luca swallows. He knows it's true: Everyone lies. He knows that if he chooses compassion, he chooses complicity. His last name, in Italian, means "the door." Now he stands at the portal of George O'Leary's career, holding his fate. LaPorta can open. LaPorta can shut.

Luca sits, guts turning, in his office in June 1978. He sits, guts turning, in his kitchen in December 2001. Again he weighs a life against a lie.

.   .   .

A letter rests in Luca's wrinkled hands. It arrived just a few days after George O'Leary stared out his hotel room's second-story window and decided that 20 feet wasn't enough to do the job.

Dear Coach LaPorta,

I want to thank Coach O'Leary for all he did for my son Rich. . . . Because of Coach O'Leary, my son behaved himself in high school and became one of his class's leaders. He developed respect for his parents (that alone was wonderful), valued his physical body, became one of a team, and stretched himself to produce "110%." . . . As an adult, my son carried his leadership and teaching skills to other boys and girls and has coached in methods O'Leary instilled in him as a teen. He is both a better parent and a better coach because of Coach O'Leary.

*I am saddened to hear of Coach O'Leary's difficulties. My
prayer is that they don't stop Coach from doing what he does
best—coach! Because somewhere there are other teens and
young men who would benefit from it. . . .*

I also thank you for your wisdom in hiring O'Leary. . . .
                    Sincerely,
                    Barbara Wiggins,
                    Rich Wiggins's Mom

·   ·   ·

Luca is 77. He's determined the fates of liars and birth-certificate
forgers—passed judgment in the Danny Almonte case just last
summer—during his quarter century on the board of Little League
Baseball International. As a boy during the Depression, working at
his family's gas station, he was astonished when adults volunteered
to pump their own gas so they could squeeze out an extra nickel's
worth and then plead that their hands had slipped. But then, Luca
himself filched dimes from the till, from his own blood, and
clamped his lips when his grandfather confronted him.

What should he have done that day, that moment after
George gave him *the look*? Could he have averted the personal
catastrophe that lay in silent wait for George for the next 23
years, gathering, girding? What would *you* have done?

Say nothing. That's all the old man wants of you for now. First
you must know George and the soil that grew his lies, maybe
your lies, my lies. First you must know the net effect of his 55
years on earth and lay that against the net effect of the sin.

Here. Take one. Read it. It's George's curriculum vitae. Not the
bogus one claiming that he lettered in football for three years at the
University of New Hampshire and holds a master's degree in education from New York University. Not a bare-bones list of jobs and
dates. A man is so much more than that—doesn't *vitae* mean "of life"?
Then you can decide. Then you'll have the right to make Luca's choice.

GEORGE J. O'LEARY
BIRTH DATE: **Aug. 17, 1946**
STATUS: **Married with four children**
EXPERIENCE: **1955–60 Altar boy**

George was seven when he first played with fire. "*Who* had the matches?" demanded his mother. George and his four siblings shrugged and shook their heads. A liar? In Peggy O'Leary's house? A liar would kneel in salt or get an earful of God and His mother. There *had* to be accountability in Peggy O'Leary's house.

She wasn't a cartoon ogre. She was a splendidly spunky sort—still is—a dandy fox-trotter with sparkling blue eyes and no hesitation about laughing at herself. A woman born to raise boys, all four of them: a classic Irish mom. She pointed to the bathtub and the singe marks made by the matches. "The Blessed Mother's watching!" she cried. Our Lady. *Notre Dame.* The statuette in the living room. "She'll tell me who did it!" Mrs. O'Leary cried.

George swallowed. He was about to become an altar boy. A few days passed, George tiptoeing around his mother and God's mother until the supper dishes were done. That's when the family always knelt under Our Lady's gaze and said the rosary, the boys machine-gunning their 10 Hail Marys apiece so they could get back to playing ball and dying a thousand deaths as their sister, Margaret, stretched each *theeeee* and *thyyyyy* from here to kingdom come.

Then it happened. George reached again for the matchbox above the sink. Every kid played with matches but George had been warned, and now he was going to play with fire a second time. Mrs. O'Leary burst into the kitchen, grabbed him and banished him to his bedroom. "When your father comes home," she shouted, "you'll be taken away to live in the Home for Wayward Children!"

Dusk fell. Dad entered the high-rise projects where the O'Learys lived on the Lower East Side of Manhattan. A wee scrap of a man, just over 5½ feet tall and 140 pounds, but full to the brim with pep and piss and pun was George the Father. He'd drop to the floor in his 50s to bang out push-ups, clapping his hands after each one, and when he blinked the telltale twinkle from his eye and told his kids that the jagged scar across his gut—the result of an ulcer operation that removed three quarters of his stomach—actually stemmed from his belly dive onto a grenade to save a buddy during World War II, they believed him. After all, he'd been a paratrooper, and who on earth was a more loyal soul than he?

Dad headed to George's bedroom, hot-footed by his wife's glower. He shut the door and confronted his son. Dad was renowned for his brutal honesty, but Dad, God rest his soul, was a pushover. The sight of a forlorn child seemed to mine misery from the ninth year of his own life, when his father had vanished. "You can't play with matches, George," he rebuked his son. Job done, he melted. It wasn't really that serious, Son, and give Mom a day or two, she'd lighten up, and maybe he could sneak young George a bite to eat or slip him a nickel for candy.

George's older brother, Peter, had a high IQ and magnificent wrists, was a .500-hitting high schooler whom opponents would defend with four outfielders. Terry, a year younger than George, was a straight-A student with a grade-A jump shot, a future Suffolk County high school tournament MVP. Margaret, three years younger, was sweetness itself, no worries there. George? Well, let's be honest: George was no slickie. *Thick* and *blunt* were the adjectives his family hung on him, a mostly B and C student who couldn't dance or carry a tune in a houseful of hams and who was teased for the half inch of elevation he got on his jump shot. But, Jesus, Mary and Joseph, there was no more loyal brother or buddy in a tight spot and no more hard-nosed bundle of will and self-assurance on a ball field. He'd play two-on-two tackle football on pavement, and then when he wrenched his neck in a helmet-to-helmet collision during his sophomore year in high school, the bedside contraption rigged by the family doctor to hold George's neck in traction lasted two days. "This is bull," snapped George, who dismantled the device, practiced the next day and played the following weekend.

By then there were eight children, and the O'Learys had outgrown the Manhattan apartment and moved to a modest Cape Cod in blue-collar Central Islip, Long Island. But a kid still couldn't hide anything in that home, not with the four boys jammed into one bedroom, the four girls into another, a grandma and great uncle in the third bedroom, George's mother and father in the last one and the church waiting outside the door with hellfire unless you confessed. George didn't even try to carve out his own place. He bunched elbow-to-elbow with all the other males on Saturdays in front of the black-and-white television, hollering the Irish home against the best that the WASPs could throw at them, no one ever saying it, only feeling it: Notre Dame football was everything honest and right and if *that* Fighting Irish Catholic 11 could *own* the American pie, then the dozen crammed in this house could at least have a slice of it.

When the game on TV ended, the boys tumbled outside and lived it all over again, deep into dark. Then came Sunday and even more Irish in the house, grandparents born and bred in the old land, along with aunts and uncles and cousins, gathering in the basement to sing the old songs on birthdays, anniversaries and holidays.

So how could the roast beef just *disappear*? It couldn't! Out with it, demanded Mrs. O'Leary. Her children blinked at her, all denying knowledge. Well, then, we'll see. For three days she served sad leftovers for supper, waiting for the children to crack, but by then they'd been hardened, known suppers during hard times that were just a plateful of mashed potatoes tinted ominously red by baby-food beets. The Blessed Mother works in mysterious ways, her wonders to perform. Sarge, the family mutt, sauntered in from the backyard with the string from the roast beef dangling from his arse, and the O'Learys at last sat down to some decent grub.

Have you located it yet? Where could a lie, an exaggeration that would make a national disgrace of a man, take root in that house?

A home where no one dared preen or puff himself, where Dad dismissed airs or boasts with just three letters—"SPS," for Self-Praise Stinks—and any boy who made himself out to be one inch more than he was risked humiliation. "All right, who is it?" Mrs. O'Leary asked, chortling one day as she finished the laundry. "Who's the big head who thinks he needs an extra-large jock?"

No one owned up. Not George, not Terry, not Peter, and for damn sure not Sarge.

1964–68 Sandbagger, Bartender, Road Paver, Landscaper, Mover, Student

When you're 18, there's no explaining it. Sometimes everything you love is everything you hate. Maybe it was the smell of four boys in a bedroom just after a ball game, maybe it was singing the same song from the Auld Sod for the 32nd time, maybe it was that eternal flame underneath that eternal pot of Mrs. O'Leary's boiling potatoes. Maybe it was the fact that Dubuque was the only college that showed a glimmer of interest in George. Maybe that's why he was suddenly on the road, the first O'Leary to leave the fold, barreling through a cornfield on a 24-hour Greyhound bus ride to Iowa, a boy who'd never been farther from home than the Jersey shore.

A glimmer, mind you. Not a scholarship. Maybe a grand in financial aid, a bit of an insult, really, after George had quarterbacked his high school team—more on grit than on grace—to an undefeated season. At Dubuque he found himself one of five quarterbacks, promptly converted to bottom-of-the-depth-chart fullback, an out-of-place Noo Yawker on a bad Division III team cheered by a few hundred fans, the glory of his senior season and the warmth of his big family fading, fading . . . gone.

He knew more than the damn coach did. He was sure of it. He barely stepped on the football field all fall. No, that's a lie. He cut across it at night to get to the Disabled American Veterans Bar to quaff a half-dozen Hamm's. The future coach of Notre Dame? They'd have howled in the locker room if you'd pointed at *him* and said *that*. He scraped by academically, quit football and wouldn't have returned for his sophomore year if he hadn't felt so listless that he couldn't stir himself to apply to another school. There was one highlight that second year: the road trip. To South Bend. He walked the hallowed grounds of Notre Dame and sensed the magic that his grades and football skills wouldn't let him touch.

A third helping of Iowa was out of the question. His dad, who'd worked his way up from school custodian to school board president and postmaster of Central Islip, had come to be known as the God-father, the townsman with the most connections and deepest devotion to arranging jobs for any man he deemed a good man. He saw the lost look in his boy's eyes and grew uneasy. He turned to Walt Mirey, an administrator in the C.I. school district who'd played football at New Hampshire. Somehow Dad had to wedge the kid through college. Mirey got him in. Dad exhaled. So long, George!

George? What was he doing back at the front door? A week and a half into August preseason camp, George quit the team, quit before he began and took a bus home. Cripes, what was the point? He'd be ineligible for a year because of the transfer, owed a bundle for student loans and couldn't bear another four-eyed professor slowly squeezing his privates in a midterm vise.

He walked through the door. He couldn't meet his father's stare. He hated letting down the kind of man who, the first time he ever flew in an airplane, jumped out of it, on a paratrooper training mission in Georgia. The kind who always forgave you.

"So . . . what're you going to do, George?" his father asked.

"I don't know. Go in the service, maybe."

"You need to get back to college, George. You're not a quitter. You're better than that."

Three days of unbearable silence later George returned to New Hampshire. His playing life was over, his pilot light barely aflame, but in the next two years he worked enough as a part-time bartender, landscaper, mover and paver to know what he *didn't* want, so he hit the books, or at least tapped them, enough to get a B.S. in phys ed.

And he met a girl. Bumped into her at a party and was so taken by her that just before the next bash at his frat house, he concocted a doozy. He talked Sharon Littlefield into coming as a blind date for a nonexistent friend of his, then offered his regrets when she showed up and the buddy didn't—but, hey, now that she was there, why not be *his* date? She didn't mind, because there was nothing slick about his deception; truth is, he was a little rough around the edges. She liked his blue eyes, his blond hair and his swagger, and she so prized her own privacy and independence that it was O.K. that he was a loner. They married before he graduated. She would look back on that first date, four children later, as such a wonderful little lie.

1969–74 Phys-Ed Teacher,
Driver's Ed Teacher,
Assistant Football Coach

Surprise! The son of Central Islip's school board president secured his first real job in 1969—as a teacher and assistant football coach at Central Islip High. "It was almost," says George's youngest brother, Tom, "as if he'd become Dad's project."

Take a young man. Place him in front of a group of kids just a few years younger than he is. He must give them direction when he's barely begun to find his own. He must seal off all his own doubts so they'll believe and follow. Make sure they never do what he did: quit. What's a young coach but an elaborate bluff, a careful construction of small lies? What's a successful coach but one so convincing that even he comes to believe the bluff, and turns it into truth?

But this was a *good* lie, right? A boy becoming a man in a world where everyone lies had to figure that out. This sort of lie his country rewarded, for its coaches played the role that tribal elders—the ones entrusted to take boys and turn them, through rites of passage, into men—played in other lands. George started driving up and down the East Coast, attending football clinics at which these elders held court, in quest of knowledge and a model.

In Washington, D.C., he found one. Here was fire, here was aura, here was Woody Hayes. You *have* to do it right, the Ohio State coach thundered, and your players *have* to do it right, *every* time! Accountability! Integrity! Trust! In four more towns George heard Woody. Woody's slogans became George's slogans. Woody's hero, Patton, became George's. Woody's realization—that raw honesty could be an astonishingly effective motivating tool—became George's eureka. George caught fire. Then breathed it.

He descended the cellar steps of Ralph G. Reed Junior High School, a few blocks from C.I. High. Beneath the low ceiling pipes he painted a wide purple circle on the floor. That's what George began doing, drawing circles. If you weren't in the circle, weren't with him on his mission, as his old high school teammate and coaching partner, Tommy Black, put it, "you might think that he had a stick up his ass." But if you *were* in the circle, you'd thrash anything that threatened it. George filled the purple circle with weights and bars and benches, raised them on platforms, lit them with track lights to make the circle more sacred, christened it the Pride Area and demanded that his players return to it three days a week, year round. No conversation was permitted there. Only screaming. George and dozens of boys raised an ear-shattering din as they encircled a puff-cheeked offensive lineman straining to surpass his personal-best bench press—*You can do it, Billy. It's fourth and-one. How much do you want it? How much?!*

"Wow," thought Billy Neuse, a Long Island guy who used to slam Hamm's with George in Dubuque and caught up with him in Central Islip, "is that the same guy?"

1975–79 High School Head Coach

Watch closely now. George just left the web of family and favors, of connections and loyalty. George just left Dad.

His heels clacked through the cavernous halls of Liverpool High in upstate New York. A man could get lost there: Nearly 4,000 students surged through the corridors, and most couldn't tell George how to find the main office. A man could be found there: Ten miles away stood Syracuse University and something impossible to see from Central Islip—a major-college football program.

It was 1977. He was 31. He looked at the sea of strange faces. They hadn't a clue that he'd labored six years as an assistant, waiting for the C.I. head coach to step aside, then gone 16–1–1 in two seasons as head coach and been named Suffolk County coach of the year. No one knew him in Liverpool, the way no one had known his grandparents 70 years earlier when they had left behind a land where everything was set in stone to come to one where everything was fluid and people kept moving, kept selling themselves to strangers, jockeying for position, an upgrade. Where a man was free to tell anyone anything to prove his worth, or his product's worth, and the line between marketing and lying was so fine that he could find himself right on top of it before he knew he was there, then stumble across it by sheer momentum. As George's brother Tom would ask, "Is anyone trying to tell me that résumés are truthful? In the America we live in, the willingness to lie on a résumé is an indication of how much you want the job."

Something was missing in the persona George had built, some mortar that would better hold the bricks in place, some grout that would make the wall more impenetrable. A man who made quitting seem so repulsive, so weak, who convinced so many boys that anything was possible if they refused to quit. . . . Why, *he* couldn't have quit, could he? So, sure, he said, there where no one knew him, sure, he'd played college ball at New Hampshire. Somehow the lie contained a deeper truth about George, an updated one. The man he'd become would've gutted it out at New Hampshire, not to mention Dubuque—which he *didn't* mention.

Funny, the lie didn't really stick in the altar boy's throat. It didn't torture Mrs. O'Leary's son. Hell, how had Dad, virtually blind in his left eye, passed the physical to become a paratrooper? By memorizing the eye chart! By pulling a fast one to get his foot in the door. And if Dad hadn't hit a tree on his last training jump and the doctor who examined him hadn't discovered his disability, he probably would've been killed in Italy like so many of his training partners and that deception would've been hailed in his eulogy as proof of his courage and patriotism.

In truth, the subject of George's past rarely arose. "He was such an awe-inspiring coach, it seemed like he was born that way," says Tim Green, an All-America defensive lineman who played under George in high school and college, then became a lawyer, writer and TV commentator. "People were terrified of him. One time at practice someone said ouch. George said, '*Ouch?* Who the hell just said *ouch?* My goddam wife doesn't say ouch! My goddam little girl doesn't say ouch! Everybody hit the ground! One hundred up-downs!' Sure, some walked away from him bruised, but we all walked away from him better. To have great rewards you must have great effort. George showed me how. He gave me the blueprint."

He inherited a 1–9 squad at Liverpool. He began to change what the players saw when they looked in the mirror. He would yank their face masks and head-slap them with his clipboard when they lost focus. He would station a kid in the center of a ring of players, a circle of fire, and call out names so they'd charge and drill the boy from all angles, one by one. He sent them out of the team bus with the Notre Dame fight song ringing in their ears, full of belief in themselves. They went 3–6 his first year, then went 8–1 and won their conference title.

At a summer camp based in a suffocating converted barn 100 miles from Liverpool, George instituted dawn wake-ups and bunk inspections and three-a-day practices and late-night team meetings. It worked because George demanded even more of himself than of the boys, and because he'd crack them up, in the midst of their misery, with a well-timed one-liner. It worked because George cared so much, because he asked how your mom and dad were doing and if there was anything else he could do to help you get that scholarship, and because come Saturday in autumn, you kicked the crap out of anyone who had the audacity to think he belonged on the same grass as you, after all you'd been through. In George's third year his team went 10–0, surrendered just *33 points* all season and was ranked No. 2 in the state as George, for the second straight year, was named Onondaga County coach of the year.

His wife received a phone call. It was their daughter's kindergarten teacher, worried because the family portrait that little Trish had been asked to draw included her mother and three siblings—but no father. Was there trouble at home? No. Sharon tried to explain: The marriage was fine, and Trish did see her dad now and then, but usually when he was on the sideline, and usually all she saw was the back of his head.

George received a letter. "You are the kind of person with whom it is a pleasure to be associated—both professionally and personally," wrote Liverpool High executive principal David Kidd. "Your dedication, ethics and loyalty are recognized by everyone."

1979–94 Asst. Coach, Syracuse
Defensive Coordinator, Georgia Tech
Asst. Coach, San Diego Chargers

It wasn't enough.

George's ballpoint hovered over four blank lines. The heading above them, on the Syracuse University personal information form, read *Athletic background (sports played in high school, college, professional; letters won, honors, championships etc. Please be specific).*

He'd made it. The big leap. The rare jump from high school coach to major-college assistant, bypassing the usual rungs—

graduate assistant, Division III coach—that took a man there. Just in time, too, after the coach at Baldwinsville High had sneaked into the woods and snapped pictures of George holding practices out of season and gotten Liverpool's sports teams put on probation for a year. It was April 1980. George had been in his new job for three months, wowing Syracuse coach Frank Maloney as a defensive line coach and a recruiter. It wasn't enough.

George's ballpoint came down. *Basketball 3 yrs.—All-League—County Champion.* His team, in fact, had lost in the Suffolk County championship game on George's missed shot at the buzzer. It wasn't enough.

College, he wrote. This information would go into his bio in game programs and the media brochure. Other coaches on the staff would read it. They'd all played college ball. *Univ. of New Hampshire*, he wrote. His players would read it too. He wasn't a quitter. He was better than that: *3 yr lettered*, he wrote. More mortar. More grout. How could he dream that a child not yet born would grow up to become a student assistant in the Syracuse sports information department, would fax this very sheet of paper to a reporter 21 years later and demolish George's life?

George spat a stream of brown juice into a Styrofoam cup. A new habit. One more thing, besides the college football letters, he now had in common with the Syracuse defensive coaches. He began filling out a second document, entitled *Personal Data Sheet*, in which he was asked to spell out his academic credentials. He began to list the graduate schools he'd attended and the credits he'd earned. He had 31. It wasn't enough. *Presently have B.S. +48*, George wrote, adding 17 credits.

Hell, it was no big deal, just another coach's ploy, wasn't it? Like thrusting his badly scarred left hand with its permanently bent pinkie—the result of a tumble at age five, when he landed on a broken bottle at the bottom of a sump—into the face of a player who seemed always to complain of injuries and screaming, "See that? *That's* college football!" Just a way of creating more authority, more aura, more men who made more victories. Just, like raw honesty, another tool. Right?

George hatched a first-round NFL draft pick on the Syracuse defensive line, Tim Green, and two second-rounders: Mike Charles and Blaise Winter—an abused kid, born with a cleft palate, for whom George became a father figure. George became assistant head coach. George became hot property. Funny: That past he'd puffed up? No one who hired him after that would ask to see his résumé. Bobby Ross didn't ask when he snatched George from Syracuse and made him his defensive coordinator at Georgia Tech in 1987, nor when George's defense refused to allow a touchdown in the *first 19 quarters* of '90 as Tech began its march to a share of the national championship. Ross sure didn't peruse the résumé before he took George to the Chargers as his defensive line coach in '92 and San Diego's front four promptly led the AFC in sacks on its way to the Chargers' first playoff appearance in a decade. Homer Rice, then athletic director at Georgia Tech, never gave the résumé a glance when he coaxed George back to cure Tech's defense in '94. The man *produced,* at every level. The man was real.

But, still, something must've been missing. George still didn't have what he lusted for; he remained an assistant. In 1987 a member of Tech's sports information department, preparing coaches' bios for the fall football program, popped into George's office to ask a few questions. When the interview was done, the boy who couldn't stop playing with matches had a master's degree.

1995–2001 Head Coach, Georgia Tech

It was ticking now. So softly that even he couldn't hear it. So softly that no one could, and nearly every article and anecdote about George hinged on his extraordinary honesty, his *painful* honesty, and all the perpendicular adjectives—upstanding, upright, up-front, straightforward—echoed again and again.

How could anyone hear the time bomb ticking as George paced before his team in 1995, his authority threatened for the first time as a college head coach, his face contorted in a snarl, his cheeks red as fire, his tobacco juice spraying his shirt, and he screamed out his paramount rule, his *only* rule: "DON'T LIE TO ME!"

Someone had sung to George: The training rules he'd put into effect that weekend had been violated. "I want anyone who was drinking," he cried, "to stand up!" Now he'd see if his bedrock values—trust, accountability, integrity—had sunk in. *"Now!"*

Ryan Stewart, one of George's leaders, a senior strong safety on his way to the NFL, agonized in his seat. He'd had a beer and a half. If he stood, he'd be up at 5:30 running or monkey-rolling or somersaulting, maybe till he vomited. If he stood, he'd force the three teammates who'd split the six-pack with him to stand up too. The silence gathered. George's face was no longer red. It was purple. *"Who didn't understand what I said?"*

The fear thickened. If George already knew that Ryan had been drinking, and Ryan didn't stand, everything between them would be broken, and his pro career might be jeopardized. Ryan loved playing for George. George made Ryan believe in himself. Ryan was about to cry.

He stood. The three other beer-and-a-halfers stood. Then six were standing. Then 10. Then a dozen. Lies couldn't last under George. His blue eyes bulged. *"The whole team will be punished!"* he roared.

It was George's world now. It was *his* field you played on, he'd remind you, *his* food you ate, *his* dorm you roomed in, *his* time when you woke, worked, ate and fell asleep. The first day of August camp he gave each of his players a packet: Every day for the next five months, their lives were scheduled. Every opponent had already been game-planned, every practice mapped out. Practices lasted two hours and seven minutes: 24 five-minute periods, sprinting between stations. He might let you miss one. *If* you ratted out a teammate.

You didn't dare show up for a meeting or a meal or a team bus exactly when his itinerary told you to. You'd miss it by 15 minutes and get left behind—it happened even to the athletic director. George's meetings ended, literally, before they were scheduled to start. You didn't dare come his way with facial hair, earrings, headphones or a hat on backward. You didn't let a cell phone ring in a team meeting unless you wished to see it bounce off the wall and go to pieces on the floor. You didn't utter a word in a coaches' meeting without assuming he'd chicken-scratch it onto one of the four legal notepads he brought to each session and sail it back at you at a meeting two months later. You didn't move a plant or lift a blind in his office. He'd know. You didn't work or play under him unless you'd learned to walk on all sorts of surfaces—on pins, on needles, on eggshells and through fire.

Ten cups of coffee and 10 fingernails—that's what he went through each day. Four hours' sleep, and he started all over again: 16-hour days, seven days a week, his Irish music blasting on the car ride home to keep him awake, his two dogs waiting frantically by the door for the man whose pockets bulged with pig's ears, cookies, beef jerky and biscuits for them. Once a year he'd take off a half day to drink beer, sing the old songs and zing one-liners at pals. Once a year: St. Patrick's Day. Irish souvenirs and proverbs covered his office desk and walls, but he never had the time to go to Ireland. For years his friends and relatives had kidded him, asking the Fighting Irishman when he'd take over the Fighting Irish, because if ever a man was made for a place, it was George for Notre Dame.

Sure, that was a dream, but who had time for dreaming? The lights went out during a Georgia Tech evening practice in '95, then flashed back on. An electrician, trying to pinpoint the problem, inserted his screwdriver into the fuse box by the field. An explosion sent him tumbling down an embankment, smoke coming from beneath his hat, and brought the football trainers on the run. Players stopped in mid-drill and stared in fear as the electrician rose slowly to his feet. "He's O.K!" screamed George. "Run the damn play!"

Obsession is contagious. Tech won an ACC title and, beginning in 1997, five straight bowl berths. The legions grew, players who'd dive on grenades for George. Off to the side stood casualties such as Dustin Vaitekunas, a 6' 7" offensive lineman whose grit left George so unimpressed two years ago that he flipped a ball to the kid and sent four defensive linemen at him so he'd know how it felt to be an unprotected quarterback. Vaitekunas didn't get up for 10 minutes; he quit the team, and his mother threatened to have George arrested for assault. Media and academic types were outraged, scarcely believing George's claim that he hadn't intended for his front four to flatten the boy. But his players—who depended on brotherhood and commitment as they stood on a field where any one of 11 men might attack from any side—rallied around George. As long as he stayed on a football field, George could be justified. "If he was on fire, I wouldn't walk across the street to piss on him," says Michael Dee, a Tech safety in the mid-'90s, "but I'd want him as my coach."

Maybe now George could chance it. Maybe now that he earned more than a million a year on a multiyear contract, now that he'd won two ACC coach of the year awards and national coach of the year in 2000, he could quietly ask that his two lies be stricken from Tech's publicity material.

His wife had noticed the falsehood about his playing career. "Ah, the guy in the sports information department at Syracuse told me to make it look good," George fibbed. His mom and dad had noticed it too. "Ah, it's not important. I don't know how it got in there," George said. "I gotta get it out." He thought about it. But he couldn't risk it. Fame had removed his control of the lies: they had flown everywhere now on paper and in cyberspace.

His children believed the lies. His brothers and old pals from C.I. figured they were just part of the hype machine. When George's more recent friends asked about his college career, he'd say, "I could hit you, but I couldn't catch you," then nod toward the scar on his knee and allude to a football injury—but not mention that the blow had actually occurred years after college, when he was coaching. The wave of his hand and his silence discouraged more questions, and who had questions about New Hampshire football anyway?

It was the perfect lie, and George the perfect agent for it: Who would suspect subterfuge from a sledgehammer? Who'd suspect it from a religious man with no tolerance for preening, the same modest man at a million a year as he had been at $14,322? If his secretary hadn't pulled his coach of the year awards out of a box and displayed them in his office, nobody would have laid eyes on them.

The one man George wished to shine for—the one he called minutes after every game—was dying a slow, gasping death from emphysema when Tech named George head coach. Dad never saw the glory. George leaned over his coffin and pinned a Georgia Tech button to his lapel. He was shocked, days later, to find himself sobbing with the team priest, unable to sleep. Shocked at how many mourners had materialized with previously untold tales of Mr. O'Leary's acts of kindness.

More and more George found himself slipping his barber $100 for a haircut to help him through hard times, or tucking a C-note beneath a plate after finding out that his harried waitress had five kids at home, or inviting a custodian home for Thanksgiving dinner and to sleep over. "Don't tell anyone," he'd tell people who witnessed such acts. He wanted no one to know who lived inside the wall he'd built, a wall so thick that he couldn't hear those last . . . few . . . ticks.

Notre Dame called. Its athletic director, Kevin White, who'd grown up just a few miles from Central Islip, had interviewed 50 people who were sure of three things: George's honesty, his character, and his ability. Notre Dame offered to buy out George's $1.5 million contract with Georgia Tech. Notre Dame wanted George.

A strange thing happened. George hesitated. It was the quiet uneasiness of a man who owned his reality and wondered if he should let go of it for anything, even his dream. "Imagine if Dad were here to see this," said his brothers and brother-in-law. "It's Notre Dame, George. It's *Notre Dame.*"

Dec. 9–13, 2001 Head Coach, Notre Dame

The moment he set foot on campus, all his doubts vanished—he knew this was right. He entered the grotto where the blue-sashed Virgin Mary stood amid stones blackened by the candle soot of a century of adoration. The day before, he had signed on to begin the crowning chapter of his life, at Our Lady's university. On *her* day, Dec. 8, the Feast of the Blessed Mother. He looked skyward. The Golden Dome gleamed. It was true, what they said about this place. Everything was magic.

He entered the basilica. The choir, rehearsing, hurled its song at the gilded angels and saints upon the soaring ceiling. He could hear and smell a hundred Sundays at the altar of his childhood, a thousand dusks of saying the rosary surrounded by his kneeling family. The emotion rose in his throat and tightened the knot on his blue-and-gold necktie. He knelt alone to offer thanks. At 55, he'd clawed his way forward to his past. He was home.

He entered the basketball arena. The pep band burst into the fight song he used to play to send his high school troops to battle. The cheerleaders tumbled. The crowd, clad in BY GEORGE, IT'S O'LEARY! T-shirts, rose, and so did the hair on his neck.

He flew back home to Atlanta, packed up his life and his Irish regalia and returned to South Bend two days later. At dusk on his first day on the job, he was interrupted quietly, apologetically, by the Notre Dame sports information director, John Heisler. A call had just come from Jim Fennell, a reporter for the Manchester *Union Leader* in New Hampshire. He was tracking down men who'd had the honor of playing college football 33 years ago with Notre Dame's newest coach, but, funny, his old teammates said George had never played.

George blinked. *Blindsided*. Now he had to lie again. Well, he said, it was true, he hadn't really played, uh . . . there was that knee injury one year, and then the other year he was sick, mononucleosis. Somebody must've made a mistake in the bio. Heisler left. George looked down at his thick, chafed hands. He worked until 2 a.m.

The next day, figuring the worst was over, he left for Alexandria, Va., to recruit running back Tommy Clayton. George still didn't understand. Notre Dame, George. *Notre Dame*. A phone call came late that afternoon. It was Lou Nanni, the university's vice president of public affairs and communications. Fennell had called back, holding a 21-year-old document that Syracuse had faxed to him. The lie had been written by George. Could he explain?

No, George couldn't, he must've written it, but, but. . . . Lou, this is just a speed bump, right? No, said Nanni. Calls from media outlets everywhere were pouring into the university. Nanni was surprised at what happened next. George offered to resign.

Hold on, said Nanni. They would prepare a statement admitting George's weakness as a young coach. They'd take some terrible blows, but they'd weather them together. George left to meet the recruit's parents, his gut in a knot. Nanni called back, read the statement, then asked, "George, is there anything else in your bio that's not accurate?"

A pause. A lifetime hanging. The master's degree—should he lie?

"George, there's going to be incredible scrutiny by the media," said Nanni. "If we don't get this all clear now, it *will* come out anyway."

George's voice cracked, and words began to tumble from his lips—something about credits and a degree—that didn't quite make sense. "George," said Nanni, in a nightmare of his own. "If someone were to look hard at the records concerning the master's degree at NYU, would it be fair to say they're not going to find your name there?"

Another pause. For the first time it occurred to George: He'd wandered off his field. He could survive a lie inside a white-lined rectangle, but now he was playing in someone else's ivory tower. Yes, George finally said, his voice deathly quiet and far away. They wouldn't find it.

Nanni blanched and got off the phone. White, the athletic director, called George moments later to verify.

"I'm sorry," George kept saying, "I'm sorry, I'm sorry."

White was reeling. He had to speak to the university president, Father Edward Malloy. He'd call back in a few minutes, he said.

George waited. Forty minutes of forever passed. The phone rang. A trust had been broken, said White. False academic credentials at Notre Dame were a death knell. He accepted George's resignation.

George hung up. That was it. He was done. Just a couple of little matches . . . and everything was up in flames. Sure, he might've had to resign from any other university, but the fact that it had happened at Notre Dame, that was the wind turning this into a conflagration, sending it burning from page 4C in the newspapers to page 1A.

His hand began to work across his face. It was just after midnight. All the consequences, one horror and humiliation after the next, began to spread through him. The joke, the sick joke, was on him. Notre Dame hadn't cared whether he had a master's degree or whether he'd lettered in college football. The lies had been wasted. George O'Leary, the chipmunk trying to pass for a squirrel, when everyone saw him as a lion.

His mind reeled: to the assistants he'd brought from Tech to Notre Dame, suddenly jobless. To the lives of his entire staff at Tech, thrown asunder for nothing. To himself, unemployed, unemployable, holding the bag for the $1.5 million buyout that Notre Dame wouldn't pay now. To his family name—ruined. Oh, Jesus, his mother, his mother. . . .

He stared out the second-floor window. He considered the

distance. Eighth floor, maybe, he thought. But not from here. He stood. He had to get out of there, leave, go somewhere, *now*. No. Not allowed. Aviation regulations. Mandatory rest time. Notre Dame's private pilots couldn't fly till 4 a.m. For four hours he sat there, holding on through the dark, trying to survive.

He flew to South Bend, grabbed a few belongings, hurried back to the plane to return to Georgia in the sickly light of dawn. He got into his car at a private airport near Atlanta and began the hour-and-a-half drive to his lake house. Tears began streaming down his cheeks.

The phone was ringing as he entered the empty house. Oh, God. Mom. Eighty years old. "George . . . what happened?" she cried. She heard him struggling not to break down.

"Mom . . . I made a mistake. But it was never a factor in getting any job."

"But. . . ."

"I really don't want to talk about it, Mom."

He went to the finished basement. His 29-year-old son, Tim—who, like his younger brother, Marty, had played for their father at Tech—came through the front door, fearful for George. He found him on a sofa in the basement, staring into nothingness, notepad in lap, pen in hand, reaching to write a list when there was nothing left to list.

His wife and daughters arrived. They dared not hug him. They couldn't even go near him. He was almost catatonic. The phone rang endlessly. Tim turned away the callers. Sharon was too tearful to speak. George's friends arrived, but he refused to see them.

Friday blurred into Saturday. George hadn't moved from the sofa. He wouldn't eat. Wouldn't change his clothes. Couldn't look in a mirror to shave or wash up or comb his hair. It was frightening to watch a man try to hold in that much grief, that much shame, that much anger. His brothers Peter and Tom arrived from New York, pushed past Tim and went downstairs. His friends showed up again. Everyone was crying. George sat and stared at his own wake.

Days passed. His friends feared that his basement would be his tomb. In bits and pieces he began to hear what the world was saying. It was even worse than he'd dreaded. America seemed more shocked by lying from a football coach than from a politician or a businessman. The country still attached honor to sports. There was glee as well, cackling at the sight of two American institutions going down at once: the crusty old-fashioned football coach and, my God, *Notre Dame.* Jay Leno called him "George O'Really?" The radio talk shows went wild. The O'Learys in New York shuddered and hurried past front pages blaring LIAR, LIAR and NOTRE SHAME. In 12 months George had gone from national coach of the year to national joke of the year.

Perhaps all the laughter was the nervous release of a deep uneasiness. People with big plans everywhere opened their laptops, called up their résumés and began hitting the delete button. Rick Smith, a newly named Georgia Tech assistant, didn't edit his bio fast enough and went from a 150-grand-a-year defensive coordinator to a 60-buck-a-day substitute teacher.

Two weeks after the horror began, George started to comb his hair and clean up. He went to a different store to get doughnuts in the morning, hoping people wouldn't recognize him, and he slipped out of Sunday Mass early to avoid meeting the eyes of the priest. As he drove, he prayed the rosary on a set of old brown beads worn smooth by his father's hands on his deathbed.

His old players felt as if they'd been kicked in the stomach, but when they caught their breath, most stood up, eyes blazing, for George. His brother Peter, the president of the Suffolk County Detectives Association, on Long Island, said, "It was like me being named FBI director and three days later being fired because I farted in church." Peggy O'Leary lit candles and cried herself to sleep over a son who wouldn't come to the phone when she called on Christmas Day. What she'd told him 50 years ago—funny how it had turned out to be right. Even when no one else has seen you, even when you're sure you've gotten away with a lie, you won't get it past the Blessed Mother. Our Lady. Notre Dame.

And George? He kept waking up at night, raging at the world and at himself: "Two sentences in my bio. Two sentences insignificant to what I was doing. Academic fraud, they're calling it. How could that be, when I never used it to get a job? Nobody ever asked for a résumé before they hired me to coach in college or the pros. I never profited from it. Look, I was stupid, I screwed up. I'm responsible for everything. But where's forgiveness? I keep kicking myself: You did it to yourself. You were set—financially, emotionally. For 30 years you put in 16 hours a day, to end up like this? Now you're nothing. Why? I was just trying to get ahead. To prove something to people who didn't know me. I just didn't believe in myself enough."

2002 Assistant Coach, Minnesota Vikings

A white-haired man moved swiftly through the airport in Atlanta with a cell phone pressed to his ear, pretending to hold a conversation so none of the people staring at him would approach. He stepped onto an airplane to Minneapolis that morning in mid-January and arranged his purgatory. George O'Leary had sown too much loyalty to be abandoned in hell.

Mike Tice, George's old high school quarterback who'd wept when he heard the shocking news, wanted this man at his side as he took over the Vikings, the purple and gold—the same colors to which the two had brought glory at Central Islip High. "I get the benefit of it all," said Tice. "I get to have a better coach than me."

A few weeks later George reported for his first day on the job. The sky was black. The temperature was 15°. The time was 6:30 a.m. He hadn't felt the tingle yet but was pretty sure it would come. He pulled into the Vikings' parking lot, first one there, 30 seconds before Tice.

So what do we have here? A man who was tarred and feathered—and is already largely rehabilitated. A man off the hook for the $1.5 million payout, which Georgia Tech let slide, and earning roughly $300,000 a year. A man who's walking into a circle where men will take a step forward to slap him on the back and say, "What a bunch of bull," and "What a raw deal you got over something so small"—while people outside the circle will take a step back and see, from a wider angle, that it's not small, because what becomes of a society if no one's word means a thing?

What no one can know is what will happen on the field, George's old safe place, the first time he snarls and demands complete honesty from a player who knows his sin.

.   •   •   •

And Luca? Over in Liverpool, N.Y., the old Italian continued to toss and turn at night, thinking of George and all the kids he'd steered to manhood, weighing the decision that he and his superintendent had made a quarter century ago—that the net worth of a man like George was more, much more, than the cost of his weakness. And shaking his head in sad wonder at the fear that whispers the oldest and biggest lie to us all: You're not good enough, you're not good enough, you're not good enough. And deciding that, still, he and his boss had been right to let George get away with playing with matches, even in the face of all that had come to pass, because . . . well, because his grandmother was right.

"'*Piglia i buoni,*' she always said to me," says Luca. "It means, 'Take the good'—in people. You have to give them the benefit of the doubt. You have to give the rose a chance to bloom, or it's a dark world."

So. That was Luca's choice. Now it's your turn.

The American Scholar

WINNER, ESSAYS

A Piece of Cotton

Among the many commentaries written after 9/11, "A Piece of Cotton," Anne Fadiman's meditation on the meaning of the flag, emerges as a model of essay writing. She weaves vivid swatches of history, philosophy and patriotism into an exploration of her family's ambivalence toward the national standard.

Anne Fadiman

A Piece of Cotton

W hen we bought an old brick farmhouse last summer in a small New England town, the elderly couple who had lived there for many years left us a set of plastic lawn chairs, a garbage can, a tool bench, a wheelbarrow, and an American flag. On September 13, with our children's help, we raised it to half staff. Our six-year-old son enjoyed pulling the halyard; on its way up the peeling white-painted pole, next to the big maple tree in the front yard, the flag made an interesting and satisfying sound, partway between a squeak and a ring. We'd read up on half-masting protocol, which dictates raising the flag briskly to the peak and then slowly bringing it halfway down. George said, "This flag is lowered now, but it will rise again, just as our country will." It is useful to have children around at such times: they authorize clichés that their parents deeply believe but might otherwise hesitate to voice.

Neither George nor I had ever owned a flag, not even a little one to wave on the Fourth of July. The closest George had come was the pair of stars-and-stripes bell-bottoms he had worn in the sixties (in violation of section 176d of the United States Flag Code: "The flag should never be used as wearing apparel, bedding, or drapery"). The closest I had come was the handkerchief-sized Whole Earth banner that I had affixed to the aerial of my brother's car before we drove from our home in California to college in Massachusetts in the fall of 1970. We took the whole earth idea seriously: what a provincial notion, I remember thinking, to fly a flag that implied one was a citizen of only *part* of the earth!

If you had asked me then what it meant to be a flag owner—or, as I would have called it, a flag-waver, as if holding a flag in one's hand was inherently more ridiculous than stringing it up a pole—I would have said "Vietnam." But my answer would have been false. My disdain for the flag wasn't really political. It was social. When I burrow back into my seventeen-year-old self as thoroughly as the intervening decades allow, here's what I fear she was thinking: If you were a flag-waver, you lived in a split-level house with vinyl siding in a suburb of Omaha. You had a crew cut. Your children belonged to the 4-H Club and had a dog that, without irony— there was no irony within a five-hundred-mile radius of Omaha— they had named Fido. You read *Reader's Digest* and listened to Andy Williams. You ate tuna casserole and frozen peas for dinner, followed by lime Jell-O with little pieces of banana suspended in it. You had never traveled east of Wichita (or maybe west; I had never been to either Omaha or Wichita, and knew only that they were both somewhere in the amorphous middle of things).

"Sept. 11 made it safe for liberals to be patriots," the critic George Packer wrote recently in *The New York Times*. Like me, Packer once considered flag-waving an embarrassing display of bad taste ("sentimental, primitive, sometimes aggressive"), though he associated it more with the working class than with the Cleaveresque middle class. Either way, it wasn't the sort of thing our families indulged in. When people like Packer and me were teenagers, we had little interest in the socioeconomic tiers that separated the upper middle class, to which we belonged, from what we might have called the "underprivileged class" (a group with which we professed heartfelt solidarity, whether or not we'd ever met any of its members). And in those days, in those circles (which pretended to be egalitarian but were in fact unthinkingly, unapologetically, unbelievably snobbish), America was itself déclassé, a simpleminded concatenation of Uncle Sam and log cabins and Smokey the Bear. I mean, really: if you wanted a stimulating dinner companion, would you pick Betsy Ross or Jean-Paul Sartre?

•   •   •

In March of 1918, a year after the United States entered World War I, a mob surrounded a Montana man named E. V. Starr and tried to force him to kiss an American flag. Starr refused, saying, "What is this thing anyway? Nothing but a piece of cotton with a little paint on it and some other marks in the corner there. I will not kiss that thing. It might be covered with microbes."

The previous month, Montana had enacted a flag desecration statute that became the model for the 1918 federal Sedition Act, outlawing "disloyal, profane, scurrilous, or abusive language" about the United States government or its flag. Starr was charged with sedition, fined $500, and sent to the state penitentiary for ten to twenty years of hard labor. Ruling on Starr's appeal, the federal district court judge who heard the appeal wrote:

> In the matter of his offense and sentence, obviously petitioner was more sinned against than sinning. . . . [The mob's] unlawful and disorderly conduct, not his just resistance, nor the trivial and innocuous retort into which they goaded him, was calculated to degrade the sacred banner and to bring it into contempt. Its members, not he, should have been punished.

Although he called the court that had sentenced Starr "stark, staring, raving mad"—no penalty that severe had ever been meted out, or would ever be meted out again, in a United States flag desecration case—the judge ruled that the state law was nonetheless constitutional and that he had no other choice than to uphold the conviction.

The unfortunate Starr's only bit of luck was that the Montana mob did not assault him, unlike the automobile workers in Lansing, Michigan, who, the same winter, after a fellow employee wiped his hands on a flag, had chopped a hole in the ice that covered the Grand River, tied a clothesline to the man's foot, and submerged him until he apologized; or the saloon patrons in Thermopolis, Wyoming, who, the previous year, had lynched a man for shouting "Hoch lebe der Kaiser." (In the latter case the victim was cut down in the nick of time by the city marshal. *The Chicago Tribune* reported: "Revived with cold water, he was forced to kneel and kiss the American flag. He then was warned to get out of town. He did.")

I read about these cases—they are collected in a fascinating and disturbing book called *Desecrating the American Flag: Key Documents of the Controversy from the Civil War to 1995*, edited by Robert Justin Goldstein—while I was attending a conference in Colonial Williamsburg, the omphalos of Americana. It felt strange to underline E. V. Starr's question in a hotel room crammed with hooked rugs and embroidered samplers. What *is* this thing, anyway? I thought. Is it just a piece of cotton? Is it, as Katha Pollitt put it, explaining why she had refused her daughter's request to hang a flag in their window, a symbol of "jingoism and vengeance and war"? Or is it, as a group of New York women wrote in the dedication of a silk flag they had sewn for Union soldiers in 1861, "the emblem of all you have sworn to defend: / Of freedom and progress, with order combined, / The cause of the *Nation*, of *God*, and *Mankind*"?

After September 11, I saw for the first time that the flag—along with all its red, white, and blue collateral relations—is what a semiotician would call "polysemous": it has multiple meanings. The flag held aloft by the pair of disheveled hitchhikers who squatted next to their backpacks on Route 116, a mile from our home, meant *We will not rape or murder you.* The red, white, and blue turban worn by the Sikh umbrella vendor a friend walked past in Dupont Circle, not far from the White House, meant *Looking like someone and thinking like him are not the same thing.* The flag on the lapel of a Massachusetts attorney mentioned in our local paper—on seeing it, his opposing counsel had whispered to a colleague, "I'm so screwed, do you have a flag pin I can borrow?"—meant *I am morally superior.* The flags brandished by two cowboy-hatted singers at a country fair we attended on the day the first bombs fell on Afghanistan meant *Let's kill the bastards.* The Old Glory bandanna around the neck of the well-groomed golden retriever I saw on a trip to Manhattan meant *Even if I have a Prada bag and my dog has a pedigree, I'm still a New Yorker and I have lost something.* The flag in our front yard meant *We are sad. And we're sorry we've never done this before.*

·   ·   ·

Newspapers printed full-page color flags for flagless readers to tape on their windows. NBC put stars and stripes on its peacock. The Macdougal Street Tattoo Company in Greenwich Village gave pro bono patriotic tattoos—something new under the sun—to nearly five hundred World Trade Center rescue workers. A Pennsylvania man had a flag shaved into his buzz cut. A New York restaurant called The Tonic introduced a dessert called Stars and Stripes: white mascarpone panna cotta encircled by red and blue pomegranate- and grape-flavored stars. The design of a new 34-cent flag stamp, captioned UNITED WE STAND, was rushed through several layers of U.S. Postal Service red tape in record time so that a billion stamps could be available by November 1. The space shuttle *Endeavor* carried more than six thousand flags to the International Space Station and brought them back for distribution to the families of those killed on September 11. Our son made a flag from a leaf and a twig to mark the final days of his vegetable garden, and asked if he should fly it at half staff.

When I visited my mother in Florida, I paused at the window of the gift shop in the Fort Myers airport. Outside, a National Guardsman with an M-16 patrolled the corridor. Inside, on a bed of gold-flecked gauze, reposed the largest collection of red, white, and blue objects I had ever seen: flags, streamers, key chains, pens, fans, T-shirts, baseball caps, figurines, coffee mugs, beer steins, shot glasses, menorahs, postcards with photographs of flags surrounded by oranges and flamingos, bumper stickers that said THESE COLORS NEVER RUN, starfish emblazoned with the words GOD BLESS AMERICA. The meaning of these objects had nothing to do with either Washington or Afghanistan; the flag was a "theme," like the "Underwater Theme" we'd chosen for our high school senior prom. ("Japan?" "Too hard to draw all those geishas." "Outer Space?" "Too much black and white." "Underwater?" "Now there's an idea.") I had recently seen a coffee-table book of flag-oriented antiques, each beautifully photographed and embellished with little air-brushed shadows, arranged on the pages like jewels in a Tiffany vitrine. *Patriotic Shield Pin Box. Uncle Sam Hat Brooch. Brass and Enamel Belt Buckle. Admiral Perry Whiskey Flask. Wheatlet Trading Card.* They all looked incredibly expensive, but what they had gained in value over the years they had lost in meaning: they were no longer about patriotism in wartime, they were about being collectible. The Fort Myers gift shop window was indistinguishable from a page in that book. It was already meaningless. All it needed was a caption: "Americana—Assorted Ephemera & Folk Art, 2001."

But just because most of the flag paraphernalia was dreck didn't mean that all of it was. I was caught short by the reproduction of Edward P. Moran's flag-filled 1886 painting *Statue of Liberty Enlightening the World*, placed in *The New York Times* by the Museum of the City of New York, accompanied by a quotation from Le Corbusier: "New York is not a completed city. . . . It is a city in the process of becoming. Today it belongs to the world. Without anyone expecting it, it has became the jewel in the crown of universal cities. . . . New York is a great diamond, hard and dry, sparkling, triumphant!" Just typing those words, nearly three months later, brings on the peculiar feeling of congestion I still feel every morning when I read the *Times* obituaries and start thinking about the widow who gave birth to twins on September 15 or the woman who lost both a husband and a son. I had lived in New York for twenty-five years, twenty-two of them within walking distance of the World Trade Center. The trauma center nearest the site was the hospital where our daughter was born; Engine 24/Ladder 5, where Mayor Giuliani, covered in ash, set up his temporary command post, was our corner firehouse. I felt ashamed when I caught myself thinking of this as a neighborhood tragedy rather than a global one; it was the solipsistic fallacy of believing that the telephone pole you're closest to is taller than all the rest, just because it *looks* taller. Our Massachusetts friends said to us, "You must be so relieved to have moved!" And though we did feel relief, our feelings were complicated and contradictory. We loved New York all the more because of what had been done to it. George said it was like the upwelling of tenderness one might feel upon hearing that an old lover had been grievously injured. I knew, though it seemed like a dishonorably trivial emotion, that one of the reasons Moran and Le Corbusier affected me was homesickness.

It was good to see George watching the World Series one night. Until then, we had been unable to watch any television that did not deal with September 11. Flying above center field at Yankee Stadium was a torn flag. It was shaped like an oriflamme, the banner the king's army carried in twelfth-century France, split at one end with flying edges like two flames. The flag, which had flown somewhere inside the World Trade Center, had been found in the rubble and nearly disposed of (Flag Code section 176k: "The flag, when it is in such condition that it is no longer a fitting emblem for display, should be destroyed in a dignified way, preferably by burning"). The Port Authority intervened, and Sgt. Antonio Scannella, a police officer who had lost thirteen of his squad's eighteen members, became the flag's unofficial caretaker, saying, "You can't throw an American flag in the garbage." When Max Von Essen, the son of the New York City Fire Commissioner, sang "The Star-Spangled Banner" (the only national anthem I can think of that's specifically about a flag), my throat caught in an unfamiliar way.

Why did the lopsided flag that billowed across our television screen pull strings that had previously been unpullable? I think it moved me *because* it was damaged, like the city itself. A clean rectangle whose proportions conform precisely to the Executive Order issued in 1912 by President Taft—hoist (height) 1.0, fly (length) 1.9, hoist of union (blue field) .5385, fly of union .76, width of each stripe .0769, diameter of each star .0616—calls up less passionate associations than, for instance, the flag flown by the Sixteenth Regiment of Connecticut volunteers in the Civil War. When surrender was inevitable, the soldiers tore the flag into fragments to keep it from falling into enemy hands. A historian named F. C. Hicks wrote in 1926:

> The regiment, some five hundred strong, was sent to a prison camp where most of the men remained until the close of the war. Each piece of the colors was sacredly preserved. When a soldier died his piece was entrusted to a comrade. At the end of the war the weary prisoners returned to their homes, each bringing his bit of star or stripe with him. All these torn fragments were patched together and the regimental colors, nearly complete, are now preserved in the State House at Hartford.

· · ·

To read about our nation's vexillological history—"vexillology," the study of flags, is an excellent crossword-puzzle word that derives from the Latin *vexillum*, or banner—is to experience a series of bitter disillusionments. Betsy Ross did not design the stars and stripes; she sewed flags for the navy in the spring of 1777, but there is no evidence that the flag as we know it was conceived before June 14 of that year, when the Continental Congress, which had previously been more concerned about designing a national seal, finally got around to the flag: "RESOLVED: that the flag of the United States be made of thirteen stripes, alternate red and white; that the union be thirteen stars, white in a blue field, representing a new constellation." (Many historians now attribute the circular shape of that constellation to Francis Hopkinson, a delegate from New Jersey, though late-eighteenth-century flags show the stars disposed in a variety of arrangements, including a single vertical line and an X.) George Washington did not cross the Delaware with flag in hand; the Battle of Trenton was fought six months before the Flag Resolution. The flag's design did not immediately engrave itself on the memories of all who beheld it; in 1778, Benjamin Franklin and John Adams informed the King of the Two Sicilies that the stripes were "alternately red, white, and blue," and on a ceramic jug manufactured in Liverpool at about the same time, an American ship flew a flag with blue and yellow stripes. "The Star-Spangled Banner" did not immediately become the national anthem; though it was written by Francis Scott Key during the Battle of Fort McHenry in 1814 (and set to the tune of "To Anacreon in Heaven," a British drinking song celebrating a bibulous Greek poet who is said to have choked to death on a grape), it was not officially adopted until 1931.

In fact, as Scot M. Guenter explains in *The American Flag 1777–1924: Cultural Shifts from Creation to Codification*, it was not until Rebel forces fired on the flag at Fort Sumter on April 12, 1861, that the flag, which earlier had been used mainly for identifying naval and commercial vessels, was transformed into a symbol men were willing to die for. If it took the Civil War to sacralize the flag— as the historian George Henry Preble wrote in 1880, "its prose became poetry"—it took the commercialism of the ensuing decades to turn its poetry back into prose. In 1905, an anti-desecration circular lamented the use of the flag in advertisements for "bicycles, bock beer, whiskey, fine cambric, bone knoll, sour mash, tar soap, American pepsin chewing gum, theatres, tobacco, Japan tea, awnings, breweries, cigars, charity balls, cuff buttons, dime museums, floor mats, fireworks, furriers, living pictures, picnic grounds, patent medicines, poolrooms, prize fights, restaurants, roof gardens, real estate agencies, sample rooms, shoe stores, soap makers, saloons, shooting galleries, tent makers, variety shows, [and] vendors of lemon acid." Tame stuff, perhaps, compared with David Bowie, his face painted red, white, and blue and a miniature vodka bottle resting on his naked clavicle (caption: "Absolut Bowie"), or with the nightmarish ads that clog the Internet ("Render this Osama Voo-Doo doll completely Pin-Laden! 6-inch doll for a Stocking Stuffer Price of $9.99! Comes with 6 red, white, and blue extra-sharp Patriot Pins").

•   •   •

In 1989, the School of the Art Institute of Chicago mounted an exhibit called "What Is the Proper Way to Display the American Flag?" In order to reach the leather-bound ledger in which they were asked to record their responses, viewers had to walk on a flag laid on the floor. "For days," reported *The Detroit News*, "veterans picked the flag up off the floor, folded it in the ceremonial military fashion and placed it on the shelf. Their faces were almost always stoic; one was visibly in tears at the sight of grimy footprints on the flag. Moments later, however, the flag was unfolded by supporters of the art, usually students with indignant faces, who shook out the flag like a bedsheet, and then draped it on the floor."

The same year, in a controversial case called *Texas v. Johnson*, Supreme Court Justice Anthony Kennedy explained why he had concluded, with great reluctance, that flag-burning is a form of free speech and therefore protected by the First Amendment.

"Though symbols often are what we ourselves make of them," he wrote, "the flag is constant in expressing beliefs Americans share, beliefs in law and peace and that freedom which sustains the human spirit. The case here today forces recognition of the costs to which those beliefs commit us. It is poignant but fundamental that the flag protects those who hold it in contempt."

·   ·   ·

We kept our flag at half staff longer than President Bush decreed that we should, and then, after raising it to full staff, we continued to fly it after most of our neighbors had put theirs away. Maybe we were making up for lost time. Maybe we needed to see our flag flying in order to convince ourselves that even though protesters marching near a mosque in Bridgewater, Illinois, had waved flags and chanted "U.S.A.! U.S.A.!," we could choose another meaning in Whately, Massachusetts: the one a Chicago flag committee had in mind in 1895 when it called the stars and stripes "our greater self."

I had not looked closely at our flag when we raised it, so I decided to take it down one day to see whether it was made of cotton or silk. It was a raw afternoon in early December; freezing rain was falling on gray patches of snow. Section 174c of the Flag Code prohibits display in inclement weather, but a handful of local diehards were still flying their flags rain or shine, twenty-four hours a day, so we had followed suit. The flag was sodden and looked like a shrouded bat. When I lowered it and detached the grommets from the halyard, I could see that it was made of nylon. Black letters printed on the hoist, so faded I could barely make them out, read DURA LITE. The red stitching that connected the stripes was beginning to bleed. The embroidered white stars were fraying. As I refastened the brass clip, I tried hard to keep the old, wet, shabby flag from touching the ground.

The Atlantic Monthly

The Fifty-first State?

In predicting the consequences of an American war on Iraq, James Fallows laid out the clearest answer to the one question no one seemed to have asked: "What comes next?" By carefully selecting a chorus of experts—both those he refers to as members of "the war party" and their opponents—and drawing upon current events and history, he brilliantly forecasts the long-term consequences and opportunities presented by a second Iraqi war.

James Fallows

The Fifty-first State?

Going to war with Iraq would mean shouldering all the responsibilities of an occupying power the moment victory was achieved. These would include running the economy, keeping domestic peace, and protecting Iraq's borders—and doing it all for years, or perhaps decades. Are we ready for this long-term relationship?

Over the past few months I interviewed several dozen people about what could be expected in Iraq after the United States dislodged Saddam Hussein. An assumption behind the question was that sooner or later the United States would go to war—and would go with at best a fraction of the international support it enjoyed eleven years ago when fighting Iraq during the Gulf War. Most nations in the region and traditional U.S. allies would be neutral or hostile unless the Bush Administration could present new evidence of imminent danger from Iraq.

A further assumption was that even alone, U.S. forces would win this war. The victory might be slower than in the last war against Iraq, and it would certainly cost more American lives. But in the end U.S. tanks, attack airplanes, precision-guided bombs, special-operations forces, and other assets would crush the Iraqi military. The combat phase of the war would be over when the United States destroyed Saddam Hussein's control over Iraq's government, armed forces, and stockpile of weapons.

What then?

The people I asked were spies, Arabists, oil-company officials, diplomats, scholars, policy experts, and many active-duty and retired soldiers. They were from the United States, Europe, and the Middle East. Some firmly supported a pre-emptive war against Iraq; more were opposed. As of late summer, before the serious domestic debate had begun, most of the people I spoke with expected a war to occur.

I began my research sharing the view, prevailing in Washington this year, that forcing "regime change" on Iraq was our era's grim historical necessity: starting a war would be bad, but waiting to have war brought to us would be worse. This view depended to some degree on trusting that the U.S. government had information not available to the public about exactly how close Saddam Hussein is to having usable nuclear warheads or other weapons of mass destruction. It also drew much of its power from an analogy every member of the public could understand—to Nazi Germany. In retrospect, the only sin in resisting Hitler had been waiting too long. Thus would it be in dealing with Saddam Hussein today. Richard Perle, a Reagan-era Defense Department official who is one of the most influential members outside government of what is frequently called the "war party," expressed this thought in representative form in an August column for the London *Daily Telegraph*: "A pre-emptive strike against Hitler at the time of Munich would have meant an immediate war, as opposed to the one that came later. Later was much worse."

Nazi and Holocaust analogies have a trumping power in many arguments, and their effect in Washington was to make doubters seem weak—Neville Chamberlains, versus the Winston Churchills who were ready to face the truth. The most experienced military figure in the Bush Cabinet, Secretary of State Colin Powell, was cast as the main "wet," because of his obvious discomfort with an effort that few allies would support. His instincts fit the general sociology of the Iraq debate: As a rule, the strongest advocates of pre-emptive attack, within the government and in the press, had neither served in the military nor lived in Arab societies. Military veterans and Arabists were generally doves. For example: Paul Wolfowitz, the deputy secretary of defense and the intellectual leader of the war party inside the government, was in graduate school through the late 1960s. Richard Armitage, his skeptical counterpart at the State Department and Powell's ally in pleading for restraint, is a Naval Academy graduate who served three tours in Vietnam.

I ended up thinking that the Nazi analogy paralyzes the debate about Iraq rather than clarifying it. Like any other episode in history, today's situation is both familiar and new. In the ruthlessness of the adversary it resembles dealing with Adolf Hitler. But Iraq, unlike Germany, has no industrial base and no military allies nearby. It is split by regional, religious, and ethnic differences that are much more complicated than Nazi Germany's simple mobilization of "Aryans" against Jews. Hitler's Germany constantly expanded, but Iraq has been bottled up, by international sanctions, for more than ten years. As in the early Cold War, America faces an international ideology bent on our destruction and a country trying to develop weapons to use against us. But then we were dealing with another superpower, capable of obliterating us. Now there is a huge imbalance between the two sides in scale and power.

If we had to choose a single analogy to govern our thinking about Iraq, my candidate would be World War I. The reason is not simply the one the historian David Fromkin advanced in his book *A Peace to End All Peace*: that the division of former Ottoman Empire territories after that war created many of the enduring problems of modern Iraq and the Middle East as a whole. The Great War is also relevant as a powerful example of the limits of human imagination: specifically, imagination about the long-term consequences of war.

The importance of imagination was stressed to me by Merrill McPeak, a retired Air Force general with misgivings about a preemptive attack. When America entered the Vietnam War, in which McPeak flew combat missions over the jungle, the public couldn't imagine how badly combat against a "weak" foe might turn out for the United States. Since that time, and because of the Vietnam experience, we have generally overdrawn the risks of combat itself. America's small wars of the past generation, in Grenada, Haiti, and Panama, have turned out far better—tactically, at least—than many experts dared to predict. The larger ones, in the Balkans, the Persian Gulf, and Afghanistan, have as well. The "Black Hawk Down" episode in Somalia is the main exception, and it illustrates a different rule: when fighting not organized armies but stateless foes, we have underestimated our vulnerabilities.

There is an even larger realm of imagination, McPeak suggested to me. It involves the chain of events a war can set off.

Wars change history in ways no one can foresee. The Egyptians who planned to attack Israel in 1967 could not imagine how profoundly what became the Six Day War would change the map and politics of the Middle East. After its lightning victory Israel seized neighboring territory, especially on the West Bank of the Jordan River, that is still at the heart of disputes with the Palestinians. Fifty years before, no one who had accurately foreseen what World War I would bring could have rationally decided to let combat begin. The war meant the collapse of three empires, the Ottoman, the Austro-Hungarian, and the Russian; the cresting of another, the British; the eventual rise of Hitler in Germany and Mussolini in Italy; and the drawing of strange new borders from the eastern Mediterranean to the Persian Gulf, which now define the battlegrounds of the Middle East. Probably not even the United States would have found the war an attractive bargain, even though the U.S. rise to dominance began with the wounds Britain suffered in those years.

In 1990, as the United States prepared to push Iraqi troops out of Kuwait, McPeak was the Air Force chief of staff. He thought that war was necessary and advocated heavy bombing in Iraq. Now he opposes an invasion, largely because of how hard it is to imagine the full consequences of America's first purely preemptive war—and our first large war since the Spanish-American War in which we would have few or no allies.

•   •   •

We must use imagination on both sides of the debate: about the risks of what Saddam Hussein might do if left in place, and also about what such a war might unleash. Some members of the war party initially urged a quick in-and-out attack. Their model was the three-part formula of the "Powell doctrine": First, line up clear support—from America's political leadership, if not internationally. Then assemble enough force to leave no doubt about the outcome. Then, before the war starts, agree on how it will end and when to leave.

The in-and-out model has obviously become unrealistic. If Saddam Hussein could be destroyed by a death ray or captured by a ninja squad that sneaked into Baghdad and spirited him away, the United States might plausibly call the job done. It would still have to wonder what Iraq's next leader might do with the weapons laboratories, but the immediate problem would be solved.

Absent ninjas, getting Saddam out will mean bringing in men, machinery, and devastation. If the United States launched a big tank-borne campaign, as suggested by some of the battle plans leaked to the press, tens of thousands of soldiers, with their ponderous logistics trail, would be in the middle of a foreign country when the fighting ended. If the U.S. military relied on an air campaign against Baghdad, as other leaked plans have implied, it would inevitably kill many Iraqi civilians before it killed Saddam. One way or another, America would leave a large footprint on Iraq, which would take time to remove.

And logistics wouldn't be the only impediment to quick withdrawal. Having taken dramatic action, we would no doubt be seen—by the world and ourselves, by al Jazeera and CNN—as responsible for the consequences. The United States could have stopped the Khmer Rouge slaughter in Cambodia in the 1970s, but it was not going to, having spent the previous decade in a doomed struggle in Vietnam. It could have prevented some of the genocide in Rwanda in the 1990s, and didn't, but at least it did not trigger the slaughter by its own actions. "It is quite possible that if we went in, took out Saddam Hussein, and then left quickly, the result would be an extremely bloody civil war," says William Galston, the director of the Institute for Philosophy and Public Policy at the University of Maryland, who was a Marine during the Vietnam War. "That blood would be directly on our hands." Most people I spoke with, whether in favor of war or not, recognized that military action is a barbed hook: once it goes in, there is no quick release.

The tone of the political debate reflects a dawning awareness of this reality. Early this year, during the strange "phony war" stage of Iraq discussions, most people in Washington assumed that war was coming, but there was little open discussion of exactly why it was necessary and what consequences it would bring. The pro-war group avoided questions about what would happen after a victory, because to consider postwar complications was to weaken the case for a pre-emptive strike. Some war advocates even said, if pressed, that the details of postwar life didn't matter. With the threat and the tyrant eliminated, the United States could assume that whatever regime emerged would be less dangerous than the one it replaced.

As the swirl of leaks, rumors, and official statements made an attack seem alternately more and less imminent, the increasing chaos in Afghanistan underscored a growing consensus about the in-and-out scenario for Iraq: it didn't make sense. The war itself might be quick, perhaps even quicker than the rout of the Taliban. But the end of the fighting would hardly mean the end of America's commitment. In August, as warlords reasserted their power in Afghanistan, General Tommy Franks, the U.S. commander, said that American troops might need to stay in Afghanistan for many years.

If anything, America's involvement in Afghanistan should have been cleaner and more containable than what would happen in Iraq. In Afghanistan the United States was responding to an attack, rather than initiating regime change. It had broad international support; it had the Northern Alliance to do much of the work. Because the Taliban and al Qaeda finally chose to melt away rather than stand and fight, U.S. forces took control of the major cities while doing relatively little unintended damage. And still, getting out will take much longer than getting in.

Some proponents of war viewed the likelihood of long

involvement in Iraq as a plus. If the United States went in planning to stay, it could, they contended, really make a difference there. Richard Perle addressed a major anti-war argument—that Arab states would flare up in resentment—by attempting to turn it around. "It seems at least as likely," he wrote in his *Daily Telegraph* column, "that Saddam's replacement by a decent Iraqi regime would open the way to a far more stable and peaceful region. A democratic Iraq would be a powerful refutation of the patronizing view that Arabs are incapable of democracy."

Some regional experts made the opposite point: that a strong, prosperous, confident, stable Iraq was the last thing its neighbors, who prefer it in its bottled-up condition, wanted to see. Others pooh-poohed the notion that any Western power, however hard it tried or long it stayed, could bring about any significant change in Iraq's political culture.

•   •   •

Regardless of these differences, the day after a war ended, Iraq would become America's problem, for practical and political reasons. Because we would have destroyed the political order and done physical damage in the process, the claims on American resources and attention would be comparable to those of any U.S. state. Conquered Iraqis would turn to the U.S. government for emergency relief, civil order, economic reconstruction, and protection of their borders. They wouldn't be able to vote in U.S. elections, of course—although they might after they emigrated. (Every American war has created a refugee-and-immigrant stream.) But they would be part of us.

During the debate about whether to go to war, each side selectively used various postwar possibilities to bolster its case. Through the course of my interviews I found it useful to consider the possibilities as one comprehensive group. What follows is a triage list for American occupiers: the biggest problems they would face on the first day after the war, in the first week, and so on, until, perhaps decades from now, they could come to grips with the long-term connections between Iraq and the United States.

The First Day

Last-minute mayhem. The biggest concern on the first day of peace would arise from what happened in the last few days of war. "I don't think that physically controlling the important parts of the country need be as difficult as many people fear," Chris Sanders, an American who worked for eighteen years in Saudi Arabia and is now a consultant in London, told me. "But of course it all depends on how one finds oneself in a victorious position—on what you had to do to win."

What would Saddam Hussein, facing defeat and perhaps death, have decided late in the war to do with the stockpiled weapons of mass destruction that were the original justification for our attack? The various Pentagon battle plans leaked to the media all assume that Iraq would use chemical weapons against U.S. troops. (Biological weapons work too slowly, and a nuclear weapon, if Iraq had one, would be more valuable for mass urban destruction than for battlefield use.) During the buildup to the Gulf War, American officials publicly warned Iraq that if it used chemical weapons against U.S. troops, we would respond with everything at our disposal, presumably including nuclear weapons. Whether or not this was a bluff, Iraq did not use chemical weapons. But if Saddam were fighting for survival, rather than for control of Kuwait, his decisions might be different.

The major chemical weapons in Iraqi arsenals are thought to be the nerve gas sarin, also called "GB," and liquid methylphosphonothioic acid, or "VX." Both can be absorbed through the lungs, the skin, or the eyes, and can cause death from amounts as small as one drop. Sarin disperses quickly, but VX is relatively nonvolatile and can pose a more lasting danger. U.S. troops would be equipped with protective suits, but these are cumbersome and retain heat; the need to wear them has been an argument for delaying an attack until winter.

Another concern is that on his way down Saddam would use chemical weapons not only tactically, to slow or kill attacking U.S. soldiers, but also strategically, to lash out beyond his borders. In particular, he could use them against Israel. Iraq's SCUD and "al-Hussein" missiles cannot reach Europe or North America. But Israel is in easy range—as Iraq demonstrated during the Gulf War, when it launched forty-two SCUDs against Israel. (It also launched more than forty against the allied troops; all these SCUDs had conventional explosive warheads, rather than chemical payloads.) During the Gulf War the Israeli government of Yitzhak Shamir complied with urgent U.S. requests that it leave all retaliation to the Americans, rather than broadening the war by launching its own attacks. Nothing in Ariel Sharon's long career suggests that he could be similarly restrained.

A U.S. occupation of Iraq, then, could begin with the rest of the Middle East at war around it. "What's the worst nightmare at the start?" a retired officer who fought in the Gulf War asked me rhetorically. "Saddam Hussein hits Israel, and Sharon hits some Arab city, maybe in Saudi Arabia. Then you have the all-out religious war that the Islamic fundamentalists and maybe some Likudniks are itching for."

This is more a worst-case prediction than a probability, so let's assume that any regional combat could be contained and that we would get relatively quickly to the challenges of the following, postwar days.

The First Week

Refugees and relief. However quick and surgical the battle might seem to the American public, however much brighter

Iraq's long-term prospects might become, in the short term many Iraqis would be desperate. Civilians would have been killed, to say nothing of soldiers. Bodies would need to be buried, wounds dressed, orphans located and cared for, hospitals staffed.

"You are going to start right out with a humanitarian crisis," says William Nash, of the Council on Foreign Relations. A retired two-star Army general, Nash was in charge of post-combat relief operations in southern Iraq after the Gulf War and later served in Bosnia and Kosovo. Most examples in this article, from Nash and others, involve the occupation of Kuwait and parts of Iraq after the Gulf War, rather than ongoing operations in Afghanistan. The campaign in Afghanistan may have a rhetorical connection to a future war in Iraq, in that both are part of the general "war on terror"; but otherwise the circumstances are very different. Iraq and Afghanistan are unlike in scale, geography, history, and politics, not to mention in the U.S. objectives and military plans that relate to them. And enough time has passed to judge the effects of the Gulf War, which is not true of Afghanistan.

"In the drive to Baghdad, you are going to do a lot of damage," Nash told me. "Either you will destroy a great deal of infrastructure by trying to isolate the battlefield—or they will destroy it, trying to delay your advance." Postwar commerce and recovery in Iraq will depend, of course, on roads, the rail system, air fields, and bridges across the Tigris and the Euphrates—facilities that both sides in the war will have incentives to blow up. "So you've got to find the village elders," Nash continued, "and say, 'Let's get things going. Where are the wells? I can bring you food, but bringing you enough water is really hard.' Right away you need food, water, and shelter—these people have to survive. Because you started the war, you have accepted a moral responsibility for them. And you may well have totally obliterated the social and political structure that had been providing these services."

Most of the military and diplomatic figures I interviewed stressed the same thing. In August, Scott Feil, a retired Army colonel who now directs a study project for the Association of the United States Army on postwar reconstruction, said at a Senate hearing, "I think the international community will hold the United States primarily responsible for the outcome in the post-conflict reconstruction effort." Charles William Maynes, a former editor of *Foreign Policy* magazine and now the president of the Eurasia Foundation, told me, "Because of the allegations that we've been killing women and children over the years with the sanctions, we are going to be all the more responsible for restoring the infrastructure."

This is not impossible, but it is expensive. Starting in the first week, whoever is in charge in Iraq would need food, tents, portable hospitals, water-purification systems, generators, and so on. During the Clinton Administration, Frederick Barton directed the Office of Transition Initiatives at USAID, which worked with State and Defense Department representatives on postwar recovery efforts in countries such as Haiti, Liberia, and Bosnia. He told me, "These places typically have no revenue systems, no public funds, no way anybody at any level of governance can do anything right away. You've got to pump money into the system." Exactly how much is hard to say. Scott Feil has estimated that costs for the first year in Iraq would be about $16 billion for post-conflict security forces and $1 billion for reconstruction—presumably all from the United States, because of the lack of allies in the war.

•　　　•　　　•

Catching Saddam Hussein. While the refugees were being attended to, an embarrassing leftover problem might persist. From the U.S. perspective, it wouldn't really matter whether the war left Saddam dead, captured, or in exile. What would matter is that his whereabouts were known. The only outcome nearly as bad as leaving him in power would be having him at large, like Osama bin Laden and much of the al Qaeda leadership in the months after the September 11 attacks.

"My nightmare scenario," Merrill McPeak, the former Air Force chief of staff, told me, "is that we jump people in, seize the airport, bring in the 101st [Airborne Division]—and we can't find Saddam Hussein. Then we've got Osama and Saddam Hussein out there, both of them achieving mythical heroic status in the Arab world just by surviving. It's not a trivial problem to actually grab the guy, and it ain't over until you've got him in handcuffs."

During the Gulf War, McPeak and his fellow commanders learned that Saddam was using a fleet of Winnebago-like vehicles to move around Baghdad. They tried to track the vehicles but never located Saddam himself. As McPeak concluded from reading psychological profiles of the Iraqi dictator, he is not only a thug and a murderer but an extremely clever adversary. "My concern is that he is smarter individually than our bureaucracy is collectively," he told me. "Bureaucracies tend to dumb things down. So in trying to find him, we have a chess match between a bureaucracy and Saddam Hussein."

The First Month

Police control, manpower, and intelligence. When the lid comes off after a long period of repression, people may be grateful and elated. But they may also be furious and vengeful, as the post-liberation histories of Romania and Kosovo indicate. Phebe Marr, a veteran Iraq expert who until her retirement taught at the National Defense University, told a Senate committee in August, "If firm leadership is not in place in Baghdad the day after Saddam is removed, retribution, score settling, and blood-letting, especially in urban areas, could take place." William

Nash, who supervised Iraqi prisoners in liberated parts of Kuwait, told me, "The victim becomes the aggressor. You try to control it, but you'll just find the bodies in the morning."

Some policing of conquered areas, to minimize warlordism and freelance justice, is an essential step toward making the postwar era seem like an occupation rather than simple chaos. Doing it right requires enough people to do the policing; a reliable way to understand local feuds and tensions; and a plan for creating and passing power to a local constabulary. Each can be more complicated than it sounds.

Simply manning a full occupation force would be a challenge. In the occupation business there are some surprising rules of thumb. Whether a country is big or small, for instance, the surrender of weapons by the defeated troops seems to take about 120 days. Similarly, regardless of a country's size, maintaining order seems to take about one occupation soldier or police officer for each 500 people—plus one supervisor for each ten policemen. For Iraq's 23 million people that would mean an occupation force of about 50,000. Scott Feil told a Senate committee that he thought the occupation would need 75,000 security soldiers.

In most of its military engagements since Vietnam the United States has enthusiastically passed many occupation duties to allied or United Nations forces. Ideally the designated occupiers of Iraq would be other Arabs—similar rather than alien to most Iraqis in language, religion, and ethnicity. But persuading other countries to clean up after a war they had opposed would be quite a trick.

Providing even 25,000 occupiers on a sustained basis would not be easy for the U.S. military. Over the past decade the military's head count has gone down, even as its level of foreign commitment and the defense budget have gone up. All the active-duty forces together total about 1.4 million people. Five years ago it was about 1.5 million. At the time of the Gulf War the total was over two million. With fewer people available, the military's "ops tempo" (essentially, the level of overtime) has risen, dramatically in the past year. Since the terrorist attacks some 40,000 soldiers who had planned to retire or leave the service have been obliged to stay, under "stop-loss" personnel policies. In July the Army awarded a $205 million contract to ITT Federal Services to provide "rent-a-cop" security guards for U.S. bases in Bosnia, sparing soldiers the need to stand guard duty. As of the beginning of September the number of National Guard and Reserves soldiers mobilized by federal call-ups was about 80,000, compared with about 5,600 just before September 11, 2001. For the country in general the war in Central Asia has been largely a spectator event—no war bonds, no gasoline taxes, no mandatory public service. For the volunteer military on both active and reserve duty it has been quite real.

One way to put more soldiers in Iraq would be to redeploy them from overseas bases. Before the attacks about 250,000 soldiers were based outside U.S. borders, more than half of them in Germany, Japan, and Korea. The American military now stations more than 118,000 soldiers in Europe alone.

But in the short term the occupation would need people from the civil-affairs specialties of the military: people trained in setting up courts and police systems, restoring infrastructure, and generally leading a war-recovery effort. Many are found in the Reserves, and many have already been deployed to missions in Bosnia, Kosovo, or elsewhere. "These are an odd bunch of people," James Dunnigan, the editor of Strategypage.com, told me. "They tend to be civilians who are overeducated—they like working for the government and having adventures at the same time. They're like the characters in *Three Kings*, without finding the gold."

One of the people Dunnigan was referring to specifically is Evan Brooks. In his normal life Brooks is an attorney at Internal Revenue Service headquarters. He is also an amateur military historian, and until his recent retirement was a lieutenant colonel in the Army Reserves, specializing in civil affairs. "Between 1947 and 1983," Brooks told me, "the number of civil-affairs units that were activated [from the Reserves] could be counted on one hand. Since 1987 there has not been a single Christmas where the D.C.-area civil-affairs unit has not had people deployed overseas." Brooks was the military interface with the Kuwaiti Red Crescent for several months after the Gulf War; though he is Jewish, he became a popular figure among his Muslim colleagues, and was the only American who attended Kuwaiti subcabinet meetings. "My ambition was to be military governor of Basra [the Iraqi region closest to Kuwait]," he told me, I think whimsically. "I never quite achieved it."

Wherever the occupying force finds its manpower, it will face the challenge of understanding politics and rivalries in a country whose language few Americans speak. The CIA and the Army Special Forces have been recruiting Arabic speakers and grilling Iraqi exiles for local intelligence. The Pentagon's leadership includes at least one Arabic speaker: the director of the joint staff, John Abizaid; a three-star general. As a combat commander during the Gulf War, Abizaid was able to speak directly with Iraqis. Most American occupiers will lack this skill.

Inability to communicate could be disastrous. After the Gulf War, William Nash told me, he supervised camps containing Iraqi refugees and captured members of the Republican Guard. "We had a couple of near riots—mini-riots—in the refugee camps when Saddam's agents were believed to have infiltrated," Nash said. "We brought a guy in, and a group of refugees in the camp went berserk. Somebody said, 'He's an agent!' My guys had to stop them or they were going to tear the man to shreds. We put a bag over his head and hustled him out of there, just to save his life. And when that happens, you have no idea what kind of vendetta you've just fallen in the middle of. You have no idea if it's a six-camel issue or something much more. I take that experience from 1991 and square it fifty times for a larger country. That would be a postwar Iraq."

Eventually the occupiers would solve the problem by fostering a local police force, as part of a new Iraqi government. "You have to start working toward local, civilian-led police," Frederick Barton, the former USAID official, told me. "Setting up an academy is okay, but national police forces tend to be sources of future coups and corruption. I'd rather have a hundred and fifty small forces around the country and take my chances on thirty of them being corrupt than have a centralized force and end up with one big, bad operation."

·　　·　　·

Forming a government. Tyrants make a point of crushing any challenge to their power. When a tyranny falls, therefore, a new, legitimate source of authority may take time to emerge. If potential new leaders are easy to identify, it is usually because of their family name or record of political struggle. Corazón Aquino illustrates the first possibility: as the widow of a political rival whom Ferdinand Marcos had ordered killed, she was the ideal successor to Marcos in the Philippines (despite her later troubles in office). Charles de Gaulle in postwar France, Nelson Mandela in South Africa, and Kim Dae-jung in South Korea illustrate the second. Should the Burmese military ever fall, Aung San Suu Kyi will have both qualifications for leadership.

Iraq has no such obvious sources of new leadership. A word about its political history is useful in explaining the succession problem. From the 1500s onward the Ottoman Empire, based in Istanbul, controlled the territory that is now Iraq. When the empire fell, after World War I, Great Britain assumed supervision of the newly created Kingdom of Iraq, under a mandate from the League of Nations. The British imported a member of Syria's Hashemite royal family, who in 1921 became King Faisal I of

Iraq. (The Hashemites, one of whom is still on the throne in Jordan, claim descent not only from the prophet Muhammad but also from the Old Testament Abraham.) The Kingdom of Iraq lasted until 1958, when King Faisal II was overthrown and killed in a military coup. In 1963 the Baath, or "renewal," party took power in another coup—which the United States initially welcomed, in hopes that the Baathists would be anticommunist. By the late 1970s Saddam Hussein had risen to dominance within the party.

The former monarchy is too shallow-rooted to survive reintroduction to Iraq, and Saddam has had time to eliminate nearly all sources of internal resistance. The Kurdish chieftains of the northern provinces are the primary exception. But their main impulse has been separatist: they seek autonomy from the government in Baghdad and feud with one another. That leaves Iraqi exile groups—especially the Iraqi National Congress—as the likeliest suppliers of leaders.

The INC survives on money from the U.S. government. The organization and its president, a U.S.-trained businessman named Ahmad Chalabi, have sincere supporters and also detractors within the Washington policy world. The columnist Jim Hoagland, of *The Washington Post*, has called Chalabi a "dedicated advocate of democracy" who has "sacrifice[d] most of his fortune so he can risk his life to fight Saddam." The case against Chalabi involves his fortune too: he is a high-living character, and under him the INC has been dogged by accusations of financial mismanagement. "The opposition outside Iraq is almost as divided, weak, and irrelevant as the White Russians in the 1920s," says Anthony Cordesman, of the Center for Strategic and International Studies, in Washington.

"What you will need is a man with a black moustache," a retired British spy who once worked in the region told me. "Out of chaos I am sure someone will emerge. But it can't be Chalabi, and it probably won't be a democracy. Democracy is a strange fruit, and, cynically, to hold it together in the short term you need a strongman."

Several U.S. soldiers told me that the comfortable Powell doctrine, with its emphasis on swift action and a clear exit strategy, could make the inevitable difficulty and delay in setting up plausible new leadership even more frustrating.

When British administrators supervised the former Ottoman lands in the 1920s, they liked to insinuate themselves into the local culture, à la Lawrence of Arabia. "Typically, a young man would go there in his twenties, would master the local dialects, would have a local mistress before he settled down to something more respectable," Victor O'Reilly, an Irish novelist who specializes in military topics, told me. "They were to achieve tremendous amounts with minimal resources. They ran huge chunks of the world this way, and it was psychological. They were hugely knowledgeable and got deeply involved with the locals." The original Green Berets tried to use a version of this approach in Vietnam, and to an extent it is still the ideal for the Special Forces.

But in the generation since Vietnam the mainstream U.S. military has gone in the opposite direction: toward a definition of its role in strictly martial terms. It is commonplace these days in discussions with officers to hear them describe their mission as "killing people and blowing things up." The phrase is used deliberately to shock civilians, and also for its absolute clarity as to what a "military response" involves. If this point is understood, there can be no confusion about what the military is supposed to do when a war starts, no recriminations when it uses all necessary force, and as little risk as possible that soldiers will die "political" deaths because they've been constrained for symbolic or diplomatic reasons from fully defending themselves. All this is in keeping with the more familiar parts of the Powell doctrine—the insistence on political backing and overwhelming force. The goal is to protect the U.S. military from being misused.

The strict segregation of military and political functions may be awkward in Iraq, however. In the short term the U.S. military would necessarily be the government of Iraq. In the absence of international allies or UN support, and the absence of an obvious Iraqi successor regime, American soldiers would have to make and administer political decisions on the fly. America's two most successful occupations embraced the idea that military officials must play political roles. Emperor Hirohito remained the titular head of state in occupied Japan, but Douglas MacArthur, a lifelong soldier, was immersed in the detailed reconstruction of Japan's domestic order. In occupied Germany, General Lucius D. Clay did something comparable, though less flamboyantly. Today's Joint Chiefs of Staff would try to veto any suggestion for a MacArthur-like proconsul. U.S. military leaders in the Balkans have pushed this role onto the United Nations. Exactly who could assume it in Iraq is not clear.

In the first month, therefore, the occupiers would face a paradox: the institution best equipped to exercise power as a local government—the U.S. military—would be the one most reluctant to do so.

.　　.　　.

Territorial integrity. This is where the exercise of power might first be put to a major test.

In ancient times what is now central Iraq was the cradle of civilization, Mesopotamia ("Mespot" in Fleet Street shorthand during the British-mandate era). Under the Ottoman Empire today's Iraq was not one province but three, and the divisions still affect current politics. The province of Baghdad, in the center of the country, is the stronghold of Iraq's Sunni Muslim minority. Sunnis dominated administrative positions in the Ottoman days and have controlled the army and the government ever since, even though they make up only about 20 percent of

the population. The former province of Mosul, in the mountain-
ous north, is the stronghold of Kurdish tribes, which make up 15
to 20 percent of the population. Through the years they have
both warred against and sought common cause with other Kurdish tribes across Iraq's borders in Turkey, Iran, and Syria. Mosul
also has some of the country's richest reserves of oil. The former
province of Basra, to the southeast, borders Iran, Kuwait, and the
Persian Gulf. Its population is mainly Shiite Muslims, who make
up the majority in the country as a whole but have little political
power.

The result of this patchwork is a country like Indonesia or
Soviet-era Yugoslavia. Geographic, ethnic, and religious forces
tend to pull it apart; only an offsetting pull from a strong central
government keeps it in one piece. Most people think that under
the stress of regime change Iraq would be more like Indonesia
after Suharto than like Yugoslavia after Tito— troubled but
intact. But the strains will be real.

"In my view it is very unlikely—indeed, inconceivable—that
Iraq will break up into three relatively cohesive components,"
Phebe Marr, the Iraq expert, told the Senate Committee on Foreign Relations. But a weakened center could mean all sorts of
problems, she said, even if the country were officially whole. The
Kurds could seize the northern oil fields, for example. The Turk-
ish government has long made clear that if Iraq cannot control
its Kurdish population, Turkey— concerned about separatist
movements in its own Kurdish provinces—will step in to do the
job. "Turkey could intervene in the north, as it has done before,"
Marr said. "Iran, through its proxies, could follow suit. There
could even be a reverse flow of refugees as many Iraqi Shia exiles
in Iran return home, possibly in the thousands, destabilizing
areas in the south."

The centrifugal forces acting on postwar Iraq, even if they did
not actually break up the country, would present a situation different from those surrounding past U.S. occupations. America's

longest experience as an occupier was in the Philippines, which the United States controlled formally or informally for most of a century. Many ethnic, linguistic, and religious differences separated the people of the Philippine archipelago, but because the islands have no land frontier with another country, domestic tensions could be managed with few international complications. And in dealing with Japan and Germany after World War II, the United States wanted, if anything, to dilute each country's sense of distinct national identity. There was also no doubt about the boundaries of those occupied countries.

Postwar Iraq, in contrast, would have less-than-certain boundaries, internal tensions with international implications, and highly nervous neighbors. Six countries share borders with Iraq. Clockwise from the Persian Gulf, they are Kuwait, Saudi Arabia, Jordan, Syria, Turkey, and Iran. None of them has wanted Saddam to expand Iraq's territory. But they would be oddly threatened by a post-Saddam breakup or implosion. The Turks, as noted, have a particular interest in preventing any country's Kurdish minority from rebelling or forming a separatist state. The monarchies of Saudi Arabia and Jordan fear that riots and chaos in Iraq could provoke similar upheaval among their own peoples.

"In states like the United Arab Emirates and Qatar, even Saudi Arabia," says Shibley Telhami, the Anwar Sadat Professor of Peace and Development at the University of Maryland, "there is the fear that the complete demise of Iraq would in the long run play into the hands of Iran, which they see as even more of a threat." Iran is four times as large as Iraq, and has nearly three times as many people. Although it is Islamic, its population and heritage are Persian, not Arab; to the Arab states, Iran is "them," not "us."

As Arab regimes in the region assess the possible outcomes of a war, Telhami says, "they see instability, at a minimum, for a long period of time, and in the worst case the disintegration of the Iraqi state." These fears matter to the United States, because of oil. Chaos in the Persian Gulf would disrupt world oil markets and therefore the world economy. Significant expansion of Iran's influence, too, would work against the Western goal of balancing regional power among Saudi Arabia, Iran, and postwar Iraq. So as the dust of war cleared, keeping Iraq together would suddenly be America's problem. If the Kurds rebelled in the north, if the Shiite government in Iran tried to "reclaim" the southern districts of Iraq in which fellow Shiites live, the occupation powers would have to respond—even by sending in U.S. troops for follow-up battles.

The First Year

"De-Nazification" and "loya-jirgazation." As the months pass, an occupation force should, according to former occupiers, spend less time reacting to crises and more time undertaking long-term projects such as improving schools, hospitals, and housing. Iraq's occupiers would meanwhile also have to launch their version of "de-Nazification": identifying and punishing those who were personally responsible for the old regime's brutality, without launching a Khmer Rouge-style purge of everyone associated with the former government. Depending on what happened to Saddam and his closest associates, war-crime trials might begin. Even if the United States had carried out the original invasion on its own, the occupiers would seek international support for these postwar measures.

In the early months the occupiers would also begin an Iraqi version of *"loya-jirga*zation"—that is, supporting a "grand council" or convention like the one at which the Afghans selected the leadership for their transitional government. Here the occupation would face a fundamental decision about its goals within Iraq.

One option was described to me by an American diplomat as

the "decent interval" strategy. The United States would help to set up the framework for a new governing system and then transfer authority to it as soon as possible—whether or not the new regime was truly ready to exercise control. This is more or less the approach the United States and its allies have taken in Afghanistan: once the *loya jirga* had set up an interim government and Hamid Karzai was in place as President, the United States was happy to act as if this were a true government. The situation in Afghanistan shows the contradictions in this strategy. It works only if the United States decides it doesn't care about the Potemkin government's lapses and limitations—for instance, an inability to suppress warlords and ethnic-regional feuds. In Afghanistan the United States still does care, so there is growing tension between the pretense of Afghan sovereignty and the reality of U.S. influence. However complicated the situation in Afghanistan is proving to be, things are, again, likely to be worse in Iraq. The reasons are familiar: a large local army, the Northern Alliance, had played a major role in the fight against the Taliban; a natural leader, Karzai, was available; the invasion itself had been a quasi-international rather than a U.S.-only affair.

The other main option would be something closer to U.S. policy in occupied Japan: a slow, thorough effort to change fundamental social and cultural values, in preparation for a sustainable democracy. Japan's version of democracy departs from the standard Western model in various ways, but a system even half as open and liberal as Japan's would be a huge step for Iraq. The transformation of Japan was slow. It required detailed interference in the day-to-day workings of Japanese life. U.S. occupation officials supervised what was taught in Japanese classrooms. Douglas MacArthur's assistants not only rewrote the labor laws but wrote the constitution itself. They broke up big estates and reallocated the land. Carrying out this transformation required an effort comparable to the New Deal. American lawyers, economists, engineers, and administrators by the thousands spent years developing and executing reform plans. Transformation did not happen by fiat. It won't in Iraq either.

John Dower, a professor of history at MIT, is a leading historian of the U.S. occupation of Japan; his book *Embracing Defeat* won the Pulitzer Prize for nonfiction in 2000. Dower points out that in Japan occupation officials had a huge advantage they presumably would not have in Iraq: no one questioned their legitimacy. The victorious Americans had not only the power to impose their will on Japan but also, in the world's eyes, the undoubted right to remake a militarist society. "Every country in Asia wanted this to be done," Dower says. "Every country in the world." The same was true in postwar Germany. The absence of international support today is one of many reasons Dower vehemently opposes a pre-emptive attack.

·　　·　　·

Oil and money. Iraq could be the Saudi Arabia of the future. Partly because its output has been constrained by ten years' worth of sanctions, and mainly because it has never embraced the international oil industry as Saudi Arabia has, it is thought to have some of the largest untapped reserves in the world. Saudi Arabia now exports much more oil than Iraq—some seven million barrels a day versus about two million. But Iraq's output could rapidly increase.

The supply-demand balance in the world's energy markets is expected to shift over the next five years. Import demand continues to rise—even more quickly in China and India than in the United States. Production in most of the world is flat or declining—in OPEC producing countries, by OPEC fiat. The role of Persian Gulf suppliers will only become more important; having two large suppliers in the Gulf rather than just one will be a plus for consumers.

So in the Arab world the U.S. crusade against Saddam looks to be motivated less by fears of terrorism and weapons of mass destruction than by the wish to defend Israel and the desire for oil.

Ideally, Iraq's re-entry into the world oil market would be smooth. Production would be ramped up quickly enough to generate money to rebuild the Iraqi economy and infrastructure, but gradually enough to keep Saudi Arabia from feeling threatened and retaliating in ways that could upset the market. International oil companies, rather than an occupation authority, would do most of the work here. What would the occupiers need to think about? First, the threat of sabotage, which would become greater to the extent that Iraq's oil industry was seen in the Arab world more as a convenience for Western consumers than as a source of wealth for Iraq. Since many of the wells are in the Kurdish regions, Kurdish rebellion or dissatisfaction could put them at risk. Oil pipelines, seemingly so exposed, are in fact not the likeliest target. "Pipes are always breaking, so we know how to fix them quickly," says Peter Schwartz, of the Global Business Network, who worked for years as an adviser to Shell Oil. At greatest risk are the terminals at seaports, where oil is loaded into tankers, and the wells themselves. At the end of the Gulf War, Iraqi troops set fire to 90 percent of Kuwait's wells, which burned for months. Wellheads and terminals are the sites that oil companies protect most carefully.

Another challenge to recovery prospects in general would be Iraq's amazingly heavy burden of debt. Iraq was directed by the United Nations to pay reparations for the damage it inflicted on Kuwait during the Gulf War. That and other debts have compounded to amounts the country cannot hope to repay. Estimates vary, but the range—$200 billion to $400 billion—illustrates the problem.

"Leaving Iraq saddled with a massive debt and wartime-reparations bill because of Saddam is an act of moral and ethical cowardice," says Anthony Cordesman, of the Center for Strategic and International Studies, a military expert who is no one's idea of a bleeding heart. "We must show the Arab and Islamic worlds that we will not profiteer in any way from our victory. We must persuade the world to forgive past debts and reparations." Cordesman and others argue that as part of regime change the United States would have to take responsibility for solving this problem. Otherwise Iraq would be left in the position of Weimar Germany after the Treaty of Versailles: crushed by unpayable reparations.

This would be only part of the financial reality of regime change. The overall cost of U.S. military operations during the Gulf War came to some $61 billion. Because of the contributions it received from Japan, Saudi Arabia, and other countries in its alliance, the United States wound up in the convenient yet embarrassing position of having most of that cost reimbursed. An assault on Iraq would be at least as expensive and would all be on our tab. Add to that the price of recovery aid. It is hard to know even how to estimate the total cost.

·   ·   ·

Legitimacy and unilateralism. An important premise for the American war party is that squawks and hand-wringing from Arab governments cannot be taken seriously. The Saudis may say they oppose an attack; the Jordanians may publicly warn against it; but in fact most governments in the region would actually be glad to have the Saddam wild card removed. And if some countries didn't welcome the outcome, all would adjust to the reality of superior U.S. force once the invasion was a fait accompli. As for the Europeans, they are thought to have a poor record in threat assessment. Unlike the United States, Europe has not really been responsible since World War II for life-and-death judgments about military problems, and Europeans tend to whine and complain. American war advocates say that Europe's reluctance to confront Saddam is like its reluctance to recognize the Soviet threat a generation ago. Europeans thought Ronald Reagan was a brute for calling the Soviet Union an "evil empire." According to this view, they are just as wrong-headed to consider George W. Bush a simpleton for talking today about an "axis of evil."

Still, support from the rest of the world can be surprisingly comforting. Most Americans were moved by the outpouring of solidarity on September 11—the flowers in front of embassies, the astonishing headline in *Le Monde:* "*NOUS SOMMES TOUS AMÉRI-CAINS*." By the same token, foreigners' hatred can be surprisingly demoralizing. Think of the news clips of exaltation in Palestinian camps after the attacks, or the tape of Osama bin Laden chortling about how many people he had killed. The United States rarely turned to the United Nations from the late 1960s through the mid-1980s, because the UN was so often a forum for anti-American rants. Resentment against America in the Arab world has led to a partial boycott of U.S. exports, which so far has not mattered much. It has also fueled the recruitment of sui-cide terrorists, which has mattered a great deal.

The presence or absence of allies would have both immediate and long-term consequences for the occupation. No matter how welcome as liberators they may be at first, foreign soldiers even-tually wear out their welcome. It would be far easier if this inescapably irritating presence were varied in nationality, under a UN flag, rather than all American. All the better if the force were Islamic and Arabic-speaking.

The face of the occupying force will matter not just in Iraq's cities but also on its borders. Whoever controls Iraq will need to station forces along its most vulnerable frontier—the long flank with Iran, where at least half a million soldiers died during the 1980–1988 Iran-Iraq war. The Iranians will notice any U.S. pres-ence on the border. "As the occupying power, we will be respon-sible for the territorial integrity of the Iraqi state," says Charles

William Maynes, of the Eurasia Foundation. "That means we will have to move our troops to the border with Iran. At that point Iran becomes our permanent enemy."

The longer-term consequences would flow from having undertaken a war that every country in the region except Israel officially opposed. Chris Sanders, the consultant who used to work in Saudi Arabia, says that unless the United States can drum up some Arab allies, an attack on Iraq "will accomplish what otherwise would have been impossible—a bloc of regional opposition that transcends the very real differences of interests and opinions that had kept a unified Arab bloc from arising." Sanders adds dryly, "If I were an American strategic thinker, I would imagine that not to be in my interest."

The Long Run

So far we've considered the downside—which, to be fair, is most of what I heard in my interviews. But there was also a distinctly positive theme, and it came from some of the most dedicated members of the war party. Their claim, again, was that forcing regime change would not just have a negative virtue—that of removing a threat. It would also create the possibility of bringing to Iraq, and eventually the whole Arab world, something it has never known before: stable democracy in an open-market system.

"This could be a golden opportunity to begin to change the face of the Arab world," James Woolsey, a former CIA director who is one of the most visible advocates of war, told me. "Just as what we did in Germany changed the face of Central and Eastern Europe, here we have got a golden chance." In this view, the fall of the Soviet empire really did mark what Francis Fukuyama called "the end of history": the democratic-capitalist model showed its superiority over other social systems. The model has many local variations; it brings adjustment problems; and it encounters resistance, such as the anti-globalization protests of the late 1990s. But it spreads—through the old Soviet territory, through Latin America and Asia, nearly everywhere except through tragic Africa and the Islamic-Arab lands of the Middle East. To think that Arab states don't want a democratic future is dehumanizing. To think they're incapable of it is worse. What is required is a first Arab democracy, and Iraq can be the place.

"If you only look forward, you can see how hard it would be to do," Woolsey said. "Everybody can say, 'Oh, *sure*, you're going to democratize the Middle East.' " Indeed, that was the reaction of most of the diplomats, spies, and soldiers I spoke with—"the ruminations of insane people," one British official said.

Woolsey continued with his point: "But if you look at what we and our allies have done with the three world wars of the twentieth century—two hot, one cold—and what we've done in the interstices, we've already achieved this for two thirds of the world. Eighty-five years ago, when we went into World War I, there were eight or ten democracies at the time. Now it's around a hundred and twenty—some free, some partly free. An order of magnitude! The compromises we made along the way, whether allying with Stalin or Franco or Pinochet, we have gotten around to fixing, and their successor regimes are democracies.

"Around half of the states of sub-Saharan Africa are democratic. Half of the twenty-plus non-Arab Muslim states. We have all of Europe except Belarus and occasionally parts of the Balkans. If you look back at what has happened in less than a century, then getting the Arab world plus Iran moving in the same direction looks a lot less awesome. It's not Americanizing the world. It's Athenizing it. And it is doable."

Richard Perle, Secretary of Defense Donald Rumsfeld, and others have presented similar prospects. Thomas McInerney, a retired three-star general, said at the Senate hearings this past summer, "Our longer-term objectives will be to bring a democratic government to Iraq . . . that will influence the region significantly." At a Pentagon briefing a few days later Rumsfeld asked rhetorically, "Wouldn't it be a wonderful thing if Iraq were similar to Afghanistan—if a bad regime was thrown out, people were liberated, food could come in, borders could be opened, repression could stop, prisons could be opened? I mean, it would be *fabulous.*"

The transforming vision is not, to put it mildly, the consensus among those with long experience in the Middle East. "It is so divorced from any historical context, just so far out of court, that it is laughable," Chris Sanders told me. "There isn't a society in Iraq to turn into a democracy. That doesn't mean you can't set up institutions and put stooges in them. But it would make about as much sense as the South Vietnamese experiment did." Others made similar points.

Woolsey and his allies might be criticized for lacking a tragic imagination about where war might lead, but at least they recognize that it will lead somewhere. If they are more optimistic in their conclusions than most of the other people I spoke with, they do see that America's involvement in Iraq would be intimate and would be long.

It has become a cliché in popular writing about the natural world that small disturbances to complex systems can have unpredictably large effects. The world of nations is perhaps not quite as intricate as the natural world, but it certainly holds the potential for great surprise. Merely itemizing the foreseeable effects of a war with Iraq suggests reverberations that would be felt for decades. If we can judge from past wars, the effects we can't imagine when the fighting begins will prove to be the ones that matter most.

Outside

FINALIST, FEATURE WRITING

Terminal Ice

News stories on global warming invariably hint at the perils of melting ice caps and rising seas but offer little perspective. In "Terminal Ice," author Ian Frazier immerses us among the icebergs with an unforgettable tale that allows us to appreciate the link between society and what happens at the top and bottom of our planet.

Ian Frazier

Terminal Ice

**Hot enough for you?
Yeah, us too. Go to
the bottom of the
planet—or the top—
and you can't miss
the warning signs of
a warm apocalypse.
And at the heart of the
mystery, like broken
shards of a colder
climate, float the
icebergs, ghost-white
messengers trying to
tell us something we
can't quite fathom.**

We are melting, like the Wicked Witch of the West. Soon there will be nothing left of us but our hat. From Chile to Alaska to Norway to Tibet, glaciers are going in reverse. Artifacts buried since the Stone Age emerge intact from the ice; in British Columbia, sheep hunters passing a glacier find protruding from it a prehistoric man, preserved even to his skin, his leather food-pouch, and his fur cloak. All across the north, permafrost stops being perma-. In the Antarctic, some penguin populations decline. In Hudson Bay, ice appears later in the year and leaves earlier, giving polar bears less time to go out on it and hunt seals, causing them to be 10 percent thinner than they were 20 years ago, causing them to get into more trouble in the Hudson Bay town of Churchill, where (as it happens) summers are now twice as long. One day in August of 2000 an icebreaker goes to the North Pole and finds not ice, but open ocean. The news is no surprise to scientists, who knew that the remote Arctic in summer has lots of ice-free areas. For the rest of us, a disorienting adjustment of the geography of Christmas is required.

Globally, there's a persistent trickling as enormities of ice unfreeze. The Greenland ice sheet loses 13 trillion gallons of fresh water a year, contributing a measurable percentage to the world's annual sea-level rise. Every year, the level of the sea goes up about the thickness of a dime. Other meltwater, and the warming of the planet, which causes water to expand, contribute too. A dime's thickness a year doesn't worry most people, so long as it doesn't get worse, which most scientists don't think it necessarily will any time soon, though who can say for sure? The first nation to ratify the Kyoto Protocol on Climate Change is the island of Fiji, one eye on the Pacific lapping at its toes.

And every year, first attracting notice in the seventies, picking up speed in the steamy eighties and steamier nineties, giant icebergs begin splashing into the news. Usually they arrive in single-column stories on an inside page: "An iceberg twice as big as Rhode Island has broken away from Antarctica and is drifting in the Ross

Sea . . . It is about 25 miles wide and 98 miles long." "The largest iceberg in a decade has broken off an ice shelf in Antarctica . . . as if Delaware suddenly weighed anchor and put out to sea."

Over the years, a number of Rhode Islands and Delawares of ice, and even a Connecticut, drift into type and out again. The more notable ones are sometimes called "celebrity icebergs," and in the cold Southern Ocean (all the biggest icebergs are from Antarctica) an occasional berg has a longevity in the spotlight that a human celebrity could envy. Iceberg C-2—as scientists labeled it—drifts for 12 years and 5,700 miles, nearly circumnavigating Antarctica, before breaking into pieces of non-newsworthy size.

Glaciologists say there's probably no connection between global climate change and the increase in the numbers of big Antarctic icebergs. They say the ice shelves at the edge of the continent, from which these icebergs come, have grown out and shrunk back countless times in the past. Our awareness of the icebergs has mainly to do with satellite technology that allows us to see them as we never could before. Still, when you've recently been through the hottest year of the past six centuries, and suddenly there's a 2,700-square-mile iceberg on the loose—well, people talk.

·   ·   ·

In recent times I did a lot of reading about icebergs, some of it at the library of a western university where the air outdoors was so full of smoke from forest fires that people were going around in gas masks. To the old question of whether we will end in fire or ice, the answer now seems to be: both. Fire's photogenic, media-friendly qualities may cause us sometimes to overlook its counterpart and to forget the spectacular entrance ice made onto the modern apocalyptic scene just 90 years ago. Ice plus the *Titanic* spawned nightmares of disaster that never seem to fade. There was a song people used to sing about the *Titanic*, part of which went:

> *It was on her maiden trip*
> *When an iceberg hit the ship . . .*

Of course, the iceberg didn't hit the ship, but the other way around. So forcefully did the iceberg enter our consciousness, however, we assume it must have meant to. Looming unannounced from the North Atlantic on April 14, 1912, it crashed the swells' high-society ball, discomfiting Mrs. Astor, leaving its calling card in the form of a cascade of ice on the starboard well deck, slitting the hull fatally 20 feet below the waterline, and then disappearing into the night. In an instant this "Shape of Ice," as the poet Thomas Hardy called it, had become more famous than all the celebrities on board. In its dreadful individuality, it had become The Iceberg.

An inflatable toy version of it is sitting on my desk. It came with a *Titanic* bath toy some friends gave my children a while ago. The inflatable iceberg is roughly pyramidal, with three peaks—two of them small, and a larger one in the middle. Whoever designed the toy must have seen the widely published photograph supposedly showing The Iceberg, or perhaps saw a cinematic iceberg based on the photo. Hours after the sinking, observers on a German ship reported an iceberg of this shape near the scene, and one of them took the famous photo. Two weeks later, another transatlantic steamer said it saw a different-looking iceberg surrounded by deck chairs, cushions, and other debris in a location where The Iceberg could have drifted. As is the case with many suspects, no positive identification could ever be made.

Northern Hemisphere icebergs like The Iceberg melt quickly once they drift down into the Atlantic, with its warming Gulf Stream. Almost certainly, within a few weeks of shaking up the world, The Iceberg had disappeared. Its ephemerality has only increased its fame; solid matter for just a few historic moments, it continues indefinitely in imaginary realms—for example, as a spooky cameo in the top-grossing movie of all time. The message of The Iceberg, common wisdom has it, concerns the inscrutability of our fate and the vanity of human pride. But when I meditate on ice and icebergs, I wonder if The Iceberg's message might have been simpler than that. Maybe the news The Iceberg bore was more ancient, powerful, planetary, and climatic. Maybe The Iceberg's real message wasn't about us, but about ice.

•   •   •

Icebergs are pieces of freshwater ice of a certain size floating in the ocean or (rarely) a lake. They come from glaciers and other ice masses. Because of the physics of ice when it piles up on land, it spreads and flows, and as it does its advancing edge often meets a body of water. When the ice continues to flow out over the water, chunks of it break off, in a process called calving. Some of the faster-moving glaciers in Greenland calve an average of two or three times a day during the warmer months. Icebergs are not the same as sea ice. Sea ice is frozen salt water, and when natural forces break it into pieces, the larger ones are called not icebergs but ice floes. Icebergs are denser and harder than sea ice. When icebergs are driven by wind or current, sea ice parts before them like turkey before an electric carving knife. In former times, sailing ships that got stuck in sea ice sometimes used to tie themselves to an iceberg and let it pull them through.

A piece of floating freshwater ice must be at least 50 feet long to qualify as an iceberg, according to authorities on the subject. If it's smaller—say, about the size of a grand piano—it's called a growler. If it's about the size of a cottage, it's a bergy bit. Crushed-up pieces of ice that result when parts of melting icebergs disintegrate and come falling down are called "slob ice" by mariners. Students of icebergs have divided them by shape into six categories: blocky, wedge, tabular, dome, pinnacle, and drydock. The last of these refers to icebergs with columnar sections flanking a water-level area in the middle, like high-rise apartment buildings around a swimming pool.

At the edges of Antarctica, where plains of ice spread across the ocean and float on it before breaking off, most of the icebergs are tabular—flat on top, horizontal in configuration. In the Northern Hemisphere, because of the thickness of glacial ice and the way it calves, most icebergs are of the more dramatically shaped kinds. Tabular icebergs tend to be stable in the water and scientists sometimes land in helicopters on the bigger ones to study them. Northern Hemisphere icebergs, with their smaller size and gothic, irregular shapes, often grow frozen seawater on the bottom, lose above-water ice structure to melting, and suddenly capsize and roll. Venturing onto such icebergs is a terrible idea.

Antarctica has about 90 percent of all the ice in the world; most of the rest of it is in Greenland. Those two places produce most of the world's icebergs—about 100,000 a year from the first, about 10,000 to 15,000 from the other. Glaciers in Norway, Russia, and Alaska produce icebergs, too. The *Exxon Valdez* went aground in Alaska's Prince William Sound partly because it had changed course to avoid icebergs. Scientists have not been observing icebergs long enough to say if there are substantially more of them today. They know that the total mass of ice in Greenland has decreased at an accelerated rate in recent years. In Antarctica, because of its size and other factors, scientists still don't know whether the continent as a whole is losing ice or not.

•   •   •

Some people have jobs that involve thinking about ice and icebergs all day long. A while ago I went to the National Ice Center in Suitland, Maryland, and met a few of them. The Ice Center is affiliated with the National Oceanic and Atmospheric Administration, the Coast Guard, and the Navy. The offices of the Ice Center are in one of the many long, three-story government buildings with extra-large satellite dishes on their roofs in a fenced-in, campuslike setting just across the Potomac from

Washington. Antennae poking up from behind clumps of trees add to the spy-thriller atmosphere. The Ice Center's supervisor, a lieutenant commander in the Navy—many of the people who work at the Center are military personnel—introduced me to Judy Shaffier, ice analyst. She is a slim woman in her mid-thirties with a shaped haircut and avid dark eyes accustomed to spotting almost invisible details. An ice analyst looks at satellite images of ocean ice on a computer screen, compares the images to other weather information, and figures out what they mean. "It's a great job, really neat to tell people about at a party or something," Shaffier said. "But it takes explaining. When I say I analyze ice, sometimes people don't get that I mean *ice*. They think it must be one of those government-agency acronyms."

Much of the Ice Center is closed to visitors. That's the part where it pursues its main purpose, which is to provide classified information on ice conditions to the military. For example, a nuclear submarine can break through ice three feet thick or less; the Center can tell a submarine how close to surfaceable ice it is. Many countries—Japan, Denmark, Great Britain, Russia, France, Sweden—have ice-watching agencies similar to the Ice Center. Any country involved in global ocean shipping needs ice information sometimes. Providing it to merchant ships, scientific expeditions, and the general public is the nonclassified part of the Center's job.

Shaffier led me into a room with darkened windows and computers all along the walls. The glow of screens in the dimness lit the faces of ice analysts tapping on keyboards, summoning up satellite pictures of ice-covered oceans and seas. "I was trained as a meteorologist originally," Shaffier said. "I started analyzing ice in '94. Mostly what we do here is sea ice. Each of us has areas we concentrate on. Mine are the Yellow Sea, the Sea of Okhotsk, the Ross Sea, and the Sea of Japan. I feel like I really know the ice in those seas. Tracking icebergs is kind of secondary. We do it to keep everyone informed about possible dangers in the shipping lanes—in the Southern Hemisphere only, because another agency handles North Atlantic bergs. Also, I guess we do it for scientific and geographic reasons, or because icebergs are just interesting.

"For us to track an iceberg it must be at least ten nautical miles long," she continued. "We label each one according to the quadrant of Antarctica where it broke off. The quadrants are A through D, and after the letter we add a number that's based on how many other bergs from that quadrant we've tracked since we started doing this back in 1976. The A quadrant, between 90 west longitude and zero, has shelves that calve big icebergs all the time, and we've tracked a lot of bergs from there. A-38 was a recent one. And if a berg breaks up into pieces, any piece that's bigger than ten nautical miles gets its own label, like A-38A, A-38B, and so on."

The subject turned to giant "celebrity" icebergs, and whether she had a favorite.

"In March of 2000 I was sitting at this computer," she said. "Another analyst, Mary Keller, was sitting at the next one, and suddenly she said, 'My God! It's a huge iceberg!' A huge piece had broken off a shelf in the B quadrant since we'd last checked a day or so before. There had been no stress fractures visible in the ice sheet; the calving was completely unexpected. This iceberg was the 15th in B, so we labeled it B-15. I had never seen a berg that size. It was awesome—158 by 20 nautical miles. After it broke off it kind of ratcheted itself along the coast, sliding on each low tide, slowly moving from where it began, and in the process it eventually split into two pieces, one of about a hundred miles long and another of about 80. B-15 was the most exciting iceberg I've watched since I've been here."

Shaffier and I spent hours looking at computer images that hopscotched the icy places of the globe. Some of the pictures were visible-light photographs; some were made by infrared imagery that indicated different ice temperatures by color. Iceberg ice is 20 or 30 Celsius degrees colder than sea ice, old sea ice is a few degrees colder than new sea ice; in general, the colder the ice, the more difficult it is to navigate through. In passing, we checked up on B-15A—the giant was partly blocking the entry to West Antarctica's McMurdo Sound, apparently stuck on underwater rocks.

"Let's look at the Larsen Ice Shelf, or what's left of it," Shaffier said. "Did you hear what just happened to Larsen B? The Larsen Shelf is in a part of West Antarctica where local temperatures have gone up four or five degrees over the past decades, and a few years ago a big part of the shelf, Larsen A, disintegrated almost completely. People said that the rest of the shelf, Larsen B, would probably go in the next two years. Well, a few weeks ago, it went. Over a thousand square miles of ice—*poof*. One day the shelf was there, the next day it started to break up, and 35 days later the satellite images showed nothing but dark water and white fragments where solid white ice used to be. In about a month this major geographic feature of Antarctica ceased to exist."

Later, a glaciologist I talked to explained how the breakup of Larsen B probably occurred: Higher surface temperatures created pools of meltwater that accumulated on the ice during the summer months until the water flowed into ice crevices; once in the crevices, the water became a hydraulic wedge, forcing its greater weight down through the ice and cracking it apart. When pieces of the ice broke off, they pushed over the pieces next to them, like books falling on a shelf. The process had a swiftness and a magnitude glaciologists had never seen before, and it created the largest movement of ice in a single event in recent times. Unlike the calving of giant icebergs, the Larsen Shelf breakup occurred because of a sharp rise in local temperatures, which scientists believe was almost certainly the result of global warming.

"Actually, I've never seen an iceberg except in pictures," Shaffier told me. "The only ice on my computer screen I've ever seen in person was ice on Lake Erie near Brook Park, Ohio, where I used to live. Next fall I might get a place on the supply ship going down to McMurdo. I'd love to do that. I want to see the ice up close, but even more, I want to hear it. The images on my screen are silent, of course. But think about when an iceberg 200 miles long by 21 miles wide breaks off Antarctica. Think what that sound must be."

According to scientists, probably no one has ever heard that sound, or been present when a giant Antarctic iceberg calved. Whether that event is even accompanied by sound audible to humans, no one can yet say. Instruments that listen for underwater oceanic sounds sometimes pick up vibrations like a cello bow across strings—only much lower, below human hearing—which are believed to come from the friction of giant icebergs, though none of the vibrations have yet been matched to a specific calving. When giant icebergs run into something, however—when they collide with the ocean bottom or the land—they cause seismic tremors that register at listening stations halfway around the world.

•   •   •

I wanted to see an iceberg myself. Like Judy Shaffier, I had never seen one live. I took a cab from my house in New Jersey to Newark Airport and flew to Halifax, Nova Scotia, one of those far northern airports where connecting passengers half-sleepwalk in a twilight of individual time zones. From Halifax I flew to St. John's, Newfoundland, on an uncrowded plane over the coastline and then across ocean that was mailbox blue. I had my face close to the window, craning my neck to scan. A finger of Newfoundland appeared directly below the plane. In the other direction, on the ocean far to the east, I saw a blip of white. It got bigger as the plane approached, and I could make out what seemed to be two white oil-storage tanks rising from the ocean's surface. They looked so plausible, I was sure that was what they were. At slightly closer range, the deception fell away, and I saw they were both parts of a single iceberg; and moreover, one of the dry-dock kind

I'd read about. This sighting excited me beyond all measure. From home to iceberg was about two hours of flying time.

The plane banked to the west and descended to land at St. John's, and at about a thousand feet it came over a high bluff above a fjordlike little bay, and in the middle of it was a large, tent-shaped iceberg. The plane passed over the iceberg in a second, and five minutes later was at the gate. I hurried to the luggage claim, got my bag, picked up my rental car, and drove back to the bay where the iceberg was. At a turnout by the road skirting the bay, I got out. The berg rode there, rotating slightly back and forth, about 200 yards away. Its top had a sort of spinal effect, with knobs in a curving row like vertebrae. Small waves broke around it, and it seemed to give off a mist.

Icebergs are really white. Usually you don't see this kind of white unless you've just been born or are about to die. It's a hazmat-suit, medical-lab, hospital white. There are some antiseptic-blue overtones to it, too, and a whole spectrum of greens where the berg descends into the depths out of sight. In these latitudes, sea and land and sky wear the colors of hand-knit Scottish sweaters: the taupes, the teals, the tans, the oyster grays. Surrounded by these muted shades, icebergs stand out like sore thumbs, if a sore thumb could gleam white and rise five stories above the ocean and float.

I drove hundreds of miles up and down the Newfoundland coast looking for icebergs. When I spotted an iceberg in close, run aground on a point or in a cove, I went toward it in the car as far as I could and then hiked the rest of the way. One such hike led through meadows, down forest trails, and across slippery shoreline rocks all inclined in the same direction. Finally I got to the iceberg, which looked somewhat like a jawbone. It even had tooth-shaped serrations in the right place as it seesawed chewingly in the waves. Gulls on fixed wings shot past the headland entanglements of weather-killed trees, clouds turned in huge pinwheels above, waves crashed, the iceberg chewed. I had forgotten to bring water and my mouth was dry.

Among the small channels and troughs in the rocks, iceberg fragments were washing back and forth. I leaned down and scooped out a flat, oval piece about ten inches long. The sea had rounded and smoothed the hard, clear ice like a sea-smoothed stone. In it were tiny bubbles of air that had been trapped among fallen snowflakes millennia ago; the air had eventually become bubbles as later snowfalls compressed the snow to ice. Bubbles in icebergs are what cause them to reflect white light. Almost certainly, this piece of ice originally was part of the Greenland ice cap. A glacier like the Jakobshavn Glacier on Greenland's western coast probably calved this ice into Baffin Bay, where it may have remained for a year or more until currents took it north and then south into the Labrador Current, which brought it here.

I licked the ice, bit off a piece. It broke sharply and satisfyingly, like good peanut brittle. At places the Greenland ice cap is two miles thick. Climatologists have taken core samples clear through it. Chemical analysis of the ice and the air bubbles in these cores provide a picture of climate and atmosphere during the past 110,000 years. For a period covering all of recorded human history, the Greenland ice timeline is so exact that scientists can identify specific events with strata in the core sample—the year Vesuvius buried Pompeii, say, marked by chemical remnants of the Vesuvian eruption. In ice core samples dating from the Golden Age of Greece, they've found trace amounts of lead, dispersed into the atmosphere by early smelting processes and carried to Greenland on the winds. Lead traces in the ice increase slowly from Greek and Roman times, stay at about the same level during the Middle Ages, go up a lot after the beginning of the Industrial Revolution, crest during the 20th century, with its leaded automobile fuels, and drop way off after the introduction of unleaded gasoline. Chemicals and other residues in the Greenland ice cores told scientists about temperatures, droughts, the coming and going of ice ages—more about paleoclimates than they had ever known. In particular, they showed how unstable global climate has been, how abruptly it sometimes changed, and how oddly mild and temperate were the recent few thousand years in which people developed civilization.

Scientifically useful concentrations of chemicals don't affect the purity of Greenland ice. Devices that measure impurities in parts per million usually register none in iceberg ice; to find substances other than air and water in it, measurement must be in smaller concentrations, like parts per billion or per trillion. As I sucked the iceberg piece, contemplating its ancientness, trying to taste the armor of Caesar or the ash of Krakatoa in infinitesimal traces, the pristine cold water seemed to evaporate through my membranes with no intervening stage. Before I finished the fragment, my thirst was gone.

· · ·

Denny Christian, director of technical support for the Center for Cold Ocean Resource Engineering (C-CORE) in St. John's, is an iceberg guy. Whenever I asked around on the subject of icebergs, his name came up. C-CORE is a company that handles extreme-conditions research-and-development problems, many having to do with oceanic ice. Denny Christian has photographed icebergs, towed them, measured them, and done experiments on them. When he was younger he used to put crampons on his feet and climb on them. With other ice technicians he has landed on them in helicopters and shut the engines down and walked around; he told me he would never do anything so reckless today. A few years ago, against his better judgment, he ferried out two scientists who wanted to climb on a berg and helped them aboard. Then he stood off in his skiff and watched. He heard a noise, saw some of the iceberg come out of the sea, and the next thing he knew the scientists were clinging to the side of the ice they'd been standing on, 50 feet above the waterline. In another few seconds, the berg had gone over on top of them. By luck and quick boat-handling he was able to fish them out alive.

Denny Christian is tall, stoop-shouldered, snub-nosed, in his mid-sixties. His ancestors were Norwegian. When he strongly wishes to make a point, he widens his eyes with an attention-getting, Norwegian ferocity; other than that, his manner is laconic and mild. Usually he has the stoic patience you get from being around the unobligingness of nature. The only person he ever threw out of his office was a man who went on in great detail about a scheme he had to tow icebergs someplace or other with a submarine he planned to buy. Listening to crazy iceberg schemes is a recurring part of Denny Christian's job.

He and I sat in his office talking icebergs and going through folders of iceberg photos he has taken in his 20 years at C-CORE. The icebergs came in every category of shape and featured many natural parodies of architectural styles from caveman days to now. Some bergs suggested cliff dwellings, some castles; some were like fortresses, or space needles, or ultramodern Jetsons-type mansions in Beverly Hills. A striking iceberg that I had seen photos of before had two foothill eminences joined at the top by a soaring St. Louis Gateway Arch of ice. I stopped at a photo of a large tabular berg with men in red carrying chainsaws and clambering on it.

"These guys were some French environmentalists who wanted to carve a big iceberg in the shape of a whale with other endangered species riding on its back, and then send it down the East Coast of America to make a point about saving the environment," Denny said. "I helped them with the project, but I told 'em, 'You better wear these bright-red life jackets so we can find you if you fall in and *die*.'" His eyes went wide. "Fortunately the Gulf War came along about that time and their money ran out, and we never heard from them again."

Right now most of the work Denny does at C-CORE is for a group of oil companies that have drilling platforms in the North Atlantic about 350 miles east of St. John's. The oil drillers are worried about icebergs crashing into their platforms or sinking their tankers. Among other problems, C-CORE studies the likelihood of iceberg impacts, how damaging they might be, and how to avert them. Two summers ago Denny harnessed some small icebergs and smashed them into a steel panel rigged with instruments, to learn more about such collisions. Recently he has been studying the iceberg-tracking effectiveness of high-frequency radar that can see over the horizon out to about 250 miles. Every so often he charters a plane and flies out to check the radar's accuracy with his own eyes. When he told me he planned to take one of these "ground-truthing" flights in the next day or two, I asked if I could go along.

First we had to drive to Gander, about four hours from St. John's, to get the charter plane. Michelle Rose, a college intern at C-CORE who assists Denny sometimes, accompanied us. The wind was blowing hard when we reached the airport, but the charter pilots didn't seem to mind. Soon we were bumping and bouncing in a twin-engine plane through the updrafts over the North Atlantic, out of sight of land. Then the plane descended to a low altitude, the turbulence subsided, and we were cruising steadily 500 feet above the waves.

Denny had given the pilots GPS readings corresponding to places where the radar had indicated icebergs. The first one appeared on the plane's right side—a blocky berg with a line of dirt on it like a slash. Denny said that was glacial till that the glacier had scraped from the ground before calving. This next one, a pinnacle berg, had two bright-blue lines on it that formed a V. Blue lines, he said, are from meltwater that flows into glacial crevices and freezes there; ice from meltwater lacks the bubbles in glacial ice, and reflects blue. As we passed each berg, Denny photographed it and shouted data—shape, size, GPS coordinates—and Michelle Rose wrote it down on a clipboard. The distribution of icebergs did not seem to fit the radar picture very closely, but that slipped from everybody's mind.

Some icebergs we didn't get a good look at on the first pass, and so we swooped back for another. An iceberg like the Rock of Gibraltar caught the sun on a facet of its never-to-be-scaled white peak as we went by. A humpbacked berg nosed through the waves with homely persistence as if going somewhere. We checked out eight icebergs in all. Each was completely by itself in a sun-sparkled immensity of ocean, each had contours and particularities as distinctive as a face. The imitations they did of habitable places inspired a hopelessness that was almost sublime. Not much in nature makes you feel as lonesome as an iceberg does. Perhaps that's the reason we don't give them names: the uncomfortable parallel to our own diffusible selves.

· · ·

Through Denny Christian I met a St. John's captain named Ed Kean. When the ocean still held lots of cod, four generations of Ed Kean's Newfoundland ancestors fished for them. Ed has an all-purpose 75-foot boat with twin diesel engines and a five-ton crane amidships. The boat's name is *Mottak*, which he says is Inuit for "boat." He uses it for a miscellany of jobs. When a ship undergoing repairs offshore needs a large part ferried out to it, Ed does that. If a film crew shows up wanting to make a nature documentary for Japanese television, he takes them around. April through September, when icebergs are in local waters, Ed harvests iceberg ice. In the *Mottak* he searches for likely-looking pieces—the size of VW Beetles or small sports cars is about right—and when he finds them he sends his crewmen in a skiff and they wrap the iceberg pieces in nets and tow them back to the boat. Then Ed winches them out of the sea and into the hold. Back in port, he sells the ice to the Canadian Iceberg Vodka Corporation, which makes their triple-distilled Iceberg Vodka from it. Last year Ed sold the company almost a million liters of melted icebergs.

Before I knew what Ed looked like, I recognized him from his walk. He walks with the rolling gait of a sailor, feeling the floor for a moment with each foot before setting it down. Until I met him, I assumed that this nautical way of walking was extinct, or a conceit of literature. Ed roll-walked across the lobby of the Holiday Inn, where I was staying, and shook my hand. We'd arranged to meet there so I could go out on his boat and watch him gather iceberg ice. We drove out to where he docks his boat, in a little harbor northeast of St. John's. Fishermen seem to have an accent different from the crisp, clipped speech of other Newfoundlanders; as near as I can tell, it's part Irish, part Cockney. "Beautiful day for 'arvestin' oiceberg oice," Ed said, as he scanned the blue sky.

Also on board the *Mottak* that day were two crew members, both named Tony, both tanned dark brown and with deeply lined, sun-reddened eyes; Denny Christian, hoping to see an unusual iceberg Ed had promised to show him; Denny's wife, Thelma, an iceberg enthusiast like her husband; me; and a producer-director, a cameraman, a soundman, and an on-camera personality named Kevin, all from a cable television show called *The Thirsty Traveler*. This show began on a food network in Canada. In each half-hour episode it visits a different part of the world and samples an emblematic local alcoholic drink. In just the last few weeks, the crew had done sake in Japan, tequila in Mexico, and ouzo in Greece. Now they were doing Newfoundland, and iceberg-water vodka.

The ocean rose in gentle swells as the *Mottak* headed south along the coast, past an island called Bell Island. Denny joined me at the rail and said that the water we were on used to hide German submarines. Twice during World War II, a U-boat came into this narrow stretch between the island and the shore, waited for an opportunity, and torpedoed boats loaded with ore from the Bell Island iron mines. On clear days when the light is right, you can see the sunken tankers on the bottom. Scores of sailors died in the attacks, and each time the sub got away. Denny pointed to the coastline, indented all along its length with big and little coves. "People used to say that sometimes U-boats would pull into one of the coves, and then the German sailors would put on civilian clothing and come into St. John's and go to the movies," he confided.

After we'd been dieseling for a couple of hours, Ed pointed to an iceberg straight ahead. Another hour and a half passed as the berg grew larger with almost undetectable slowness. At about a quarter-mile, you could see that the berg was immense, tabular, and completely brown on top; at a hundred yards, it looked as if badly financed developers had abandoned a housing project on it while still at the bulldozing stage. Dirt and gravel and large rocks were strewn all over in heaps and piles. Denny said he had never seen this much glacial till on an iceberg. The sun was hot by now, the wind had become brisk, and the melting edges sent mini-avalanches of gravel raining down. If an iceberg can be described as having a fit, this one was. Rocks clacked and splashed all around it, little waterfalls streamed from it every few feet, pieces of ice fell off the sides and shattered and bobbed. When iceberg ice melts quickly, the bubbles released from it make a sound like soda water fizzing. A piece of ice as big as a bedroom fell splintering into the sea, and its myriad fragments, when they came back to the surface, fizzed full-throatedly.

With a rifle, Ed fired a couple of shots at the iceberg. The idea was to knock loose a conveniently sized piece. From the white cliff, some ice chips flew, but nothing big fell down. After the second shot, Thelma shouted that she had seen a fox—that an arctic fox had come to the edge of the berg, peered over, and ducked back. Denny said it happens sometimes that foxes and other animals get stranded on icebergs when they drift free. All of us stood and waited for the fox to reappear at the ledge of dirty ice and gravel 30 feet above the boat deck, but it didn't. Thelma kept saying that she was sure she'd seen it, and that the fox had looked miserable and skinny.

After some to-ing and fro-ing at the request of the TV people—approaching the iceberg now this way, now that, for the best angle and light—Ed motored around to its shoreline side. Acres of ocean dotted with iceberg pieces extended in all directions. The Tonys launched the skiff and began to harvest; securing nets around unwieldy car-size pieces of ice floating in 41-degree water can't be as easy as they made it seem. As the cameraman filmed, Kevin, the on-air person, gamely jumped into the skiff and assisted with the net-handling. Overseeing from the deck, Ed supplied his own dialogue: "Oh, you'll 'ave to do better'n that, boys!" he sang out when they brought a smaller-than-usual piece alongside.

The air filled with the pleasant click of grapples, the substantial thumps of boated ice, the whining of the crane, the slap of the waves. During a lull, an iceberg piece too big to bring aboard drifted up beside the *Mottak*'s stern. This piece was about the size of six parking spaces and almost level with the water. It had a section like a pulpit rising from one side. I lay facedown on the stern and leaned my head over to within inches of the living ice. At this distance it glistened with the dull, wet gray of cubes in an ice cube tray, and its surface was pitted with little depressions. With a push I could have slid onto it and drifted away. Just as I was thinking that, a corner of the stern knocked, not hard, against it: In an instant, the entire piece of ice split in two. The section with the pulpit angled precariously upward from the water and then rotated its former top to deep below. The movement had the succinctness of a wall revolving to reveal a hidden door. It sent a sympathetic, shivery rush from my spine to the backs of my knees.

Ed filled the hold with iceberg pieces and piled others on the deck. Late in the afternoon, he headed for port, first making another close pass by the big iceberg. Thelma was watching out for the fox, and she and Denny and one of the Tonys caught a glimpse of it near where it had been before. They said it was running along the edge of the iceberg, trying to keep up with the progress of the boat. Thelma wanted to call the Humane Society and get them to send a helicopter to pick up the fox. Its prospects did not look good out there, miles from land and with no company but the gulls. Thelma stayed in the stern, scanning the iceberg with binoculars, as we motored away.

*   *   *

In a booklet written for iceberg enthusiasts, a St. John's engineer and history buff named Stephen E. Bruneau mentions a locally famous iceberg called the Virgin Berg. It was an iceberg "hundreds of feet high and bearing an undeniable likeness to the Blessed Virgin Mary" (as one account described it) that appeared off St. John's harbor in June of 1905. Thousands of people went to a high hill above St. John's to watch it drift by, and the fishing boats that came out to follow it became a flotilla as it continued on its way south along the coast. Catholic and Protestant Newfoundlanders took it as a sign—generally, as a mark of divine favor for the Catholic side.

Probably there were also a few skeptics who saw it as just a big piece of ice in the water. My own mild fanaticism for icebergs can sometimes be hard to explain to unconvinced acquaintances. I notice the bewilderment in their eyes, and it infects me: Why, exactly, should anyone get so worked up about a piece of ice? Like the Newfoundland faithful of a hundred years ago, each of us sees in an iceberg what we are disposed to see. And yet . . . if icebergs have no significance other than the fanciful notions we project, why do they look as they do? A white iceberg lit by the sun in a field of blue ocean simply *looks* annunciatory. It might as well have those little lines radiating from it—the ones cartoonists draw to show something shining with meaning. In its barefaced obviousness, an iceberg seems the broadest hint imaginable; but what is it a hint of?

When I went to the Ice Center, Judy Schaffier gave me a list of ice-watch Web sites run by government agencies in a dozen countries. All across the United States and Canada are institutes and university departments that devote some or all of their resources to studying the world's ice. From the earth and the sky, ever more sophisticated instruments constantly record tiny changes in the ice. A satellite that measures global sea levels, a key part of ice studies, takes 500,000 sea-level readings a day. Laser altimeters deployed on satellites can detect the minutest shifts of ice position with essentially no error. And yet with all this information flooding in, broad conclusions are hard to come by. Science is specialization, and almost no expert in a particular area wants to step out into summary or generalizing. The experts tend to approach big ideas like global warming with the greatest hesitancy. Apparently, nobody wants to be the one to tell us (for example) that our SUVs have got to go.

What science will hazard instead of conclusions is a series of ifs. Ten thousand or 20,000 square miles of ice broken off Antarctica hardly diminishes that continent's total ice area of five million square miles, but *if* the shedding of ice continues at an increasing rate, and *if* the ice loss causes the glaciers inland to move faster toward the sea, and *if* seawater flows in where glacial ice used to be and reaches certain sub-sea-level parts of the continent and melts the ice there, and *if* as a consequence the entire West Antarctic Ice Sheet goes—well, then we would have the schnitzel, to speak plainly. That much ice added to the ocean might raise world sea levels anywhere from 13 to 20 feet. Such a rise would submerge parts of the island of Manhattan and of the Florida peninsula, not to mention many other coastal areas worldwide where about half the planet's population lives.

News stories in the months following the *Titanic* disaster examined the preceding few years' weather conditions in the Arctic and North Atlantic and concluded that a number of meteorological features had been "unusual." The winter of 1910–11 had been "unusually" snowy and severe, the summer of '11 and the spring of '12 had been "unusually" warm, the icebergs had drifted "unusually" far south. Such descriptions bring to mind the TV weather forecasters who still speak of temperatures as being "unseasonably" warm; most of the years in the last two decades have been warmer than any recorded in decades previous, so what does "unseasonable" mean nowadays? In fact, from an expanded perspective of time, there is nothing unusual about so many icebergs being as far south as the place where the *Titanic* went down. Over the past millennia, as climatic events came and went, icebergs invaded the Atlantic in armadas. Stones dropped from melting Canadian icebergs have been found in sea sediments off the coast of Portugal. The North Atlantic climate over the last tens of thousands and hundreds of thousands of years has been characterized by periods of continent-wide glaciation, massive melting, and the intermittent huge discharge of icebergs.

As easily as The Iceberg fits a morality tale about human pride, it fits a climatologist's possible scenario of global-warming ifs. If increased moisture held in the warmer atmosphere results in more precipitation in the North Atlantic region, and if that precipitation leads to more runoff into the ocean, and if warmer summers result in a greater melting of glacial ice in Greenland, and if lots more icebergs set sail, and if all that leads to a greatly increased amount of fresh water poured every year into the North Atlantic—then, possibly, the complicated process of tropical warm water rising, flowing north, giving off its heat, and cooling and sinking (the process that creates the great ocean currents) will be disrupted. And if those currents stop, and the heat they bring to Northern Europe and parts of the United States and Canada no longer arrives, those regions will very likely become colder, like other places at similar latitudes that ocean currents don't warm.

Of course no one imagined any such scenarios back in 1912. Most people knew little or nothing about climatology. Yet it might turn out that a foreshadowing of major climate change in that part of the world was the real message The Iceberg carried for us out of the North Atlantic night.

And then again, maybe not. Discussions of global warming always deal in elaborate scary possibilities, while always including enough disclaimers and unknowns to blunt the fear. Considering all that's at stake, I want to tell us what we should do immediately to change our lives and avert environmental catastrophe. But I can't bring myself to, somehow. All I can do is put in a good word for the sweeping conclusion and broad generalization. There aren't enough of them around—enough high-quality ones, I mean. I think we have yielded the sweeping-conclusion field to the wackier minds among us. Scenarios based on the Mothman Prophecies are colorful, but not a lot of help in the long run. Sensibly, most of us fort up behind our ever-growing heaps of information. But eventually, and maybe soon, we should draw a conclusion or two about where the globe is heading; and after that, maybe even act.

A lot of what is exciting about being alive can't be felt, because it's beyond the power of the senses. Just being on the planet, we are moving around the sun at 67,000 miles an hour; it would be great if somehow we could climb up to an impossible vantage point and just for a moment actually *feel* that speed. All this data we've got piling up is interesting, but short on thrills. Time, which we have only so much of, runs out on us, and as we get older we learn that anything and everything will go by. And since it will all go by anyway, why doesn't it all go right now, in a flash, and get it over with? For mysterious reasons, it doesn't, and the pace at which it proceeds instead reveals itself in icebergs. In the passing of the seconds, in the one-thing-after-another, I take comfort in icebergs. They are time solidified and time erased again. They pass by and vanish, quickly or slowly, regular inhabitants of a world we just happened to end up on. The glow that comes from them is the glow of more truth than we can stand.

The Nation

Backlash Babies

Katha Pollitt is a proudly reconstructed feminist, yet one who never shies from noting weaknesses and contradictions in conventional thinking about women's issues and other issues of social importance. She has an impressive ability to combine wit and passion in her forceful, concise commentary. Her columns are gems of polished writing.

Katha Pollitt

Backlash Babies

**If women allow
motherhood to
relegate them to
secondary status
in the workplace
and at home, then
women will never
achieve equality.
Katha Pollitt
considers the
kids vs. career
dilemma.**

A long time ago I dated a 28-year-old man who told me the first time we went out that he wanted to have seven children. Subsequently, I was involved for many years with an already middle-aged man who also claimed to be eager for fatherhood. How many children have these now-gray gentlemen produced in a lifetime of strenuous heterosexuality? None. But because they are men, nobody's writing books about how they blew their lives, missed the brass ring, find life a downward spiral of serial girlfriends and work that's lost its savor. We understand, when we think about men, that people often say they want one thing while making choices that over time show they care more about something else, that circumstances get in the way of many of our wishes and that for many "have kids" occupies a place on the to-do list between "learn Italian" and "exercise."

Change the sexes, though, and the same story gets a different slant. According to Sylvia Ann Hewlett, today's 50-something women professionals are in deep mourning because, as the old cartoon had it, they forgot to have children—until it was too late, and too late was a whole lot earlier than they thought. In her new book, *Creating a Life: Professional Women and the Quest for Children*, Hewlett claims she set out to record the triumphant, fulfilled lives of women in mid-career only to find that success had come at the cost of family: Of "ultra-achieving" women (defined as earning $100,000-plus a year), only 57 percent were married, versus 83 percent of comparable men, and only 51 percent had kids at 40, versus 81 percent among the men. Among "high-achieving" women (at least $65,000 or $55,000 a year, depending on age), 33 percent are childless at 40 versus 25 percent of men.

Why don't more professional women have kids? Hewlett's book nods to the "brutal demands of ambitious careers," which are still structured according to the life patterns of men with stay-

at-home wives, and to the distaste of many men for equal relationships with women their own age. I doubt there's a woman
over 35 who'd quarrel with that. But what's gotten Hewlett a
cover story in *Time* ("Babies vs. Careers: Which Should Come
First for Women Who Want Both?") and instant celebrity is not
her modest laundry list of family-friendly proposals—paid leave,
reduced hours, career breaks. It's her advice to young women: Be
"intentional" about children—spend your twenties snagging a
husband, put career on the back burner and have a baby ASAP.
Otherwise, you could end up like world-famous playwright and
much-beloved woman-about-town Wendy Wasserstein, who we
are told spent some $130,000 to bear a child as a single 48-year-
old. (You could also end up like, oh I don't know, me, who married and had a baby nature's way at 37, or like my many
successful-working-women friends who adopted as single, married or lesbian mothers and who are doing just fine, thank you
very much.)

Danielle Crittenden, move over! Hewlett calls herself a feminist,
but *Creating a Life* belongs on the backlash bookshelf with *What
Our Mothers Didn't Tell Us*, *The Rules*, *The Surrendered Wife*, *The
Surrendered Single* (!) and all those books warning women that
feminism—too much confidence, too much optimism, too many
choices, too much "pickiness" about men—leads to lonely nights
and empty bassinets. But are working women's chances of domestic
bliss really so bleak? If 49 percent of ultra-achieving women don't
have kids, 51 percent do—what about them? Hewlett seems determined to put the worst possible construction on working women's
lives, even citing the long-discredited 1986 Harvard-Yale study that
warned that women's chances of marrying after 40 were less than
that of being killed by a terrorist. As a mother of four who went
through high-tech hell to produce last-minute baby Emma at age
51, she sees women's lives through the distorting lens of her own
obsessive maternalism, in which nothing, but nothing, can equal

looking at the ducks with a toddler, and if you have one child, you'll be crying at the gym because you don't have two. For Hewlett, childlessness is always a tragic blunder, even when her interviewees give more equivocal responses. Thus she quotes academic Judith Friedlander calling childlessness a "creeping non-choice," without hearing the ambivalence expressed in that careful phrasing. Not choosing—procrastinating, not insisting, not focusing—is often a way of choosing, isn't it? There's no room in Hewlett's view for modest regret, moving on or simple acceptance of childlessness, much less indifference, relief or looking on the bright side—the feelings she advises women to cultivate with regard to their downsized hopes for careers or equal marriages. But Hewlett's evidence that today's childless "high achievers" neglected their true desire is based on a single statistic, that only 14 percent say they knew in college that they didn't want kids—as if people don't change their minds after 20.

This is not to deny that many women are caught in a time trap. They spend their twenties and thirties establishing themselves professionally, often without the spousal support their male counterparts enjoy, perhaps instead being supportive themselves, like the surgeon Hewlett cites approvingly who graces her fiancé's business dinners after thirty-six-hour hospital shifts. By the time they can afford to think of kids, they may indeed have trouble conceiving. But are these problems that "intentionality" can solve? Sure, a woman can spend her twenties looking for love— and show me one who doesn't! But will having a baby compensate her for blinkered ambitions and a marriage made with one eye on the clock? Isn't that what the mothers of today's 50-somethings did, going to college to get their Mrs. degree and taking poorly paid jobs below their capacities because they "combined" well with wifely duties? What makes Hewlett think that disastrous recipe will work out better this time around?

More equality and support, not lowered expectations, is what

women need, at work and at home. It's going to be a long struggle. If women allow motherhood to relegate them to secondary
status in both places, as Hewlett advises, we'll never get there.
Meanwhile, a world with fewer female surgeons, playwrights and
professors strikes me as an infinitely inferior place to live.

Fortune

FINALIST, COLUMNS AND COMMENTARY

Phoning It In

Few writers communicate with the zing of Stanley Bing, Fortune's pseudonymous back-page columnist. Whether it's fleeing an annual shareholders meeting, getting swamped by useless e-mails or zoning out as others phone in, he holds a funhouse mirror up to corporate life and proves there's a wealth of humor even in a recession.

Stanley Bing

Phoning It In

Maybe it's the time of year. Or maybe it's the time of man, I don't know. But there's something going around, and it's worth evaluating.

I first noticed it in myself, since I'm around myself more than I'm with other people, which may be part of the problem. A certain . . . inability to take things seriously. Not that I'm taking them lightly. I'm just not taking them.

I called my friend Tom. "I think I'm phoning it in," I told him. It's an expression. He'd heard it before.

"Yeah!" he said, brightening the way you do when you hear that somebody else has something that afflicts you. "Are you having trouble focusing on things?"

"I don't know," I said, "but I appear to be having trouble focusing on things."

"Why do you think that is?" said Tom, but I had lost interest already since we weren't talking exclusively about me, although we were, sort of.

Later that day I called Mark out on the coast. Mark is a killer. I mean, he doesn't actually kill people, but he would if he could. It's one of the corporation's most valuable assets. "What do you want to do about the Ehrlanger situation?" I didn't care about the Ehrlanger situation, but it was an issue on his watch, and I thought he might want to talk about it.

"I don't give a fig about the Ehrlanger situation," he said, although that was not the actual term that he utilized.

"You don't?" I said. "Well, if you don't, I don't, that's for sure." Then we talked about the stock price for a while, which is code for a whole bunch of stuff that has to do with freedom and release from servitude. Then we hung up.

I asked myself . . . so what? So what if this week it seemed that a bunch of guys were phoning it in from Planet Mambo? What's the big deal?

I sat there for a while and thought about Sandy Weill and Jack Grubman, suspected of manipulating the rating of AT&T, the first because he wanted to rule Citigroup alone and the second because he wanted to get his tot into some snotty nursery school. How much of what we do is like that? Stuff that looks like business but is really just a bunch of guys scratching an itch? Once you start to think that way, it's hard not to phone in the activities that feel inauthentic. And when you begin gauging the authenticity of the work you do, it's a short step to picking up that psychic receiver and phoning in the whole deal.

I put on my jacket and went outside for a walk. You know what I saw everywhere? Thousands of people quite literally phoning it in, walking down the street yakking into their little handheld receivers, nowhere near a place where people do any actual business.

The whole society, phoning it in from digital space. Who exactly, I inquired of myself, was *not* phoning it in? Anybody? I went back to my office and thought about that for a while, and as I was thinking, about six people came into my office with a bunch of stuff. I couldn't really tell you what it was, but it was very important and had to be adjudicated immediately. And all six had something in common. Can you guess what it was?

Then Landry called for maybe the fourth time that day. Landry is a good operator. She gives a big fig about everything, even stuff that isn't worth a fig. She gave me this long and involved story about a huge slight that was inflicted on her operation by some other entity someplace, and I was looking out the window and thinking, whoa, look at that BMW Z8.

"You know what, Landry?" I said at last, because I couldn't think what else to say. "Why don't you just handle it the way you want to? Your instincts are good. Go with 'em."

"Yeah?" said Landry. "Thanks! I will!" And she went away feeling good about herself, so I managed the situation all right, except that was by accident, because I was really just, you know, phoning it in.

So then I sat there thinking, what is it with Landry and the six other warriors who breached my ruminations and made me deal with stuff? Are they smarter? No. Faster? Maybe, but that's not it. How come they're the only ones who are not phoning it in? Then it came to me.

Let's put it this way. Jack Grubman remembers where he was when J.F.K. was shot. So do Tom and Mark and I. These other guys rushing in with problems that need solving don't. Because they're too young. And we're not. We're young enough to smell the open road. But we're too old to care about stuff that doesn't seem worth caring about. At least not this week.

So the question is, Can we reclaim our lack of perspective and get back in harness? Or has the time come for us to hang up our phones and hit whatever portion of the highway remains to be seen? When I figure it out, I'll let you know. Until then, I'll have my people call your people.

Christopher Hitchens

Jewish Power, Jewish Peril

With synagogues being burned in Europe, ancient anti-Semitic lies finding new currency in the Arab and Muslim worlds, and even American Jews feeling distinctly unnerved, the author explores the ironies behind Israel's founding—and the seemingly ineradicable hatred of his "tribe."

Two old Jewish men are sitting on a park bench in Berlin in the early 1930s. Things are not yet so bad, but that doesn't mean they won't get worse. One of the two is solemnly reading a Jewish newspaper. The other is scanning a Nazi paper, and laughing out loud. Finally, the first man stops reading and says, "It's bad enough that you read that pro-Hitler rag. But to laugh at it!" The second responds with a shrug. "What if I read your paper? It tells me about Jewish windows being broken, Jewish shops boycotted, Jewish children beaten up in school. So . . . if I read the Hitler paper it tells me that we Jews control the whole world."

Like all jokes on this subject, the above story involves a dangerous flirtation with bad taste, with tragedy, and with irony. Irony has been an essential constituent of Jewish life ever since Maimonides wrote that, while the Messiah will one day come, "he may tarry." That shrug—half hopeful and half pessimistic—is present in Woody Allen and in Lenny Bruce. And the tragic element is so raw and so recent that there isn't any need to go over it. American Jews may be the most successful minority in American history, which is as much as to say that they are the most successful minority ever. But no other ethnicity has ever had to witness the physical destruction of perhaps one-third of its entire membership, carried out by a highly civilized European country that had been the model for assimilation, and involving the deliberate state murder of children. Still, no other American minority can also claim a stake in a local superstate of its very own, at the other end of the Mediterranean, where for the first time in history Jews can debate whether it would be proper to employ nuclear weapons on the Sabbath.

•   •   •

As I began to write this article, synagogues had been fire-bombed in several French towns and in one north London suburb, and a suicide assassin had massacred Jews who just minutes earlier had arrived from synagogues for a Passover dinner in the Israeli coastal town of Netanya. In response, American Jews in California had taken out an advertisement urging Woody Allen and others to boycott the Cannes Film Festival, on the grounds that the days of Vichy were back. Similar themes were being stressed by many Jewish and Israeli writers, who spoke darkly of the imminence of another Holocaust. Very often recently, this "Never Again" note has been struck by liberal and even radical Jews who seem to regret their former softness. Nat Hentoff, civil libertarian and longtime friend of the civil-rights movement, told *New York* magazine that "if a loudspeaker goes off and a voice says, 'All Jews gather in Times Square,' it could never surprise me."

I have to say that if such a voice were ever raised or broadcast, I would be much more than surprised, and very much more than shocked. I also think I could count on a very large number of Jews failing to report to Times Square, and an even larger number of non-Jews willing to support this refusal. Perhaps I should say here that I am related on my mother's side to this ancient argument and that, according to the Law of Moses, the Israeli Law of Return, and the Nuremberg laws, I can be counted as a member of the ancient tribe. This isn't much use, either to the tribe or to myself, since I don't believe there is a single word of truth in either Exodus or Genesis, would never consider asking a Palestinian to move out and make room for me, and do not believe that the human species is subdivided into races. I maintain that I have the best evidence of Darwin and DNA on my side, as well as many recent anti-Biblical and anti-mythical discoveries made by Israeli archeologists. Ze'ev Herzog, professor of archaeology at Tel Aviv University, has concluded that "the Israelites were never in Egypt, did not wander in the desert, did not conquer the land in a military campaign, and did not pass it on to the Twelve Tribes of Israel. Furthermore, the united monarchy of David and Solomon, which is described by the Bible as a regional power, was at most a small tribal kingdom." (Archaeological myths are often the most toxic. The legend of Masada involves believing as a positive and noble aspect of the story that Jewish resistance to Rome culminated in a suicide-murder.) Nonetheless, I like to think that I would be despised or hated by any movement defining itself as anti-Semitic. And on my shelf is an American Nazi pamphlet, denouncing the "Zionist Occupation Government" (or "ZOG") that covertly rules these United States. This illiterate screed isn't just a joke: it comes from the same swamp as those who murdered the Jewish radio host Alan Berg in Denver in 1984, and ultimately from the same mind-set that produced the atrocity in Oklahoma City. In these hate-clotted pages, I am—for the first and only time in my life—listed with both Henry Kissinger and Norman Podhoretz as a member of the international Jewish/Zionist conspiracy. As in the case of the tale with which I began: who knew I had such secret power?

.　　.　　.

Nativist and Christian though that 1989 pamphlet is, it was written partly in praise of the Ayatollah Khomeini. And the most horrifying recent development on the international scene is the emergence, in the Arab and Muslim world, of the debauched myths and falsifications of medieval Christianity. Saudi Arabian and Egyptian and Palestinian sources, some of them official, have been circulating *The Protocols of the Elders of Zion*, and reviving the accusation that no Passover meal is complete without the blood of a non-Jewish child to thicken the dough for the matzos. It is degrading even to argue with this kind of thing: the Protocols have been repeatedly and conclusively shown to be a crass forgery, originating in the witch trials of the Middle Ages and updated for the modern world via the reactionary secret police of the Russian czars and the publishers of *Mein Kampf*. (In neither circle, incidentally, were Arabs or Muslims regarded very highly.) Here again we find a version of the same sick joke: the Jews are supposed to be diabolical and clever enough to plot a secret world rule, and stupid enough to write the whole plan down. But please don't let the title fool you. The hideous cunning of the whole thing is that, in the secret book of their private deliberations, the "Elders" never mention Zionism or Palestine at all. The Jews' plan is that, from being the most dispersed and reviled minority in history, they go straight to a worldwide takeover and supreme power. Just like that. (The scary plot is hatched, according to this hoax, at midnight in the Jewish cemetery in Prague, near the later resting-place of Franz Kafka.)

•   •   •

Confronted with the re-appearance of this filthy libel, even Jews who inhabit global and regional superpowers, such as the United States and Israel, can be pardoned for feeling edgy. Anti-Semitism is not like other prejudices. Many white people do not like other people with supposedly African genes, but they don't accuse them, or even suspect them, of taking over Wall Street as a prelude to world domination. Nor do they accuse them of murdering Jesus Christ (one of the emptier accusations against the Jews, I have always thought, since if Christ hadn't been killed there would be no Christianity, and presumably the Christians think that god had some say in the decision to offer his only son). Some Protestants think that Catholics form a secret society. Some Catholics think that Freemasons form an invisible government. Many secular crackpots believe that the Illuminati or the Trilateralists or the Knights Templar are really running the world. But anti-Semitism is a kind of venomous distillation of all this conspiracy mania, and it is directed at a group which, when it can't be attacked as a race, can be indicted as a religion. Or, when it can't be attacked as a capitalist plutocracy, can be arraigned as the evil genius behind Communism. Or, and in each case, both. The Nazis portrayed Jews both as bloated profiteers and as gaunt, sinister Bolsheviks. This infection occurs in almost all societies, and breaks out at the oddest times, and is derived from paranoia. It is completely evidence-proof. (The Protocols were endorsed by *The Times* of London in 1920 and later reprinted and distributed all over the United States by Henry Ford, though no increase in missing children at Passover-time had ever been reported.) Jew hatred has a special appeal to the quasi-educated and the pseudo-intellectual, as well as to the ignorant who fear modernity and the big city. It is more like a form of mental disorder, or collective hallucination, than a form of racism. Though there are societies, such as India, where it has never been a problem, and the United States has seemingly been successfully inoculated against it, there are grounds for thinking that it is somehow ineradicable. Certainly that is what the Zionist movement believes.

To many others, also, it now seems self-evident that the presence of this sort of toxin is proof enough by itself that the state of Israel needs an unqualified defense. Most of the anxious propaganda about anti-Semitism earlier this summer was mobilized in favor of General Ariel Sharon, or by the supporters of Benjamin Netanyahu, who thinks that Sharon is a sissy. But how obvious is this connection when you come to examine it?

· · ·

The Protocols were fabricated by hired anti-Jewish reactionaries in Paris, almost certainly in 1897 or 1898, according to *Warrant for Genocide*, Professor Norman Cohn's magisterial 1966 study of the subject, and certainly between 1894 and 1899. What else was hap-

pening at that precise moment in history? France was being con-
vulsed by the case of Captain Alfred Dreyfus, a Jewish army officer
who had been framed for treason. In this, the mother of all French
scandals, the issue of justice for a single Jew had split the army, the
church, the press, the parliament, and the whole society. A Viennese Jewish journalist named Theodor Herzl, covering the trial,
was so appalled by French mobs yelling against the Jews that he
decided to call for all Europe's Jews to abandon the sick continent
and seek their own national home. He founded the movement
known as Zionism in 1897. His slogan was that "a land without a
people" should be a national home for "a people without a land." In
other words, he made the serious mistake of asserting that Palestine was effectively uninhabited.

This huge miscalculation was overlooked by some Jews
because of the terrible pogroms in the late 1880s, which had
driven millions of refugees out of czarist Russia. A handful of the
religious among them wanted to go to Jerusalem, where Jews
were scarce, but the majority opted for exile in the "Christian"
world. Not everybody in Western Europe or America was pleased
to see these new arrivals. In Britain, for example, in the first years
of the 20th century, a Conservative politician named Arthur Balfour made a political reputation by opposing "alien" Jewish
immigration. Meanwhile, in 1899, Dreyfus had been pardoned,
which meant that for the first time a Christian European nation
had decided that the right of a single Jew under the law was
worth a national climb-down. But Herzl's petitioning and cam-
paigning continued, through the energy of his disciple (and
Israel's first president), Chaim Weizmann, and extended itself
through the First World War. In 1917 it culminated in the anti-
Semite Balfour issuing "the Balfour Declaration," which is the
effective founding document of the state of Israel. Balfour was
not the first or last anti-Semite to urge Jews, in effect, to clear off
to Palestine or to Uganda or Cyprus or Madagascar or other

remote or isolated places briefly considered by Herzl himself as alternative "homelands." An old slogan of anti-Zionist and leftist Jews was that, "when Jew-baiters say 'Jews get out,' the Zionists offer to be the travel agents." And this does not exhaust the irony. The British Cabinet at that time contained only one Jewish member, Edwin Montagu, and he was passionately opposed to the declaration on the grounds that (a) it was a capitulation to anti-Semitic bigotry, with its suggestion that Palestine was the natural destination of the Jews, and that (b) it would be a grave cause of alarm to the Muslim world. Balfour's wording had included the proviso that "nothing shall be done which may prejudice the civil and religious rights of existing non-Jewish communities in Palestine," but not even the most committed Zionist will claim that that part of the promise has been kept. The fact must be faced: even if the Protocols had never been confected, and even if the settlers in Palestine were Dutch or British, there would still be an Arab nationalist resistance to the loss of their land.

. . .

Much of this history has been forgotten, because of the unimaginable disaster which later overwhelmed European civilization and very nearly annihilated European Jewry. However, a respect for truth requires one to remember that for the first three decades of the argument the only serious anti-Zionists were Jewish. There were leftist Jews who thought that the Arabs of Palestine were being done an injustice. There were Orthodox Jews who thought that Zionism was a blasphemy, because no return to Jerusalem was possible before the arrival of the Messiah. And there were liberal assimilationist Jews who thought that the future of the Jewish people lay in the Diaspora throughout the Western world, the scene of all its triumphs from Spinoza to Einstein. (Those Jews who today boycott *The New York Times* for being bleeding-heart about the Palestinians would smack their brows if they could see how Arthur Hays Sulzberger kept the whole American Zionist movement at arm's length before and even during the Second World War.) Between about 1942 and 1948, the American Council for Judaism enjoyed wide support for its anti-Zionist arguments (it is still worth reading Thomas Kolsky's 1990 scholarly history of the period, *Jews Against Zionism*). Be serious and ask which is more likely: that Nat Hentoff is right and America will intern and exterminate its Jewish population, or that Israel will succeed forever in governing resentful Arabs? The first outcome is to the very highest imaginable degree improbable. The second is simply impossible.

In a recent essay for the Jewish weekly *Forward* in New York, for which I ought to say I have been an occasional book reviewer, the liberal pro-Israeli critic Paul Berman detected a certain coarsening among those who take the Palestinian side. He was able to cite some disgusting examples of euphemism, concerning the vile tactic of suicide-murder, among Western intellectuals who were ready to explain the murder of children as a symptom of "despair." He even detected concessions to anti-Semitism in the pages of *The New York Review of Books*—which might be described as a flagship of secular liberal Judaism—particularly in the anti-Sharon essays it had published from Professor Tony Judt of New York University. Yet when it came to it, Berman was unable to cite any explicitly anti-Jewish propaganda in such sources. "It is the unintended inferences," he concluded somewhat lamely, "that seem to me the most frightening of all." Well, let's agree by all means that there are reasons enough for hypersensitivity. I, for example, always think I can tell something from the mere way that a person pronounces the word "Jew." (The longer he takes to pronounce it, the more on guard one should be.) Harold Abrahams in *Chariots of Fire* says memorably of prejudice that you "catch it on the edge of a remark."

Nonetheless, there is a danger in overprescribing, as well as in underdiagnosing. If everything is anti-Semitic, then the term loses its vital distinction. In a recent debate with a rabbi from the Simon Wiesenthal Center, I ridiculed the idea that Vichy and Kristallnacht have resurfaced in France. First, it's provably not true. But second, and hardly less important—what would there be left to say if these horrible phenomena really *did* recur? I care enough about this issue to keep my hatred pure, and to reserve it for those who truly merit it.

·   ·   ·

In April there was a huge demonstration in Washington, D.C., in favor of the Palestinians. To the astonishment of many bystanders, in the front rank of this demonstration stood a phalanx of bearded and hatted ultra-Orthodox Jews. They carried the flag of the P.L.O. and waved placards denouncing Zionism root and branch. They were not for a two-state solution: they were for a Palestinian state from the Jordan to the Mediterranean. These are the members of Neturei Karta. For them, the Messiah will indeed tarry, in fact won't even bother to call in advance, until the bogus atheist state of Israel has disappeared. (You can read about anti-Zionist Hasidim in Chaim Potok's 1967 novel *The Chosen*, or view them in the movie of the same name.) I have seen these people before, in Brooklyn and in the Mea Shearim quarter of Jerusalem, where they spit on the Israeli flag. I hung around with them at the demonstration for a while, collected some of their arcane literature, and noticed the more usual contingents of left and liberal and secular Jews who oppose the occupation, some of them wincing as hoarse and furious young Arabs shouted "*takbir!*," invoking Islam and jihad. I realized again why this long story has no neat or tidy resolution: maybe no resolution at all.

•   •   •

If the insane sickness of Fascism were to strike the "Christian" world again, and all the Jews had to flee—the six million or so American Jews, the 600,000 in France, the large populations in Argentina, Russia, Canada, Ukraine, and Britain—there would not be room in Palestine unless the state of Israel were to approximately double its size as well as to evict many if not all of the three million Muslim and Christian Palestinians. (A repellent option, with whose advocates Sharon himself has flirted.) One could hardly expect this to be tolerated even by the most moderate Arabs, who are in enough of a rage as it is (and not entirely because of the circulation of the Protocols, either). This would not be the only assimilation problem: Israeli writer David Grossman points out that, as it is, more Israeli Arabs speak Hebrew than American Jews. If, on the other hand, there were to be a peace agreement which led to the dismantling of the settlements, and the settlers had to be "assimilated" within a smaller Israel, an even more Zionist movement would spring up among the former colonists, who would start to dream—and not just to dream—of a "return" to the lost West Bank homeland of Hebron and Nablus. This would be the perfect counterpart to the scheme in Philip Roth's 1993 novel, *Operation Shylock*, where Israeli-born Jews dream of liberation and escape by rejoining the Diaspora.

Meanwhile, having promised safety to the Jews by means of a state in Palestine, the Israeli government issues almost daily warnings of the imminent destruction of the whole community. Having proposed Zionism as a means of declaring proud independence from fluctuations in Gentile goodwill, Israel has become utterly reliant upon foreign aid—especially an annual American subsidy of $3 billion—in its endless battle with its neighbors. And, having proposed Zionism as a cure for anti-Semitism, Israel recruits the support of anti-Semitic fundamentalists such as Pat Robertson and Billy Graham, who see the Jewish state as a prelude to the conversion of the Jews, to be followed happily enough by Armageddon and the consigning of the non-converts to hell. Some of these ironies are in Israel's favor: the kids who burned those French synagogues this past spring were lumpen Arab immigrants trying to make a crude and violent point about Palestine, and at least France's leading anti-Semite, Jean-Marie Le Pen, has promised to deport all of *them*. But some of the ironies are not helpful: there is no decent way to compare destitute Arab refugees in Gaza to the members of the SS, as Menachem Begin used to do. One sign of modern anti-Semitism is the obsessive, nasty need of some people to compare Israel to Nazi Germany. It would actually be good if all sides dropped this outrageous analogy, which is designed to cheapen something, namely the Shoah, or Final Solution, the memory of which must not be abused.

· · ·

The survival of the Jewish people has for centuries been a means of taking the moral temperature of a society. Those who take that temperature are quite rightly conditioned to notice even a slight elevation. It is sometimes said that all Jews must have a bag mentally packed, ready to flee. To the extent that this is true it will, alas, always be true. The creation of a Jewish state, it can now be argued, merely re-states an old dilemma in fresh terms. Neither Israel nor messianism can cure the irrational: Myself, even as a wretchedly heretic and bastard member of the tribe, I perhaps conceitedly think that there may be something to the cliché about Jews' being inherently and intuitively smart. Smart enough to see that if ethno-religious nationalism isn't good for other people, it may not even be good for the Jews.

Smart enough to doubt the divinity of antique man-made scrolls. Smart enough even to see that the Promised Land may be a secular multi-ethnic democracy, none the worse for being a second home to many other wanderers and victims, too. America, in a word. The best hope and, yes, perhaps the last one.

The New Yorker

FINALIST, ESSAYS

Bumping Into Mr. Ravioli

Many children have imaginary playmates, but New Yorker *writer Adam Gopnik started to worry when his daughter developed an invisible friend named Charlie Ravioli, who was always too busy to play with her. His essay, "Bumping Into Mr. Ravioli," is more than just a funny story; it's a perceptive look into our crowded schedules and hit-and-run social relationships—and how we got that way.*

Adam Gopnik

Bumping Into
Mr. Ravioli

A theory of busyness,
and its hero

My daughter Olivia, who just turned three, has an imaginary friend whose name is Charlie Ravioli. Olivia is growing up in Manhattan, and so Charlie Ravioli has a lot of local traits: he lives in an apartment "on Madison and Lexington," he dines on grilled chicken, fruit, and water, and, having reached the age of seven and a half, he feels, or is thought, "old." But the most peculiarly local thing about Olivia's imaginary playmate is this: he is always too busy to play with her. She holds her toy cell phone up to her ear, and we hear her talk into it: "Ravioli? It's Olivia . . . It's Olivia. Come and play? O.K. Call me. Bye." Then she snaps it shut, and shakes her head. "I always get his machine," she says. Or she will say, "I spoke to Ravioli today." "Did you have fun?" my wife and I ask. "No. He was busy working. On a television" (leaving it up in the air if he repairs electronic devices or has his own talk show).

On a good day, she "bumps into" her invisible friend and they go to a coffee shop. "I bumped into Charlie Ravioli," she announces at dinner (after a day when, of course, she stayed home, played, had a nap, had lunch, paid a visit to the Central Park Zoo, and then had another nap). "We had coffee, but then he had to run." She sighs, sometimes, at her inability to make their schedules mesh, but she accepts it as inevitable, just the way life is. "I bumped into Charlie Ravioli today," she says. "He was working." Then she adds brightly, "But we hopped into a taxi." What happened then? we ask. "We grabbed lunch," she says.

It seemed obvious that Ravioli was a romantic figure of the big exotic life that went on outside her little limited life of parks and playgrounds—drawn, in particular, from a nearly perfect, mynah-bird-like imitation of the words she hears her mother use when she talks about *her* day with *her* friends. ("How was your day?" Sighing: "Oh, you know. I tried to make a date with Meg, but I couldn't find her, so I left a message on her machine. Then I bumped into Emily after that meeting I had in SoHo, and we had coffee and then she had to run, but by then Meg had reached me on my cell and we arranged . . .") I was concerned, though, that Charlie Ravioli might also be the sign of some "trauma," some loneliness in Olivia's life reflected in imaginary form. "It seems odd to have an imaginary playmate who's always too busy to play with you," Martha, my wife, said to me. "Shouldn't your imaginary playmate be someone you tell secrets to and, I don't know, sing songs with? It shouldn't be someone who's always *hopping* into taxis."

We thought, at first, that her older brother Luke might be the original of Charlie Ravioli. (For one thing, he is also seven and a half, though we were fairly sure that this age was merely Olivia's marker for As Old as Man Can Be.) He *is* too busy to play with her much anymore. He has become a true New York child, with the schedule of a Cabinet secretary: chess club on Monday, T-ball on Tuesday, tournament on Saturday, play dates and after-school conferences to fill in the gaps. But Olivia, though she counts days, does not yet really *have* days. She has *a* day, and into this day she has introduced the figure of Charlie Ravioli—in order, it dawned on us, to insist that she does have days, because she is too harried to share them, that she does have an independent social life, by virtue of being too busy to have one.

Yet Charlie Ravioli was becoming so constant and oddly discouraging a companion—"He cancelled lunch. Again," Olivia would say—that we thought we ought to look into it. One of my sisters is a developmental psychologist who specializes in close scientific studies of what goes on inside the heads of one- and two- and three-year-olds. Though she grew up in the nervy East, she lives in California now, where she grows basil in her garden and jars her own organic marmalades. I e-mailed this sister for help with the Ravioli issue—how concerned should we be?—and she sent me back an e-mail, along with an attachment, and, after several failed cell-phone connections, we at last spoke on a land line.

It turned out that there is a recent book on this very subject by the psychologist Marjorie Taylor, called "Imaginary Companions and the Children Who Create Them," and my sister had just written a review of it. She insisted that Charlie Ravioli was nothing to be worried about. Olivia was right on target, in fact. Most under-sevens (sixty-three per cent, to be scientific) have an invisible friend, and children create their imaginary playmates not out of trauma but out of a serene sense of the possibilities of fiction—sometimes as figures of pure fantasy, sometimes, as Olivia had done, as observations of grownup manners assembled in tranquillity and given a name. I learned about the invisible companions Taylor studied: Baintor, who is invisible because he lives in the light; Station Pheta, who hunts sea anemones on the beach. Charlie Ravioli seemed pavement-bound by comparison.

"An imaginary playmate isn't any kind of trauma-marker," my sister said. "It's just the opposite: it's a sign that the child is now confident enough to begin to understand how to organize her experience into stories." The significant thing about imaginary friends, she went on, is that the kids know they're fictional. In an instant message on AOL, she summed it up: "The children with invisible friends often interrupted the interviewer to remind her, with a certain note of concern for her sanity, that these characters were, after all, just pretend."

I also learned that some children, as they get older, turn out to possess what child psychologists call a "paracosm." A paracosm is a society thought up by a child—an invented universe with a distinctive language, geography, and history. (The Brontës invented a couple of paracosms when they were children.) Not all children who have an imaginary friend invent a paracosm, but the two might, I think, be related. Like a lonely ambassador from Alpha Centauri in a fifties sci-fi movie who, misunderstood by paranoid earth scientists, cannot bring the life-saving news from his planet, perhaps the invisible friend also gets an indifferent or hostile response, and then we never find out about the beautiful paracosm he comes from.

"Don't worry about it," my sister said in a late-night phone call. "Knowing something's made up while thinking that it matters is what all fiction insists on. She's putting a name on a series of manners."

"But he seems so real to her," I objected.

"Of course he is. I mean, who's more real to you, Becky Sharp or Gandalf or the guy down the hall? Giving a manner a name makes it real."

I paused. "I grasp that it's normal for her to have an imaginary friend," I said, "but have you ever heard of an imaginary friend who's too busy to play with you?"

She thought about it. "No," she said. "I'm sure that doesn't occur anywhere in the research literature. That sounds *completely* New York." And then she hung up.

•   •   •

The real question, I saw, was not "Why this friend?" but "Why this fiction?" Why, as Olivia had seen so clearly, are grownups in New York so busy, and so obsessed with the language of busyness that it dominates their conversation? Why are New Yorkers always bumping into Charlie Ravioli and grabbing lunch, instead of sitting down with him and exchanging intimacies, as friends should, as people do in Paris and Rome? Why is busyness the stuff our children make their invisible friends from, as country children make theirs from light and sand?

This seems like an odd question. New Yorkers are busy for obvious reasons: they have husbands and wives and careers and children, they have the Gauguin show to see and their personal trainers and accountants to visit. But the more I think about this the more I think it is—well, a lot of Ravioli. We are instructed to believe that we are busier because we have to work harder to be more productive, but everybody knows that busyness and productivity have a dubious, arm's-length relationship. Most of our struggle in New York, in fact, is to be less busy in order to do more work.

Constant, exhausting, no-time-to-meet-your-friends Charlie Ravioli-style busyness arrived as an affliction in modern life long after the other parts of bourgeois city manners did. Business long predates busyness. In the seventeenth and eighteenth centuries, when bourgeois people were building the institutions of bourgeois life, they seem never to have complained that they were too busy—or, if they did, they left no record of it. Samuel Pepys, who had a Navy to refloat and a burned London to rebuild, often uses the word "busy" but never complains of busyness. For him, the word "busy" is a synonym for "happy," not for "stressed." Not once in his diary does Pepys cancel lunch or struggle to fit someone in for coffee at four-thirty. Pepys works, makes love, and goes to bed, but he does not bump and he does not have to run. Ben Franklin, a half century later, boasts of his industriousness, but he, too, never complains about being busy, and always has time to publish a newspaper or come up with a maxim or swim the ocean or invent the lightning rod.

Until sometime in the middle of the nineteenth century, in fact, the normal affliction of the bourgeois was not busyness at all but its apparent opposite: boredom. It has even been argued that the grid of streets and cafés and small engagements in the nineteenth-century city—the whole of social life—was designed self-consciously as an escape from that numbing boredom. (Working people weren't bored, of course, but they were engaged in labor, not work. They were too busy to be busy.) Baudelaire, basically, was so bored that he had to get drunk and run out onto the boulevard in the hope of bumping into somebody.

Turn to the last third of the nineteenth century and the beginning of the twentieth, though, and suddenly everybody is busy, and everybody is complaining about it. Pepys, master of His Majesty's Navy, may never have complained of busyness, but Virginia Woolf, mistress of motionless lull, is continually complaining about how she spends her days racing across London from square to square, just like—well, like Charlie Ravioli. Ronald Firbank is wrung out by his social obligations; Proust is constantly rescheduling rendezvous and apologizing for being overstretched. Henry James, with nothing particular to do save live, complains of being too busy all the time. He could not shake the world of obligation, he said, and he wrote a strange and beautiful story, "The Great Good Place," which begins with an exhausting flood of correspondence, telegrams, and manuscripts that drive the protagonist nearly mad.

What changed? That James story helps supply the key. It was trains and telegrams. The railroads ended isolation, and packed the metropolis with people whose work was defined by a complicated network of social obligations. Pepys's network in 1669 London was, despite his official position, relatively small compared even with that of a minor aesthete like Firbank, two centuries later. Pepys had more time to make love because he had fewer friends to answer.

If the train crowded our streets, the telegram crowded our minds. It introduced something into the world which remains with us today: a whole new class of communications that are defined as incomplete in advance of their delivery. A letter, though it may enjoin a response, is meant to be complete in itself. Neither the Apostle Paul nor Horace Walpole ever ends an epistle with "Give me a call and let's discuss." By contrast, it is in the nature of the telegram to be a skeletal version of another thing—a communication that opens more than it closes. The nineteenth-century telegram came with those busy-threatening words "Letter follows."

Every device that has evolved from the telegram shares the same character. E-mails end with a suggestion for a phone call ("Anyway, let's meet and/or talk soon"), faxes with a request for an e-mail, answering-machine messages with a request for a fax. All are devices of perpetually suspended communication. My wife recalls a moment last fall when she got a telephone message from a friend asking her to check her e-mail apropos a phone call she needed to make vis-à-vis a fax they had both received asking for more information about a bed they were thinking of buying from Ireland online and having sent to America by Federal Express—a grand slam of incomplete communication.

In most of the Western world outside New York, the press of trains and of telegraphic communication was alleviated by those other two great transformers: the car and the television. While the train and the telegram (and their love children, subways and commuter trains and e-mail) pushed people together, the car and the television pulled people apart—taking them out to the suburbs and sitting them down in front of a solo spectacle. New York, though, almost uniquely, got hit by a double dose of the first two technologies, and a very limited dose of the second two.

Car life—car obsessions, car-defined habits—is more absent here than almost anywhere else in the country, while television, though obviously present, is less fatally prevalent here. New York is still a subject of television, and we compare "Sex and the City" to sex and the city; they are not yet quite the same. Here two grids of busyness remain dominant: the nineteenth- and early-twentieth-century grid of bump and run, and the late-twentieth- and early-twenty-first-century postmodern grid of virtual call and echo. Busyness is felt so intently here because we are both crowded and overloaded. We exit the apartment into a still dense nineteenth-century grid of street corners and restaurants full of people, and come home to the late-twentieth-century grid of faxes and e-mails and overwhelming incompleteness.

We walk across the Park on a Sunday morning and bump into our friend the baker and our old acquaintance from graduate school (what the hell is she doing now?) and someone we have been avoiding for three weeks. They all invite us for brunch, and we would love to, but we are too . . . busy. We bump into Charlie Ravioli, and grab a coffee with him—and come home to find three e-mails and a message on our cell phone from him, wondering where we are. The crowding of our space has been reinforced by a crowding of our time, and the only way to protect ourselves is to build structures of perpetual deferral: I'll see you next week, let's talk soon. We build rhetorical baffles around our lives to keep the crowding out, only to find that we have let nobody we love in.

Like Charlie Ravioli, we hop into taxis and leave messages on answering machines to avoid our acquaintances, and find that we keep missing our friends. I have one intimate who lives just across the Park from me, whom I e-mail often, and whom I am fortunate to see two or three times a year. We are always . . . busy. He has become my Charlie Ravioli, my invisible friend. I am sure that he misses me—just as Charlie Ravioli, I realized, must tell his other friends that he is sorry he does not see Olivia more often.

.   .   .

Once I sensed the nature of his predicament, I began to feel more sympathetic toward Charlie Ravioli. I got to know him better, too. We learned more about what Ravioli did in the brief breathing spaces in his busy life when he could sit down with Olivia and dish. "Ravioli read your book," Olivia announced, for instance, one night at dinner. "He didn't like it much." We also found out that Ravioli had joined a gym, that he was going to the beach in the summer, but he was too busy, and that he was working on a "show." ("It isn't a very good show," she added candidly.) Charlie Ravioli, in other words, was just another New Yorker: fit, opinionated, and trying to break into show business.

I think we would have learned to live happily with Charlie Ravioli had it not been for the appearance of Laurie. She threw us badly. At dinner, Olivia had been mentioning a new personage almost as often as she mentioned Ravioli. "I talked to Laurie today," she would begin. "She says Ravioli is busy." Or she would be closeted with her play phone. "Who are you talking to, darling?" I would ask. "Laurie," she would say. "We're talking about Ravioli." We surmised that Laurie was, so to speak, the Linda Tripp of the Ravioli operation—the person you spoke to for consolation when the big creep was ignoring you.

But a little while later a more ominous side of Laurie's role began to appear. "Laurie, tell Ravioli I'm calling," I heard Olivia say. I pressed her about who, exactly, Laurie was. Olivia shook her head. "She works for Ravioli," she said.

And then it came to us, with sickening clarity: Laurie was not the patient friend who consoled you for Charlie's absence. Laurie was the bright-toned person who answered Ravioli's phone and told you that unfortunately Mr. Ravioli was in a meeting. "Laurie says Ravioli is too busy to play," Olivia announced sadly one morning. Things seemed to be deteriorating; now Ravioli was too busy even to say he was too busy.

I got back on the phone with my sister. "Have you ever heard of an imaginary friend with an assistant?" I asked.

She paused. "Imaginary friends don't have assistants," she said. "That's not only not in the literature. That's just . . . I mean—in California they don't have assistants."

"You think we should look into it?"

"I think you should move," she said flatly.

Martha was of the same mind. "An imaginary playmate shouldn't have an assistant," she said miserably. "An imaginary playmate shouldn't have an agent. An imaginary playmate shouldn't have a publicist or a personal trainer or a caterer—an imaginary playmate shouldn't have . . . *people*. An imaginary playmate should just *play*. With the child who imagined it." She started leaving on my pillow real-estate brochures picturing quaint houses in New Jersey and Connecticut, unhaunted by busy invisible friends and their entourages.

.   .   .

Not long after the appearance of Laurie, though, something remarkable happened. Olivia would begin to tell us tales of her frustrations with Charlie Ravioli, and, after telling us, again, that he was too busy to play, she would tell us what she had done instead. Astounding and paracosmic tall tales poured out of her: she had been to a chess tournament and brought home a trophy; she had gone to a circus and told jokes. Searching for Charlie Ravioli, she had "saved all the animals in the zoo"; heading home in a taxi after a quick coffee with Ravioli, she took over the steering wheel and "got all the moneys." From the stalemate of daily life emerged the fantasy of victory. She had dreamed of a normal life with a few close friends, and had to settle for worldwide fame and the front page of the tabloids. The existence of an imaginary friend had liberated her into a paracosm, but it was a curiously New York paracosm—it was the unobtainable world outside her window. Charlie Ravioli, prince of busyness, was not an end but a means: a way out onto the street in her head, a declaration of potential independence.

Busyness is our art form, our civic ritual, our way of being us. Many friends have said to me that they love New York now in a way they never did before, and their love, I've noticed, takes for its object all the things that used to exasperate them—the curious combination of freedom, self-made fences, and paralyzing preoccupation that the city provides. "How did you spend the day?" Martha and I now ask each other, and then, instead of listing her incidents, she says merely, "Oh, you know . . . just . . . bumping into Charlie Ravioli," meaning, just bouncing from obligation to electronic entreaty, just spotting a friend and snatching a sandwich, just being busy, just living in New York. If everything we've learned in the past year could be summed up in a phrase, it's that we want to go on bumping into Charlie Ravioli for as long as we can.

Olivia still hopes to have him to herself someday. As I work late at night in the "study" (an old hallway, an Aalto screen) I keep near the "nursery" (an ancient pantry, a glass-brick wall), I can hear her shift into pre-sleep, still muttering to herself. She is still trying to reach her closest friend. "Ravioli? Ravioli?" she moans as she turns over into her pillow and clutches her blanket, and then she whispers, almost to herself, "Tell him call me. Tell him call me when he comes home."

The Atlantic Monthly

FINALIST, REVIEWS AND CRITICISM

Home Alone

Caitlin Flanagan is the rare critic who manages to be profoundly edifying and wildly entertaining at the same time. Unpredictable, persuasive and effortlessly challenging—without the slightest hint of academic tone—her distinct voice turns every review into an engaging model of original thinking.

Caitlin Flanagan

Home Alone

It's all too easy to deride Martha Stewart, but the attacks on her often point up how much there is to admire.

Christopher Byron has had the misfortune of writing a lengthy book on Martha Stewart's business dealings that went to press before news broke of what would surely have been its centerpiece—the ImClone scandal. Nor have the fates been kind to him in the matters of prose style or basic storytelling ability. *Martha Inc.* is a book with rather high literary aspirations, but they go bust from the get-go: in the opening sentences of Chapter One, Stewart's father, Eddie Kostyra, is described as a "self-absorbed narcissist." One of Christopher Byron's desires—and not a bad one—is to give readers a sense of Martha Stewart's true nature. Regrettably, his means for achieving this goal border on the comical, as he marshals all of Western art and culture (and, one senses, the entirety of his Yale undergraduate education) to his aid. In the course of the book Stewart is compared to the Romanovs, Richard Nixon, "the ghostly wife of King Popiel the Heartless," elevator music, the Jim Carrey character in *The Truman Show*, the Karl Malden character in *One-Eyed Jacks*, the Jeff Daniels character in *The Purple Rose of Cairo*, a "demonically possessed character out of a horror movie," an unspecified character "out of a Bo Widerberg movie," a central character in *Who's Afraid of Virginia Woolf?*, the Cheshire Cat, Dorothy Gale, Jay Gatsby, Marie Antoinette, Macbeth, Evita Peron, John Fitzgerald Kennedy Jr., Walt Disney, a witch, a saint, a participant in Torquemada's Theater of Tortures, the Ohio State football team, the Chicago Bulls, Chairman Mao, and (perhaps most unlikely of all, and for an entire chapter) Nancy Drew. That this curious assemblage is incapable of suggesting any one human being—and least of all Martha Stewart—eludes Byron, although midway through the book we find a defeated little remark that amounts to an authorial waving of the white flag: Stewart, he decides, is really just "like everyone." She has "good qualities and bad qualities, and still other qualities that seemed to occupy a kind of 'work in progress' niche in between." Well, then maybe we ought to let poor old Richard Nixon rest in peace.

Byron makes Stewart appear distasteful, but no one could be more distasteful than Byron himself, as he dredges up news about Stewart's hysterectomy, does his level best to glean facts from her sealed divorce file, and reports on the intimate sleeping arrangements of her teenage daughter. In Byron's hands Stewart can't catch a break. When she and her husband relocated their young family from Manhattan to Turkey Hill Farm, in Westport, Connecticut, "scarcely had the couple moved to the country than they found enough money to dump the child in a fancy country day school a mile from Turkey Hill and left her to fend for herself." It's a remark that prompts the reader to wonder what the preferable alternative was—enrolling the little girl in a public school farther from home and attending classes with her? (He seems also to have forgotten that in the book's preface he explained proudly that he and his glamorous subject "had actually been leading parallel lives"; in fact, Byron and his wife "had sent [their] daughter to the same country day school where the Stewarts had sent theirs.") We get the by now familiar litany of offenses (hopped up with a few spicy new additions) that prove conclusively that Martha Stewart is the rottenest, nastiest person ever to draw breath: she was mean to a trick-or-treater, frightened a Boy Scout, jumped to the head of a line at a tag sale, ran over a kitten, and irritated an employee at a Chinese restaurant so badly that he blurted out, "I don't give a fuck." She honked at slowpokes in a bank drive-through. She unplugged a guest-room mini-fridge in which a visitor had been storing yummy "coffee, juice, leftovers and snacks." She once borrowed a large pot and never returned it. A guest at one of her breakfast meetings was made "instantly nauseous" by the fare. Even Stewart's breathtaking triumphs (such as seizing and maintaining control of a Charlie Rose interview) are portrayed in the same grim light as are her disastrous lapses of judgment (such as actually dating Charlie Rose). Sometimes Byron's tone is that of a censorious eighth-grade girl, as when he reports that "Martha is not a good mixer at parties." Much has been made in the press of the fact that contrary to expectation, *Martha Inc.* is not the nastiest biography of Stewart yet published. But not for lack of trying. Byron wants us to understand that Stewart is an egomaniac (perhaps even a self-absorbed narcissist), and this should not require much heavy lifting on his part. But oftentimes his evidence lacks punch. When a Cuban tour guide tells her that he learned English by tuning in Tom Brokaw's news broadcasts using a home-made antenna, we get this bit of silliness:

Whether Martha was genuinely interested or irritated that her "guide" was talking about a rival celebrity isn't known. But whatever her feelings at the new direction in the conversation, she nonetheless quickly managed to steer things back toward something that made her the center of events once again. She said, "I can buy you a satellite dish and send it to you."

Stop this monster before she maims and kills!

Byron performs arabesques of conclusion upon the weakest scaffolding of facts. We learn, for example, that the Kostyra family home "had a single full bath, and two washrooms—one in the basement and the other off the kitchen, where Eddie would shave and relieve himself during mealtimes, whether the family liked it or not." The source for this unlovely revelation seems to be one of Stewart's "Remembering" columns (a regular feature of her *Martha Stewart Living* magazine), in which she remarks of the household facilities, "One of the half-bathrooms was a toilet and a sink off the kitchen—that was really Dad's private domain." How we get from this unremarkable statement to Dad's "reliev[ing] himself during mealtimes" is, I think, what makes so much of this book "The Incredible Story" that it is. Byron is quite rabid on the subject of the "Remembering" columns. In the kind of footnote that makes one think it was really a pity he gave up the law in favor of writing, he tells us, "At the time of this book's writing, ninety-five such columns had been published. Copies of all were obtained and digested for this book." A lesser student of human evil might assume that in ninety-five columns about her childhood, a person might commit a few inconsistencies and repetitions; but Byron is a stickler for absolute accuracy in such matters. Stewart wrote in 1982 that she first visited Europe with her husband, but then wrote in a "Remembering" column that she first went to the Continent with her mother— and Byron cries foul. He is certainly not the first to sense that collectively these columns leave a telling record of their author's interests and intentions, but surely it is the biographer's job—if his method is to involve a careful examination of these things— to make something more of their various obfuscations and revisions than the observation that they all appear to have been "dashed off on the way to the airport."

But the book just comes apart at the seams when it addresses its intended main subject—not the personality of Martha Stewart but, rather, her business acumen and success. Byron, a financial reporter, serves up plenty of blather about "a Harvard B-school concept known as 'synergy' " and the intricacies of television syndication deals and the dot-com revolution. He tells us that Stewart is "the human embodiment of an abstract marketing message," but what, exactly, that message might be is beyond him. I knew that we might be in the hands of someone distinctly unsuited to write about a woman whose financial success is based, in large part, on cooking and fine dining when he described the faces of the girls in her high school yearbook as appearing to be "frozen in aspic." But at every turn he fails to understand what, precisely, Stewart is selling, and to whom and how. For her followers he has at best a kind of pity, finding in them a group of hausfraus completely worn down by the one-two punch of women's liberation and housework, and desperate for a messiah. Stewart's fans, we learn, are women "in fly-over America," women who "toiled in Norman Rockwell's silent rituals of life and death and yearned for something more." They are women "who came home exhausted from jobs they didn't really want, to confront equally exhausted husbands and resentful latchkey children," women severely disillusioned by the fact that the women's movement has "morphed into an array of more than 500 increasingly shrill special interest groups, with a thousand different issues and arenas for action"—this disillusionment somehow causing them to run willy-nilly toward Stewart's world of gracious living and entertaining. At worst Byron has contempt for

Stewart's fans, especially those who are Kmart shoppers, whom he characterizes as broke, tasteless, rural, and harried. That the chain's executives seem also to have underestimated its customers is clear, although Stewart (perpetually blasted as elitist) never has—which is perhaps why the retailer is in Chapter 11 while Martha Stewart Living Omnimedia is thriving.

Over and over, Byron presents scenes in which Stewart doesn't "get" Kmart shoppers; "She didn't really understand what was appropriate merchandise for Kmart . . . and what was not," says a former Kmart consultant, to which Byron adds, "Martha had become like the single out-of-step soldier in the army—yet week after week, month after month, she kept pushing to get the whole army to shift to her cadence." He reports that what Kmart wanted from Stewart was merely a little of her allure, a few of her "daffodil daydreams." What she gave the retailer—and what any more competent outfit ought to have been able to turn into a gold mine—was a line of products called Martha Stewart Everyday, which was founded on a simple principle: not that Betty Friedan has left all of womankind hungering for pastels but, rather, that cheap things don't have to be ugly. For dime-store prices she came up with some attractive merchandise, decorated with a restraint not often seen in discount items, that women (and, in not insignificant numbers, gay men) loved buying. Shortly after Kmart announced its financial woes, the *New York Observer* ran a Simon Doonan column titled "Domestic Slaves of New York Confess Dependency on Kmartha," in which he reported panic buying of Martha Stewart Everyday ware and said that "these middle-class groovers are not slumming for a hit of reverse chic: They are sincerely appreciative of the amazing value and quality that Martha offers." Typical of the line is a very pretty white eyelet shower curtain with a scalloped hem, a product with which I am intimately familiar, because it is hanging in my bathroom. And typical of Byron's inability to understand these products or their appeal is his characterization of Stewart as a control freak "who turned up at every meeting, determined to elbow and nudge her way into every decision made in her name . . . all the way down to demanding to know the thread-count per square inch in sheets and towels sold under her name." It's a foolish remark, because, of course, the only really important thing about sheets is their thread count. He later notes snidely that reporters at a publicity event for Stewart's linens thought the patterns were lovely but "once [they] touched the sheets they were reminded where they came from," because "they weren't as soft as [Ralph] Lauren's or Calvin Klein's." Why? Because the thread count was too low, you idiot.

•   •   •

Martha Inc. is so bloated, repetitive, and overwrought that the reader is much more often frustrated by Byron's meanderings and hypotheses than enlightened by his perceptions. Happily, another recent biography tackles the subject of Stewart's business success with clarity and precision: the Martha Stewart volume in the Women of Achievement series, which you can find in the young-adult section of your local public library. (Stewart is apparently someone whom educational publishers think schoolchildren ought to know about; there are also Martha Stewart volumes in the People to Know and the Library of Famous Women series.) Skip the introductory essay on women's history that is printed in each volume (written by Matina S. Horner, the president emerita of Radcliffe College, it evokes Abigail Adams and Ralph Waldo Emerson, two thinkers who may be fine guardians of the volumes on Eleanor Roosevelt and Elizabeth Cady Stanton, but who may strike too resounding a gong for Women of Achievement such as Cher, Gloria Estefan, and Barbara Walters).

Charles J. Shields, the author of the Stewart volume, trots us through the high points of Stewart's early life and career in short order, making astute observations as to how these various experiences may have shaped her as a businesswoman. Compared with Byron's fervid ramblings, this clear analysis is a welcome relief. In his attempt to provide a brief, vivid sketch of Stewart's domineering father, Byron puts his shoulder to the wheel: Eddie Kostyra was a Captain Queeg, a Stanley Kowalski, a "nobly born" character from an Hilaire Belloc rhyme, both faces of Janus. It's a bravura display of the Byron technique, but it can't compare with Shields's fascinating revelation that Eddie Kostyra's mother "had taught him how to cook, sew, and garden, in the hope of encouraging his creative side," and that Eddie decorated the high school gym for the prom during Martha's junior year. Of her early modeling career Byron says that Stewart lacked the "erotic and sexually charged" quality of the sixties model Veruschka and failed to capture the attention of Richard Avedon as had Twiggy. Why he sees a need to compare Stewart's modeling work (conducted part-time while she was a student in high school and college) with that of two of the most famous fashion models of the era is unclear, although he misses an obvious point that Shields does not: "Working with photographers gave her a sense of how things should look, or be presented." Byron on Stewart's work as a stockbroker: "What was Martha's job? The same job any good-looking young woman got in the 1960s in a world dominated by men: Walk into the room, sit down, and cross her legs." Shields on the same topic: "She was learning the ropes of big business and its key elements—investment, negotiation, and finance." (Whether she was also learning the rudiments of insider trading has turned out to be one of the most gleefully debated questions of the summer. To borrow a page from the Byron style book, not since Marie Antoinette got hauled off to the Conciergerie—or Leona Helmsley to federal prison—has there been the potential of such a thrilling new addition to the female prison population.) Shields gives us Stewart's own take on her Kmart experiences, which brings the conflict between her and the retailer into much sharper focus than any of Byron's hyperbole: "When I first started with Kmart, I was very enthusiastic to build a fine business with them. Little did I know that management was extremely weak and their inventory control and computer programs a complete disaster."

What no biography of Stewart has yet accomplished is an insightful analysis of the core questions that her phenomenal success prompts. Many writers—especially male writers, such as Byron and Jerry Oppenheimer, the author of *Martha Stewart: Just Desserts* (1997)—have been fascinated by her famously mercurial temperament and the unsavory details of her personal life. But other than indulging in juicy speculation (such as Oppenheimer's creepy fascination with Stewart's heavy menstrual periods and Byron's notion that she had a hysterectomy as a form of birth control, a notion that only a man could believe and only a jerk could promulgate), they don't know what to do with these supposed secrets except to humiliate Stewart by making them public. The notion of an attractive late-midlife woman who offers homemaking advice on television but leads an off-camera life marked by nastiness and single-girl liberty is rife with comedic possibility (it is the basis for the Sue Ann Nivens character on *The Mary Tyler Moore Show*), and this type draws the cruelest of the biographers. But these writers' books fail because they assume that Stewart's success is based on the stupidity of women, their inability to see through her many inconsistencies and hypocrisies. If only those dumb clucks would read the "Remembering" columns more critically! They'd cancel their subscriptions in an instant! Byron misses nothing less than the heart of Stewart's appeal to women.

·　　·　　·

In the first place there is the incontrovertible fact of her tremendous style. The photography in her various publications seems to reduce all of female longing to its essential elements. A basket of flowers, a child's lawn pinafore draped across a painted rocking chair, an exceptionally white towel folded in thirds and perched in glamorous isolation on a clean and barren shelf: most of the pictures feature a lot of sunlight, and many show rooms that are either empty of people or occupied solely by Martha, evoking the profound and enduring female desires for solitude and silence. No heterosexual man can understand this stuff, and no woman with a beating heart and an ounce of femininity can resist it. I can unpack a paragraph of Martha Stewart prose with the best of them, but I also fall mute and wondering at the pages of *Martha Stewart Living*.

Stewart's aesthetic has been steadily evolving over the past two decades, and at this point it has reached a peak of almost unbearable perfection. To compare her two wedding volumes— published in 1987 and 1999—is to see just how far things have come. The first appeared at the precise moment when Americans by the millions were returning to formal weddings; in fact, its publication was so timely and so influential that it's hard to know to what extent Stewart predicted the craze and to what extent she created it. The book has a documentary quality: it features photographs of actual weddings she catered during the summers of 1984 and 1985 and also some that she heard about and asked if she might photograph and include in the book. The pictures are full of the mess and indignity of real life. There are a few unattractive brides and a couple of chubby ones (as well as several couples of such heartrending youth and hopefulness that I banished a vague notion of doing a longitudinal study of the fate of these marriages as soon as it flitted through my head). There are wedding guests in shorts and shirtsleeves, several preparing to board a Greyhound bus, a couple of Porta Potties nestled into a leafy corner of a reception site. On one table there's a two-liter bottle of Coca-Cola, on another a fifth of cheap Scotch. But to look at the more recent volume is to see all this unpleasantness burnished away. Actual brides are for the most part relegated to small black-and-white photographs; the full-color spreads feature models and careful art direction and receptions unsullied by actual guests. The venues for these stage-set weddings seem to be a collection of New England chapels of the highest caliber. Whitewashed shingles and gleaming wooden pews provide austere backdrops for garlands of flowers, wreaths of flowers, paper cones of flowers; espaliered bushes are covered in clouds of white tulle and tied with silk ribbons; walkways are blanketed in thick drifts of petals; oak trees are hung with white Japanese lanterns. Flower girls wear wreaths of roses and carry more of them; winter weddings feature severe Christmas trees and tall centerpieces of sugared fruit. My attraction to these images has nothing to do with "Norman Rockwell's silent rituals of life and death," nor is it compromised by my knowledge of Stewart's complex personal life. It is rooted in a truth far less mysterious: women like pretty things. Stewart's magazines (she has four titles: *Living, Baby, Kids,* and *Weddings*) all seem to depict some parallel universe in which loveliness and order are untrammeled by the surging chaos of life in session, particularly life as it is lived with small children. In an issue of *Martha Stewart Kids,* I recently saw a photograph of a pair of old-fashioned white baby shoes with their laces replaced by two lengths of grosgrain ribbon. The result was impractical in the extreme, and very, very pretty. Which is a fair summation of many Stewart projects. In one of his few apt observations, Christopher Byron calls Stewart's "the face of the age." I would also say that the look of her magazines has become the look of women's magazines of the age: the photography, art direction, and layouts in many contemporary publications—including the recent magazine *Real Simple,* the redesigned *Child,* and all the craft and decorating features in *Rosie* (the revamped *McCall's*)—are clearly and deeply influenced by Stewart's.

Much of the Stewart enterprise, of course, involves a certain level of fantasy and wish fulfillment, having to do not only with the old dreams of wealth and elegance but also with the new one of time. That many of Stewart's projects are time-consuming is in fact part of their appeal. A risibly complicated recipe for sandwiches that are a "tempting snack for a 1-year-old," which ran in a recent issue of *Baby* (flower-shaped, their bright-yellow centers were created by mashing cooked egg yolk with butter, rolling the resulting paste into a tube, wrapping the tube in parchment paper, refrigerating it, and then slicing it into half-inch-thick rounds), is attractive not in spite of its ludicrous complexity but because of it—*imagine having enough time to do something like that!* The question of whether Stewart is indeed the "teacher" she has always professed to be or whether she is a kind of performance artist is an old one; I think that a significant number of women—including some of Stewart's staunchest defenders—appreciate what she does but never personally attempt it. *Martha Stewart Living* is filled with recipes for complicated restaurant-type food—caramelized fennel, warm goat cheese with wasabi-pea crust, and the like—but the ads are for Wendy's Mandarin Chicken Salad, and Hormel's pre-cooked roast beef, and Jell-O. One gets the sense that women enjoy reading about the best way to select a leg of lamb, but when it's dinnertime, they give an exhausted shrug and settle for the ease and convenience of Campbell's 2-Step Beefy Taco Joes, the recipe for which appears in a Campbell's ad in the magazine's recent hundredth issue.

The true engine of her success has much to do with a remark Stewart makes in Chapter One of her first book, the phenomenally successful *Entertaining* (1982).

Entertaining provides a good excuse to put things in order (polish silver, wash forgotten dishes, wax floors, paint a flaking windowsill) and, sometimes, to be more fanciful or dramatic with details than usual. It is the moment to indulge in a whole bank of flowering plants to line the hall, or to organize a collection of antique clothes on a conspicuous coat-rack, or to try the dining-room table at an odd angle.

The second sentence, of course, is the stuff of a thousand jokes and parodies—not just a vase of flowers but a "bank" of them; the elaborate clothing display that no normal householder has the resources or the willingness to pull off. But the first sentence is the one to keep your eye on, with its unremarkable but attractive suggestion of a house put in order: a windowsill painted, floors gleaming under a new coat of wax. In the hundredth issue of *Martha Stewart Living*, Stewart says that she recently came across a memo she wrote at the magazine's inception, one that she feels expresses her vision as clearly today as it did then. "Our reader," the memo states, "still wants to iron, to polish silver, to set a sensible table, to cook good food." She's right, of course, millions of women still "want" to do these things, although an astonishing number of them (myself included) don't do much ironing or polishing anymore, and are repeatedly frustrated by the nightly return to the kitchen. Our desire to reconnect with these tasks—which we fear are crucial to a well-run home—is commensurate with our uncertainty about what, exactly, they entail. Just as Disneyland presents a vision of Main Street, USA, that is very far afield from the real thing, so Stewart presents a vision of domesticity that involves as much make-believe as practicality, that is filled with allure and prettiness rather than the drudgery and exhaustion of which we are all so wary. She lectures not on the humdrum reality of sweeping the kitchen floor every night but on the correct way to store two dozen specialty brooms. Not on washing the dishes meal after relentless meal but on the advisability of transferring dishwashing liquid from its unattractive plastic bottle to a cut-glass cruet with a silver stopper. The Stewart fantasy encompasses the feminine interest in formal weddings and gracious entertaining, but principally—and more powerfully—it turns on a wistful and almost shameful attraction to ironing boards and newly washed crockery and good meals sensibly prepared. And on this wan longing, Stewart has built an empire.

.   .   .

None of which is to suggest that I have any fondness for Stewart, whom I find the most unpleasant person on television. She is stern and exacting about things for which I have only the fondest and gentlest associations: flower beds and freshly laundered clothes and home-cooked food. That millions of people are happy to be lectured on "family" and "tradition" by a woman whose own marriage imploded and whose relations with her only child have been famously stormy used to drive me wild with frustration; but lately I've softened on the old girl. She is the producer of a myth about American family life that is as old as Hollywood—and if we expected the men who make our best-loved "family movies" to comport themselves honorably as husbands and fathers, we'd be sunk at matinee time. Her faltering confessions about her private domestic bewilderments (she should have "read more psychology books," she has said about her early career as a mother; it was "a big mistake" to have had an only child) provide her most humanizing moments. And I find something touching and almost elegiac in her memories of the family that raised her, for all the ridicule they receive: "We all sat down to dinner at the same time, and we all got up at the same time and we were very close-knit."

Clearly, something powerful is at work here, some weaving together of the dream of a "close knit" family with rigid adherence to complicated baking and gardening protocols. There was a time when the measure of a home was found in the woman who ran it—who was there all day long, who understood that certain aspects of "hominess" had less to do with spit and polish than with continuity and permanence. As these old standards wane, a new one has emerged, and it is Stewart's. No human effort is so fundamentally simple and pleasurable that she cannot render it difficult and off-putting (we are to be grateful that thus far she has not produced a marriage manual). But almost any project she cooks up is less daunting than the one it is meant to replace: keeping a family together, under one roof, home.

Vanity Fair

U.S. Confidential

James Wolcott sneaks into America's subconscious and dissects our thoughts. Wolcott's conversational prose gets to the heart of current events (terrorism coverage, tabloid news and white-collar criminals) without sounding overwrought or hypercritical. He simply presents the facts, offers perspective and then leaves room to rethink the original idea.

James Wolcott

U.S. Confidential

The tabloid age began in the 50s with Generoso Pope's gore-spattered <u>National Enquirer</u>, and his obsession with Jackie O. touched off a celebrity hunt that would culminate in Princess Diana's death. But through mayhem and martyrdom, the scandal sheets have reflected America's gamy id, breaking news from the national gutter.

I n the March 26 issue of the *Globe*, the ugly sister of the Big Three gossip mags (the other two being the more presentable *National Enquirer* and the *Star*), Celine Dion, the Canadian singer with the intensely dramatic personal life, made a profound—yes, profound—observation. Asked why she chose to change her son's diapers rather than have nannies do the honors, Dion replied that it was the best way to monitor the child's health and well-being. "The poop says it all," she proclaimed. "When you want to know the truth, look to the poop."

Look to the poop—that's the guiding principle of the supermarket tabloid. Granted, the tabloids cater to a slob mentality that one associates with mullet haircuts and muumuus. Their editorial policy often combines the ethical standards of Watergate burglars with the prissy hypocrisy of horny preachers. They invade privacy, pay informants, misquote, exaggerate, distort, fabricate, set up honey traps (such as the gotcha stings that ambushed Frank Gifford and political adviser Dick Morris), fish through medical records, and punch up grainy spy photographs that make stars look bloated, ravaged, or demented (Whitney Houston with her mouth unhinged, as if in mid-primal scream). And yet, to experienced gold prospectors, buried somewhere in those clumps of bogus quotes and contrived hysteria (REGIS QUITS!; JENNIFER ANISTON' NUDE PHOTO SCANDAL— BRAD'S FURY OVER HIS TOPLESS WIFE!) is a truth about America's mayhem entertainment and political culture that you won't find reading the editorial pages or listening to public radio. Whether it's O. J. Simpson's Bruno Magli shoes or Monica Lewinsky's stained dress, Mike Tyson toking up or Mariah Carey melting down, the tabloids present a composite photorealist portrait of a country as wealthy, powerful, and fixated on spectacle as Rome in its imperial prime regularly and irrationally spazzing out. It isn't the whole picture of America, but neither is Robert Altman's or Don DeLillo's. What the tabloids give us is thermal imagery of the mass libido.

Cultural-declinists who bemoan the "dumbing down" of America often fail to observe how so much of what was once septic and

sub-moronic in the media slowly becomes house-trained, gentri-
fied. Angling and aspiring to a better class of sleaze—that, too, is
the American way. Supermarket tabloids, which once polluted
newsstands like inkblot squirts from warped psyches, their bla-
tantly doctored photos, genuine atrocity shots, gruesome headlines, and leering text leaving a grimy residue, have spiffed themselves up in recent years to appeal to a more sophisticated sucker.
They now dish a mildly deodorized dirt, the pastel colors of the
papers evoking an artificial bouquet of floral accents. Instead of
Dumpster-diving solely into celebrity garbage, as in the past, the
tabloids have taken to foraging into the affairs of Beltway players,
breaking page-one stories that the serious news outlets can't
ignore, no matter how much it gnaws at them. (I can see Bernard
Kalb of CNN's *Reliable Sources* staring at the ceiling now, ruing
another journalistic erosion.) It was *The National Enquirer* that
busted the news that the Reverend Jesse Jackson had been a bad
bunny with an employee of his Rainbow/PUSH Coalition, and that
went full throttle investigating the Clinton pardon giveaway. To
some, this campaign for respectability and political impact has
come at a cost. Like a seedy carnival converted into a theme park,
the tabs aren't as much tawdry fun as they used to be—their animal
spirits have become corporatized. "Today's *National Enquirer* is the
Las Vegas of journalism," wrote the cultural reporters Jane and
Michael Stern. "You know it was built on dirty money and bad
taste, but it is now clean and safe for the whole family."

·   ·   ·

What Bugsy Siegel was to the creation of Las Vegas, another
shady visionary was to the invention of the supermarket tabloid. In
1952 a 25-year-old former C.I.A. employee named Generoso Pope
Jr. purchased a sorry excuse for a Sunday paper called the *New York
Enquirer*. Pope's father was the kingpin owner of the nation's largest
Italian-language paper, *Il Progresso Italo-Americano*, whose pages

enthusiastically barked the praises of Fascist dictator Benito Mussolini. Pope Sr. was also pals with Mob boss Frank Costello, whom
he asked to be Gene junior's godfather. According to Bill Sloan's
valuable history of tabloids, *I Watched a Wild Hog Eat My Baby!*,
Costello also served as godfather in the Mario Puzo sense, backing
Pope's bid for the *New York Enquirer* and providing frequent infu-
sions of cash. As Sloan notes, the murky alliance of Mafia money
and vague C.I.A. connections has fed a lot of conspiracy theories
over the decades regarding the tabloid's possible role as a sewage
outlet for disinformation and influence peddling. (There's little
debate that historically the tabs have shown greater relish skinning
the hides of liberal Democrats—the Kennedys, the Clintons, Jesse
Jackson, Gary Condit—than they have conservative-Republican
corn dogs.)

Inspired by the ogling he once saw caused by a car crash, Pope
converted the *New York Enquirer* from an anemic also-ran into a
splattered intersection of sex, gore, and gossip where the readers
were the rubberneckers. Like Robert Harrison, who founded the
celebrity rap sheet *Confidential* the same year the *New York
Enquirer* was sold (and was the subject of one of Tom Wolfe's best
early profiles, "Purveyor of the Public Life"), Pope took Weegee's
snapshot sensationalism and Walter Winchell's rat-a-tat spiel so far
down-market you couldn't see sunlight. (Compared with the *film
noir* high contrasts of Weegee's best work, the pictures in the old
Enquirer looked like coffee grounds.) It was in the 50s and early
60s, as the *Enquirer* gradually went national (changing its name in
1954), that it earned the trashy notoriety it has since struggled to
outgrow. Headlines such as I CUT OUT HER HEART AND STOMPED ON
IT! and TEENAGER TWISTS OFF CORPSE'S HEAD . . . TO GET GOLD TEETH
hollered from covers of issues pocked with photos of tortured animals, starved children, mutilated corpses, and grotesque human
deformities. Published on the cheap, *The National Enquirer* made a
mint. Copycats sprang up from the slimepool, managing to be even
cruder than the original (evolution in reverse). Some of the shock-

horror stereotyping is now laughably quaint, such as the fixation on slam-bam lesbians (actual headlines: MATE SWAPPING AT A LEZZIE LOVE CAMP; LESBIAN GANG ATTACKS BEAUTY QUEEN) and the itchy excitement over interracial sex (WHITE MEN LIKE IT BLACK: A NEGRO BEAUTY TELLS WHY), but the absence of style, even the kind of punk style that Tom Wolfe christened the "*aesthetique du schlock*," gives the early tabloids a flophouse dinginess that no degree of pop-cult nostalgia can make sparkle. The morbid voyeurism they practiced was delivered as a jab to the eye, bypassing civilized defenses and aesthetic distance. The emaciated victims in some of these photos seem caged by the camera, pet food for the tender imaginations of serial killers and the director John Waters.

The *Enquirer* and its competition tried so hard to outdo one another in the hacked-limbs, boiled-baby buffet that newsstands looked as if they were hosting cannibal parties. Despite the boom in sales in the late 50s, the trend couldn't last, and not only because the gore was reaching flood levels. The landscape was shifting. The corner newsstand was becoming a disappearing relic of city life, like the trolley car and the Superman phone booth. Thousands of local newsstands and family-owned shops boarded up in the mid-60s as major chains branched into the neighborhoods. Generoso Pope Jr. had the sensibility of a snail, but he did possess the cunning agility to see around the next corner and radically adjust course. He understood that the only way tabloids could thrive as their urban habitat declined was by being sold in supermarkets, and that supermarkets wouldn't stock a tabloid as long as it printed spew. Choosy grocery shoppers tend to shun butchered corpses greeting them on the magazine rack at the checkout line. It was time to give the tabloid a scrub job. As Bill Sloan puts it, Pope Gene, as he was known, "issued the most sweeping 'papal decree' of his career: No more gore!" The *Enquirer* was going to become as blue-sky inspirational as *Reader's Digest*. Out with the sideshow geeks and mad slashers, in with Little Timmy valiantly battling leukemia and feisty grandmas fending off muggers with their purses.

The *Enquirer*'s staff was aghast. It was like asking an experienced team of grave robbers to take up gardening. Rival tabs and industry onlookers viewed this as a staggering miscalculation that would lose the old faithful, who would defect to the racier titles, and fail to lure a new flock. The naysayers felt vindicated as the *Enquirer*'s circulation took an immediate dive, its sales dropping by about 250,000 copies—one-quarter of its paid readership. This wasn't a circulation fall-off; it was a form of mass suicide. However, Pope proved the far-sighted victor: urban newsstands continued to vanish, the shakier tabloids folded, and the millions of dollars of profits that had padded the *Enquirer*'s bottom line during its first gallop of success bought it enough time, marketing talent, and leverage to implement a mass-distribution strategy that would make *The National Enquirer* as indispensable to every American's bathroom library as *TV Guide* and crossword puzzles.

Pope was also a content-visionary, the first idea merchant to seize and exploit the boundless love-hate fascination with Jackie Onassis. After a snippy tell-all cover story in which a former nanny disparaged Jackie's child-rearing practices sent newsstand sales through the roof, Pope unleashed packs of high-paid hyenas on the trail of her and her Greek tycoon husband, Aristotle. The *Enquirer*'s lust for the Jackie O. money shot escalated into a rolling orgy as every other tabloid and Eurotrash magazine joined the mad pursuit. The pesky motor-scooter paparazzi of Fellini's *La Dolce Vita* multiplied and mobilized into convoys of cutthroat opportunists bankrolled with bribe money to tickle the palms of nannies, maids, bellhops, busboys, window washers, hospital staff, valet-parking attendants, and other helpful snitches. Jackie couldn't sunbathe without a 1,000-mm. lens taking aim from the bushes. She was eventually able to settle into a life and career of relative normalcy in Manhattan, but others weren't so lucky. It was open season on the world-famous, and open season never closed. The ferocity and velocity of these scavenger hunts would converge and crescendo in a traffic tunnel in Paris on a summer night in 1997 as the furies unleashed by the Jackie phenomenon finally claimed a sacrificial bride, Princess Diana.

In 1974, Pope's *National Enquirer* faced the first heavyweight challenge to its supermarket hegemony: the arrival of the *National Star*, published by Rupert Murdoch, whose London scandal sheet *News of the World* had inspired Pope's ongoing makeover of the *Enquirer*. The publishers Pope had bested before were insignificant scroungers who thought small—this was different. Murdoch's entry into the field was like having Bigfoot show up on your welcome mat. His News Corporation had the resources, willpower, experience, and jugular instinct to trade thunder with an entrenched brand name, and could draw upon its roster of tabloid dailies to staff the *Star* with a ferret colony of Australian and British hacks. Murdoch introduced the *National Star* (its name later shortened to the *Star*) with an expensive ad campaign that was like the first round of a major arms race. The *Enquirer* counterattacked with a brilliant ad campaign whose catchy tag line was "Enquiring minds want to know."

Not since the tabloid heyday of the 30s, when Menckenesque cynics and ambulance chasers turned reporting into a contact sport, had there been such a scramble for red meat that would sell copy. (Lysa Moscowitz-Mateu, one of the co-authors of the tabloid memoir *Poison Pen*, describes sneaking into a hospital to interview the actor Ray Sharkey, who was dying of AIDS, and ratting out acquaintances from 12-step programs.) And because the *Enquirer* and the *Star* had more money to lavish than metropolitan dailies in the Depression, some of the competitive stunts turned into sick extravaganzas. When Princess Grace died in a car crash in 1982, a team of nine *Enquirer* reporters flew on the Concorde to Paris (other sources say it was a chartered Learjet), where they linked up with nine stringers summoned from different parts of Europe and Africa. Then they swarmed Monaco, where they locked up exclusive rights

With the morgue shots of Elvis and River Phoenix in their coffins, the snaps of a decrepit Dean Martin climbing out of a car, a puffy Liza Minnelli without makeup, and a strung-out Dana Plato (the child star from the sit-com *Diff'rent Strokes* who died of an overdose in 1999), the *National Enquirer* book hints at something that smacks the reader in the face each week in the papers themselves—the probing, mocking emphasis on decay, disease, and mortality. The tabloids traffic in vile bodies, delighting in spreads on fading stars who have dilapidated due to drugs, booze, anorexia, or binge eating. Weight fluctuations make the tabs giddier than Joan Rivers in a sea of fashion victims. The only thing they get off on more than celebrity skinnies (grab Calista Flockhart by the ankles and make a wish) are celebrity chubbies—they'll actually run helpful arrows pointing to the cottage-cheese deposits of cellulite. And God help any sex symbol or even modest cutie who's had the bad taste to age ungracefully—the tabloids take glee in juxtaposing photos of the smooth, radiant features of their youth with the geological ruins that they've become. No wonder some Hollywood stars spend their sunset years in seclusion, not wanting to have the disparity between then and now flung in their faces. Oh, the tabloids will do the occasional "Fifty and Fabulous!" feature to showcase former TV babes who are still filling their leotards just fine, but it's Anna Nicole Smith annexing the surrounding area with her hips or Elizabeth Taylor being carried out on a stretcher that really flips their switch.

Age has crept up on the tabloids themselves, eroding their grip on shoppers. Circulation has trended down since the delirious highs of the 70s and 80s. "In 1994, *The National Enquirer* had a circulation of more than 3.1 million readers," the *American Journalism Review* reported. "In 1999, it had 2.1 million readers. *Star*'s circulation dropped from nearly 2.8 million in 1994 to 1.8 million in 1999." It's no mystery what's been biting the tabs. Their success spawned a litter of clones that whittled away their base. Tabloid print begat tabloid TV with Murdoch's *A Current Affair* (1987), whose broadcast coups included bootleg videotapes of "rough sex" killer Robert Chambers tearing the head off a doll and Rob Lowe doing X-rated push-ups atop an under-age girl. *A Current Affair* was a synergistic fit, hyping the *Star*'s cover stories and providing face time for Murdoch's top gunslingers from the *Star* and *New York Post* (such as Steve Dunleavy and his fabulous pompadour). Tabloid TV exploded in syndication and before long the monkey-see-monkey-do networks were defacing the memory of Edward R. Murrow with magazine programs that covered tabloid subjects with an aerosol foam of sickly sweet sentimentality and phony solicitude. Interviewers adopted the tender tone of grief counselors as they tried to tweeze every sliver of sadness out of widows and orphans. A similar solemnity afflicted print. Once prim newsweeklies increasingly poached on tabloid turf by classing up the same subjects with a smart coating of pop sociology (O.J. as racial Rorschach test, Madonna as postmodern shape-shifter—that sort of thing).

· · ·

As social taboos lost their stigma, the tabloids lost their power to intimidate. It's difficult to ruin reputations when reputations have become so fungible. Giggly, hung-over actors and rock stars blurt out indiscretions to Howard Stern that celebrities in the past hired publicists to hush up. Since the 90s, public disgrace has become a good career move, the springboard to rehabilitation and acceptance. You check into Betty Ford, do penance on *Oprah* or *Primetime Live*, choke up at the right poignant moment, and wait for the ratings to come in to count the sympathy vote. Even going after closeted stars is no longer the trophy hunt it once was. Stars now "out" themselves and stage-manage the official announcement. (Rosie O'Donnell got two hours of prime time on ABC to state the obvious.)

A pivotal event for the tabloids was the death of Princess Diana in 1997. Whether or not the paparazzi racing after her and Dodi Fayed were culpable for the fatal crash, the reports of the photographers' frantic, boorish behavior before and after triggered a wave of revulsion from which the tabloids have never fully recovered. The history of the supermarket tabloid is demarcated by an ever more climactic series of car accidents: the one that inseminated Generoso Pope Jr.'s idea for the *New York Enquirer*; Princess Grace's, which turned tabloid publishers into spectacle producers; and Princess Diana's, which seemed to lay bare the destructive wish fulfillment lurking in the hysteria of celebrity worship all along—the malevolence under the exploitation. Her tragic crack-up was the last in an unholy trinity. As with Elvis and the Kennedys, the tabloids persist in resurrecting her image, unable to let go. That's one of the problems with tabloids today—too many ghosts.

•   •   •

While tabloidization has spider-veined throughout the media culture, the supermarket tabloids themselves have become a monopoly power supply. Since the death of Generoso Pope Jr. in 1988 and the sale of Murdoch's *Star* in 1990, a byzantine series of buyouts and consolidations have resulted in all of the major tabloids' being published by American Media Inc., owned by Evercore Capital Partners. All of the papers are based in Florida and overseen by David Pecker, John Kennedy Jr.'s former partner at *George* and a man given to grand Pooh-Bah posturing. A title queen, he's listed on the *National Enquirer* masthead as "Chairman, President & Chief Executive Officer," and no one else is allowed to speak on behalf of American Media under penalty of exile. The dirty tricks that once typified the tabloid scene are no longer tolerated, as competition has given way to play-nice cooperation. Blockbuster stories are now divvied up rather than fought over. "If a big

Hollywood story breaks," Pecker told the *American Journalism Review*, "then the *Enquirer* would do the investigative stories, the *Star* would cover the impact to the celebrity's career, and the *Globe* would really do the spicy parts of the story." This is why the *Globe* has long been the taste choice of discerning tabloid connoisseurs like myself.

Pecker's dream to make American Media the Condé Nast of Laundromat literature became more of an uphill climb after anthrax claimed the life of one employee and forced the evacuation of the editorial headquarters in Boca Raton last October, the first known post-9/11 act of bioterrorism. It's still unclear why its offices were targeted, although its proximity to a flight school used by the terrorists and the tabloids' attacks on Osama bin Laden led conspiracy buffs to suspect payback. But in the teeth of dwindling circulation and poor morale, Pecker and American Media aren't retrenching, like so many print titles—they're ramping up. The *Enquirer* and *Star* increased their pages in March, promising supersized portions of the celebrity poop: "more news, more information, more exclusive interviews, more entertaining photos—and more FUN!" Sounds exhausting, but if the tabloids continue to falter, no one can say they didn't go down fighting. For all their intrusions and idiocy, the tabs serve as useful, wild-card deflators of the sham, hypocrisy, and *All About Eve* intrigues of America's entertainment culture, which has become the world's entertainment culture. At their best, they read like rough drafts of a James Ellroy novel—contemporary history in the gamy raw. They may often be guilty of practicing "gutter journalism," but the last 50 years have taught us there's a lot going on in the gutter. It's where secrets swim.

Texas Monthly

FINALIST, PUBLIC INTEREST

Death Isn't Fair

Stories about capital punishment in Texas are not new—anything but. But in "Death Isn't Fair," senior editor Michael Hall dramatically and scientifically shows how the state's system is fundamentally flawed—set up to make sure that even the demonstrably innocent cannot escape death row. It's a disturbing yet dispassionate plea for justice.

Michael Hall

Death Isn't Fair

Cops who threaten torture. Prosecutors who go too far. Defense lawyers who sleep on the job. And an appellate court that rubber-stamps it all. Let's be tough on crime, but let's also see that justice is done. It's time to fix the capital punishment system in Texas.

As Ernest Willis tells it, he woke up in a house on fire. It was around four in the morning in Iraan, an oilfield town in West Texas, on June 11, 1986. He had fallen asleep on the living room couch fully clothed except for his eel-skin boots, which lay beside him on the floor. It was the smoke that awakened him, and he ran to the rear bedroom to get the woman who had passed out there a few hours earlier, but the flames and smoke pushed him back. He ran to the front bedroom, where his cousin Billy had gone with another woman a few hours before, but flames again forced him back. He ran through the house and out the door, yelling, "Fire!" and then around the side and rear, banging on windows. As Willis stood in the back yard, Billy came diving naked through a bedroom window. Betsy Beleu and Gail Allison, whom the Willis cousins had just met the day before, never made it out.

At first, the police thought the fire, which came after a night of drinking and pill popping at the house, whose owners had been arrested earlier in the day, was drug-related. Maybe someone had been freebasing or cooking heroin. Later they thought that maybe it was set by an ex-husband of one of the women or a Mexican drug dealer named Santana who Allison had said was after her husband. They found no evidence of arson—for example, no one smelled gasoline—but they were suspicious of Willis. He just wasn't acting right. He didn't seem to be coughing as much as his cousin, he didn't seem concerned about the dead women, and his clothes and hair weren't singed. He'd said (and Billy had confirmed) that he had run through a burning house, yet his feet weren't burned. He stood around smoking and acting distant as firefighters fought the blaze. Later, Willis failed a polygraph test, and the police developed a theory that marks on the floor were "pour patterns," suggesting that an accelerant like gasoline had been used. But they had no evidence to support their suspicions: no fingerprints, no bodily fluids, no flammable liquids in the house or on Willis' clothes or body, no witnesses, no motive.

Nevertheless, four months later Willis was arrested, charged with arson and murder, and taken into the ruthless grasp of the Texas death penalty process. Though the state had a weak circumstantial case, the cops and the prosecutors adamantly pressed ahead. Cliff Harris, then the chief of deputies and now the Pecos County sheriff, recalls, "When we took it to the grand jury, we didn't feel that we had the evidence to get him indicted." District attorney J. W. Johnson told the *Odessa American* after the trial that he had thought he had only a 10 percent chance of winning a conviction. Willis had no history of mental illness, but he was given high doses of anti-psychotic drugs, making him appear zombielike at trial—a look that prosecutors used to full advantage, vilifying him whenever they could. He was represented by well-meaning but inexperienced lawyers who made serious errors that doomed him to death row. Finally, he was abandoned by the appeals process that is supposed to be a safety net for questionable cases like his. Now he waits on death row while his final appeal before execution works its way through federal court.

It is the combination of unfairness and persistence that has put Texas under national and international scrutiny. We have been criticized for executing people who are mentally retarded, for executing people who were juveniles at the time of their offense, for trying to execute—before the federal courts stepped in to prevent it—people whose lawyers slumbered in court. These are the kinds of cases that get national attention, but there are many more that go unnoticed. Like Willis'. His case had it all: overzealous police officers and prosecutors, inadequate defense counsel, and an appellate court, the Texas Court of Criminal Appeals, that seemed almost desperate for him to die. The 57-year-old former roughneck is a poster child for what is wrong with the capital punishment system in Texas.

No one can know with absolute certainty that Willis is innocent. But innocence is not the issue here. Nor is capital punishment. Texas is a law-and-order society. We execute more criminals than any other state and most countries. Support for this policy is overwhelming; capital punishment is favored by 68 percent of Texans, compared with 59 percent of all Americans. Texas is going to have capital punishment as long as the United States Supreme Court allows it.

The issue is fairness. Our adversarial process of justice rests on an essential assumption: that the fight is fair. We should be tough on criminals, but when the moment comes that the last appeal is denied and the accused faces death by injection, we want to be able to look at ourselves in the mirror and believe that the State of Texas gave the condemned man a fair trial. The statistics say that this is not always the case. Since 1976, when the U.S. Supreme Court reinstated the death penalty after abolishing it four years earlier, 927 people have been sentenced to death in Texas. Of these, 285 have been executed (as of press time), and 188 have escaped the needle by having their sentences reduced, most of them for procedural violations. Some call these violations "technicalities," but they can be fundamental, such as the withholding of exculpatory evidence by prosecutors. Twelve of the 188 went free—their convictions reversed or overturned or their cases dismissed or sent back for a new trial that resulted in an acquittal. It's hard to know how many of them were actually innocent, as opposed to benefiting from some serious procedural violation by the state, but there are a handful who we can almost certainly say didn't do the crime but were sentenced to die.

And there are still men on death row who were put there unfairly. In addition to Ernest Willis, there is César Fierro, who confessed to murder after police officers in El Paso threatened him with the torture of his mother and stepfather by police officers in Juárez; the El Paso police have admitted this, but Fierro remains on death row. Michael Blair was convicted of murder on discredited scientific evidence; even though recent DNA tests appear to exonerate him, he too remains on death row. Wrongs like these will always occur. Our criminal justice system is a government system, and the government—in this case, the courts, the cops, the district attorneys—will inevitably make mistakes. The issue is whether we are willing to correct them, as other states have done. The Republican pro–death penalty governor of Illinois, George Ryan, instituted a moratorium on executions in 2001 until the state could work out the bugs in its death penalty process, which Ryan called "fraught with errors." In May 2002 the governor of Maryland, also a death penalty proponent, followed suit. The Texas Legislature voted down a proposed moratorium in 2001, though lawmakers couldn't ignore the criticism of the death penalty system. So they made three changes: a new DNA testing program, a revised method for providing court-appointed defense lawyers, and a prohibition on executing the mentally retarded—the latter a bill that was vetoed by Governor Rick Perry.

We live in an era of little sympathy for criminals, especially violent ones. Gone are the old notions that "there but for the grace of God go I" and "it is better for one hundred guilty people to go free than for one innocent person to be executed." Today, you will find death penalty proponents who argue the opposite— that it is unfortunate if occasionally a possibly innocent person is put to death, but the public interest requires that those found guilty of capital murder be executed. The assumption is that only the bad guys get caught up in the system, and that is generally true. But every once in a while, it's the hapless ones, the losers, who go to sleep on a strange couch and are unlucky enough to wake up in a house that's on fire.

Death by Lottery

Ernest Willis was a sad sack, a drunk, a onetime oil-field hand from New Mexico who was cursed with a bad back, caused by a 1970 accident, that often prevented him from working. By age forty he had had six wives, three DWIs, and four back surgeries, the most recent one a month before the fire, and he had developed a fondness for pain pills. In addition to the DWIs, he had been in trouble with the law on a couple of occasions—once, in his twenties, when he was arrested for cruising by the drive-through window of a fast-food restaurant naked and drunk, and another time, a couple of years ago, for making obscene phone calls. But he had no violent criminal past, not even a juvenile record. Lately he hadn't been able to work and was living on food stamps, so he had moved to Odessa to live with Billy, a guy who sometimes made and sold bathtub speed. They had come to Iraan hoping their luck would change.

Instead, Willis' got worse: He lost the capital punishment lottery. Only about one in a hundred killings ends up as a death penalty case. Who decides? The local district attorney. What does he base his decision on? There's no simple answer. Prosecutors have enormous discretion and are accountable to no one, except to the voters who elect them. You might think that politics would cause all DAs to be death penalty advocates, but this is not borne out by the facts. Since 1976, only 116 of Texas' 254 counties (fewer than half) have sentenced a person to death; more than half the counties (138) have *never* sent anyone to death row. In theory, the odds were with Willis in Pecos County; before his case, according to prosecutor Johnson, authorities had not sought the death penalty since the days of Judge Roy Bean, when the rope was used, not the needle. So what made Johnson decide that the Willis case should be treated as capital murder? He insists he didn't. "I presented the evidence and witnesses to the grand jury," Johnson says, "and they are the ones who made a determination it was capital murder."

Most district attorneys would admit to taking a more active role. Retired Harris County DA Johnny Holmes, who won more death sentences than any DA in Texas history, always made the call on whether to seek the death penalty. "The most important issue to me," he says, "is whether a reasonable cross section of the public in this jurisdiction, sitting as a jury, would vote to impose death. There are many factors that go into that decision." Interviews with prose-cutors and defense attorneys produced a long list of such factors: politics, the heinousness of the crime, the chance of winning, how good the defense attorney is, the willingness of a defendant to accept a plea bargain for a lengthy sentence, and how much publicity the case is getting. "I think the press has a lot to do with it," says Robert Icenhauer-Ramirez, an Austin criminal defense attorney for 23 years. "If the case is high-profile and the DA figures he will have an easy time making the case, he'll go for the death penalty. I've had horrendous cases with horrible facts that got no publicity. The DA will treat them as non–death penalty cases."

One of the biggest factors is money. Many counties have never sent anyone to death row because they can't afford to. It costs anywhere from $50,000 to $100,000 to plan and prosecute a cap-ital murder case. Some counties don't have their own medical examiners and have to hire one to do an autopsy. Some don't have a crime lab and have to pay another county to test forensic evidence. Some counties have only one judge; since a trial can take two to three months, they have to pay a visiting judge to take care of all the other cases backed up behind the murder trial. Judges and DAs are beholden to county commissioners, who control the purse strings. Norman Lanford was a former district judge in Harris County as well as a visiting judge in vari-ous other counties. Out there, he says, "The commissioners would tell judges, 'Don't ever do a capital murder case. We can get a road grader for that kind of money.'"

In other words, if you *have* to kill someone during a robbery, do it in Waller County, which has never prosecuted anyone for capital murder. Don't, however, do it next door, in Harris County. Like most urban counties, it has a prosecution machine. The DA has a budget of $37 million and 233 attorneys (54 of whom do nothing but try the eight to fourteen capital murder cases a year and another 10 who just work on appeals), access to the Houston Police Department and Department of Public

Safety crime labs, as well as secretaries, psychologists, forensics experts, investigators, and the budget to hire expert witnesses. The same is true in Dallas, San Antonio, El Paso, and Austin. Prosecutors there are specialists at trying capital murder cases.

At his trial, Willis appeared lost in a fog. His court-appointed lawyer, Steven Woolard, gave him a legal pad and a pencil. "He said to doodle, do anything—just look busy," Willis says now. "He asked me if it was the pain medication causing me to act like this. I thought I was acting normal. I didn't know." In fact, while Willis sat in the Pecos County jail awaiting trial, someone—no one remembers who, but it had to be someone connected with the state's side of the case—ordered that he be given high daily doses of Haldol and Perphenazine, two anti-psychotic medicines, along with the pain pills for his back. Haldol especially is given to people with severe mental illness, and according to a doctor who testified in a 1996 hearing to reopen the Willis case, the standard dosage for a person who is "barking at the moon, a danger to other people and himself," is fifteen milligrams a day. Willis was given forty milligrams a day, on top of an undetermined daily dosage of Perphenazine.

Nor can anyone remember why the medication was ordered. Back in June, shortly after the fire, Willis had told deputy sheriff Larry Jackson about sometimes feeling tense and nervous, but he had no history of mental illness or psychosis, and the jailers all said he had been a model prisoner. "Ernest was never any problem," says then-deputy Cliff Harris. "He was always quiet." Willis did what he was told and took the pills.

Prosecutors Johnson and Albert Valadez both say they were never aware of the doping and that Willis didn't appear to be acting strangely. Yet, the trial transcript reveals that Johnson repeatedly used the defendant's doped-up demeanor against him, calling him an "animal" and a "satanic demon" and referring to "this deadpan, insensitive, expressionless face" and "cold fish eyes"— symptoms that, according to psychologists testifying at a later hearing, are typical side effects of anti-psychotic drugs.

The jury didn't believe Willis' story that he had woken up in a burning house or his attorneys' theory that the fire was accidental. The prosecution's theory of cold-blooded arson was much easier to believe. All the jurors had to do was look at the remorseless monster sitting there blank-faced, with "these weird eyes," as Johnson said, that would "pop open like in some science-fiction horror film." The verdict was guilty; the jury took only an hour to give him death. Later, juror Roy Urias said he was convinced of Willis' guilt "by his failure to deny the charges against him. Specifically, when the prosecutor referred to Mr. Willis as 'vicious,' with his 'fish eyes,' I expected Mr. Willis to deny the accusations. I also expected a denial when the prosecutor presented the photographs of the charred bodies of the victims. Instead, Ernest Willis remained seated, completely expressionless." Of course, he was in no condition to do much else.

The prosecution also failed to turn over a psychological report about Willis that might have saved him from death row during the punishment phase of the trial. To give the death penalty, the jury must find that the defendant is a future danger to society and that there are no mitigating reasons to spare him from capital punishment. Court records indicate that Johnson had hired a San Angelo psychologist named Jarvis Wright to test Willis, but Wright wrote that he had found nothing in the defendant's personality to indicate such danger. The prosecution didn't reveal the report to the defense, as the U.S. Supreme Court requires.

Prosecutors, like all lawyers, are officers of the court, which means that their first duty is not to win but to see that justice is done. Yet this responsibility is all too often overlooked in the heat of battle. It's a war out there, and the state wants to win. In fact, prosecutors have to win. They are under far more pressure than defense lawyers, who, most of the time, are trying to get the least possible sentence for clients who are almost certainly guilty. The DA is a politician, an elected servant of the people, and he constantly needs to prove that he is winning the war against crime. And in war, anything goes. Prosecutors and police officers sometimes lie, evade the truth, and suppress evidence. They don't do it because they are evil; rather, they do it because they are certain the defendant is evil. So in their relentless pursuit of a conviction, they sometimes fail to disclose information that would help him, as they are required to do. They don't disclose the names of other confessors or witnesses who saw something that would help the defendant. They don't tell the whole truth. It's not in their interest. The attitude of defense lawyers toward prosecutors is summed up by veteran Houston defender Randy Schaffer: "You will always have prosecutors and police cutting corners, whether it's a death penalty case or a traffic stop. It's indigenous to the beast—what they do. And the more severe the case, the more likely they'll do it."

Two aforementioned cases, those of César Fierro and Michael Blair, illustrate the lengths to which the state and its agents will go to get a conviction. In 1980 Fierro was convicted of killing a cab driver the year before in El Paso. The evidence against him was the testimony of a sixteen-year-old boy who said he was with Fierro at the time of the killing, and Fierro's confession. At his trial, Fierro, a Mexican citizen who lived in both El Paso and Juárez, said that detectives had coerced his confession by threatening to have Mexican police officers torture his mother and stepfather, who lived in Juárez, with the dreaded *chicharra*, an electric generator that the Juárez police were infamous for using, applying it to an interviewee's genitals, occasionally after wetting him or her down. At trial the lead detective, Al Medrano, denied colluding with the Mexican police, and the jury convicted Fierro and sent him to death row. Fifteen years later appellate attorneys for Fierro found in his file a report written by Medrano, in which he told how he had indeed contacted the Juárez police. Armed with rifles, they raided Fierro's parents' home in the middle of the night and took them to the city's police station. Later that day Fierro, in El Paso police custody, was told where his parents were. Medrano handed Fierro the phone, and he spoke briefly with Jorge Palacios, the Mexican police chief. He hung up and immediately signed a confession.

The Fierro case involves conduct the police obviously are not supposed to engage in, but equally troublesome is something the state is *allowed* to do: rely on forensic evidence that—TV shows such as *CSI* notwithstanding—often sounds more convincing than it really is, from bite marks to blood spatters. Improved scientific methods have cast doubts on the reliability of the traditional tests used to support this kind of evidence. One of the most unreliable techniques is hair-comparison analysis. In 1996 the Justice Department did a study of 240 crime labs and found hair-comparison error rates ranging from 28 percent to 68 percent. The testimony is outlawed in Michigan and Illinois, but unfortunately for Michael Blair, it is admissible in Texas.

Blair, a convicted child molester, was arrested for one of the highest-profile crimes in Texas: the 1993 murder of seven-year-old Ashley Estell, who was kidnapped from a crowded Plano soccer tournament. The police had no fingerprints, body fluids, or eyewitnesses who could place Blair and the girl together that morning. After several days, however, Charles Linch, the trace-evidence analyst from the Southwestern Institute of Forensic Sciences, concluded that hairs found in Blair's car "appeared similar" to Ashley's, and hairs in a clump found at another park two miles from the abduction site looked like they belonged to the suspect and the victim. This evidence gave the police probable cause to arrest Blair.

At his trial, the police produced three witnesses who had come forward after Blair's arrest, when his photo was blanketing the local news, and a fourth who said she'd seen a car that bore a tenuous resemblance to Blair's Ford EXP near the area where the body was recovered. The only substantive evidence came from Linch, who said that three hairs found in Blair's car had the same "microscopic characteristics" as Ashley's. Two tiny black hairs, found on and near the body, were too small for comparison, but Linch said they had Mongolian characteristics, which could apply to Blair, who is half Thai. And, Linch said, a fiber found on Ashley's body was similar to fibers from a stuffed rabbit found in Blair's car. In his closing arguments, Collin County prosecutor J. Bryan Clayton said of the hairs, "You can call it a link, you can call it association, you can call it a match, or any other darned thing they want to call it." The jurors did, and Blair was convicted and sent to death row.

In 1998, however, the case against Blair began to unravel when a series of newer mitochondrial DNA tests revealed that *none* of the hairs belonged to either him or Ashley. The latest of the four test results, on the clump of hair, came only two months ago. And, defense lawyers say, the fiber was from a stuffed rabbit bought at Target that was indistinguishable from any one of half a million stuffed animals. It's clear now: Blair was convicted and sentenced to death on junk science.

Dubious forensic evidence also played a central role in the Ernest Willis case. Arson investigation is an inchoate "science"; in 1987, when Willis was convicted because prosecutors said pour patterns indicated he had dumped an accelerant throughout the house, it was even more so. The first national standards for fire investigation weren't even published until 1992. "For many years fire experts looked at things like spalled concrete or crazed glass and speculated, dreamed up theories," says Arizona State University law professor and noted authority on forensic evidence Michael Saks. "Finally, after sending umpteen people to prison, they did empirical testing. They set buildings on fire and went in and looked for spalled concrete and crazed glass. It turns out those things are unrelated to whether a fire was arson or not. It was all guesswork and imagination."

Perhaps the most unreliable experts are those who, during the punishment phase, predict that a defendant will be a continuing danger to society. Such evidence is necessary before a jury can impose the death penalty. Though the American Psychiatric Association has said such predictions are wrong two thirds of the time, Texas prosecutors have relied on a handful of psychiatrists who can be counted upon to answer, emphatically and almost every time, yes, this person is a future danger, thus dooming him or her to die. The most notorious was James Grigson, of Dallas, a psychiatrist who was known in legal circles as Dr. Death because of the scores of Texas capital murder cases in which he testified, using phrases like "absolutely certain" or "one hundred percent sure." Many times he never even interviewed the person he testified about.

Defense attorneys must object to such flimsy evidence to preserve the right to object to it on appeal, but they know they will be overruled. In the view of many defense attorneys, judges are not neutral referees, assuring that a trial is fair, but adversaries, especially in capital punishment cases. Former judge Lanford says, "Generally, the judge is the second or third prosecutor in the courtroom. The state is going to win on most things." Many district judges are former prosecutors; some even worked for the prosecutor's office that is trying the case before them. In Harris County 20 of the 22 judges in local felony courts previously worked in the DA's office. Like prosecutors, judges are elected; they will be tough on crime, especially in capital punishment cases. Most defendants have only one chance for a fair trial: a court-appointed lawyer who knows how to defend a death penalty case. In Texas, that chance isn't very good.

The Defense Rests—Literally

I put my heart and soul into the defense of Ernest Willis," says Steven Woolard, the lead counsel in the case. "But if I were a judge today, there's no way I would have appointed me then." Not many attorneys were available in Pecos County in 1986, Woolard recalls, and he and another lawyer were named by Judge

Brock Jones to defend Willis. Woolard was zealous but inexperienced: At the time, he had been practicing law for less than four years. He had never tried a death penalty case.

Willis' attorneys never tried to poke holes in the prosecution's unlikely theory that a pillhead with "surgical failed back syndrome" (Willis, vomiting from pain, had seen two doctors the day of the fire), who had drunk a six-pack of Coors, could have gone out—would have *wanted* to go out—at three-thirty in the morning to siphon ten to fifteen gallons of gas into a can, douse the house from one end to the other, set the place on fire, and then get rid of the can without waking anyone up or getting even a drop on his hands, feet, or clothes. They rarely objected when Johnson called Willis an "animal." Worst of all, during the punishment phase of the trial, they asked only two perfunctory questions of the state's two witnesses, who claimed Willis had a "bad" reputation but gave no details, and they rested their case without calling character witnesses who might have persuaded the jury to spare Willis' life. Many years later Pecos County deputy sheriff Larry Jackson (now deceased) told the *Dallas Morning News*, "If he'd had sufficient counsel, he wouldn't be on death row. . . . They messed this old boy around for years."

Kevin McNally, a Kentucky attorney who analyzes cases for evidence of bad lawyering, testified in a hearing to determine whether Willis should get a new trial that the punishment-phase lawyering was "in the bottom one half of one percent" of the two hundred cases he had looked at. That would make it the very worst. He referred to witnesses Woolard knew about but didn't call: family members and friends, some of whom came forth at this hearing and testified that Willis was a loving father, a good boss, and a decent man. Willis' brother Alton related a story about a family gathering at Lake Stamford, when Willis had seen a boy accidentally back a truck into the lake. The man J. W. Johnson had called a "satanic demon" had pulled off his boots, dived into the water, broken a window, pulled the kid out, and then refused money for saving his life. "Most capital defense lawyers would trade their right arm" for this kind of mitigating evidence, McNally said. Today Woolard says he didn't call the character witnesses because of concerns about their credibility: "Their presentation, manner of dress, cultural affectations." In other words, they were rednecks. In Pecos County, of all places.

Once again, the Willis case shows the extent to which the death penalty system is like a lottery. A few counties, such as Dallas, have public-defender systems with experienced attorneys. In most counties, however, the trial judge appoints attorneys for indigent defendants from a list of available volunteers. Some are experienced lawyers, but many more are inexperienced (sometimes only a couple of years out of law school); they are easily confused by the arcane rules of capital punishment cases and cowed by the prosecutorial juggernauts. Court-appointed attorneys are frequently solo practitioners with little support staff to investigate, find witnesses, and keep track of motions to file. They object when they shouldn't and don't object when they should. As in the Willis case, they don't question the obvious or do the basic work to save their clients' lives; as in Michael Blair's case, they don't hammer away at flimsy evidence. They cut corners. Sometimes they just give up. A *Dallas Morning News* investigation in 2000 found that one quarter of all death row inmates had been defended by attorneys who had been or were later disciplined by the State Bar of Texas for everything from lying to neglecting their cases.

One of the reasons for the bad lawyering is bad pay, which chases away good people and makes a good defense impossible. Court-appointed defense attorneys often lack the budgets to hire their own experts to attack those of the prosecution. In Willis' case, Woolard hired a fledgling arson investigator, whose credentials Johnson mocked mercilessly. "I felt inhibited somewhat," says Woolard now about his choice. "I had to justify expenses to [trial judge Brock] Jones." Unlike prosecutors, judges, police officers, or jailers, court-appointed attorneys are the only ones in the criminal justice system who work for less than the going rate for their profession. County officials can think of a lot of ways they would rather spend tax dollars than defending accused murderers. So appointed lawyers have to battle to get paid. "You take a voucher to the judge after the case," says an Austin defense attorney. "Let's say you worked three hundred and fifty hours. The judge would cut it in half." Such penny-pinching stifles the lawyers' incentive to investigate and put on a vigorous defense. In the case of Federico Macias, the federal court that overturned a guilty verdict because of ineffective assistance of counsel noted in its opinion that the trial attorney had been paid roughly $11.84 an hour. "Unfortunately," the court said of defense counsel, who had failed to interview the witnesses who would one day exonerate the defendant, "the justice system got only what it paid for."

Proof of the low quality of court-appointed lawyers in Texas came in a state bar committee study of 2,983 Texas defense attorneys, prosecutors, and judges that appeared in 2000. Called "Muting Gideon's Trumpet" (the reference is to a book about the case of *Gideon* v. *Wainwright*, in which the U.S. Supreme Court said that every indigent criminal defendant had to be provided with a lawyer), the study revealed a system in which judges appointed attorneys who were friends or campaign contributors, especially if they were good at speeding the case through the court. The study confirmed that many state trial judges operated a patronage system: Attorneys who were beholden to judges for work turned around and made campaign contributions to those same judges. Former judge Lanford remembers a colleague, George Walker, who gave death penalty cases to a friend, the late Joe Cannon. "Joe was a nice man, but he was incompetent to handle capital cases," Lanford recalls. "He was George's buddy. He got the cases because he moved them. There was pressure— keep costs down, keep things moving."

Such a system inevitably wound up embracing incompetence.

Cannon was one of the infamous sleeping lawyers; he bragged about hurrying through trials. In the murder trial of Calvin Burdine, Cannon slept during the questioning of witnesses, and though he knew about mitigating character witnesses, he failed to bring them into court to testify. Burdine was convicted and got the death penalty. Then there was Ronald Mock, who kept getting appointments (and a steady paycheck) despite sloppy lawyering that caused him to be disciplined five times by the state bar. Mock defended more than a dozen men who wound up on death row.

To the Legislature's credit, the patronage system that bumbled so many men to death row has been improved by the passage, in 2001, of the Fair Defense Act. Though it is still up to individual counties how they appoint attorneys to defend the poor, the act says that judges have to adopt stricter procedures for appointing attorneys, specify their qualifications, and pay a "reasonable fee." Counties also have to set standards (at least five years of criminal-law experience) and require continuing-education seminars in defending criminals. For the first time, the state has provided money to supplement what counties pay for indigent defense—a total of $19.7 million for 2002 and 2003. That is approximately 10 percent of the total cost; most states pay half. The law has been in force only since January 2002, so it's difficult to gauge its effectiveness. Jim Bethke, the director of the Task Force on Indigent Defense, says, "Anecdotally, things have improved." But some defense lawyers remain unimpressed. "Texas has developed a culture of bad legal representation," says veteran Austin attorney Rob Owen, who has defended more than fifty death penalty cases. "Just paying more money per hour provides more money for poor representation."

Ernest Willis would be dead today if not for his appellate lawyers. Back in 1989, Willis had lost his direct appeal before the Court of Criminal Appeals (CCA), the one that automatically follows a guilty verdict. After that came his writ of habeas corpus, an appeal that concerns new evidence and violations of constitutional rights (also filed before the CCA). Attorneys with the Texas Resource Center, a now-defunct federally funded organization that represented poor death row inmates, and then Latham and Watkins, a large international firm with offices in New York, put on the kind of vigorous defense for Willis that court-appointed lawyers in Texas could not afford. For instance, Latham and Watkins, working pro bono for Willis since 1995, has used five lawyers, a private investigator, a professor of psychiatry, a forensic psychologist, a neuropharmacologist, and an arson investigator. Willis' appellate attorneys looked at the county jail logs and discovered the daily dopings. They tracked down the psychological evaluation that said Willis was not a future danger. And they looked into the strange story of David Long, a convicted ax-murderer who used to make and sell bathtub speed with Billy Willis. The born-again Long had met Ernest Willis in the dayroom at the Ellis prison unit in 1990. Eventually he confessed to the prison psychiatrist that he had set fire to the Iraan house. The psychiatrist believed Long and set up a videotaped confession in 1990, during which Long confessed in detail, saying he had driven from Round Rock to Iraan that night, drinking and shooting speed. When he got to the house, he started the fire with a mix of Wild Turkey and Everclear, his favorite drink. Long had motive ("I hated the dude," he said about Billy, toward whom he had various druggy grudges) and a history of violence: In 1983, after being fired by his boss, Long had used whiskey to set the man's trailer on fire. "I killed him because I hated the son of a bitch," he said in a 1986 confession.

In 1995 lead attorney Jim Blank, of Latham and Watkins, went to the CCA with the new evidence. The court ruled in 1996 that trial judge Jones should hold hearings to determine whether Willis was entitled to a new trial. The wheels of justice ground slowly; hearings were held intermittently during the next three years. Blank brought forward the previously ignored witnesses, who testified to Willis' good character. He found an arson expert who said the state's pour-pattern theory was all wrong—the patterns on the floor could have been caused by any number of things. The expert had also done an experiment to see if Long's Wild Turkey and Everclear cocktail was capable of setting fire to carpet and wood; it was. Blank got Woolard to admit on the stand to several serious trial errors, including failing to offer any character witnesses. ("I loaded my guns for the guilt-innocence question and felt so very strongly about that," Woolard offered.)

Jones was convinced: Willis had not gotten a fair trial. In June 2000, in a 33-page opinion, he ordered a new trial based on the withheld psychological profile, the mind-numbing drugs, and the ineffective assistance of counsel. All Ernest Willis needed was for the CCA to uphold Jones's order, and he would get the shot at freedom he deserved.

Disorder in the Court

The court of criminal appeals is no ordinary court. The idea of a separate court of last resort for criminal cases is one that has been embraced by only one other state, Oklahoma. The court has always had its critics. Its isolation in a single area of the law caused it long ago to develop a fondness for legal hypertechnicalities at the expense of justice. It used to have a reputation for being pro-defendant, overturning cases for minor procedural defects. In the forties the CCA famously reversed the conviction of a murderer who had stomped an old woman to death because the indictment didn't say he stomped her with his feet. Through the eighties, the court kept its reputation for overturning convictions and ordering new trials, reversing up to a third of its cases. The CCA was all Democratic until 1992, when the first Republican judge was elected. Outrage in 1993 over a brutal Houston murder—in which the CCA ordered a new trial because the cards containing the names of potential jurors were shuffled an extra time—led to the elections in 1994 of Republicans Sharon Keller and Steve Mansfield, and by 1999 all nine judges were Republicans. As with elections for DAs, elections for the CCA have increasingly emphasized how tough the candidate would be on criminals. Keller, now the presiding judge, has campaigned on the idea that failure to give the death penalty is a human rights violation. (She declined to be interviewed for this story.) In 2001 Judge Tom Price, the closest thing to a voice of moderation on the court, received an official reprimand from the Commission on Judicial Conduct for his 2000 campaign literature, which included the statement: "I have no feelings for the criminal. All my feelings lie with the victim."

Indeed. Since 1994, the CCA has reversed only thirteen death penalty convictions on direct appeal, about 3 percent of the total cases—the lowest death penalty reversal rate of any state court of last resort in the country. The court is even tougher on habeas corpus appeals; since 1995, the CCA has granted new trials on death penalty writs only *twice*—out of more than five hundred writs coming its way. "From the seventies through the nineties, I got reversals on sixty percent of my habeas writs," remembers Houston defense attorney Randy Schaffer. "Since the mid-nineties, I doubt if I get ten percent reversed. Did I get real stupid? I don't think so. The judges stopped looking at the damn cases."

When Judge Jones made his recommendation for a new trial for Willis, he was going out on a limb. Trial judges, who must face the local electorate, don't arbitrarily recommend new trials for death row inmates. For this reason, appellate courts usually defer to trial judges, who are closest to the action. Not the CCA. "If the trial judge recommends that relief be refused, the court will follow the trial judge," says Charlie Baird, a Democrat who served on the CCA until the end of 1998. "But if the trial judge recommends relief be granted, the court will figure out some way to get around that recommendation."

In the change from Democrat to Republican, the court changed its philosophy but not its character: It is still hypertechnical. The most notorious example of this did not involve the death penalty. Roy Criner had received a 99-year sentence for the rape of a woman who was also murdered. In 1998 a DNA test proved that the sperm in the victim wasn't Criner's, and the trial judge ordered a new trial. In a 5–3 opinion written by Judge Keller, the CCA denied Criner a hearing on the new evidence. "The DNA evidence . . . does not establish his innocence," she wrote, noting that Criner could have used a condom or not ejaculated. Former judge Baird, who dissented, is still outraged: "The problem with Keller's position was that those arguments were never made by the state. Keller left any semblance of being an impartial judge behind and became a partisan advocate for the prosecution. And it begs the question, Why would anyone want an innocent man to stay in prison?" Judge Price later wrote that the decision had made the CCA a "national laughingstock." Keller didn't help matters when she gave an interview in 2000 for *Frontline*, discounting the DNA evidence and calling the victim "promiscuous." About Criner's little innocence problem, she said, "He has to establish unquestionably that he is innocent, and he hasn't done it." When asked how a person could prove he was innocent, she replied, "I don't know. I don't know." She's right: It's almost impossible under the court's standard, which is "clear and convincing evidence." If exonerating DNA isn't "clear and convincing," what is? (Criner was eventually freed after the Board of Pardons and Paroles recommended that he be pardoned.)

The CCA has also made it almost impossible to show that the state violated a defendant's right to a fair trial. The court typically describes mistakes or misconduct during a trial as "harmless error." In other words, the defendant would have been convicted anyway. Perhaps the most infamous examples of harmless error occurred in the sleeping-lawyer cases, one of which involved Calvin Burdine. Even though the trial court said he should get a new trial, the CCA overruled. (A federal judge rejected the CCA's opinion in June, and he will get a new trial next year.)

The most troublesome use of harmless error was in 1996, when the CCA ruled on the capital murder conviction of César Fierro, the suspect who had confessed after being warned that his parents would be tortured in Mexico. In a July 1994 affidavit, the DA at the time of the trial, Gary Weiser, said, "I believe that Medrano and Palacios colluded to coerce Fierro's confession." Had he known, he says, he would have recommended that the judge suppress the confession and dismiss the case unless he could have corroborated other testimony. The trial judge found a "strong likelihood" that the confession had been coerced and said Fierro should get a new trial. Alas, the CCA overruled a judge once again. Yes, Keller wrote, the police had lied about coercing a confession, but the trial court would have found Fierro guilty anyway. "[W]e conclude that applicant's due process rights were violated," she wrote. "But, because we conclude that the error was harmless, we deny relief." Though he believes Fierro committed the murder, Weiser thinks he deserves to go free. "I was a prosecutor for ten years, and I put a lot of people to death," he says. "I never lost one. But to execute a man on illegally produced evidence—it's *wrong*. It's not justice. *Nobody* should be convicted on illegally obtained evidence." Once again: If violating a citizen's right to due process and threatening torture isn't harmful, what is?

One of the more baffling things about the CCA is its failure to respect the fact that competent counsel is an essential part of the constitutional guarantee of a fair trial. The CCA's position is that any licensed attorney meets the competency standard. For example, in 1997 a death row inmate named Ricky Kerr wrote the CCA, saying he was worried that his neophyte court-appointed appellate lawyer was overlooking his constitutional claims and that he wanted a new attorney. The court refused. The attorney subsequently botched the appeal, which the CCA dismissed. A federal judge stayed Kerr's execution and called the CCA's actions in the case "a cynical and reprehensible attempt to expedite petitioner's execution at the expense of all semblance of fairness and integrity."

The CCA's critics say that the court is result-oriented, ruling on ideology. Asked to explain the court's sometimes bizarre opinions, former judge Baird says, "They are beyond comprehension. They cannot be understood because they are the product of judges who are intellectually dishonest. They first determine the result they want, and then they distort the law to fit that result." But a former colleague of Baird's, Mike McCormick, who served on the court from 1980 to 2000, thinks critics have an agenda of their own: "Calling a court result-oriented, well, it depends whether you're on the winning side or the losing side."

The real question is whether the role of the court should be restricted to construing the law or broadened to include dispensing justice. McCormick believes the CCA's job is to interpret the law: "One individual judge's concept of justice is not what the court is all about." And what about cases like Ernest Willis', where it looks like an injustice is being done, where it looks like the guy really might not have committed the crime? "If you have evidence of actual innocence," says McCormick, "the vehicle to get it in the system is the governor and clemency."

The Board of Pardons and Paroles is often the last chance for the condemned. It isn't much of a chance, though, and it isn't much of a board either. The eighteen members, all appointed by the governor, have never gotten together to vote in the past quarter of a century. They've never even conducted a hearing. They individually consider the cases and then vote, by fax and e-mail. "We vote on our best gut feeling," says member Paul Kiel, "with all the information we have." A pardon can be granted by the governor only on the board's recommendation. But the board has granted only two death penalty pardons since 1990, and both were requested by prosecutors. In short, the board has neither the desire nor the authority to deliberate issues of innocence. Board chairman Gerald Garrett says that innocence should be up to the judicial system. "I don't think we should casually set aside rulings of the courts," he says. It's a catch-22 worthy of the whole Texas death penalty system: No one cares about the possibility of innocence.

And so, six months after Judge Jones ordered a new trial for Ernest Willis, the Court of Criminal Appeals, in a six-page reply, denied all relief. The state's court of last resort found that Willis hadn't proved that he took the anti-psychotic drugs involuntarily; that perhaps the state had an "essential state policy" in giving them that Judge Jones never asked about; that Woolard used "reasonable professional judgment" in not calling character witnesses; and that the suppressed psychological report regarding future dangerousness was "inconclusive," an interpretation the psychologist, Jarvis Wright, disagreed with, later saying in an affidavit that he saw "no evidence that Mr. Willis would pose a future danger." Doping, cheating, bumbling—if these don't trouble the Court of Criminal Appeals, what will?

What Now?

Jim Blank has filed a habeas petition in federal court and hopes for oral arguments in Midland soon. But the odds aren't good—since Congress passed the Anti-Terrorism and Effective Death Penalty Act in 1996, the federal courts have been severely limited in granting habeas relief. Willis is beginning his sixteenth year on death row. In October 2000 he married for the seventh time, to Verilyn Harbin, the sister of former death row inmate Ricky McGinn, who was executed that same year. The two started writing each other a few years ago, then met and fell in love through the Plexiglas windows of the visitor's cage. She says, "He is the most loving person I've ever met." He says if not for her, he would have given up already.

Meanwhile, former Pecos County prosecutor Johnson, now a defense attorney, still thinks Willis is guilty. "Twelve grand jurors and twelve members of the jury—that's twenty-four people who made the decision unanimously," he says. He and other defenders of the Texas death penalty process insist that the system works. This, says Judge Michael Keasler, of the CCA, is the reason the court doesn't overturn more cases: "They're tried well. That's a tribute to the jobs the trial judges, prosecutors, and defense lawyers are doing." Try telling that to the federal judges who have castigated the system. Or to Blank. He and his firm have worked billable hours in excess of $1 million trying to get Willis off death row. Ultimately, the only death row inmates who stand a chance in Texas are those with pro bono attorneys—lawyers with the resources, experience, and desire to take on the state. And this is the final proof that the system doesn't work. Every Texan who has walked free from death row has done so with outside help—filmmakers, TV stars, preachers, activists, and pro bono lawyers, not the attorneys appointed by the state to represent them. They got out in spite of the system, not because of it.

It's an unfair system, and we need a statewide debate on how to straighten it out. The 2001 legislative session showed that capital punishment sits heavily on people's minds. Lawmakers made some changes, but more are needed: For example, beef up the Fair Defense Act, ensure that claims of innocence backed by new evidence get a hearing, restructure the Board of Pardons and Paroles, change the way we select judges to the CCA—or maybe just abolish the damned thing. At the very least, the Legislature should institute a two-year moratorium on executions, the length of one legislative cycle, while it studies the problem. In the long run, this won't prevent any justifiable executions, but it will make sure that every execution is, in the best sense of the word, justified.

GQ

FINALIST, PROFILE WRITING

Lucky Jim

The story of the truly unlucky hero of "Lucky Jim" could easily overwhelm a less-gifted writer, but Elizabeth Gilbert deftly avoids melodrama as she follows her subject from able-bodied man to amputee to quadriplegic. "Lucky Jim" is tragic, harrowing and ultimately inspiring—without ever indulging in sentimentality.

Elizabeth Gilbert

Lucky Jim

The most amazing thing happened to Jim MacLaren one day while running an Ironman race. He lost his body.

J im MacLaren doesn't have any memory of the first accident. He can't tell you what it feels like to be hit by a New York City bus and thrown eighty-nine feet in the air, to have your bones shattered and your legs crushed, to have your organs pulverized and to be pronounced dead on arrival at the hospital, because he can't recall any part of it.

The last thing he remembers about that accident is happily cruising down Fifth Avenue on his motorcycle, on "one of those balmy October nights when anything seems possible." As well it should have. Jim MacLaren was, as of that moment, a handsome, intelligent, ambitious and well-liked 22-year-old who had the world on a string. He'd recently graduated from Yale, where he'd excelled as a scholar, a football player and a theater star—not a bad trifecta for a fatherless kid from a moneyless family. He'd spent the previous evening dancing with debutantes at a society party and was returning home from a job interview that had gone extremely well. He was wearing a crisp white oxford shirt, his favorite jeans and a brand-new pair of Italian shoes. He looked wonderful, and he felt wonderful.

He never saw the 40,000-pound bus that ran the red light on 34th Street and demolished him. Nor does he have any memory of the paramedics who scraped him off the sidewalk (certain he was already a corpse) and delivered him to Bellevue Hospital. The next thing Jim remembers—after disappearing into a coma for eight days—is waking up in intensive care and learning that his left leg had been amputated below the knee.

So that was the first accident.

Over the next eight years, Jim MacLaren made a concerted effort to become the best one-legged man he possibly could. He endured a brutally painful rehabilitation but was ever uncomplaining about his loss. He graduated from the prestigious Yale School of Drama, acted on stage and television, found plenty of girlfriends. What's most astonishing, though, is that Jim now became a more accomplished athlete as an amputee than he'd ever been as an able-bodied man.

He initially took up swimming to get back in shape after the accident. Then he began riding his bicycle with a special prosthetic. Within a year of losing his leg, Jim was running. First limping, then walking, then hopping, then running. He started signing up for 10-K road races. During his first race, Jim's prosthetic rubbed the stump of his amputated leg so raw and bloody that he had to walk and stumble the last four miles, stopping frequently to change his bandages and dress his open wound, but he did finish and was exhilarated by the accomplishment. Which is why, the following November, he ran the New York City Marathon. Then it was on to the Boston Marathon, where he broke the world speed record for amputee contenders. Jim MacLaren was now the fastest one-legged endurance runner on earth.

Still as engaging a personality as ever, Jim started making a living as a motivational speaker, encouraging people with and without physical disabilities to never accept the notion of personal limitations. He also pursued a serious study of Eastern philosophy, which helped put his amputation into a larger metaphysical context. He was moved and edified by the Buddhist idea that all pain comes from attachment and that therefore we must not become attached to anything in this universe that is impermanent—including, for example, our own bodies. Our bodies are temporary vessels, after all. Attaching our identities to some ego-based perception of physical self is a sure path to misery. Instead, we must define ourselves only by what is eternal within us—namely, our highest level of pure consciousness, our divinity, our one true self. The more attachments we can shed, the closer we can come to enlightenment.

Even as he studied this idea, though, Jim kept pushing that temporary body of his to higher limits. He found extreme physical challenge to be a means of knowing himself better. Pain and endurance were becoming doorways through which he could pass toward greater self-awareness.

How strong is my will? How far can I go without fear? Who am I, really?

Soon he could run a marathon in just over three hours, routinely finishing in the top third of able-bodied contenders. And then he took up triathlons. Yes, triathlons. Once he'd survived a few of those, he set out to conquer the Ironman, one of the most brutal organized sporting events ever imagined. Two and a half miles of swimming, 112 miles of biking and a full 26.2-mile marathon, all in one race, all in one day. And all on one leg.

Which explains what Jim MacLaren was doing in Southern

California on that cool June afternoon in 1993. He was participating in an Ironman. Jim was excelling. He was speeding through the town of Mission Viejo on his bicycle, tearing ass at thirty-five miles per hour. The sidewalks were crowded with spectators, and he was dimly aware of their cheers. He had just pulled ahead of a thick snarl of cyclists. He was leading the pack. Suddenly, Jim heard the crowd gasp. He turned his head to see what was going on, and there was the steel grille of a black van heading straight toward him. He realized he was about to be hit by a goddamn car.

It was supposed to have been a closed racecourse. But for some unknown reason, a cop guarding an intersection decided to let one car through, and he misjudged how fast the bicyclists were coming. As Jim MacLaren was approaching, the cop was gesturing to the driver of the van to hit the gas. The driver, a 50-year-old man on his way to church, was merely obeying orders. He floored it. He didn't see Jim until Jim was on his windshield.

This time Jim vividly remembers being hit. He remembers the screams from the crowd. He remembers his body flying across the street and smashing into a lamppost headfirst, snapping his neck. He remembers riding in the ambulance and being aware that he could not feel his limbs. He was put under anesthesia for emergency surgery on his spine, and when he woke up he was in the trauma ward. He could not move. His head was shaved. There was a bolt screwed into the back of his skull, preventing him from shifting his head even a millimeter. Jim remembers this well. But what he remembers most clearly is this image: All the nurses were in tears.

"We're so sorry," they kept saying.

Jim MacLaren was now a quadriplegic. He was 30 years old. And this is where his story begins.

·　　　·　　　·

I first heard about Jim from a friend who had been a roommate of his at Yale and who described him as "a marvel and a mystery."

"What happens to a person after two accidents like that?" I asked. "How does he survive? How does he reconcile? How does he not kill himself?"

"That's the mystery part."

I first spoke with Jim MacLaren on the telephone one morning in the spring. I told him I wanted to write about him.

"For *GQ*?" he asked, and laughed. "OK, but I don't really look the part these days. Armani doesn't exactly make Velcro flies on their pants, you know?"

And I first met Jim MacLaren on the side of a road. It was a sunny afternoon in coastal California. Jim had suggested I come over and meet him at the campus of the Pacifica Institute, where he is currently working on his doctorate. The Pacifica Institute is a small private university buried in the hills of Santa Barbara and dedicated to the graduate study of mythology and psychology. The school is also home to papers of the great mythologist Joseph Campbell. Jim is writing his dissertation on wounds and the wounded male throughout mythological history.

"Meet me down on the road by the front entrance," he said. "We can go up to the campus and have lunch."

The day was cool and dry. The landscape was all parched browns and olive greens. I drove until I reached the gates of Pacifica, and there, waiting on the shoulder of the lonely and dusty road, was Jim MacLaren—Yale graduate, football star, actor, amputee, triathlete, quadriplegic, scholar. He was in a wheelchair, but he did not look anything close to helpless. He was a big and handsome man, broad through the chest. He was wearing shorts, and there was a peglike prosthesis attached to the stump of his left leg. His other leg was muscular and tan. A catheter bag half filled with urine hung from the side of his wheelchair, and a thin hose snaked up from it and disappeared under his shorts.

He was lighting a cigarette with fingers that were frozen into painful-looking talons, bent and twisted like little Joshua trees. I rolled down my window.

"Jim MacLaren, I presume?"

He smiled. "How'd you recognize me?"

"You *smoke*?" I said.

"Don't start," he warned.

.   .   .

The reason Jim MacLaren can light his own cigarettes has to do with the nature of his spinal injury. He is what is known as an incomplete quadriplegic. This means that although all four limbs were damaged when he broke his neck, he still has limited nerve activity, allowing him some movement and sensation. He can raise his arms a bit, he can bend forward in his wheelchair, he can use his hands somewhat (twisted though they are), and sometimes he can even lift his legs by a few degrees. This tiny range of movement means everything—the difference between an independent life and one with round-the-clock caretakers. The incompleteness of Jim's injury is why he can live alone. With excruciatingly protracted effort, Jim can bathe himself, dress himself, feed himself and even drive a van (specially outfitted with only hand controls). This all came as a big surprise to Jim's doctors; they'd initially diagnosed him as a complete quadriplegic, meaning he would never have any feeling or motion below the point of injury.

"So I've been very lucky," Jim told me.

We were now sitting in the garden of the Pacifica Institute, eating lunch in the sun. Jim is a true sun lizard. His body is deadly intolerant to cold; chills burrow down into his bones and nerves and torment him without mercy, but sunlight can bake out the pain even better than codeine sometimes. And Jim is almost always in pain. This is the kicker about an incomplete spinal injury—there is still just enough damaged-nerve activity left in his spine to keep him in agony. It's a terrible biological irony. If Jim's injury were more serious, it would actually cause him less suffering. He would feel nothing from the neck down. His limbs would atrophy, and he could forget about his body. As it stands, though, his nerves are spastic and unpredictable. He wakes up some mornings, he says, "feeling like I'm encased in wet cement with electrical currents running through it." His legs convulse uncontrollably, his bowels revolt, he goes blind with pain. Other days he's fine. Day by day, he never knows what he's going to get from his body, or when.

So when Jim says he's been "very lucky," well . . . go ahead and take that with the biggest grain of salt you need to get it down.

•   •   •

What they do in hospitals to someone who has suffered a major spinal injury is unthinkable and torturous, something from a nightmare or the basement of a serial killer. After another surgery to clean the bone chips from Jim's spinal fluid, the doctors put him in a halo—a steel ring that encircled his head and bolted directly into his skull. They had to do this procedure without anesthesia, and Jim screamed for mercy while they drilled the screws into his forehead. Then the halo was attached with four long bars to steel plates clamped tightly on either side of Jim's body. This was to keep him immobilized during recovery, so his spine would risk no further injury. Jim was locked in this halo for three months. There has never been a more dreadfully misnamed apparatus than the medical device known as "the halo."

During his time in the halo, Jim got such bad respiratory infections that an orderly had to come by every few hours with a long tube, forcing it up his nose and down into his lungs to clean out the infected fluid. Other people came to dig inside his rectum with their hands, pulling out the feces because he could not empty his own bowels. Others came to take his blood, to catheterize his bladder, to force-feed him or to tighten the screws on his halo.

Jim had known physical agony before. After his first accident, he'd been sent to a rehab center legendary for its toughness, a kind of boot camp for new amputees. There Jim worked with a physical-therapy aide named Oscar, a big, bald, muscular black guy who was tougher, Jim says, "than Apollo Creed." Oscar used to hoist Jim onto a machine to exercise what was left of his leg, make him do squats and lifts. Jim would do a few repetitions, and then Oscar would gently lift him off, lay him down on the ground, cover him with a towel and let him sob uncontrollably for a while. Then they'd do it all over again. So Jim had endured pain before.

But not like this.

The nights were interminable. Paralyzed and in the halo, he couldn't reach the call button for the nurse. He lay awake, anguished at being left alone but equally frightened of whoever might come into his room next and what they might do to him. His body was a hot chaos of pain. Every time someone touched him, he screamed. "I was all body," he remembers. "I was all animal impulses, operating from the most primitive core of my being. I was too afraid to cry—I'd lost control of my diaphragm muscle and was physically unable to cough. I was afraid that if I started crying, all my tears would fill up in my lungs and throat and literally choke me to death."

As he describes it now, he had no soul anymore. He had no self. He had no identity, no "Jim MacLaren," no history, no future, no hope. Because all this stuff is a luxury in the face of real trauma. The metaphysical question of *Who am I?*—that universal question of humanity that had echoed through Jim's consciousness for years, was now brutally silenced. He wasn't even a "who" anymore; he was a "what."

•   •   •

After three months in this dark underworld of pain, Jim was released from the steel halo. Moved to a rehabilitation center in Colorado, he was assigned to a floor with thirty-seven other patients who had recently become quadriplegics or paraplegics. Like Jim, most of these patients were young men. They were athletic, healthy men who'd been out there in the world only a few weeks earlier, living at their prime and doing the things that snap guys' necks—climbing rocks, racing motorcycles, driving with the top down and riding in rodeos.

"There was a lot of anger on that ward," Jim says. "But it was good anger. Funny anger. Sarcastic, brave, young man's anger. It wasn't as grim as you might think."

Tentatively, in this battered company, Jim's sense of self began to reemerge. His human consciousness crept out from hiding, and he began to recognize that there was something familiar about his situation. Loss, pain, incapacitation, rehabilitation, endurance? Jim had been through this already. The amputee-triathlete-survivor within him took over. This was the inner voice that said "You know how to do this, Jim. Work your ass off in rehab, eat the pain, focus on regaining your independence, keep your spirits up, and get the hell out of this place."

Over the next months, Jim became—to nobody's surprise—the model recovering quadriplegic. He was upbeat and stoic and unflinchingly focused. He kept his distance from the other patients so that he could concentrate instead on his own recuperation. He lobbied to get the best therapist in the place and then arranged to have an old issue of a triathlon magazine sent to the guy, featuring an article about this wondrous amputee athlete.

"Look," Jim said. "I want you to read this. This is who I am. This is how hard I'm willing to work."

There is a particular energy to the momentum of recovery,

and Jim now swung his whole existence into that energy. He advanced, he pushed, he strove. He defied prognosis after prognosis and recovered faster than anyone had expected. But here's the thing—everyone *had* expected that. Because he's *Jim MacLaren*, damn it, and that's what Jim MacLaren does when he's beaten down. He rises up. He never quits. He's a marvel and a mystery, right?

Which is why, just six months after breaking his neck, Jim was back in the world. He was living on his own, with only visits from caretakers. About a year after his accident, he made a difficult voyage to Hawaii to speak before a convention of Ironman athletes. He was wheeled out onstage to a standing ovation. When the applause finally died down, Jim began with, of all things, a dark joke: "For years I sat out there in that audience and listened to the best Ironman champions in the world speak from this very podium. I always wondered what it would take for a guy like me to be invited up here. I never realized it would be so simple—all I had to do was break my neck."

There was a bone-chilling silence.

Jim thought, *Whoops. . . .*

Apparently, these people weren't ready for a joke like that. Nobody in the real world was ready for this. Quickly, Jim changed his tone, went back to his old rousing motivational-speaker oration about endurance and the strength of the human spirit. He gave the people what they wanted, and they (with considerable relief) rewarded him with riotous applause and tears of emotion. After the speech, they all gathered around him, telling him what a hero he was, how healthy he seemed, how they all expected to see him running in the Ironman next year.

"Doesn't Jimmy look *great*?" everyone said. "Isn't Jimmy doing incredibly well?"

In fact, though, he wasn't. He wasn't doing well at all.

Yes, there is a galvanizing momentum to recovery, but then there comes a moment when the recovery has gone as far as it can possibly go and momentum can't carry you anymore. There eventually comes a wall where healing stops and the truth of what you're left with settles in. And Jim had just hit that wall. His body had healed as much as it was ever going to. And all the determination in the world could not change these facts: He would never be out of pain again; he would never lift his arms above his head again; he would never be able to control his bladder again. And he would absolutely never walk again. Not even if he spent ten hours a day in physical therapy, as his old triathlete buddies kept suggesting he do. ("Why aren't you in the gym right now?" they'd ask. "Why aren't you trying harder to beat this, Jimmy?")

Because it couldn't be beat, that's why. That was it—the truth, plain and simple. And the day he realized that truth was the day the invincible Jim MacLaren finally began to lose it.

.   .   .

The next year was an ugly tailspin of rage, sorrow, calamity and dysfunction. Jim won a big settlement for his accident—$3.7 million. After considerable medical and attorney's fees, that still left him with a fair amount of money. He decided to move to Kona, Hawaii, putting an ocean between himself and everyone who loved him.

"I announced to all my friends that I was moving to the beach to spend my time contemplating my destiny and writing my memoirs," Jim recalls. "Everyone thought this was a great idea and believed it. Everyone supported it. But it was bullshit. I was just running away."

Jim was running away because he didn't want anyone to know the truth, which was that he had become addicted to cocaine. He'd started using the drug about two years after he broke his neck. He'd met this woman, and she'd offered some coke to him. ("Go ahead," she'd said, full of sympathy. "You've suffered so much, you deserve it.") And Jim thought, *Yeah, I do deserve it.* He took the stuff, and it made him disappear for a little while. It took the nightmare of his reality away. Soon he was buying it, doing it alone, needing it—and surrounding himself with the kinds of friends who encouraged the behavior. Junkies, prostitutes, dealers and lost souls.

"You wouldn't believe how many people were willing to give me cocaine and let me kill myself because they felt sorry for me," he says. "These weren't cruel people, but they were just like, 'Dude, have another line—what else are you gonna do with your damn life?' "

And he drank. There's nothing worse he could have done to his battered body, but he drank and did cocaine every night until his body went away from him, until he didn't have to belong to it anymore.

His old friends called from California, from Colorado, from Yale. Left messages. *How you doin', Jim?* He wouldn't call them back for weeks; then he'd apologize—*Sorry, I've been really busy, been working on my book. . . . Yeah, it's going great. . . .*

Then one night, he found himself drunk out of his mind and drugged to the gills at three in the morning, wheeling his chair up the middle lane of some desolate highway. He realized he was on Alii Drive—the most famous stretch of road on the Hawaiian Ironman racecourse. He'd been here before—had run marathons up this road. Now he shut his eyes and could almost hear the lost echo of the crowd's roar. Alii Drive had been the site of Jim MacLaren's greatest triumph, but now look at him. Wheeling around at night, seeing double, trying to figure out where he could score more cocaine at this hour. Unwashed, alone, crippled. He looked up, or as far up as he could, given that his head couldn't tilt back and he was too blind drunk to see the sky.

"Why are you doing this to me?" he yelled. "Why are you fucking doing this?"

•   •   •

As a human being, you have two choices as to how you view the events of your life. Either you can believe every act is random, or you can believe every act occurs for a preordained reason. But what if you believe every act occurs for a reason and then hideous, unspeakable things happen to you? Well, you are faced with two choices once more. Either you can believe you are cursed, or you can believe you are somehow blessed. Jim MacLaren—who lost a leg at 22 and became a quadriplegic at 30—has decided to believe he is blessed.

This has indeed been a decision. Jim made it shortly after that dark night on Alii Drive. He woke up and knew there was a choice he had to make, and soon. Was he going to die, or was he going to live? He'd surrounded himself with people who were essentially saying to him with each gram of cocaine and each grimace of pity, "Go ahead and kill yourself, Jim. You've suffered enough. I give you permission to leave this life."

"But I didn't *want* to leave this life," he says. "I was 33 years old. That's too young to say you're finished. I wanted to live. I didn't want to live as a fucking quadriplegic, but I couldn't change that. And since I couldn't change it, I knew I'd have to make some kind of peace with it."

Not some facile, life-is-beautiful, made-for-television, triumph-of-the-human-spirit peace but a true and sustaining and deeply personal peace. And the only chance he had for gaining any peace, he realized, was to start seeing things very differently. He needed a total change in perception, a paradigm shift. He wasn't sure exactly how to do this yet, but he knew one thing: If he couldn't start finding some serious blessings in all this disaster, he did not stand a chance in hell.

•   •   •

So he went inside. What else could he do? He took his intellect, his energy and his spiritual hunger and he turned it all inward, setting forth on a journey to find out all over again, but with a newfound humility, "OK, seriously now—who am I? Who am I *really*?"

"The first thing I had to do was identify my absolute deepest fear about all this," Jim says. "What was it? What was the worst thing about having to spend life as a quadriplegic? Was I afraid of death? Not really. I'd had two near-death experiences already, with the white light and the tunnel and the whole deal. They were both amazing encounters, not scary either time. I knew that death no longer frightened me. Was I afraid of losing my sexuality? No, I knew as long as I had taste and smell and sensation, I could lead a sensual life. Was I afraid of helplessness? Not really. Managing on my own is a drag, but it's just logistics. Was I afraid of pain? No. I know how to deal with pain. Pain is a bitch, but I know how to beat it, how to wrestle physical pain to the ground. So what was I afraid of? The answer was pretty clear: I was afraid of being alone with myself, with my mind, with the dark things that lived in me, like fear and doubt and loneliness and confusion. I was afraid of *metaphysical pain*."

Jim MacLaren knew he was going to have to spend much of his life in solitude and stillness. He was often confined to his bed for days at a time. As though wrestled to the ground by God Himself, he had been forced into his own company. This was petrifying, but now Jim faced this terror and wondered if he could learn to see it differently.

"Maybe, I thought to myself, this wasn't really a curse at all. Maybe it was actually the most exquisite blessing of my life. Maybe it was the opportunity for true catharsis, if I chose to make it one—an opportunity to see my true self beyond all the noise."

Jim MacLaren? Meet Jim MacLaren.

Continuing to seek answers, Jim began to speculate that

maybe he needed to have the second accident because he'd never fully learned the correct metaphysical lessons from the first one.

"Yeah, sure, after I lost my leg, I talked the talk about how *I am not this body*, but did I really understand that yet? I had the words down, and I appreciated the concept, but I didn't really have the experience yet to carry that wisdom beyond words. As an amputee, I was still vain about my looks, still seeking attention and affirmation from women, still getting approval from the world through applause, still trapped in my ego."

So maybe destiny had looked down at Jim MacLaren and said, "Hate to do this, pal, but you still don't quite get it," and then pushed him in front of a van—not as a punishment but as a favor—saying, "*Now* will you let go of all your attachment to this mortal body? Now will you examine who you really are?"

Or, as Goethe said, "Die, so you can live."

Inspired, Jim turned to his books. He went back to the ancients. He examined all the classical images of wounded men—the crippled god Hephaestus, the blinded Oedipus, the long-suffering Job. What was God trying to do to Job, anyhow, by stripping him so ruthlessly of his family, his health, his fortune? Testing his faith, right? But something more than that, Jim suspected. And then Jim finally saw it on the tenth reading of that biblical book. God was trying to bring Job closer to Him. After all, Job starts off the story as a faithful but somehow detached worshiper of the Lord. By the end, however, his suffering has erased all formality and he speaks to God directly, challengingly, intimately—just the way God speaks to him.

Maybe this is what had happened to Jim that dark night in Kona in his wheelchair when he'd yelled up at the sky. No priests or rituals or prayers were needed—he had been able to yell directly in God's face, *I am here right now and I am talking to you. Answer me!* Jim had believed that was his low point, but now he saw another possible truth: Perhaps he had been closer than ever to the divine. Perhaps that had been his *highest* moment.

Jim came to believe there were other blessings. For the first time, he could see something most people go through their entire lives blind to—namely, that we are not in charge of what happens to us in this lifetime. We are in charge only of how we *perceive* what happens to us in this lifetime.

"I started looking around and seeing people everywhere—especially successful middle-class American men—walking around in complete denial, smugly thinking to themselves, *I sure am doing a good job running my life here.* But I could see now that their sense of control was nothing but a mirage. Safety, entitlement, power—these are all fantasies. We don't drive our destinies. Not in that way."

Jim realized, to his relief, that once you stop trying to control events you can't control anyway, you can drop all that wasted energy and focus on the one thing you *are* in charge of. As the teachings of Buddha and Socrates show, you have only one task as a human being: To know yourself.

"Look," Jim says. "I have honestly come to believe that I needed these accidents in my life. I completely believe that. Not in terms of paying dues or getting punished by God, but in terms of getting my attention and bringing me deeper inside myself to a place where I could find honesty and peace. Was it destined? Did I literally choose to have these awful things happen to me? No, not in so many words, I don't believe so. But I do believe this—I believe I was born *begging* for experiences that would show me who I really am. And that's what I've been given."

Sitting across from Jim at lunch, listening to him recount his story, I suddenly decided to interrupt and tell him a story of my own. I told him about a bicycle accident I'd had a few weeks before I met him. I was riding my bike at night in New York City, going too fast, getting thrills from dodging taxis and passing buses. I was crossing 37th Street, thinking, *I am so cool!* when I hit a pothole and went flying. I landed on my head, broke my helmet, took all the skin off my shoulder. But after a few minutes of shaking with adrenaline and pain, I was able to get back on my bike and—very gingerly—ease my way home.

I told this story to Jim only because I'd just realized that my little accident took place a mere three blocks from the street where he'd lost his leg. Raising the inevitable question: *Why?* Two separate accidents in two isolated moments. Why did they have such astonishingly different consequences?

"Is it even worth asking why I got *this*," I say, lifting my sleeve and showing the tiny scar on my shoulder, "and you got . . . *that?*"

"Sure, it's worth asking. Any question is worth asking. Why do different people have different destinies? It's an interesting intellectual subject. We could sit here and speculate about it forever, if that's what you want to do. But we'll never know why. And if we did somehow miraculously find out why, would that change anything?"

"So should we just move on to some other question?" I asked.

Jim smiled. "Well, that's what I've done."

.   .   .

These days, Jim lives in a huge loft in downtown Pasadena. On good mornings, he can get out of bed, eat, clean out his bowels, attach his catheter, shower, dress and be ready to leave the apartment in just under three hours. Almost the same amount of time it used to take him to run a marathon, and nearly as physically grueling. It's painful, but he gives his body the time it needs, and then the rest of day belongs to him. If the weather is nice and he feels strong enough and doesn't have a paper to write, he'll get in his wheelchair and head into the city's Old Town. He'll park at an outdoor café, order up a triple espresso and read in the sun, blissfully alone and blissfully comfortable with his own company.

Or sometimes he spends the day with his girlfriend. Her name is Alessandra. Jim calls her Ally, or Ally-mander, or Ally-cat. She's beautiful, blond, smart. They met in an Internet chat room and have been together for two years.

"People look at me and call me a saint for being with a guy in a wheelchair," says Ally, "and it's so insulting. First of all—the idea of *me* as a saint . . ."

This makes both Jim and Ally laugh so hard that the conversation has to stop for several minutes.

"Anyway," Ally continues, wiping her eyes. "I'm with him because he's the most intelligent and sexy man I've ever known. Period."

As for the sex, yes, they have it. Maybe not the way you have it, but they do have it. Jim does have limited sensation in his penis, but he has to be careful because an orgasm could be a serious health risk. (It could put him into a state of hyperreflexia—pulse goes down, blood pressure goes up; he could have a stroke or a spasm or even die.) So he expresses his sexuality differently now—with hands, mouth, voice, imagination and lots of time.

Of course, Jim and Ally have to deal with the limitations of his body every day. For one thing, they don't get a lot of privacy in public. People stare at Jim. People stare shamelessly. After all these years, Jim is used to this sort of thing. He recognizes that his is a public body now. But it still drives his girlfriend nuts when people stare. The three of us all headed into the Old Town one afternoon, with Jim rolling along as Ally and I walked beside him. Every person we passed either gaped openly at Jim, did a double take or stared with purpose at the ground before his own feet, fiercely determined not to gawk at the quadriplegic. Jim took no notice of this, but Ally grew increasingly tense. By the time a young couple nudged each other with absolute indiscretion and actually pointed at Jim, Ally lost it.

"What the fuck is the *matter* with people?" she exploded.

"They're just curious, Ally-mander," Jim said, reaching for her hand. "It's nothing."

Indeed, Jim attracts an enormous amount of attention. And

it's not only gruesome fascination, either. He has earned a strange kind of status through his injury. People constantly come to Jim with their own tragedies in hand, seeking solace or wisdom from him. Even perfect strangers see him as some holy sage of pain, someone who can help them heal their own wounds.

"I'm a walking projection," Jim says, and then clarifies, "No— I'm a *rolling* projection."

Acquaintances who barely know Jim make him the first person they consult when calamity strikes. People call him at all hours from hospitals, jails, funeral homes and rehab centers, everybody begging for the same thing—*Please, help lead me out of this fear*. Jim tries to help when he can, but he says sometimes it's hard to come across as completely sympathetic. For instance, when he gets a desperate midnight phone call from someone whose brother or son or wife has been in a dreadful car accident and he hears that the loved one has lost a limb, it's all Jim can do to affect a somber tone and not say what he's thinking. Which is, Thank God! Hallelujah! Just an amputation? That's *nothing*. We can *totally* handle that.

And it isn't always easy, because Jim still struggles. Jim MacLaren, let's be very clear about this, did not enjoy losing his leg, and he does not enjoy being in a wheelchair. He looks for the blessings where he can find them, and he tries to keep a sense of humor, but there are days when it's not funny and it's not enlightening. Days when he wakes up in so much pain he can't get out of bed at all. Days when he can no longer stand the endless battle over trying to control his bowels ("I'm more obsessed with my feces than the Marquis de Sade," he jokes darkly). Days when yet another infection lodges in his catheter incision and his testicles swell to the size of softballs. Days when he wonders how he's going to possibly survive this abuse for another forty years.

"There are moments when I realize all over again what happened to me," Jim says, "and it's still unbelievable. I mean, come *on!* Jesus Christ, for fuck's sake, how much can one person endure? But I can't stay in that place for long or I'll lose my mind. Instead, I have to ask, What is wholeness, really? What is a full life? What are my actual obstacles? And whenever I find myself frustrated with my handicap or looking with envy at an able-bodied man, I ask myself this: If I could get up out of this wheelchair right now and walk across the room, would that really get me there? I mean, would that *really* get me to the place I most want to go with my life? Because let's be honest here—the other side of this room is not my ultimate destination. My ultimate destination is self-knowledge and enlightenment. Do I have to get there on foot? Or can I find some other path?"

·　　·　　·

The day before Jim MacLaren broke his neck, he woke up in his house in Boulder, Colorado, stirred out of bed earlier than usual by some strange and unfamiliar energy. He left his then girlfriend, Pam, sleeping and went outside to sit in his backyard to eat his breakfast alone. The sun was coming up, reflecting off the mountains, and the morning light was filmy and gold. Jim could hear his neighbor's young children playing next door. He could hear birdsong and the tremor of leaves. He'd brought a book outside with him to read, but it lay in his lap unopened; he couldn't focus on it. He couldn't pay attention to his breakfast, either. He wasn't even thinking about the Ironman he'd be competing in the next day. None of this mattered, suddenly. All Jim wanted was to sit in stillness and experience the inexplicable bliss that was surrounding him in this moment.

And then the bliss started to grow, to rise within him. Jim moved from a state of contentment into a state of joy, and soon even the joy could not be contained, and it became a euphoria that spilled out over his whole body, lifting the hair on the back of his neck and running goose bumps across his skin. He was overcome by a thrilling sense of what he could later only describe as *anticipation*. He'd never felt anything like this, and he never wanted it to end. He was laughing and crying at the same time, elated beyond his senses.

Jim's girlfriend heard the noise and rushed out of the house to see what was wrong.

"What is it, Jim?" she asked. "What's going on?"

He looked up at her through his tears and smiled. He was 30 years old. He was twenty-four hours away from becoming a quadriplegic, and he could not contain his excitement.

"Pam," he said, and he was never more certain of anything in his life, "Pam—listen! Something *amazing* is about to happen to me!"

Harper's

The Boy Who Loved Transit

An uncommonly seamless blend of fluid writing and fastidious reporting, "The Boy Who Loved Transit" tells the story of Darius McCollum, a thirty-seven-year-old New Yorker who has spent much of his life in jail for impersonating a transit officer. Writer Jeff Tietz outlines the numerous ways in which the court system has failed McCollum, but the piece is much more than a sermon against injustice; it's a complex portrait of an inscrutable character who, in Tietz's hands, comes alive.

Jeff Tietz

The Boy Who
Loved Transit

How the system
failed an obsession

Before leaving his girlfriend's apartment in Crown Heights, on the morning of his nineteenth arrest for impersonating and performing the functions of New York City Transit Authority employees, Darius McCollum put on an NYCTA subway conductor's uniform and reflector vest. Over his feet he pulled transit-issue boots with lace guards and soles designed to withstand third-rail jolts. He took transit-issue work gloves and protective goggles. He put a transit-issue hard hat on his head. In his pockets he carried NYCTA work orders and rerouting schedules and newspaper clippings describing his previous arrests: for driving subway trains and buses and various other vehicles without authorization, possessing stolen property, flagging traffic around NYCTA construction sites, forging documents. He also carried a signed letter on NYCTA letterhead:

To: All Concerned Departments
From: Thomas Calandrella
        Chief Track Officer
Re: Darius McCollum

Effective this date of January 10, 2000, Darius McCollum is a member of a special twelve member Special Study Group; and will analyze the operations of track safety and track operations. SSG will report directly to this office and will be issued all related gear for the respected purposes of this department and will receive assistance of any relating department.

To his belt Darius clipped a flashlight and a key ring the size of a choker. From this ring six smaller rings hung like pendants. Along the curves of the small rings, 139 keys climbed symmetrical and fanlike. Each key granted access to a secure area of the train, bus, or subway system of the New York City Transit Authority. The collection was equivalent to the number of keys an employee would acquire through forty years of steady promotions. Just before he left the apartment, Darius picked up an orange emergency-response lantern.

Six weeks earlier, Darius had been paroled from the Elmira Correctional Facility, near Binghamton, New York, where he had served two years for attempted grand larceny—"attempted" because he had signed out NYCTA vehicles for surface use (extinguishing track fires, supervising maintenance projects) and then signed them back in according to procedure. Darius has never worked for the NYCTA; he has never held a steady job. He is thirty-seven and has spent a third of his adult life in prison for victimless offenses related to transit systems.

He was at work by 7:20, eating buttered rolls and drinking coffee in a GMC pickup with a small signal crew above the Nos-

trand Avenue stop on the Number 3 line. The truck was hitched
to an emergency generator temporarily powering the station
lights; during a repair job Con Edison had spliced into the wrong
cable. Traveling through the system three days earlier, Darius had
encountered the crew members and told them that he was a
track-department employee waiting for his truck to be fixed. In
the meantime, he said, his only responsibility was the occasional
street-flagging operation. The signal guys were on what they, and
therefore Darius, called "a tit job": baby-sitting the generator and
periodically reporting on the electrical work. Darius sat in the
station with the signal guys, surveying the Con Ed work and
watching girls.

That slow morning there was a lot of conversation about the
transit union. Its president, Willie James, was on his way out.
Darius, who is voluble and almost perpetually affable, was defer-
entially critical of James, who, he said, "came from buses and
favored the bus guys." Darius voiced or echoed complaints about
the effects of union inaction: low pay, retirement after twenty-
five years instead of twenty, the difficulty of getting basic equipment. For nearly two decades Darius had attended NYCTA
workers' rallies and union meetings. At the meetings he had
argued for, among other things, better lighting in tunnels and
the right to wear earplugs against ambient noise. He had agreed
that positive drug tests should result in mandatory ninety-day
suspensions and counseling but objected to withholding salary
during that time. He took detailed notes as he traveled through
the system so that he could accurately critique management
actions.

At noon Darius volunteered to go to his girlfriend's apartment and bring back lunch for the crew. Darius had met his girlfriend a week earlier, on the subway. It was a snowy night; they
were alone in the car. Darius said she looked cold. She nodded
and smiled and pointed to his uniform. He told her where he
worked in the track department and how he approached various

kinds of emergency situations and that he did street flagging and drove heavy equipment. She didn't understand anything he said because she was from Ecuador and didn't speak English. Her name was Nelly Rodriguez. She was forty-five and had five children and worked as a seamstress in a garment factory. They exchanged phone numbers; later her sister translated for them.

Within a week Nelly had asked Darius for his Social Security number and invited him to move in. Several months later they would be married, and Darius would confess to Nelly, having fabricated a story about his nineteenth arrest, that he was a lifelong subway impostor, and she would say, through her sister, "If it's your problem it's our problem, and I'm not going to tell anybody," and then successfully inveigle him into signing over the rights to his story to a small Manhattan production company for a relatively tiny sum (several newspapers had covered his arrest). Eventually a lawyer hired by Darius's parents would void this agreement, and Darius would yield to their unremitting pressure and request a divorce. When he is asked now if he worried about his quick start with Nelly, Darius says, "No, because I had already said a long time ago that I had not planned to get married until I was at least in my thirties. . . . I wanted to get married when I was a little more settled, when I had a little better insight."

In Nelly's kitchen, Darius ate a plate of the fish and rice and beans that she had cooked the night before. He sealed the rest in Tupperware and brought it back to the crew. He told the guys to take their time finishing up; he had to check on his truck at fleet operations. Then he left to visit a friend, a token-booth clerk at Fifty-seventh Street in Manhattan.

Darius's friend was at lunch when he arrived, so he let himself into the station's command tower to wait. The control room had a big signal board that tracked train movement and a tinted picture window with a platform view. The vacant tower had recently been automated, but Darius remembered when the seven empty lockers had been full and when, in the recessed kitchen with its miniature sink and stove, there had been pots in the bottom cabinet and food in the top. He had often stopped by to chat about work, or read the newspaper, or get a doughnut and a cup of coffee.

Darius sat surveilling the lights on the board: a clear-skinned dark black guy of average height in an unusually complete Transit Authority uniform. Darius is only slightly overweight, but everything about him appears tender and fleshy: the heels of his hands and the little underhung bellies of skin between the knuckles of his fingers, his small paunch, the cushions of his cheeks, his chubby iridescent lips. His movements are almost always leisurely—when he's being chased by transit cops he lopes onerously, counting on his knowledge of the system's crannies—and he stands slightly stooped, the shallow curve of his back in conformity with all the small padded curves of his body. Darius has big circular eyes that quickly admit delight, a serene form of which he was feeling as he absorbed the scrupulous, luridly represented shuttling of the trains. He can't explain why, but he is always content in the subway: elementally content, at unrivaled ease, unable to think about anything outside the system.

•   •   •

Darius grew up near the 179th Street yard, the terminus of the F train, in Jamaica, Queens. He was a bright, early-talking child. His obsession with the subway manifested itself as soon as he began riding trains with his mother, at age three: his desire to see a train's headlights materialize in the tunnel black always threatened to propel him over the platform edge. The force of this attraction never diminished. Darius did well in school, but an opaque inwardness isolated him from other children and worried his teachers; he never formed enduring friendships or felt comfortable in class.

Darius spent hundreds of hours watching trains at 179th

Street. He estimated the angle of every track intersection in the yard. By the time he was eight, he could visualize the entire New York City subway system. (Later he memorized the architecture of the stations.) Family and friends with subway questions began calling the McCollum household and asking for Darius. In small notebooks he recorded arrival and departure times at various stations, and documented whatever he observed: the shrill, keyed-up atmosphere an emergency stop instantly creates on a platform, the presence of transit police, mechanical problems ("E-train to Canal st 0015 L.C. Delay of train leaving Parson's Blvd Door Trouble"), passengers riding between cars ("A-train to 81st L.C. 4112—Girl riding in between cars approx. 17 Brown Coat Blue Pants Brown Shoes"). He hasn't abandoned this note-taking. His logs—

0210 D train 169st N.P.C. Meal
0217 S/B F 169th st L.C. 586
0230 S/B F Woodhaven D train
0311 N/B F 71st F.H. L.C. 1200
0317 N/B E Kew Gardens L.C. 1134 . . .

—span twenty-five years.

When Darius was eleven, a classmate, unprovoked, stabbed him in the back with a pair of scissors. The scissors punctured a lung and came within an inch of his heart. The boy opened and closed the scissors as he pulled them out, creating a wound in the shape of an irregular star. At the hospital, doctors pumped blood out of Darius's lung and re-inflated it. He didn't speak that day or the next: he just stared at his parents with awestruck eyes. At night he paced in his sleep or lay awake. When he went back to school, he would sit only with his back against the wall.

Not long after the stabbing, Darius began disappearing into the subway system for days at a time:

3/30/81 7:30 didn't go to school, but then I went on the J train up to Chambers st . . . 11:30 I went back on the J train and went to catch the D train to Brighton Beach at approx 12:45. Transf to M train and went to Stillwell a 1:05 and went to the bathroom (no food dur this time) back on the M, return to Brighton and took D train to pacific st (Bklyn) approx 2:00 took the #2 train transfered to the #6 to 28th street to Girls Club `at 3:30 pat, angie, rosemary. They gave me a sandwich and milk and then left 3:45. . . .

4/2/81 I left to #6 to Grand Central took #7 to 5th ave and took F for the rest night, and slept on the F train Balance of night till approx 6:30 am.

Darius counted on certain relatives in Queens and Brooklyn: he would stop by to eat and spend the night and then return to the subway. He often went home for provisions when his parents were asleep or at work. Samuel and Elizabeth McCollum worked long hours, but they tried to stay up later than their son and wake up before him. They tried to lock him in and lock him out; they talked to NYCTA supervisors; they called his school and arranged for morning escorts; they tried different schools; they had him hospitalized for psychiatric treatment. But each remedy had its limit, and ultimately they found that they could only interrupt his journeying. Mrs. McCollum tracked her son's movements. On one of her calendars, the word "out," meaning "location unknown," fills fourteen day-boxes in January of 1981, when Darius was first arrested for driving a train. The four days from the twenty-seventh to the thirtieth read: *late for school—in at 10:00 a.m.; home; out—drove train; court.*

By this time Darius had cultivated a constellation of admirers at the 179th Street yard. Darius has always been deeply disarming. His charm resides in his peculiar intelligence, his perpetual receptivity to transporting delight, and his strange, self-endangering indifference to the consequences of his enthusiasm. Darius never curses. He has no regionally or culturally recognizable accent. He has a quick-to-appear, caricaturishly resonant laugh, like the laugh ascribed to Santa Claus, and he can appreciate certain comedic aspects of what he does, but he often laughs too long or when things aren't funny, as when he mentions that he briefly worked on the LIRR route that Colin Ferguson took to slaughter commuters. Darius litters his speech with specialized vocabulary ("BIE incident," "transverse-cab R-110") and unusually formal phrases ("what this particular procedure entails," "the teacher didn't directly have any set curriculum studies"). He frequently and ingenuously uses the words "gee," "heck," "doggone," "gosh," and "dang."

It is difficult to find anyone who knows Darius well and does not express an abiding protective affection for him. Cops always refer to him by his first name, and often with wistful amusement, as if he were a wayward godson. In discussing his cases, they have called him "great," "endearing," and "fabulous." They mention his honesty and abnormally good memory. Sergeant Jack Cassidy, a high-ranking transit cop who has interviewed Darius more often than anyone else in the NYPD, told me, "You'll be talking to a fantastic person when you talk to Darius, and I hope prison never changes that. Give him my best. But don't tell him where I am, because he'll probably come visit me." (Darius has paid Sergeant Cassidy several friendly, unannounced visits at his office, in full transit gear.)

•   •   •

Darius's apprenticeship began with a motorman he called Uncle Craft, who drove the first train Darius took regularly. When Craft began working at the 179th Street yard, he taught Darius to drive along the generous stretch of track between the yard and the last F stop. Darius learned how to ease a train into a station, aligning it with the markers that match its length, how to read signals while simultaneously observing the track connections the signals predict (he was taught never to assume the infallibility of signals), and how to understand the timers that govern the signals. Darius was an exceptional, methodical student: he learned quickly and thoroughly, building on each skill he acquired and instantly memorizing terminology. Soon he was doing yard maneuvers and taking trains into passenger service, as both a train operator and a conductor. (By the time of his first arrest, he had driven trains dozens of times.)

To broaden his knowledge, Darius visited employees from 179th Street who had taken up new positions elsewhere. He learned to drive garbage trains and de-icer trains and to repair the electrical boxes that control signals. In renovation shops he learned how to dismantle trains and reassemble them. In control towers he learned how to direct traffic: routing trains around obstructions, replacing late trains, switching ABD trains ("abandoned due to malfunction") out of service. The more he learned the more he volunteered to do, and the easier he made the lives of the people who taught him. By the time he was eighteen, TA employees had begun calling him at home and asking him to pull shifts.

Darius was given his first uniform at fifteen: "I can't compare that feeling to anything. I felt official. I felt like this is me, like this is where I belong." Darius discusses his work in the subway with professional pride, generally using the first-person plural ("Sometimes we didn't feel that management should be doing certain things..."). His vision of himself as an NYCTA worker is officious and uncompromising: "I'm a very good train operator. Even though I drive fast, don't get me wrong: I believe in coasting, I don't believe in excessive speeds. Even if you're late don't speed, because eventually you'll catch up. As a conductor, I give a whole announcement before and during stops. . . . That's just me. Sometimes they'll make part of an announcement: 'Next stop is Queens Plaza.' Okay, the next stop is Queens Plaza, but what do we *do* there?"

The question of how Darius's immutable sense of belonging

has never been damaged by all the skillful impersonation and fakery it depends on is not one that he can answer. I spent almost fifteen hours sitting across a table from him, and I asked this question several times. He looked bemused, his eyes wandered, he half-smiled, he said he just thought of himself as a part of the system, that he felt safer and more content there than anywhere else, that for reasons he doesn't understand this paradox never occurs to him until he is behind bars for a while. He always stressed that he improved service to the "riding customers" and that, given his ability and care, he would never endanger anyone. (During one of these conversations, he said, "Oh—in the article could you put that my title is Transportation Captain? That's the title the employees gave me, because I move around the system so well.") Eventually Darius began taking the skills tests the NYCTA requires for employment, but by then he was notorious.

·   ·   ·

Reclining in the tranquillity of the Fifty-seventh Street tower, Darius heard the descending scale of a train losing its charge. He sat up and waited. He knew something had tripped the train's emergency brake, and he knew the operator would reset the brake and try to recharge the train. When the recharge attempt failed, he picked up his helmet, his vest, his gloves, his lantern, and his flashlight. He was thinking only of the train. The first four cars had made it into the station. Darius questioned the train operator and lent him his flashlight so that they could begin the routine debris search. Darius was inspecting the tracks when over the train radio he heard Command Center order an evacuation, so he unhooked the chains between the fourth and fifth cars, climbed up and unlocked the two sets of car doors, made the standard evacuation announcement, and continued down the train this way until the last passengers walked off.

(After opening each car, he stood by the doors to make sure everyone got through safely.) When the train was empty, he briefly examined its rear brakes and then resumed his debris search. Two transit cops arrived; Darius hurried back to help explain the situation.

The cops, Officers Cullen and Morales, saw passengers exiting the train in a neat stream, and they saw Darius conscientiously inspecting the track with a flashlight. They had just begun questioning the conductor and train operator when Darius rushed up and co-opted an answer: "Yeah, the train went BIE and we think it caught some debris, so we're evaluating the track—the rear brakes checked out, the passengers are all clear." When Darius had gone back to work, the train operator pulled the cops aside and whispered, "This guy's not one of us. He's an impostor."

They found that hard to believe. Everything about Darius— his gear, his carriage, his total comfort with protocol—suggested authenticity. But the train operator had recognized Darius from a Transit Authority wanted poster, and he told the cops to ask for I.D. Darius produced his study-group letter, which essentially convinced them that he was legitimate (they had encountered track-study notices many times before), but the operator was adamant, and they asked Darius to have his supervisor come vouch for him. Darius led Officer Cullen back to the tower, unlocking the door and turning on the lights and telling Officer Cullen to sit down and make himself comfortable. Darius got a drink from a water cooler and sat down at a desk to call a friend. Cullen, short and thick-limbed, with a gelled part in his hair and multiple tattoos and nine years on the force, felt faintly guilty for inconveniencing Darius.

On the phone, Darius asked to speak to someone and then said, "Oh, okay, I'll try back." His boss was out to lunch, he said. Cullen said not to worry, they could wait, and apologized for the annoyance. Out the tower window Darius glimpsed an unfriendly superintendent conferring with the train operator. Darius started laughing. He said, "All right, you got me." Officer Cullen asked him what he was talking about. Darius—now narrowly smiling and incipiently prideful—said, "You got me! I don't work for the TA. The letter's a forgery. I stole the letterhead and did the letter myself. The uniform and keys I got from people I know. I've been doing this for a long time. It's actually easy if you know what you're doing." Officer Cullen stood silent and staring, suspended in his disbelief. "Here's some articles about me," Darius said.

On the way to a formal interview with Assistant District Attorney Michael Dougherty at 100 Centre Street, Darius offered unsolicited, sophisticated descriptions of the NYCTA surface crews the police car passed. Cullen and Morales wondered how he knew so much about the minutiae of surface work; Darius responded with monologues about his mastery of the system. To the officers it seemed that he couldn't speak fast enough, that his confession had energized him and elevated his self-regard. The sight of the Brooklyn Bridge reminded Darius that he had plans to go to a barbecue the next day on the Manhattan Bridge: it was a Friday tradition of a bridge crew he had been working with. He asked if there was a chance he would get out in time. Officer Cullen said that, whether or not he got out, it might not be such a great idea.

At Centre Street, Darius was interviewed by A.D.A. Dougherty and Detective Martin Mullen. He gave no sign that he knew a transgression had occurred, that there was a permanent divide in the room and that he was alone on one side of it. With a single exception, neither interviewer noted any change in his demeanor, which was one of subdued bliss. According to Detective Mullen, "emotionally Darius was even-keeled the entire time. The fact that he was carrying these articles from his previous arrests—it was almost like he dug the publicity, like there was some prestige in the experience."

The exception came when A.D.A. Dougherty suggested that

Darius might have had something to do with the train's emergency stop. The absurd, pejorative idea that he would ever compromise service quality and passenger safety disturbed Darius. "That's exactly what I'm trained *not* to do," he said. He explained that stopping the train would have required both override permission from the City Hall control tower and access to the switch room in the back of the Fifty-seventh Street tower. Neither was available to him—though, as he admitted, he probably could have guessed the location of the switch-room key. City Hall later confirmed Darius's story, and evidence indicated that he had never been in the switch room. His theory of the event—a wheel-detector device had tripped the train's emergency brake because the train had exceeded the posted speed—was later determined to be the most plausible.

Once it became clear that Darius wouldn't plead to the charge of reckless endangerment, Dougherty and Mullen decided to let him talk. He talked for two hours and seemed willing to talk indefinitely. He was cagey when it came to identifying collaborators or detailing certain methods whose secrecy was essential to his freedom of movement; otherwise, almost any question elicited long tales of his exploits that gave way episodically to ornate, unnecessary digressions. Once I asked Darius what he was doing at Fifty-seventh Street before his arrest. My question implied that he'd been in the station. His answer began like this: "No, no. I was mainly in the tower, not the station. Now: Towers are for what is known as train-traffic control. The board lights tell you where everything is at. All right? Okay. So every single train from Fifth Avenue, on the N and the R, down to Canal Street. Not only that but there's a communications box for listening to the crew on every train. You also have what is known as fire watch. I watch the board for anything relating to a fire condition. Now, if it's something minute, I can hopefully go down and end the problem without having to call the fire department. If it's close to the third rail, use a dry chemical. If it's something major, call the fire department, call Command, have the power turned off for that section because otherwise the fire department cannot go on the tracks, that's part of their protocol. . . . And if need be you can have EMS on standby, just in case. So you always take all necessary precautions. Okay! Now on this particular day, I'm in the tower . . ."

•   •   •

Darius's obsession has always been concentrated on the subway, but a long interview with him will teach you how far beyond it he has roamed. He may describe his experiences as a substitute engineer on the freight-trains of Conrail, Norfolk Southern, Delaware & Hudson, or CSX. ("CSX is definitely my favorite. Every single engine is freshly painted.") He may tell you how to manipulate the employee-transfer protocol of the metro bus system to get a job as a shifter (cleaning and prepping buses at depots), and how to use that position to take buses out on express routes. He might explain Job 179 (conductor) on the Long Island Railroad: what track you'll be on (17 or 19), how to let the crew know when you've finished preparing the train for departure (two buzzes on the intercom), how you return to Penn Station "as equipment" (without passengers).

It is unlikely that Darius will omit the year he spent wearing an NYCTA superintendent's shield. While he was doing a stint as a conductor, he discovered that he could have a shield made in a jewelry store. He began wearing it on a vest he pulled over his TA-specified shirt and tie. He had a hard hat and pirated I.D. Darius considered himself a track-department superintendent, so he signed out track-department vehicles and radios and drove around the city, supervising track maintenance and construction projects and responding to emergencies. He was sensitive to the threat of close scrutiny by superiors, but given his high position and network of allies, that was rare. Darius worked regular hours: eight to four from Tuesday to Thursday, seven in the evening to three in the morning on Friday, and three until eleven on Saturday morning. That way he was off from Saturday morning until Tuesday morning. "Because of my title and my position," Darius told me, "I figured I had the seniority to do it."

At the end of the Centre Street interview, Darius was facing felony charges to which he had confessed. He had twice been convicted of felonies. He had just dramatically violated his parole, and he had multiple parole and probation violations on his record. But he never asked Detective Mullen or A.D.A. Dougherty about his legal situation. He shook their hands and was led out in handcuffs, his still face showing contentment.

•   •   •

On that day Darius's parents, who had retired from New York to North Carolina, awaited him uncertainly in their house outside Winston-Salem. Since his release, Mr. and Mrs. McCollum had prevailed on him to apply for a parole transfer and recommence his life in North Carolina, where Mrs. McCollum's nephew had found him a job through a state program for parolees. Darius stayed with them for a few weeks, and then went up to New York for a parole hearing. But weeks had passed; Darius's aunt, with whom he'd been staying, no longer knew where he was or what he was doing.

What he was doing, while sleeping and eating and showering at Nelly's or in NYCTA crew rooms, was driving a deicer train from Coney Island to Prospect Park on the D line; putting out track fires (a train dripping battery acid caused a small explosion at Thirty-fourth Street and Sixth Avenue, a tossed cigarette butt kindled a small rubbish fire in Brooklyn); investigating a busted water main at 110th Street on the A line; flagging traffic, on weekends, around a transit construction project at Queens Plaza

("The guys from transit that do street flagging, they look as if they're stiff, and see, when I do it, I look like I'm with DOT, because I make it look so efficient—I know how to do the hand signs"); assisting the track crew he mentioned to Cullen and Morales with inspections of the Manhattan Bridge on Mondays, Wednesdays, and Fridays; and entirely repainting a crew room after hearing a supervisor say that it would make a good project for someone. This all happened, Darius says, because he ran into some old friends at Queens Plaza soon after he got back to New York, and they invited him to hang out and take some of their shifts, and he thought he could do a few and go back to North Carolina, "but it just kept going, and that was it."

Elizabeth McCollum is unreserved and accurately judgmental and dresses well and cannot discuss her son without becoming fervent; she retired a decade ago from an administrative job at a textbook company. Samuel McCollum, a former plant supervisor, is bulky and skeptical, has an impulsive falsetto giggle, and tries, when discussing the actions of others, to discover decent motivations that have been obscured by mistakes or cruelties. Like his wife, he has been injured by the experiences of his only child: "Darius won't open up and talk about anything. He would never elaborate on an answer. That's all we ever wanted. Now, how do you get somebody like that in touch with himself?" On the day of the final arrest, Mrs. McCollum was still hopeful: "You can't let negativism cloud you, because with Darius, once that comes in, forget it." She and Mr. McCollum talked about the life Darius might have in North Carolina, and thought about getting him a driver's license and a pickup truck, which he had always wanted. They didn't say it, but they were each thinking that in their house Darius grew restless immediately.

The McCollum house stands at the edge of a rural two-lane, on a four-acre grass lot that runs to a curtain of hardwoods. The neighboring houses, similarly situated, occasionally give way to grazing horses. When I visited, the only thing in one big field down the road was a tethered mule. The problem for Darius was that he couldn't walk out the front door and easily go anywhere. The McCollums had furnished their house ardently: chiming clocks and porcelain figurines and hand-stitched antimacassars and graven glassware and pictures of sunset-silhouetted African kings left no blank space. Emptied from many rooms in many homes over a lifetime and now tensely converged in this final house, these encroaching objects in their familiarity had become largely invisible to Mr. and Mrs. McCollum, but in an attempt to understand the propensities of her son, Mrs. McCollum had preserved every document—subway notes and journals, school reports, letters from prison—that might explain him, and this expanding collection never entirely disappeared from her or her husband's awareness. Much was boxed; much lay around, visible and frequently handled; the things that Mrs. McCollum liked to look at every few days remained enshrined in convenient places. One was a letter from prison, dated June 12, 1987:

> Its me again saying hello along with a thought . . . my thought goes like this. There once lived a young man and a very bright man. This young man had . . . such good parents . . . they did everything that they saw was good for this guy. . . . The guy was actually great until he [got] into his teenage years and started hanging out around trains, trucks and buses, but one day it all caught up with him and this young man was confused. . . . This guy is away somewhere to where he can't runaway from and has to face his problems. He is sorry for everything and wants to forget about everything he has done. That is the end of that story. This is a beginning step. I am wondering what is going to happen when this young man comes home. . . . I'm sure there will be some changes but what I mean is will he be able to find his destiny.

Darius's call from Rikers Island didn't surprise Mr. and Mrs. McCollum. They had long since learned how to entertain ambitious plans for him while anticipating legal dilemmas. They replaced his court-appointed attorney with a family friend named Tracey Bloodsaw. Bloodsaw decided on a psychiatric defense and got the access order required for an examination, but corrections officers at Rikers Island, on various bureaucratic pretexts and over a period of months, refused to admit her psychiatrist. Justice Carol Berkman declined to intervene on the psychiatrist's behalf, and eventually precluded a psychiatric defense, declaring that adequate notice of such a defense had become impossible. Bloodsaw told Berkman what she thought of the ruling, explained to the McCollums that she had become a liability to Darius, and removed herself from the case.

Darius's next lawyer, Stephen Jackson, accepted a plea, and Justice Berkman scheduled a sentencing hearing. This empowered her to order—as opposed to merely authorizing—a psychiatric examination. A prison psychiatrist, after a cursory evaluation, noted that a neurological disorder called Asperger's Syndrome might explain Darius's behavior. Almost simultaneously, Jackson was contacted by members of several Asperger's support groups. Darius, whose arrests had been covered in newspapers for twenty years, had become well known among Asperger's experts and activists, and his case had been cited in at least one scholarly work. There was a strong consensus in the Asperger's community that Darius suffered from the syndrome, and dismay that his treatment had consisted entirely of jail time. Jackson decided to request an adjournment in court so that Darius could be examined and might receive a counseling-based sentence.

·　　·　　·

Stooped and silent at his sentencing, in late March of last year, Darius stood at the very edge of the courtroom, just in front of the holding-cell door through which he had been led. In accordance with the law, he faced Justice Berkman, who sat on a high plinth before a ten-foot mural of the Lady of Justice, between half-furled flags on eagle-tipped poles. The justice had black-gray hair and a squinty, repudiative face. She often listened to the lawyers with her chin on her upturned palms and her incredulous mouth open; she often rolled her eyes with unusual vigor and range, her head following, as if drawn by her eyes, until it almost touched her shoulder. Darius looked around only once, for his mother. Mrs. McCollum, anxious and carrying an accumulation of anger at the legal system, forced herself to smile at him. Darius says he wasn't thinking about anything: he knew what was going to happen.

I arrived before Darius and watched a few brusque bail hearings. The distant ceiling diminished the few spectators. Then the clerk called Darius's docket number and the lawyers identified themselves. They had spare tables at the foot of Justice Berkman's plinth. A.D.A. Dougherty—plain, young, resolute—sat alone. Stephen Jackson sat with Alvin Schlesinger, a former colleague of Justice Berkman's who had been recruited by the president of an Asperger's organization. Jackson is tall; every aspect of his appearance had been managed. His manner was measured and grandiloquent: he seemed to take a special pleasure in formality. (When I called him afterward and asked for an interview, he said, "Certainly I would be amenable at some point in time. Would you like to do it telephonically?") Schlesinger, who had retired to the country, seemed patient in a practiced, almost impervious way; after the sentencing he would drive back to Vermont without stopping, drink a double scotch, and write Justice Berkman a letter he would never send.

Jackson rose. "Your Honor," he said, "after the Court agreed to provide a plea to satisfy the indictment, I was inundated with information regarding Darius's possible psychological condition. It is apparent that he may be afflicted with Asperger's Syndrome. . . . The Court is aware of the letters that were sent to the Court providing the Court with information regarding the disease, and—"

"I'm sorry, Mr. Jackson," Justice Berkman said, staring hard at various faces in the courtroom, "but perhaps we could bottom-line this . . . having educated myself on the website and with the *DSM* and so forth, Mr. McCollum has some characteristics which are very much inconsistent with Asperger's. He's got a lot of friends. You told me he has a fiancée, and one of the major signs . . . is social dysfunction. Not just, gee, his friends think he's a little strange sometimes but an inability to relate to others. . . ." Mrs. McCollum started to get up and was pulled back down by the people on either side of her.

"In any event," Berkman said, "I don't understand what the point is. . . . So far as I can tell there's no treatment for Asperger's. That is number one. . . . Number two, Asperger's would not disable him from knowing that he's not supposed to form credentials identifying him as an employee of the Transit Authority and go in and take trains or buses or vans or cars or other modes of transportation, which I gather has been his specialty. . . . I don't see any reason to delay this further, because for some reason the press thinks that, oh, Darius is not responsible. Darius is responsible. . . . He can stop doing this, if his family and friends would stop telling him, oh, isn't this amusing. Right?" Mrs. McCollum rose rapidly and was pulled down.

Mr. Schlesinger stood and requested an adjournment so that the defense could have Darius examined and explore treatment options. Many experts felt that Darius had the disorder and to deny treatment was to risk indefinitely perpetuating his past: a limbo in the alternating forms of furtive impersonation and incarceration. Schlesinger had secured a promise from an Asperger's expert at the Yale Child Study Center to examine Darius and recommend a residential treatment facility. A.D.A. Dougherty stood and opposed the request. Given his history of parole and probation violations, Darius was a bad candidate for any treatment program. Stephen Jackson stood and pointed out the circularity: Darius is not a good candidate for treatment because of his condition, and his condition persists because he's not a good candidate for treatment.

Resisting several defense attempts to respond, Justice Berkman stabbed out: "Well, now that I've been accused of presiding over a travesty of justice and condemning Darius to a life sentence, I suppose there is no way of the Court coming out of this looking anything but monstrous. . . . This man is a danger. . . . But in the meantime we've made him a poster boy for the system's lack of compassion for the mentally ill. Well, I have a lot of compassion for the mentally ill. You know, we don't lock them up anymore. We let them have lives, and most of the mentally ill, I hear from the experts . . . lead law-abiding lives. Darius McCollum does not. That's too bad. The law says he has to face the consequences of that, because . . . he has free will, and that's the nature of humanity, and unless he wants to be treated like an animal . . . he has to exert his free will for the good . . . and to say that he is incapable of doing that is to take away his humanity. So all those people out there making faces at me"—Mrs. McCollum was shaking her head exaggeratedly—"thinking of me as the Wicked Witch of the West, are, in fact, the people who are stealing his humanity from him. . . ."

Mrs. McCollum stood up; before she could be pulled down Berkman had sentenced Darius to five years in prison. When the gavel hit, all the released talk overwhelmed her rapid words.

Jackson immediately appealed, on the ground that Justice Berkman's failure to grant an adjournment at sentencing was arbitrary. It's a weak argument: Jackson agreed to a plea and sentencing date and then waited until sentencing to ask for more time; Justice Berkman made no technical mistakes. The D.A.'s office has been disinclined to consider vacating Darius's plea and changing his sentence if he is diagnosed with Asperger's. This option, proposed by Alvin Schlesinger, who as a Supreme Court justice developed a relationship with New York County District

Attorney Robert Morgenthau, was theoretically available to the defense as soon as Darius was sentenced. Jackson, inexplicably, has yet to have Darius examined.

.   .   .

Asperger's Syndrome, which mainly affects males, is generally considered to be a mild variant of autism, with a prevalence rate several times higher. The *Diagnostic and Statistical Manual of Mental Disorders* requires five symptoms for a diagnosis: "impairment in social interaction," including "failure to develop [appropriate] peer relationships" and a "lack of social or emotional reciprocity"; "restricted, repetitive and stereotyped patterns of behavior, interests and activities," including an "encompassing preoccupation with [an area of] interest that is abnormal either in intensity or focus"; "significant impairment in social, occupational or other important areas of functioning"; and "no significant delay in cognitive [4] or language [5] development."

Among the "encompassing preoccupations" in the literature of Asperger's: Abbott and Costello, astrophysics, deep-ocean biology, deep-fat fryers, telephone-wire insulators, carnivorous dinosaurs, cows, Wagner, nineteenth-century Russian novels, storm drains, steam trains, transit timetables, Zoroastrianism, Zsa Zsa Gabor, and the genealogy of royalty. Entire lives are brought to bear on one tiny piece of the world. Because abstract thought tends to be very difficult for people with Asperger's, they satisfy their obsessions by amassing precisely defined units of information: numbers, terms, codes, dates, titles, materials, names, formulas.

Asperger's precludes normal emotional intuition. Behavioral cues are elusive: winks and shoulder-shrugging and sarcasm are often meaningless. Conversations are one-sided; patients generally deliver long, fact-crowded monologues on their areas of expertise, blind to gestures of boredom or puzzlement. General questions, which can require both speculating abstractly and intuiting a questioner's intent, are often impossible for people with Asperger's to answer. Patients may respond with a far-reaching elaboration of a single related fact or experience.

Conventions of interpersonal behavior, if they are not explicit, remain beyond comprehension, as when a small boy, generally affectionate toward his mother, asks her why, given that he can dress and feed himself, she is still necessary, or when a boy endlessly photographs people while telling them that humans are his favorite animal, or when Darius writes to his parents from prison: "Hello There, People of America lets get down and party on as we say hello and what's going on, cause I know there's something going on . . ." and:

> I am enclosing a reese's peanut butter cup coupon to let you read and see if you can win some money. Just read the directions. . . . I kind of wish that I was a Jeanie so I wouldn't have to be here. "Ha-ha." I've got a stiff neck and itching all over and cold feet and runny nose and watery eyes itchy ears o Mom I'm just in poor shape. There's a rat under my bed and a little green man on my head but there's a true blue inside of you that keeps stopping me to say that I Love You. In here: It's like Death of a Salesman with a happy ending I hope. Well you guys I guess I will go to bed to get warm so have fun and keep out of trouble. Give my regards to Broadway . . .

Explicit rules that make sense socially but aren't strictly rational seem unconvincing and often go unheeded, as when a boy in junior high asks a female classmate if he can touch her crotch as casually as if he were asking to borrow an eraser. That explicit and logical rules exist along a continuum of seriousness is unappreciated, as when a young man follows a barefoot woman around a supermarket, assiduously trying to conceal her naked feet from employees, and then stands behind her in the express lane, diligently removing one of her purchases each time she turns her head until she is no longer over the ten-item limit.

Speech is oddly formal and often unmarked by accent, as if verbal local color had been filtered out. Specialized phrases are applied in a way that is logical but, from the perspective of conventional usage, awkward or bizarre, as when an English boy describes a hole in his sock as "a temporary loss of knitting."

For people with Asperger's, self-identity has little to do with internal life; information constitutes identity. One boy who was asked to draw a self-portrait sketched an ocean liner, cracked and sinking beside an iceberg; the *Titanic* was his obsession. Another self-portrait accurately represented a tsunami-shadowed tract of California coast; its author was fascinated by plate tectonics. An autobiographical statement:

> I am an intelligent, unsociable, but adaptable person. I would like to dispel any untrue rumors about me. I am not edible. I cannot fly. I cannot use telekinesis. My brain is not large enough to destroy the entire world when unfolded. I did not teach my long-haired guinea pig Chronos to eat everything in sight (that is the nature of the long-haired guinea pig).

People with Asperger's recognize their difference. One patient said he wished he had a micro-brain on his head to process all the intuitive meaning that surrounded and evaded him. Another patient, studying astronomy, told his therapist that he knew how scientists discovered the stars, and what instruments they used to discover the stars, but not how they discovered the names of the stars. He said he felt like a poor computer simulation of a human being, and he invented algebraic formulas to predict human emotion: frustration (z), talent (x), and lack of opportunity (y) give the equation $x + y = z$.

Darius, explaining that he has never needed to socialize and really only associates with people in transit systems, said to me, "Some people think that I'm different. Okay, fine, I am different, but everybody's different in their own kind of way. Some people just don't know how to directly really react to that." Before Darius's sentencing hearing, Stephen Jackson sent him a pamphlet on Asperger's. It was the first Darius had heard of the disorder. When I asked him about the pamphlet, he said, "I'll put it like this. Out of the twelve things that's on it I think I can identify myself with at least eight or nine. And all you need is five to have, you know, that type of thing."

Asperger's patients choose obsessions the way other people choose interests: personality accounts for the choice. Sometimes, usually when they're young, patients acquire and discard fixations in swift succession, but eventually a single subject consumes them. They are born to fall down some rabbit hole, from which they never fully emerge.

·   ·   ·

The Clinton Correctional Facility, where I interviewed Darius, is a leviathan relic from 1845, just south of the Canadian border, with granite walls thirty feet high. In the intake center a guard examined the cassette and batteries in my tape recorder. I was escorted across a lawn to the main prison building. The walls leaned in—thirty feet is claustrophobically high. There were long-barreled guns and searchlights in guard towers. I felt as if I might provoke a terrible reaction by accident. We went through the prison lobby, a leaden door, a corridor, another leaden door, and arrived at the interview room, where the guard left me. Except for a table and chairs, the room was as plain as a cell. I sat waiting in a restless institutional quiet. Two guards brought Darius in. In his jumpsuit he looked lumpy and quiescent. We shook hands—Darius's handshake was bonelessly indifferent—and sat down. The guards left, one whispering to the other, "He's pretty docile."

I made a vague little speech: I was writing an article, etc. Darius nodded politely as I talked but gave no indication that he was interested in my aims or motivations or life. When I finished he asked where I was staying and how much it cost and what train I'd come on and how long it had taken. From the time of the trip he guessed that my train hadn't had an M-10 engine; he wished me luck getting one on the way back. I started asking about his career in transit, and he showed the transporting animation that Detective Mullen had observed. He sketched control panels in the air, he drove trains in mime, he asked for paper and drew the track intersections of subway stations. He often looked away to concentrate on the images he conjured.

Clinton is a maximum-security facility. Darius was there because the Department of Corrections, aware of his impersonation convictions, considered him an escape risk. To keep him safe the DOC had to segregate him from the general population, which meant confining him to his cell for, Darius said, twenty-one hours a day. That morning he had made the guards laugh by wedging a sign in his cell bars that said, "Train Out of Service." He watched TV and read general-interest magazines; he studied arrangements of facts in several specialty publications he subscribed to: *Truckers News, World of Trains, Truck 'N Trailer*; he made lists of various things, like 185 love songs he happened to think of one day; and he wrote a lot of letters requesting information. Unsatisfied by something he saw on TV, he wrote to the Department of Defense, which replied:

Unfortunately, the term "discretionary warfare" is not currently used by the Department of Defense (DoD), so I am uncertain what you mean by it. In addition, there are no 12-man Special Operations units made up of personnel who are at the rank of Colonel or above. There are however, Special Operations units made up of 12 men: the US Army Special Forces A Teams. The Special Forces A team is

made up of two officers, two operations/intelligence sergeants, two weapons sergeants, two communications sergeants, two medics and two engineers—all trained in
unconventional warfare and cross-trained in each other's
specialties.

Darius underlined the word "two" every time it appeared.

On May 31 of this year, Darius will have spent 799 days in
prison. At his first parole hearing, 912 days into his sentence, the
D.A.'s office will present his history of violations. His full sentence comes to 1,825 days. In the interview room of the Clinton
Correctional Facility, I asked Darius if he thought he would continue to impersonate transit employees and otherwise break the
law. He looked at the ceiling and took a long breath. He seemed
to have prepared his answer. "Okay," he said, "trains are always
going to be my greatest love. It's something that I depend upon
because I've been knowing how to do it for twenty-five years. So
this is like my home, my best friend, my everything. Everything
that I need and want is there. But I don't want to get caught up
with that again, and I'm probably going to need a little help. That
much I can admit. If I can find—I know there's no such program
as Trains Anonymous, but if I can get some kind of counseling it
would be really beneficial towards me."

Darius doesn't like prison and complains about its deprivations, but he never expresses despair or outrage at the severity of
his punishment. He sees his experience in terms of its daily components, without considering the entirety of his sentence—the
abstract unbroken length of time between the present and his
release. "I'll get out of here sooner or later," he says. And it
doesn't occur to him to imagine an alternative life for himself: he
never wonders what he might have been.

The Georgia Review

FINALIST, FICTION

Three Girls

The Georgia Review *is where fiction goes to take a chance, share a poignant moment or just have a good time. "Three Girls" is the story of two girl-poets in 1956 who spot Marilyn Monroe browsing in the Strand bookshop. Here, imagination rules and style takes precedence.*

Joyce Carol Oates

Three Girls

In Strand Used Books on Broadway and Twelfth one snowy March early evening in 1956 when the streetlights on Broadway glimmered with a strange sepia glow, we were two NYU girl-poets drifting through the warehouse of treasures as through an enchanted forest. Just past 6:00 P.M. Above light-riddled Manhattan, opaque night. Snowing, and sidewalks encrusted with ice so there were fewer customers in the Strand than usual at this hour but *there we were.* Among other cranky brooding regulars. In our army-surplus jackets, baggy khaki pants, and zip-up rubber boots. In our matching wool caps (knitted by your restless fingers) pulled down low over our pale-girl foreheads. Enchanted by books. Enchanted by the Strand.

No bookstore of merely "new" books with elegant show window displays drew us like the drafty Strand, bins of books untidy and thumbed through as merchants' sidewalk bins on Four-teenth Street, NEW THIS WEEK, BEST BARGAINS, WORLD CLASSICS, ART BOOKS 50% OFF, REVIEWERS' COPIES, HIGHEST PRICE $1.98, REMAIN-DERS 25¢–$1.00. Hardcover/paperback. Spotless/battered. Beautiful books/cheaply printed pulp paper. And at the rear and sides in that vast echoing space massive shelves of books books books rising to a ceiling of hammered tin fifteen feet above! Stacked shelves so high they required ladders to negotiate and a monkey nimbleness (like yours) to climb.

We were enchanted with the Strand and with each other in the Strand. Overseen by surly young clerks who were poets like us, or playwrights/actors/artists. In an agony of unspoken young love I watched you. As always on these romantic evenings at the Strand, prowling the aisles sneering at those luckless books, so many of them, unworthy of your attention. Bestsellers, how-tos, arts and crafts, too-simple *histories of*. Women's romances, sentimental love poems. Patriotic books, middlebrow books, books lacking esoteric covers. We were girl-poets passionately enamored of T. S. Eliot but scornful of Robert Frost whom we'd been made to memorize in high school—slyly we communicated in code phrases from Eliot in the presence of obtuse others in our dining hall and residence. We were admiring of though confused by the poetry of Yeats, we were yet more confused by the lauded worth of Pound, enthusiastically drawn to the bold metaphors of Kafka (that cockroach!) and Dostoevski (sexy murderer Raskolnikov and the Underground Man were our rebel heroes) and Sartre ("Hell is other people"—we knew this), and had reason to believe that we were their lineage though admittedly we were American middle class, and Caucasian, and female. (Yet we were not "conventional" females. In fact, we shared male contempt for the merely "conventional" female.)

Brooding above a tumble of books that quickened the pulse, almost shyly touching Freud's *Civilization and Its Discontents*, Crane Brinton's *The Age of Reason*, Margaret Mead's *Coming of Age in Samoa*, D. H. Lawrence's *The Rainbow*, Kierkegaard's *Fear and Trembling*, Mann's *Death in Venice*—there suddenly you glided up behind me to touch my wrist (as never you'd done before, had you?) and whispered, "Come here," in a way that thrilled me for its meaning *I have something wonderful/unex-pected/startling to show you.* Like poems these discoveries in the Strand were, to us, found poems to be cherished. And eagerly I turned to follow you though disguising my eagerness, "Yes, what?" as if you'd interrupted me, for possibly we'd had a quarrel earlier that day, a flaring up of tense girl-tempers. Yes, you were childish and self-absorbed and given to sulky silences and mercurial moods in the presence of showy superficial people, and I adored and feared you knowing you'd break my heart, my heart that had never before been broken because never before so exposed.

So eagerly yet with my customary guardedness I followed you through a maze of book bins and shelves and stacks to the ceiling ANTHROPOLOGY, ART/ANCIENT, ART/RENAISSANCE, ART/MODERN, ART/ASIAN, ART/WESTERN, TRAVEL, PHILOSOPHY, COOKERY, POETRY/MODERN where the way was treacherously lighted only by bare sixty-watt bulbs, and where customers as cranky as we two stood in the aisles reading books, or sat hunched on footstools glancing up annoyed at our passage, and unquestioning I followed you until at POETRY/MODERN you halted, and pushed me ahead and around a corner, and I stood puzzled staring, not knowing what I was supposed to be seeing until impatiently you poked me in the ribs and pointed, and now I perceived an individual in the aisle pulling down books from shelves, peering at them, clearly absorbed by what she read, a woman nearly my height (I was tall for a girl, in 1956) in a man's navy coat to her ankles and with sleeves past her wrists, a man's beige fedora hat on her head, scrunched low as we wore our knitted caps, and most of her hair hidden by the hat except for a six-inch blond plait at the nape of her neck; and she wore black trousers tucked into what appeared to be salt-stained cowboy boots. Someone we knew? An older, good-looking student from one of our classes? *A girl-poet like ourselves?* I was about to nudge you in the ribs in bafflement when the blond woman turned, taking down another book from the shelf (e. e. cummings' *Tulips and Chimneys*—always

I would remember that title!), and I saw that she was Marilyn
Monroe.

Marilyn Monroe. In the Strand. Just like us. And she seemed
to be alone.

Marilyn Monroe, alone!

Wholly absorbed in browsing amid books, oblivious of her
surroundings and of us. No one seemed to have recognized her
(yet) except you.

Here was the surprise: this woman was/was not Marilyn Monroe. For this woman was an individual wholly absorbed in selecting, leafing through, pausing to read books. You could see that
this individual was a *reader*. One of those who *reads*. With concentration, with passion. With her very soul. And it was poetry
she was reading, her lips pursed, silently shaping words. Absent-
mindedly she wiped her nose on the edge of her hand, so intent
was she on what she was reading. For when you truly read
poetry, poetry reads *you*.

Still, this woman was—Marilyn Monroe. And despite our
common sense, our scorn for the silly clichés of Hollywood
romance, still we halfway expected a Leading Man to join her:
Clark Gable, Robert Taylor, Marlon Brando.

Halfway we expected the syrupy surge of movie music, to
glide us into the scene.

But no man joined Marilyn Monroe in her disguise as one of
us in the Strand. No Leading Man, no dark prince.

Like us (we began to see) this Marilyn Monroe required no
man.

For what seemed like a long time but was probably no more
than half an hour, Marilyn Monroe browsed in the POETRY/MOD-
ERN shelves, as from a distance of approximately ten feet two girl-
poets watched covertly, clutching each other's hands. We were
stunned to see that this woman looked very little like the glamorous "Marilyn Monroe." That figure was a garish blond show-
girl, a Hollywood "sexpot" of no interest to intellectuals (*we*

thought, we who knew nothing of the secret romance between Marilyn Monroe and Arthur Miller); this figure more resembled us (almost) than she resembled her Hollywood image. We were dying of curiosity to see whose poetry books Marilyn Monroe was examining: Elizabeth Bishop, H.D., Robert Lowell, Muriel Rukeyser, Harry Crosby, Denise Levertov . . . Five or six of these Marilyn Monroe decided to purchase, then moved on, leather bag slung over her shoulder and fedora tilted down on her head.

We couldn't resist, we had to follow! Cautious not to whisper together like excited schoolgirls, still less to giggle wildly as we were tempted; you nudged me in the ribs to sober me, gave me a glare signaling *Don't be rude, don't ruin this for all of us.* I conceded: I was the more pushy of the two of us, a tall gawky Rima the Bird Girl with springy carroty-red hair like an exotic bird's crest, while you were petite and dark haired and attractive with long-lashed Semitic sloe eyes, you the wily gymnast and I the aggressive basketball player, you the "experimental" poet and I drawn to "forms," our contrary talents bred in our bones. Which of us would marry, have babies, disappear into "real" life, and which of us would persevere into her thirties before starting to be published and becoming, in time, a "real" poet—could anyone have predicted, this snowy March evening in 1956?

Marilyn Monroe drifted through the maze of books and we followed in her wake as through a maze of dreams, past SPORTS, past MILITARY, past WAR, past HISTORY/ANCIENT, past the familiar figures of Strand regulars frowning into books, past surly yawning bearded clerks who took no more heed of the blond actress than they ever did of us, and so to NATURAL HISTORY where she paused, and there again for unhurried minutes (the Strand was open until 9:00 P.M.) Marilyn Monroe in her mannish disguise browsed and brooded, pulling down books, seeking what? at last crouched leafing through an oversized illustrated book (curiosity overcame me! I shoved away your restraining hand; politely I eased past Marilyn Monroe murmuring "excuse me" without so much as brushing against her and without being noticed), Charles Darwin's *Origin of Species* in a deluxe edition. Darwin! *Origin of Species*! We were poet-despisers-of-science, or believed we were, or must be, to be true poets in the exalted mode of T. S. Eliot and William Butler Yeats; such a choice, for Marilyn Monroe, seemed perverse to us. But this book was one Marilyn quickly decided to purchase, hoisting it into her arms and moving on.

That rakish fedora we'd come to covet, and that single chunky blond braid. (Afterward we would wonder: Marilyn Monroe's hair in a braid? Never had we seen Marilyn Monroe with her hair braided in any movie or photo. What did this mean? Did it mean anything? *Had she quit films, and embarked on a new, anonymous life in our midst?*)

Suddenly Marilyn Monroe glanced back at us, frowning as a child might frown (had we spoken aloud? had she heard our thoughts?), and there came into her face a look of puzzlement, not alarm or annoyance but a childlike puzzlement: *Who are you? You two? Are you watching me?* Quickly we looked away. We were engaged in a whispering dispute over a book one of us had fumbled from a shelf, *A History of Botanical Gardens in England*. So we were undetected. We hoped!

But wary now, and sobered. For what if Marilyn Monroe had caught us, and knew that we knew?

She might have abandoned her books and fled the Strand. What a loss for her, and for the books! For us, too.

Oh, we worried at Marilyn Monroe's recklessness! We dreaded her being recognized by a (male) customer or (male) clerk. A girl or woman would have kept her secret (so we thought) but no man could resist staring openly at her, following her, and at last speaking to her. Of course, the blond actress in Strand Used Books wasn't herself, not at all glamorous, or "sexy," or especially blond, in her inconspicuous man's clothing and those salt-stained boots; she might have been anyone, female or male, hardly a Hollywood celebrity, a movie goddess. Yet if you stared, you'd recognize her. If you tried, with any imagination you'd see "Marilyn Monroe." It was like a child's game in which you stare at foliage, grass, clouds in the sky, and suddenly you see a face or a figure, and after that recognition you can't not see the hidden shape, it's staring you in the face. So too with Marilyn Monroe. Once we saw her, it seemed to us she must be seen—and recognized—by anyone who happened to glance at her. If any man saw! We were fearful her privacy would be destroyed. Quickly the blond actress would become surrounded, mobbed. It was risky and reckless of her to have come to Strand Used Books by herself, we thought. Sure, she could shop at Tiffany's, maybe; she could stroll through the lobby of the Plaza, or the Waldorf-Astoria; she'd be safe from fans and unwanted admirers in privileged settings on the Upper East Side, but—here? In the egalitarian Strand, on Broadway and Twelfth?

We were perplexed. Almost, I was annoyed with her. Taking such chances! But you, gripping my wrist, had another, more subtle thought.

"She thinks she's like *us*."

You meant: a human being, anonymous. Female, like us. Amid the ordinary unspectacular customers (predominantly male) of the Strand.

And that was the sadness in it, Marilyn Monroe's wish. To be *like us*. For it was impossible, of course. For anyone could have told Marilyn Monroe, even two young girl-poets, that it was too late for her in history. Already, at age thirty (we could calculate afterward that this was her age) "Marilyn Monroe" had entered history, and there was no escape from it. Her films, her photos. Her face, her figure, her name. To enter history is to be abducted spiritually, with no way back. As if lightning were to strike the building that housed the Strand, as if an actual current of electricity were to touch and transform only one individual in the great cavernous space and that lone individual, by pure chance it might seem, the caprice of fate, would be the young woman with the blond braid and the fedora slanted across her face. Why? Why her, and not another? You could argue that such a destiny is absurd, and undeserved, for one individual among many, and logically you would be correct. And yet: "Marilyn Monroe" has entered history, and you have not. She will endure, though the young woman with the blond braid will die. *And even should she wish to die, "Marilyn Monroe" cannot.*

By this time she—the young woman with the blond braid— was carrying an armload of books. We were hoping she'd almost finished and would be leaving soon, before strangers' rude eyes lighted upon her and exposed her, but no: she surprised us by heading for a section called JUDAICA. In that forbidding aisle, which we'd never before entered, there were books in numerous languages: Hebrew, Yiddish, German, Russian, French. Some of these books looked ancient! Complete sets of the Talmud. Cryptically printed tomes on the cabala. Luckily for us, the titles Marilyn Monroe pulled out were all in English: *Jews of Eastern Europe; The Chosen People: A Complete History of the Jews; Jews of the New World.* Quickly Marilyn Monroe placed her bag and books on the floor, sat on a footstool, and leafed through pages with the frowning intensity of a young girl, as if searching for something urgent, something she knew—knew!—must be there; in this uncomfortable posture she remained for at least fifteen minutes, wetting her fingers to turn pages that stuck together, pages that had not been turned, still less read, for decades. She was frowning, yet smiling too; faint vertical lines appeared between her eyebrows, in the intensity of her concentration; her eyes moved rapidly along lines of print, then returned, and moved more slowly. By this time we were close enough to observe the blond actress's feverish cheeks and slightly parted moist lips that seemed to move silently. *What is she reading in that ancient book, what can possibly mean so much to her? A secret, revealed? A secret, to save her life?*

"Hey you!" a clerk called out in a nasal, insinuating voice.

The three of us looked up, startled.

But the clerk wasn't speaking to us. Not to the blond actress frowning over *The Chosen People*, and not to us who were hovering close by. The clerk had caught someone slipping a book into an overcoat pocket, not an unusual sight at the Strand.

After this mild upset, Marilyn Monroe became uneasy. She turned to look frankly at us, and though we tried clumsily to retreat, her eyes met ours. *She knows!* But after a moment, she simply turned back to her book, stubborn and determined to finish what she was reading, while we continued to hover close by, exposed now, and blushing, yet feeling protective of her. *She has seen us, she knows. She trusts us.* We saw that Marilyn Monroe was beautiful in her anonymity as she had never seemed, to us, to be beautiful as "Marilyn Monroe." All that was makeup, fakery, cartoon sexiness subtle as a kick in the groin. All that was vulgar and infantile. But this young woman was beautiful without makeup, without even lipstick; in her mannish clothes, her hair in a stubby braid. Beautiful: her skin luminous and pale and her eyes a startling clear blue. Almost shyly she glanced back at us, to note that we were still there, and she smiled. *Yes, I see you two. Thank you for not speaking my name.*

Always you and I would remember: that smile of gratitude, and sweetness.

Always you and I would remember: that she trusted us, as perhaps we would not have trusted ourselves.

So many years later, I'm proud of us. We were so young.

Young, headstrong, arrogant, insecure though "brilliant"—or so we'd been led to believe. Not that we thought of ourselves as young: you were nineteen, I was twenty. We were mature for our ages, and we were immature. We were intellectually sophisticated, and emotionally unpredictable. We revered something we called *art*, we were disdainful of something we called *life*. We were overly conscious of ourselves. And yet: how patient, how protective, watching over Marilyn Monroe squatting on a foot-stool in the JUDAICA stacks as stray customers pushed past mut-tering "excuse me!" or not even seeming to notice her, or the two of us standing guard. And at last—a relief—Marilyn Monroe shut the unwieldy book, having decided to buy it, and rose from the footstool gathering up her many things. And—this was a temptation!—we held back, not offering to help her carry her things as we so badly wanted to, but only just following at a dis-creet distance as Marilyn Monroe made her way through the labyrinth of the bookstore to the front counter. (Did she glance back at us? Did she understand you and I were her protectors?) If anyone dared to approach her, we intended to intervene. We would push between Marilyn Monroe and whomever it was. Yet how strange the scene was: none of the other Strand customers, lost in books, took any special notice of her, any more than they took notice of us. Book lovers, especially used-book lovers, are not ones to stare curiously at others, but only at books. At the front of the store—it was a long hike—the cashiers would be more alert, we thought. One of them seemed to be watching Marilyn Monroe approach. Did he know? Could he guess? Was he waiting for her?

Nearing the front counter and the bright fluorescent lights overhead, Marilyn Monroe seemed for the first time to falter. She fumbled to extract out of her shoulder bag a pair of dark glasses and managed to put them on. She turned up the collar of her navy coat. She lowered her hat brim.

Still she was hesitant, and it was then that I stepped forward and said quietly, "Excuse me. Why don't I buy your books for you? That way you won't have to talk to anyone."

The blond actress stared at me through her oversized dark glasses. Her eyes were only just visible behind the lenses. A shy-girl's eyes, startled and grateful.

And so I did. With you helping me. Two girl-poets, side by side, all brisk and businesslike, making Marilyn Monroe's purchases for her: a total of sixteen books!—hardcover and paper-back, relatively new books, old battered thumbed-through books—at a cost of $55.85. A staggering sum! Never in my two years of coming into the Strand had I handed over more than a few dollars to the cashier, and this time my hand might have trembled as I pushed twenty-dollar bills at him, half expecting the bristly bearded man to interrogate me: "Where'd you get so much money?" But as usual the cashier hardly gave me a second glance. And Marilyn Monroe, burdened with no books, had already slipped through the turnstile and was awaiting us at the front door.

There, when we handed over her purchases in two sturdy bags, she leaned forward. For a breathless moment we thought she might kiss our cheeks. Instead she pressed into our surprised hands a slender volume she lifted from one of the bags: *Selected Poems of Marianne Moore*. We stammered thanks, but already the blond actress had pulled the fedora down more tightly over her head and had stepped out into the lightly falling snow, headed south on Broadway. We trailed behind her, unable to resist, wait-ing for her to hail a taxi, but she did not. We knew we must not follow her. By this time we were giddy with the strain of the past hour, gripping each other's hands in childlike elation. So happy!

"Oh. Oh God. Marilyn Monroe. She gave us a book. Was any of it real?"

It was real: we had *Selected Poems of Marianne Moore* to prove it.

That snowy early evening in March at Strand Used Books. That magical evening of Marilyn Monroe, when I kissed you for the first time.

The New Yorker

WINNER, FICTION

Jolene: A Life

If there is a gold standard in short fiction, it is The New Yorker, *which consistently publishes writers who create finely drawn characters, indelible landscapes and unforgettable prose. E. L. Doctorow mesmerizes with his dark but giddy story of a deprived young girl's inevitable fall into cultural and personal despair.*

E. L. Doctorow

Jolene: A Life

She married Mickey Holler when she was fifteen. Married him to get out of her latest foster home, where her so-called dad used to fool with her, get her to hold him, things like that. Even before her menses started. And her foster mom liked to slap her up the head for no reason. Or for every reason. So she married Mickey. And he loved her—that was a plus. She had never had that experience before. It made her look at herself in the mirror and do things with her hair. He was twenty, Mickey. Real name Mervin. He was a sweet boy, if without very much upstairs, as she knew even from their first date. He had a heel that didn't touch the ground and weak eyes, but he was not the kind to lay a hand on a woman. And she could tell him what she wanted, like a movie or a grilled-cheese sandwich and a chocolate shake, and it became his purpose in life. He loved her, he really did, even if he didn't know much about it.

But, anyway, she was out of the house now, and wearing a wedding ring to Jeff David High. Some of the boys said smutty things, but the girls looked upon her with a new respect.

Mickey's Uncle Phil had come to the justice of the peace with them, to be best man. After the ceremony he grinned and said, Welcome to our family, Jolene, honey, and gave her a big hug that lasted a mite too long. Uncle Phil was like a father to Mickey and employed him to drive one of the trucks in his home-oil-delivery business. Mickey Holler was almost an orphan. His real father was in the state penitentiary with no parole, for the same reason that his mother was in the burial ground behind the First Baptist Church. Jolene asked Mickey, as she thought permissible now that she was a relation, what his mother had done to deserve her fate. But he got all flustered when he tried to talk about it. It happened when he was only twelve. She was left to gather for herself that his father was a crazy drunk who had done bad things even before this happened. But, anyway, that was why Jolene was living now with Mickey under the same roof with his Uncle Phil and Aunt Kay.

Aunt Kay was real smart. She was an assistant manager in the Southern People's Bank across the square from the courthouse. So, between her and Uncle Phil's oil business, they had a nice ranch house with a garden out back and a picnic table and two hammocks between the trees.

Jolene liked the room she and Mickey occupied, though it looked into the driveway, and she had all she could do to keep it nice, with Mickey dropping his greasy coveralls on the floor. But she understood the double obligations of being a wife and an unpaying boarder besides. As she was home from school before anyone finished his job for the day, she tried to make herself useful. She would have an hour or so to do some of her homework and then she would go into the kitchen and put up something for everyone's dinner.

Jolene had always liked school—she felt at home there. Her favorite subject was art. She had been drawing from the time she was in third grade, when the class had done a mural of the Battle of Gettysburg and she drew more of it than anyone. She couldn't do much art now at this time in her life as a married woman, not being just for herself anymore. But she still noticed things. She was someone who had an eye for what wants to be drawn. Mickey had a white hairless chest with a collarbone that stood out across from shoulder to shoulder like he was someone's beast of burden. And a long neck and a backbone that she could use to do sums. He surely did love her—he cried sometimes he loved her so much—but that was all. She had a sixteenth birthday and he bought her a negligee he'd picked out himself at Berman's department store. It was three sizes too big. Jolene could take it back for exchange, of course, but she had the unsettling thought that as Mickey's wife all that would happen in her life to come was she would grow into something that size. He liked to watch her doing her homework, which made her realize he had no ambition for himself, Mickey Holler. He would never run a business and play golf on the weekend like Uncle Phil. He was a day-to-day person. He did not ever talk about buying his own home, or moving toward anything that would make things different for them than they were now. She could think this of him even though she liked to kiss his pale chest and run her fingers over the humps of his backbone.

Uncle Phil was tall with a good strong jaw and a head of shining black hair he combed in a kind of wave, and he had dark meaningful eyes and a deep voice, and he joked around with a lot of self-assurance—oh, he was a man, of that there was no doubt. At first it made Jolene nervous when he would eye her up and down. Or he would sing a line from a famous love song to her. *You are so beautiful to me-e!* And then he would laugh to let her know it was all just the same horsing around as he was accustomed to doing. He was tanned from being out on the county golf course, and even the slight belly he had on him under his knit shirt seemed just right. The main thing about him was that he enjoyed his life, and he was popular; they had their social set, though you could see most of their friends came through him.

Aunt Kay was not exactly the opposite of Uncle Phil, but she was the one who attended to business. She was a proper sort who never sat back with her shoes off, and, though kind and correct as far as Jolene was concerned, clearly would have preferred to have her home to herself now that Mickey had someone to take care of him. Jolene knew this—she didn't have to be told. She could work her fingers to the bone and Aunt Kay would still never love her. Aunt Kay was a Yankee and had come to live in the South because of a job offer. She and Uncle Phil had been married fifteen years. She called him Philip, which Jolene thought was putting on airs. She wore suits and panty hose, always, and blouses with collars buttoned to the neck. She was no beauty, but you could see what had interested Phil—her very light blue, icy eyes, maybe, and naturally blond hair, and she had a generous figure that required a panty girdle, which she was never without.

But now Uncle Phil got in the habit of waking them up in the morning, coming into their room without knocking and saying in his deep voice, Time for work, Mickey Holler! but looking at Jolene in the meantime as she pulled the covers up to her chin.

She knew the man was doing something he shouldn't be doing with that wake-up routine and it made her angry but she didn't know what she could do about it. Mickey seemed blind to the fact that his own uncle, his late mother's brother, had an eye for her. At the same time, she was excited to have been noticed by this man of the world. She knew that as a handsome smiling fellow with white teeth Phil would be quite aware of his effect on women, so she made a point of seeming to be oblivious of him as anything but her husband's uncle and employer. But this became more and more difficult, living in the same house with him. She found herself thinking about him. In her mind Jolene made up a story: how gradually, over time, it would become apparent that she and Uncle Phil were meant for each other. How an understanding would arise between them and go on for some years until, possibly, Aunt Kay died, or left him—it wasn't all that clear in Jolene's mind.

But Uncle Phil was not one for dreaming. One afternoon she was scrubbing their kitchen floor for them, down on her knees in her shorts with her rump up in the air, and he had come home early, in that being his own boss he could come and go as he liked. She was humming "I Want to Hold Your Hand" and didn't hear him.

He stood in the door watching how the scrubbing motion was rendered on her behind, and no sooner did she realize she was not alone than he was lifting her from the waist in her same kneeling position and carrying her that way into his bedroom, the scrub brush still in her hand.

That night in her own bed she could still smell Uncle Phil's aftershave lotion and feel the little cotton balls of their chenille bedspread in the grasp of her fingers. She was too sore even for Mickey's fumblings.

And that was the beginning. In all Jolene's young life, she had never been to where she couldn't wait to see someone. She tried to contain herself, but her schoolwork began to fall off, though she had always been a conscientious student, even if not the smartest brain in her class. But it was that way with Phil, too—it was so intense and constant that he was no longer laughing. It was more like they were equals in their magnetic attraction. They just couldn't get enough. It was every day, always while Aunt Kay was putting up her numbers in the Southern People's Bank and Mickey, poor Mickey, was riding his oil route as Uncle Phil devised it to the furthermost reaches of the town line and beyond.

Well, the passion between people can never be anything but drawn to a conclusion by the lawful spouses around them, and after a month or two of this everyone knew it, and the crisis came banging open the bedroom door shouting her name, and all at once Mickey was riding Phil's back like a monkey, beating him about the head and crying all the while, and Phil, in his skivvies, with Mickey pounding him, staggered around the combined living-and-dining room till he backpedalled the poor boy up against their big TV and smashed him through the screen. Jolene, in her later reflections, when she had nothing in the world to do but pass the time, remembered everything—she remembered the bursting sound of the TV glass, she remembered how surprised she was to see how skinny Phil's legs were, and that the sun through the blinds was so bright because daylight-saving had come along unbeknownst to the lovers, which was why the working people had got home before they were supposed to. But at the time there was no leisure for thought. Aunt Kay was dragging her by the hair through the hall over the shag carpet and into the kitchen, across the fake-tile flooring, and she was out the kitchen door, kicked down the back steps, and thrown out like someone's damn cat and yowling like one, too.

Jolene waited out there by the edge of the property, crouching in the bushes in her shift with her arms folded across her breasts. She waited for Phil to come out and take her away, but he never did. Mickey was the one who opened the door. He stood there looking at her in the quiet outside, while from the house they listened to the shouting and the sound of things breaking. Mickey's hair was sticking up and his glasses were bent broken across his nose. Jolene called to him. She was crying; she wanted him to forgive her and tell her it was all right. But what he did, her Mickey, he got in his pickup in his bloody shirt and drove away. That was what Jolene came to think of as the end of Chapter 1 in her life story, because where Mickey drove to was the middle of the Catawba River bridge, and there he stopped and with the engine still running he jumped off into that rocky river and killed himself.

•　　•　　•

More than one neighbor must have seen her wandering the streets, and by and by a police cruiser picked her up, and first she was taken to the emergency room, where it was noted that her vital signs were O.K., though they showed her where a clump of her red hair had been pulled out. Then she was put into a motel off the interstate while the system figured out what to do with her. She was a home wrecker but also a widow but also a juvenile with no living relatives. The fosters she had left to marry Mickey would take no responsibility for her. Time passed. She watched soaps. She cried. A matron was keeping an eye on her morning and night. Then a psychiatrist who worked for the county came to interview her. A day after that, she was driven to a court hearing with testimony by this county psychiatrist she had told her story to in all honesty, and that was something that embittered her as the double cross of all time, because on his recommendation she was remanded to the juvenile loony bin until such time as she was to become a reasonable adult able to take care of herself.

Well, so there she was, moping about on their pills, half asleep for most of the day and night, and of course, as she quickly learned, this was no place to regain her sanity, if she had ever lost it in the first place, which she knew just by looking at who else was there that she hadn't. About two months into the hell there, they one morning took off her usual gray hanging frock and put her in a recognizable dark dress, though a size too big, and fixed her hair with a barrette and drove her in a van to the courthouse once again, though this time it was for her testimony as to her relations with Uncle Phil, who was there at the defense table looking awful. She didn't know what was different about him till she realized his hair was without lustre and, in fact, gray. Then she knew that all this time she had been so impressed he had been dyeing it. He was hunched over from the fix he was in and he never looked at her, this man of the world. A little of the old feeling arose in her and she was angry with herself but she couldn't help it. She waited for some acknowledgment, but it never came. What it was, Aunt Kay had kicked him out, he was sleeping in his office, his business had gone down the tubes, and none of his buddies would play golf with him anymore.

Jolene was called upon to show the judge that she was, at sixteen, underage for such doings, which made Phil a statutory rapist. There was a nice legal argument for just a minute or two as to how she was a married woman at the time, an adulteress, in fact, and certainly not unknowing in the ways of carnal life, but that didn't hold water, apparently. She was excused and taken back to the loony bin and put back in her hanging gray frock and slippers, and that was it for the real world. She heard that Phil pulled eighteen months in the state prison. She couldn't sympathize, being in one of her own.

Jolene didn't think much about Mickey, but she drew his face over and over. She drew headstones in a graveyard and then drew his face on the gravestones. This seemed to her a worthy artistic task. The more she drew of Mickey the more she remembered the details of how he looked at her on the last evening of his life, but it was hard with just crayons—they would only give her crayons to draw with, not the colored pencils she asked for.

Then something good happened. One of the girls in the ward smashed the mirror over the sink in the bathroom and used a sliver of it to cut her wrists. Well, that, of course, wasn't good, but all the mirrors in the bathroom were removed and nobody could see herself, except maybe, if they stood on the bed and the sunlight was in the right place, in the windows behind the mesh screen. So Jolene began a business in portraits. She drew a girl's face, and soon they were waiting in line to have her draw them. If they didn't have a mirror, they had Jolene. Some of her likenesses were not very good, but since in most cases they were a lot better than the originals, nobody minded. Mrs. Molloy, the head nurse, thought that this was good therapy for everyone, and so Jolene was given a set of watercolors with three brushes, and a big thick sketch pad, and when the rage for portraits had played itself out she painted everything else—the ward, the game room, the yard where they walked, the flowers in the flower bed, the sunset through the black mesh, everything.

But since she was as sane as anyone, she was more and more desperate to get out of there. After a year or so, she made the best deal she could, with one of the night attendants—a sharp-faced woman, sallow in coloring but decent and roughly kind to people, name of Cindy. Jolene thought that Cindy, with the leathery lines in her face, might be no less than fifty years old. Cindy had an eye for Jolene right from the beginning. She gave her cigarettes to smoke outside behind the garbage bins, and she knew hair and makeup. She said, Red—Jolene had what they call strawberry hair, so that, of course, was her nickname—Red, you don't want to cover up those freckles. They are charming in a girl like you, they give your face a sunlight. And see, if you keep pulling back your hair into ponytails your hairline will recede, so we'll cut it just a bit shorter, so that it curls up as it wants to, and we let it frame your sweet face and, lo and behold, you are as pretty as a picture.

Cindy liked the freckles on Jolene's breasts, too, and it wasn't too bad being loved up by a woman. It was not her first choice, but Jolene thought, Once you get going, it doesn't matter who it is or what they've got—there is the same panic, after all, and we are blind at such moments. But, anyway, that was the deal, and in order to get herself out of the loony bin she agreed to live with Cindy in her own home, where she would cuddle secretly like her love child, until she could escape from there as well. With just a couple of clicks of door locks and some minutes of hiding in a supply closet, and then with more keys turning and a creak of gates, Jolene rode to freedom in the trunk of Cindy's beat-up Corolla. It was even easier, after one night, walking out Cindy's front door in broad daylight once the woman had gone back to work.

Jolene hit the road. She wanted out of that town and out of that county however she could. She had almost a hundred dol-

lars from her watercolor business. She hitched some, and rode
some local buses. She had a small suitcase and a lot of attitude to
get her safe across state lines. She worked in a five-and-ten in
Lexington and in an industrial laundry in Memphis. There was
always a Y.W.C.A., to stay out of trouble. And while she did have
to take a deep breath and sell it once or twice across the country,
it had the virtue of hardening her up for her own protection. She
was just seventeen by then, but carrying herself with some new
clothes like she was ten years older, so that nobody would know
there was just this scared girl-child inside the hip-slinger with
the platform strap shoes.

Which brought her to Phoenix, Arizona, a hot, flat city in the
desert, but with a lot of fast-moving people who lived inside
their air-conditioning.

.   .   .

She appreciated that in the West human society was less tight-
assed, nobody cared that much what you did or who your parents were and most everyone you met came from somewhere
else. Before long, she was working at a Dairy Queen and had a
best friend, Kendra, who was one of her roommates, a Northern
girl from Akron, Ohio.

The Dairy Queen was at the edge of city life with a view over
warehouses to the flat desert with its straight roads and brownish
mountains away in the distance. She had to revert back to her
real age to get this job. It involved roller-skating, a skill which she
fortunately had not forgotten. You skated out to the customers
with their order on a tray that you hooked to the car window. It
was only minimum, but some men would give you a good tip,
though women never did. And, anyway, that wasn't to last long,
because this cute guy kept coming around every day. He had long
hair, a scraggly lip beard, and a ring in his ear—he looked like a
rock star. He wore an undershirt with his jeans and boots, so you

could see the tattoos that went up and down his arms, across his shoulders, and onto his chest. He even had a guitar in the back of his 1965 plum-color Caddy convertible. Of course she ignored his entreaties, though he kept coming back, and if another girl waited on him he asked her where Jolene was. All the girls wore nametags, you see. One day, he drove up, and when she came back with his order he was sitting on the top of the front seat with a big smile, though a front tooth was missing. He strummed his guitar and he said, Listen to this, Jolene, and he sang this song he had made up, and as he sang he laughed in appreciation, as if someone else was singing.

> Jolene, Jolene
> She is so mean
> She won't be seen with me
> At the Dairy Queen.
> Jolene, Jolene
> Please don't be mean
> Your name it means to me
> My love you'll glean from me
> I am so keen to see
> How happy we will be
> When you are one with me
> Jolene, Jolene
> My Dairy Queen.

Well, she knew he was a sly one, but he'd gone to the trouble of thinking it up, didn't he? The people in the next car laughed and applauded, and she blushed right through her freckles, but she couldn't help laughing along with them. And, of course, with his voice not very good and his guitar not quite in tune, she knew he was no rock star, but he was loud and didn't mind making a fool of himself, and she liked that.

In fact, the guy was by profession a tattoo artist. His name was

Coco Leger, pronounced Lerjay. He was originally from New Orleans, and she did go out dancing with him the next Saturday, though her friend Kendra strongly advised against it. The guy is a sleaze, Kendra said. Jolene thought she might be right. On the other hand, Kendra had no boyfriend of her own at the moment. And she was critical about most everything, their jobs, what she ate, the movies they saw, the furniture that came with the rental apartment, and maybe even the city of Phoenix in its entirety.

But Jolene went on the date and Coco was almost a gentleman. He was a good disco dancer, though a bit of a showoff with all his pelvic moves, and what was the harm, after all? Coco Leger made her laugh, and she hadn't had a reason to laugh in a long time.

One thing led to another. There was first a small heart to be embossed for free on her behind, and before long she was working as an apprentice at Coco's Institute of Body Art. He showed her how to go about things, and she caught on quick and eventually she got to doing customers who wanted the cheap stock tattoos. It was drawing with a needle, a slow process like using only the tip of your paintbrush one dab at a time. Coco was very impressed with how fast she learned. He said she was a real asset. He fired the woman who worked for him, and after a serious discussion Jolene agreed to move in with him, in the two rooms above his store, or studio, as he called it.

Kendra, who was still at the Dairy Queen, sat and watched her pack her things. I can see what he sees in you, Jolene, she said. You've got a trim little figure and everything moves the way it should without your even trying. Thank you, Kendra. Your skin is so fair, Kendra said. And you've got that nose that turns up and a killer smile. Thank you, Kendra, she said again, and gave her a hug because, though she was happy for herself, she was sad for Kendra, whose really pretty face would not be seen for what it was by most men in that she was a heavyset girl with fat on her shoulders who was not very graceful on skates. But, Kendra continued, I can't see what you see in him. This is a man born to betray.

Still, she didn't want to go back to skating for tips. Coco was teaching her a trade that suited her talents. But when, after just a couple of weeks, Coco decided they should get married, she admitted to herself she knew nothing about him, his past, his family. She knew nothing, and when she asked he just laughed and said, Babe, I am an orphan in the storm, just like you. They didn't like me much where I come from, but as I understand it neither of us has a past to write home about, he said, holding her and kissing her neck. What counts is this moment here, he whispered, and the future moments to come.

She said the name Jolene Leger, pronounced Lerjay, secretly to herself and thought it had a nice lilt to it. And so after another justice of the peace and a corsage in her hand and a flowered dress to her ankles and a bottle of champagne, she was in fact Jolene Leger, a married woman once again. They went back to the two rooms above the store and smoked dope and made love, with Coco singsonging to her in her rhythm *Jolene Jolene she's a love machine*, and after he fell asleep and began to snore she got up and stood at the window and looked out on the street. It was three in the morning by then, but all the street lights were on and the traffic signals were going, though not a human being was in sight. It was all busyness on that empty street in its silence, all the store signs blazing away, the neon colors in the windows, the laundromat, the check-cashing store, the one-hour photo and passport, the newsdealer, the coffee shop, and the dry cleaner, and the parking meters looking made of gold under the amber light of the street lamps. It was the world going on as if people were the last thing it needed or wanted.

She found herself thinking that if you shaved off Coco's scraggly lip beard and if his tattoos could be scrubbed away and you took off his boots with the lifts in them and got him a haircut and maybe set a pair of eyeglasses on his nose, he would look not unlike her first husband, the late Mickey Holler, and she began to cry.

For a while, she was sympathetic to Coco's ways and wanted

to believe his stories. But it became more and more difficult. He was away in his damn car half the time, leaving her to man the shop as if he didn't care what business they lost. He kept all the moneys to himself. She realized she was working without a salary, which only a wife would do. Who else would stand for that? It was a kind of slavery, wasn't it? Which is what Kendra said, tactlessly, when she came to visit. Coco was critical of almost everything Jolene did or said. And when she needed money for groceries or some such, he would only reluctantly peel off a bill or two from his carefully hoarded wad. She began to wonder where he got all his cash—certainly not from the tattooing trade, which was not all that great once the dry, cold Arizona winter set in. And when a reasonable-looking woman did come in he carried on saying all sorts of suggestive things as if they were the only two people in the room. I really don't like that, Jolene told him. Not at all. You married yourself a good-lookin' stud, Coco said. Get used to it. And when Jolene found herself doing a snake or a whiskered fish for some muscleman, and—as you'd expect, working so close up—he'd come on to her, all Coco would say when she complained was, That's what makes the world go roun'. She became miserable on a daily basis. The drugs he was dealing took up more and more of his time, and when she confronted him he didn't deny it. In fact, he said, it was the only way to keep the shop going. You should know without I have to tell you, Jolene, no artist in this U.S.A. can make it he don't have somethin' on the side.

One day, a taxicab pulled up and a woman carrying a baby and holding a valise came into the store. She was a blonde, very tall, statuesque even, and although the sign was clearly printed on the store window, she said, Is this the Institute of Body Art of which Coco Leger is the proprietor? Jolene nodded. I would like to see him, please, the woman said, putting the valise down and shifting the baby from one arm to the other. She looked about thirty or thirty-five, and she was wearing a hat and had just a linen jacket and a yellow dress with hose and shoes, which was most unusual on this winter day in Phoenix, or in any season of the year, for that matter, where you didn't see anyone who wasn't wearing jeans. Jolene had the weirdest feeling come over her. She felt that she was a child again. She was back in childhood, she'd only been a pretend adult and was not Mrs. Coco Leger except in her stupid dreams. It was a premonition. She looked again at the baby, and at that moment knew what she didn't have to be told—its ancestry was written all over its runty face. All it lacked was a little lip beard.

And you are? Jolene asked. I am Marin Leger, the wife of that fucking son of a bitch, the woman said. As if any confirmation was needed, her large hand coming around from under the baby's bottom had a gold band impressed into the flesh of its fourth finger.

I have spent every cent I had tracking him down and I want to see him now, this very instant, the woman said. A moment later, as if a powerful magic had been invoked, Coco's Caddy rolled to the curb, and it may have been worth everything to see the stunned expression on his face as he got out of the car and both saw Marin Leger and was seen by her through the shopwindow. But, being Coco, he recovered nicely. His face lit up, and he waved as if he couldn't have been more delighted, and came through the door with a grin. Looka this, he said. Will ya looka this! he said, his arms spread wide. Because she was the taller of the two, the hug he gave her mashed his face against the baby in her arms, who commenced to cry loudly. And as Coco stepped back he suffered the free hand of the woman smartly against his cheek.

Now, darlin', just be cool, he told her. There is an explanation for everythin'. Come with me—we have to talk, he said, as if he'd been waiting for her all along. Believe it or not, I am greatly relieved to see you, he said to her. He took no further notice of the kid in her arms, and as he picked up her bag and ushered her out the door he looked back at Jolene and told her out of the side of his mouth to hold tight, to hold tight, and outside he gallantly opened the car door for Marin Leger and sat her and their baby down and went off with them in the plum-color 1965 Caddy convertible he had once driven up every day to see Jolene wiggle her ass on skates.

Jolene, Jolene, of the Dairy Queen, she is so mean, she smashed the machinery. . . . She had never been so calm in her life as she quietly and methodically trashed Coco's Institute of Body Art, turning over the autoclave, pulling down the flash posters, banging the tattoo guns by their cables against the rear exposed-brick wall until they cracked, scattering the needle bars, pouring the inks on the floor, pulling the display case of 316L stainless-steel body jewelry off the wall, tearing the paperback tattoo books in the rotating stand. She smashed the director's chairs to pieces, and threw a metal footstool through the back-door window. She went upstairs, and, suddenly aware for the first time how their rooms smelled of his disgusting unwashed body, she busted up everything she could, tore up the bedding, swept everything out of the medicine cabinet, and pulled down the curtains she had chosen to make the place more homey. She took an armful of her clothes and stuffed them into two paper sacks, and when she found in a shoebox on their closet shelf a zip-lock plastic bag with another inside it packed with white stuff that felt under the thumb like baking powder she left it exactly where it was and, downstairs again, cleaned out the few dollars in the cash register, picked up the phone, left a precise message for the Phoenix P.D., and, putting up the Back in Five sign, she slammed the door behind her and was gone.

She was still dry-eyed when she went to the pawnshop two blocks away and got fifteen dollars for her wedding band. She waited at the storefront travel agency where the buses stopped, and didn't begin to cry till she wondered, for the first time in a long time, who her mom and dad might have been, and if they were still alive, as she thought they must be if they were too young to do anything but name her Jolene and leave her for the authorities to raise.

· · ·

In Vegas, she waitressed at a coffee shop till she had enough money to have her hair straightened, which is what the impresario of the Starlet Topless told her she had to do if she wanted a job. So if she shook her head as she leaned back, holding on to the brass pole, her hair swished back and forth across her shoulders. Wearing a thong and high heels was not the most comfortable thing in the world, but she got the idea quickly enough and became popular as the most petite girl in the place. The other girls liked her, too—they called her Baby, and watched out for her. She rented a room in the apartment of a couple of them. Even the bouncer was solicitous after she lied to him that she was involved.

When she met Sal, a distinguished gray-haired man of some girth, it was at the request of the manager, who took her to a table in the back. That this man Sal chose not to sit at the bar and stare up her ass suggested to her he was not the usual bum who came into Starlets. He was a gentleman who, though not married, had several grandchildren. The first thing he did on their first date when she came up to his penthouse suite was show her their pictures. That's the kind of solid citizen Mr. Sal Fontaine was. She stood at the window looking out over all of Vegas. Quiet and soft-spoken, Sal was not only a dear man, as she came to know him, but one highly respected as the founder and owner of Sal's Line, with an office and banks of phones with operators taking calls from people all over the country wanting Sal's Line on everything from horses to who would be the next President. Without ceremony, which was his way, he put a diamond choker

on her neck and asked her to move in with him. She couldn't
believe her luck, living with a man highly regarded in the community in his penthouse suite of six rooms overlooking all of
Vegas. It had maid service every morning. From the French
restaurant downstairs you could order dinner on a rolling cart
that turned into a table. Sal bought her clothes, she signed his
name at the beauty parlor, and when they went out, though he
was so busy it was not that often, she was treated with respect by
the greeters, and by Sal's associates, mostly gentlemen of the
same age range as his. She was totally overwhelmed. With all the
leggy ass in Las Vegas, imagine, little Jolene, treated like a
princess! And not only that but with time on her hands to
develop a line of her own, of greeting cards she drew, psychedelic
in style, sometimes inspired by her experience with tattoo
designs but always with sentiments of loving family relationships
that she dreamed up, as if she knew all about it.

She never thought she could be so happy. Sal liked her to
climb all over him, he liked her to be on top, and they were very
tender and caressing of one another, certainly on her part,
because always in the back of her mind was the fear of his
overexerting himself. And he talked so quietly and he believed or
pretended to believe her life story, the parts that were made up as
well as the parts that were true.

As she became used to the life, she reflected that Sal Fontaine
did not give of himself easily. It wasn't a matter of his material
generosity. He never confided in her. There was a distance in
him, or maybe even a gloom, that for all his success he could not
change in himself. If she had questions, if she was curious, she
met a wall. He moved slowly, as if the air set up a resistance just
to him. When he smiled, it was a sad smile, despite his capped
teeth. And he had heavy jowls and hooded sad eyes made darker
by the deep blue pouches under them. Maybe he could not forget
what he had lost, his old country or his original family, who was
she to say?

She would tell him she loved him, and at the moment she said it she did. The rest of the time she sort of shrugged to herself. The contractual nature of their relationship was all too clear to her, and she began to suspect that the regard Sal's friends held for her was not what they might have expressed among themselves. Her life, once the novelty wore off, was like eating cotton candy all day long. Her long straight red hair now shone with high-lights. In the mornings, she would swim in the Olympic-size hotel pool with her hair in a single braid, trailing. She was this Jolene person who wore different Vegas-style outfits depending on the time of day or night. She saw herself in an I. Magnin fitting-room mirror one day and the word that came to her mind was "hard." When had it happened that she'd taken on that set of the mouth and stony gaze of the Las Vegas bimbo? Jesus.

One evening they were sitting watching television, and Sal said, out of the blue, that she didn't have to worry, she would be taken care of, he would settle something on her. Thank you, sweetheart, she said, not knowing exactly how or when he would do that but understanding the essential meaning: that she was in a situation designed not to last. The next morning, she took all her greeting-card designs to a print shop at the edge of town and spent two hours making decisions about the stock she wanted, the layouts, the typefaces, the amounts to print of each item, and so on. It was real business, and it made her feel good, even though she had no idea who would distribute her cards, let alone who would buy them. Step by step, she told herself in the cab back. Step by step.

A week later, the phone rang just when they were getting up, and Sal told her quickly to get dressed and go have breakfast in the coffee shop because some men were coming for a meeting. She said that was O.K., she would stay out of the way in the bed-room with a cup of coffee and the *Sun*. Don't argue, he shouted, and threw a dress at her face. She was speechless—he had never yelled at her before. She was waiting for the elevator when the doors opened and they came out, the men to meet with Sal. She saw them and they saw her, two of them looking, like so many of the men in Vegas, as if they had never felt the sun on their face.

But then in the coffee shop it dawned on her. She all at once turned cold and then sick to her stomach. She ran to the ladies' and sat there in a cold sweat. Such stories as you heard were never supposed to intrude into your own life.

How long did she sit there? When she found the courage to come out, and then out of the coffee shop into the lobby, she saw an ambulance at the front entrance. She stood in the crowd that gathered, and saw the elevator doors open and someone with an oxygen mask over his face and hooked up to an intravenous line being wheeled on a gurney through the lobby.

That it was Sal Fontaine was quickly agreed upon by everyone. Exactly what had happened to him was less clear. Finally, a police officer walking by said it was a heart attack. A heart attack.

She did not even have her purse, just the orange print mini she was wearing, and the sandals. She didn't even have any makeup—she had nothing. She saw the name of the hospital on the ambulance as it drove off and decided to go upstairs and put something on and take a cab there. But she couldn't move. She walked up the winding staircase to the mezzanine and sat in an armchair with her hands between her knees. Finally, she got up, the courage to go back to the penthouse floor. If it was a heart attack, what were the police and TV cameras doing there? Everyone in the world was in the corridor, and the door to the apartment was sealed with yellow tape and under guard, and everything was out of her reach—Mr. Sal Fontaine and all her clothes and her diamond choker, and even the money he had given her over time, despite the fact that he never allowed her to pay for anything.

She had over a thousand dollars in the drawer on her side of the bed. She knew that eventually she could reclaim it if she wanted to be questioned by the police. But whatever was to happen to her now might not be as bad as what would happen if she risked it. Even if she told them nothing, what would Sal's Line be on her chances of living to her nineteenth birthday, which happened to be the next day? He was not around to tell her.

Which is how life changes, as lightning strikes, and in an instant what was is not what is, and you find yourself sitting on a rock at the edge of the desert, hoping some bus will come by and take pity on you before you're found lying dead there like any other piece of road kill.

.   .   .

Two years later, Jolene was living alone in Tulsa, Oklahoma. She had heard from a truck driver at a whistle stop in north Texas, where she was waiting tables, that Tulsa was a boomtown with not enough people for all the jobs. She'd taken a room at a women's residential hotel and first found work, part time, in the public library shelving books, and then full time as a receptionist at a firm that leased oil-drilling equipment. She had not been with anyone in a while, but it was kind of nice, actually. She was surprised at how pleasant life could be when you were on your own. She liked the way she felt walking in the street or sitting at a desk. Self-contained. Nothing begging inside her. I have come of age, she told herself. I have come of age.

To make some extra cash, she worked after hours on call for a caterer. She had to invest in the uniform—white blouse, black trousers, and black pumps—but each time she was called it meant sixty dollars for a minimum three hours. She wore her hair in the single braid down her back and she kept her eyes lowered, as instructed, but, even so, managed to see a good deal of the upper crust of Tulsa.

She was serving champagne on a tray at a private party one evening when this six-footer with blow-dried hair appeared before her. He was good-looking and he knew it. He grabbed a glass of champagne, drank it off, and took another and followed her into the kitchen. He didn't get anything out of her except her name, but he tracked her down through the caterer and sent her flowers with a note, signed Brad G. Benton, asking her out to dinner. Nobody in all her life had ever done that.

So she bought herself a dress and went out to dinner with Brad G. Benton at the country club, where the table linen was starched and there were crystal wineglasses and padded red leather chairs with brass studs. She wouldn't remember what she ate. She sat and listened with her hands in her lap. She didn't have to say much—he did all the talking. Brad G. Benton was not thirty-five and already a senior V.P. at this stock brokerage where they kept on giving him bonuses. He didn't want just to get her in bed. He said that since Jesus had come into his heart the only really good sex remaining to him was connubial sex. He said, Of course, you need someone precious and special enough for that, like you, Jolene, and looked deeply into her eyes.

At first, she couldn't believe he was serious. After a couple of more dates, she realized he was. She was thinking Brad G. Benton must be crazy. On the other hand, this was the Bible Belt, she had seen these super-sincere people at her receptionist's job. They might be rich and do sophisticated business around the world, but they were true believers in God's written word with no ifs, ands, or buts. From the looks of things it was a knockout combination, though a little weird, like they had one foot in the boardroom and one in Heaven.

You don't know anything about me, Jolene told him, in an effort to satisfy herself of her integrity. I expect soon to know everything, he said, flashing a big handsome smile that could have been a leer.

He was so damn cocky. She almost resented that there was never any doubt in his mind as to what she would say. He insisted she quit her job and move to a hotel at his expense until the wedding day. Oh, what day is that? she said, teasing, but he was a wild man: The engagement will necessarily be short, he said, slipping a diamond ring on her finger.

A week later, they were married in the chapel of the First Methodist Church there in Tulsa that looked like Winchester Cathedral. Brad G. Benton brought her to live in his apartment in a new building that had a swimming pool in the basement and a gym on the roof. They were high enough to see out over the whole city, though there wasn't that much to see in Tulsa, Oklahoma.

So once more her fortunes had changed and little Jolene was a young matron of the upper class. She wanted to write to someone about this incredible turn in her life, but who could she write to? Who? There was no one. In that sense, nothing had changed, because she was as alone as she had always been, a stranger in a strange land.

Things in the marriage were O.K. at first, though some of Brad G. Benton's ideas were not to her taste. He was very athletic, and no sooner satisfied in one orifice than she was turned over for the other. Also, he seemed not to notice her art work. She had bought an easel and set up a little studio in what was designed to be the maid's room, because the Indian woman who cooked and cleaned had her own home to go to each evening. Jolene painted there and stretched her canvases, and she took a figure-painting class once a week where there were live models. She did well, her teacher was very encouraging, but Brad took none of this in, he just didn't notice—he was too busy with his work and his workouts and his nights out and his nights in her.

It turned out Brad G. Benton's family was prominent in Tulsa. Not one of them had come to the wedding, their purpose being to define to her what white trash meant. At first she didn't care that much. But she'd see their pictures in the newspapers being honored at charity events. They had wings of buildings named after them. One day, coming from shopping, she looked out the cab window as it passed a glass office tower that said Benton International on a giant brass cube balanced on one of its corners in the plaza out front.

She said to Brad, I would think they had more respect for you, if not for me. But he only laughed. It was not so much that he was a democrat in his ideals, as she was to realize; it was part of his life's work to do outrageous things and raise hell. It was how he kept everyone's attention. He loved to twist noses out of joint. He was contrary. He hadn't joined the Benton family enterprise, as he was supposed to—it was a holding company with many different kinds of businesses in their hands—but had gone off on his own to show what he was made of.

Jolene knew that if she wanted to prove anything to this family, if she wanted any kind of social acceptance in Tulsa, Oklahoma, she would have to work for it. She would have to start reading books and take a course or two in something intellectual and embrace the style of life, the manners, the ways of doing and talking by being patient and keeping her eyes and ears open. She would attend their church, too. As wild as he was, Brad was like his father, what he called a strong Christian. That was the one place they would have to meet and, she was willing to bet, speak to one another. And how then could the family not speak to her?

Oddly enough, she was looking as good as she ever had, and Brad took her once a week to dinner at the country club to show her off. By then, everyone in town knew this so-called Cinderella story. Grist for the mill. He was heedless, he just didn't worry about it, whereas she could hardly raise her head. One evening, his father and mother were sitting at a far table with their guests, who looked as if they were there to serve them as much as the waiters. Brad waved—it was more like a salute—and the father nodded and resumed his conversation.

Through no fault of her own, Jolene had stepped into a situation that was making her life miserable. Whatever was going on with these people, what did it have to do with her? Nothing. She was as nothing.

To tell the truth, she had made Brad for a creep that first time he came on to her at that cocktail party. He'd padded into the kitchen, stalking her like some animal, taken the empty champagne tray out of her hands, and told her redheads smelled different. And he stood there sniffing her and going, Hmm, yes, like warm milk.

·   ·   ·

After her baby was born, when Brad G. Benton started to bat her around, Jolene could not help but remember that first impression.

Every little thing drove him crazy. It got so she couldn't do anything, say anything, without he would go off half-cocked. He took to hitting her, slapping her face, punching her. What are you doing, she screamed. Stop it, stop it! It was his new way of getting off. He would say, You like this? You like it? He'd knock her around, then push her down on the bed. She grew accustomed to living in fear of getting beaten up and forced against her will. She was still to learn what they would teach at the shelter—it happens once, that's it, you leave. But now she just tried to see it through. Brad G. Benton had been to college, he came of money, and he wore good clothes, and she was flattered that he would fall for her when she didn't even have a high-school diploma. And then, of course, there were the apologies and the beggings for forgiveness and the praying in church together, and by such means she slowly became a routinely abused wife.

Only when it was all over would she realize it wasn't just having the baby; it was their plans for him, the Bentons' plans for her Mr. Nipplebee. He was an heir, after all. The minute they'd found out she was pregnant, they went to work. And after he was born they slowly gave it to Brad in bits and pieces, what their investigators had learned about her life before. Never mind that she had tried to tell Brad about her marriages, her life on the road; he never wanted to hear it, he had no curiosity about her, none. He had blessed her with his insanity. She had appeared in Tulsa as a vision, God's chosen sex partner for him, a fresh and wet and shining virgin with red hair. All those beatings were what he was told, and all those apologies were the way his love for her was hanging on. She would feel sorry for him if she could, because he was so wired, such a maniac—it was as if his wildness, his independent choice of life was being driven from him, as if it was the Devil. It was those parents slowly absorbing him back into their righteousness.

One day, Brad G. Benton appeared at the door to her little studio room when he would ordinarily be at work. She was ruling off a grid on one of her canvases, as she had been taught. Brad! she said, smiling. But there was no recognition in his eyes. He kicked the stool out from under her. He broke the easel over his knee, he bashed her canvases against the wall, tore down the drawings she had pinned up there, and then he squeezed tubes of paint into her face as he held her down on the floor. And he began hitting her as she lay there, he punched her face, he punched her in the throat. When he got off her, she could hear his breathing—it was like crying. He stood over her, kicked her in the side, and as suddenly as he had come he was gone.

She lay there moaning in pain, too frightened and shocked even to get up, until she thought of the baby. She dragged herself to the nursery. The Cherokee woman, who had heard everything, sat beside the crib with her hand over her eyes. But the baby was sleeping peacefully. Jolene washed her face, and, wrapping up her Mr. Nipplebee, she took him with her as she dragged herself to a doctor. She was told that she had had her cheekbone fractured, two broken ribs, contusions of the throat, and a bruised kidney. How did this happen? the doctor asked her. She was afraid to tell him and, besides, it hurt too much to talk. But the nurse in the office didn't have to be told. She wrote out the name and address of a women's shelter and said, Go there right now. I'll order you a cab. And in that way, with her precious in her arms and only what she was wearing, Jolene left her marriage.

She could hardly bear staying at the shelter, where there were these wimpy women looking for her friendship, her companionship. Jolene wouldn't even go to the group sessions. She stayed by herself and nursed Mr. Nipplebee.

The shelter gave her the name of a woman lawyer, and she put down a retainer. Get me a divorce as fast as you can, she told the lawyer. The money, I don't care. I'll take anything they give. I just want out of here and out of Tulsa, Oklahoma. And then she waited, and waited, and nothing happened. Absolutely nothing. This went on for some time. And the next thing Jolene knew, when she was about stripped of her savings, the lawyer quit on her. She was an older woman, who wore pin-striped suits and big loopy bronze earrings. I may be broke, Jolene said to her, but Brad G. Benton has money to burn, and I can pay you afterward out of the alimony or child care.

You didn't tell me you had a past including a stretch in juvenile detention, the lawyer said. To say nothing of a previous, as yet un-annulled marriage to a convicted drug dealer.

Jolene was so stunned she didn't think to ask how the lawyer knew that if she hadn't told her.

She was up against a scumbag husband on his own turf, so what could she expect but that there was worse to come, as there was, if he knew all along where she was hiding, and if he knew by first name everyone in town, as he probably did the very police officers who came one morning to arrest her for unlawful kidnapping of her own child, who they took from her arms, driving him off in one squad car and Jolene in another as she looked back screaming.

I don't want to hear about what is the law in this country and what is not, Jolene told the legal-aid person who was assigned to her. Do you know what it means to have your child torn from you? Do you have to have that happen to you to know it is worse than death? You want to kill yourself but you can't for thinking of the child's welfare in the hands of a sick father who never smiled at him and was jealous of him from the day he was born.

My baby, she said aloud when she was alone. My baby.

He had her coloring and button nose and carrot-red fuzz for hair. He drank from her with a born knowledge of what was expected of him. He was a whole new life in her arms, and for the very first time she could remember she had had something she wanted. She was Jolene, his mother, and could believe in God, who had never before seemed to her to be much of a fact of life.

And so now there was a hearing for the divorce Brad had filed for. And his whole miserable family was there, they loved him after all, now that he was getting rid of her and her past was thrown in her face. They had it all down, including the medical records of her S.T.D. from Coco, her living in sin, and even her suspension one term at Jeff Davis High for smoking pot. It was a no-brainer. Her legal-aid kid was out of his league, and without giving it much thought the judge ruled she was an unfit mother and granted Brad G. Benton sole custody of her Mr. Nipplebee.

On top of everything, in the fullness of her milk that she had to pump out, she must have done something wrong, because she ended up in the hospital with a staph infection that had to be drained—like the milk had gone bad and turned green. But she had a chance to think. She thought of her choices. She could kill Brad G. Benton—it'd be simple enough to buy some kind of gun and wait on him—but then the baby would be raised by the Benton family. So what was the point? She could find a job and see the baby every second Sunday for one hour, as allowed by the judge, and rely on the passing of time for the moment when nobody was looking and she could steal him back and run for it. But then on her first visitation what happened was that Brad was up in the gym and a new large Indian woman was with Mr. Nipplebee, and Brad's crone of a mother stood with her back to the door and they wouldn't let Jolene hold him but just sit by the crib and watch him sleep. And she thought, If I stay on in Tulsa for my visitations, he will grow up learning to think of me as an embarrassment, a poor relative, and I can't have that.

·   ·   ·

These days, Jolene has a job in West Hollywood inking for a small comic-book company, except they don't call them comic books—they call them graphic novels. Because most of them aren't funny at all. They are very serious. She likes the people at work—they are all good pals and go out for pizza together. But where she lives is down near the farmers' market in a studio apartment that is sacred to her. Nobody can come in, no matter how good a friend. She has a little stereo for her Keith Jarrett CDs and she lights a candle and drinks a little wine and dreams of plans for herself. She thinks someday, when she has more experience, of writing a graphic novel of her own, "The Life of Jolene."

She has a pastel sketch she once did of her precious baby. It is so sweet! It's the only likeness she has. Sometimes she looks at this sketch and then at her own face in the mirror, and because he takes after her in his coloring and features, she tries to draw what he might look like at his present age, which is four and a half.

Friends tell Jolene she could act in movies, because she may be twenty-five but she looks a lot younger. And they like her voice, which, courtesy of her ex-husband, cracks like Janice Joplin's. And her crooked smile, which she doesn't tell them is the result of a busted cheekbone. So she's had some photos taken and is sending them out to professional agents.

I mean, why not? Jolene says to herself. She has this daydream. Her son sees her up on the screen one day. And when she takes herself back to Tulsa in her Rolls-Royce Silver Cloud he answers the door and rushes into the arms of his movie-star mother.

Contributors

STANLEY BING first appeared in *Esquire* in 1984. Since then, Bing has been writing scurrilous things about his employers and providing strategic advice to those even more befuddled than he. Rather than risk expulsion from his corporate environment, he created a new name under which he could observe and criticize the executive class while at the same time aspiring to its lifestyle. This strategy has succeeded, and Bing now reports on corporate life for *Fortune*. This fall Bing will publish a collection of his columns, *The Big Bing* (HarperBusiness) and a novel, *You Look Nice Today* (Bloomsbury).

TIM CAHILL is a contributing editor of *National Geographic Adventure* and an editor-at-large with *Outside*. He is the author of eight books, including *Hold the Enlightenment: More Travel, Less Bliss; A Wolverine Is Eating My Leg* and *Pecked to Death by Ducks*.

E. L. DOCTOROW has been published in thirty languages. His novels include *Welcome to Hard Times, The Book of Daniel, Ragtime, Loon Lake, Lives of the Poets, World's Fair, Billy Bathgate* and *The Waterworks*. He has received the National Book Award, the PEN/Faulkner Award, the Edith Wharton Citation for Fiction, the William Dean Howells medal of the American Academy of Arts and Letters and the National Humanities Medal.

ANNE FADIMAN is the editor of *The American Scholar,* which has won three National Magazine Awards in the last five years. Fadiman herself has received National Magazine Awards for both reporting (when she was a staff writer at *Life*) and essays. Her first book, *The Spirit Catches You and You Fall Down*, an account of the cross-cultural conflicts between a Hmong refugee family and the American medical system, received a National Book Critics Circle Award. Her second book, *Ex Libris*, a collection of essays on reading and language, has been translated into thirteen languages. Fadiman is also the editor of *The Best American Essays 2003*.

JAMES FALLOWS is the national correspondent for *The Atlantic Monthly*, where he has worked for more than twenty years. He also writes regularly for *Slate*, *The New York Times Magazine*, *The New York Review of Books*, *The New Yorker* and *The American Prospect*. He has published seven books, including *Breaking the News: How the Media Undermine American Democracy* and *Free Flight: From Airline Hell to a New Age of Travel* (2001).

CAITLIN FLANAGAN, a contributing editor of *The Atlantic Monthly*, began her magazine-writing career in 2001 with a series of extended book reviews about conflicts at the heart of modern life—specifically, modern domestic life as it is lived by professional women. Her *Atlantic Monthly* article "Confessions of a Prep School College Counselor" was featured in *The Best American Magazine Writing 2002*. A book based on her columns, *The Wifely Duty*, will be published by Little, Brown in 2005.

IAN FRAZIER is a frequent contributor to *The New Yorker*, *The Atlantic Monthly* and *Outside*. He is the author of such books as *On the Rez*, *Great Plains*, *Family* and *The Fish's Eye: Essays About Angling and the Outdoors*.

ELIZABETH GILBERT is a writer-at-large for *GQ*, where three of her profiles have been nominated for National Magazine Awards. She has also been published in *Story*, *Ploughshares*, *The Mississippi Review*, *Esquire*, *The London Sunday Telegraph* and *The Paris Review*. She is the author of *Pilgrims*, a short-story collection; *Stern Men,* a novel; and *The Last American Man*, which was a finalist for the National Book Award for Nonfiction.

JEFFREY GOLDBERG is a staff writer and Middle East correspondent at *The New Yorker*. In 2003, he won the Overseas Press Club Award for Human Rights for his article "The Great Terror," about the Iraqi government's use of chemical and biological weapons against the Kurdish people of northern Iraq. Prior to joining *The New Yorker*, Goldberg was a contributing writer at *The New York Times Magazine*, a contributing editor at *New York*, the New York bureau chief of *The Forward*, a columnist for *The Jerusalem Post* and a police reporter for the *Washington Post*. He is currently working on a book about the Middle East, entitled *Prisoners*, which will be published by Alfred A. Knopf.

ADAM GOPNIK has been writing for *The New Yorker* since 1986 about many subjects, particularly art, Paris and children. He has twice won National Magazine Awards for his essays, and is the author of *Paris to the Moon*.

MICHAEL HALL joined *Texas Monthly* in 1997. Prior to that, Hall worked as an editor at *Third Coast* and *The Austin Chronicle*. Now a senior editor at *Texas Monthly*, he has also written for *Trouser Press*, the *Austin American-Statesman, Blender, Men's Journal* and *Grammy Magazine*.

CHRISTOPHER HITCHENS joined *Vanity Fair* as a contributing editor in September 1992, where he writes a wide-ranging monthly column. He is also a regular contributor to *The Atlantic Monthly*. Hitchens began his career as a staff writer with the *New Statesman* and later served as a foreign correspondent for London's *Daily Express*. For twenty years Hitchens wrote a biweekly column for *The Nation*. He has also served as Washington editor for

Harper's, U.S. correspondent for *The Spectator* and *The Times Literary Supplement* and was the book critic at *New York Newsday* from 1986 to 1992. Hitchens is the author of several books, including *No One Left to Lie To, The Trial of Henry Kissinger, Letters to a Young Contrarian* and *Why Orwell Matters*.

JOYCE CAROL OATES has published a number of novels, including *Blonde, Broke Heart Blues, Black Water* and *Because It Is Bitter and Because It Is My Heart.* Her stories have appeared in publications as diverse as *Harper's, Playboy, Granta* and *The Paris Review*, and have been anthologized in *The O. Henry Awards, The Pushcart Prize, The Best American Short Stories of the 20th Century* and *The Best American Mystery Stories.* She won a National Book Award in 1970 for her novel *Them.* Her most recent novel, *The Tattooed Girl*, was published in June 2003. Oates is the Roger S. Berlind Distinguished Professor of the Humanities at Princeton University.

MICHAEL PATERNITI is a writer-at-large for *GQ* and the bestselling author of *Driving Mr. Albert: A Trip Across America with Einstein's Brain.* He has been nominated six consecutive years for a National Magazine Award and has won for the *Harper's* article on which his book was based. Paterniti's work has appeared in such publications as *The New York Times Magazine, Details, Outside, Rolling Stone* and *Esquire*, as well as in a number of anthologies. A former executive editor at *Outside* and managing editor at the fiction journal *Story,* Paterniti is currently at work on his next book, which is set in Spain and involves love, betrayal and revenge.

KATHA POLLITT has written a column for *The Nation*, "Subject to Debate," since 1994. She has also contributed to *The New Yorker, Harper's, Ms.,* the *New York Times* and many other publications. She has published a collection of poems, *Antarctic Traveler*, and two collections of prose: *Reasonable Creatures: Essays on Women* *and Feminism* and *Subject to Debate: Sense and Dissents on Women, Politics, and Culture.*

GARY SMITH's career at *Sports Illustrated* has been punctuated by a number of remarkable profiles. Smith has won four National Magazine Awards, three for feature writing and one for profile writing. His stories have appeared in the annual *Best American Sportswriting* anthology seven times, and his 1996 profile of Tiger Woods, "The Chosen One," was selected for *The Best American Sportswriting of the Century.* A collection of his work, *Beyond the Game: The Collected Sportswriting of Gary Smith*, was recently published by Grove/Atlantic.

JOHN JEREMIAH SULLIVAN was an editor at the *Oxford American* and now works as a senior editor at *Harper's.* His story "Horseman, Pass By," republished here, has led to his first book, *Blood Horses: An Education*, which will be published in April 2004 by Farrar, Straus and Giroux.

JEFF TIETZ's work has appeared in *The New Yorker, The Atlantic Monthly, Harper's, TriQuarterly, New England Review* and the anthology *Best American Crime Writing.*

JAMES WOLCOTT is currently the cultural critic for *Vanity Fair.* He has also been a staff writer at the *Village Voice, Esquire, Harper's* and *The New Yorker.* Wolcott's work has also been published in *The New Republic, London Observer, The New Criterion* and the *Wall Street Journal.* His first novel, *The Catsitters,* was published in 2001, and his next book, *Attack Poodles*, will be published in 2004 by Miramax.

2003 National Magazine Award Finalists

NOTE: All nominated issues are dated 2002 unless otherwise specified. The editor whose name appears in connection with finalists for 2003 held that position, or was listed on the masthead, at the time the issue was published in 2002. In some cases, another editor is now in that position.

General Excellence

This category recognizes overall excellence in magazines. It honors the effectiveness with which writing, reporting, editing and design all come together to command readers' attention and fulfill the magazine's unique editorial mission.

Under 100,000 circulation

The American Scholar: Anne Fadiman, Editor, for Winter, Summer, Autumn issues.

The Chronicle of Higher Education: Edward Weidlein, Editor-in-Chief; Scott Jaschik, Editor, for January 18, February 8, March 15 issues.

Foreign Policy: Moisés Naím, Editor & Publisher, for March/April, July/August, September/October issues.

JD Jungle: Jon Gluck, Editor-in-Chief, for April/May, September/October, November/December issues.

Step inside design: Emily Potts, Editorial Director, for July/August, September/October, November/December issues.

100,000 to 250,000 circulation

Architectural Record: Robert Ivy, Editor-in-Chief, for March, April, July issues.

Harper's: Lewis H. Lapham, Editor, for March, October, December issues.

Mother Jones: Roger Cohn, Editor-in-Chief, for January/February, May/June, September/October issues.

Nylon: Marvin Scott Jarrett, Editor-in-Chief, for June/July, August, September issues.

Preservation: Robert Wilson, Editor, for March/April, May/June, November/December issues.

250,000 to 500,000 circulation

National Geographic Adventure: John Rasmus, Editor-in-Chief, for January/February, May, September issues.

Saveur: Colman Andrews, Editor-in-Chief, for January/February, May/June, July/August issues.

Skiing Magazine: Perkins Miller, Editor-in-Chief, for September, October, November issues.

Texas Monthly: Evan Smith, Editor, for July, November, December issues.

W: Patrick McCarthy, Chairman and Editorial Director, for March, September, December issues.

500,000 to 1,000,000 circulation

The Atlantic Monthly: Michael Kelly, Editor; Cullen Murphy, Managing Editor, for July/August, October, December issues.

Condé Nast Traveler: Thomas J. Wallace, Editor-in-Chief, for May, September, November issues.

Esquire: David Granger, Editor-in-Chief, for July, September, December issues.

House & Garden: Dominique Browning, Editor, for April, September, October issues.

The New Yorker: David Remnick, Editor, for February 18 & 25, March 25, November 18 issues.

1,000,000 to 2,000,000 circulation

Discover: Stephen L. Petranek, Editor-in-Chief, for February, March, June issues.

Entertainment Weekly: James W. Seymore, Jr., Managing Editor, for August 9 issue; Rick Tetzeli, Managing Editor, for November 15, December 20/December 27 issues.

ESPN The Magazine: John Papanek, Senior Vice President/Editor-in-Chief, for June 10, December 9, December 23 issues.

Fortune: Rik Kirkland, Managing Editor, for June 24, September 2, September 16 issues.

Real Simple: Carrie Tuhy, Managing Editor, for February, September, December/ January issues.

Vanity Fair: Graydon Carter, Editor, for February, March, August issues.

Over 2,000,000 circulation

National Geographic: William L. Allen, Editor-in-Chief, for January, April, November issues.

Newsweek: Richard M. Smith, Chairman and Editor-in-Chief; Mark Whitaker, Editor, for June 10, December 9, December 16 issues.

O, The Oprah Magazine: Oprah Winfrey, Founder and Editorial Director; Amy Gross, Editor-in-Chief, for March, August, November issues.

Parenting: Janet Chan, Vice President/Editor-in-Chief, for October, November, December/January issues.

Sports Illustrated: Terry McDonell, Managing Editor, for June 3, December 9, December 16 issues.

Personal Service

This category recognizes excellence in service journalism. The advice or instruction presented should help readers improve the quality of their personal lives.

Business Week: Stephen B. Shepard, Editor-in-Chief, for *The Coming Revolution in Health Care*, May 6.

Money Magazine: Robert Safian, Managing Editor, for *Real Estate: Your Questions Answered*, by Jon Birger, Jon Gertner, Lisa Gibbs, Maya Jackson, Jeff Nash and Cybele Weisser, December.

My Generation: Betsy Carter, Editor-in-Chief, for *Taking Care of Our Parents*, November/December.

Newsweek: Richard M. Smith, Chairman and Editor-in-Chief; Mark Whitaker, Editor, for *The Science of Alternative Medicine*, December 2.

Outside: Hal Espen, Editor, for *The Shape of Your Life*, by Paul Scott, Part I, May; Part II, June; Part V, September.

Leisure Interests

This category recognizes excellent service journalism about leisure-time pursuits. The advice or instruction presented should help readers enjoy hobbies or other recreational interests.

Esquire: David Granger, Editor-in-Chief, for *America or Bust*, July.

National Geographic Adventure: John Rasmus, Editor-in-Chief, for *Wild in the Parks*, by Jim Gorman and Tim Cahill, May.

Sports Illustrated: Terry McDonell, Managing Editor, for *Hitters Rule*, March 25.

Time Out New York: Cyndi Stivers, President/Editor-in-Chief, for *Cork Screwed*, by Randall Lane, June 13–20.

Vogue: Anna Wintour, Editor-in-Chief, for three articles by Jeffrey Steingarten, *The Sweetest Thing*, June; *Buttering Up*, July; *Cuts Above*, September.

Reporting

This category recognizes excellence in reporting. It honors the enterprise, exclusive reporting and intelligent analysis that a magazine exhibits in covering a story of contemporary interest and significance.

The Atlantic Monthly: Michael Kelly, Editor; Cullen Murphy, Managing Editor, for a three-part article by William Langewiesche, *American Ground: Unbuilding the World Trade Center*, Part One: *The Inner World*, July-August; Part Two: *The Rush to Recover*, September; Part Three: *The Dance of the Dinosaurs*, October.

Newsweek: Richard M. Smith, Chairman and Editor-in-Chief; Mark Whitaker, Editor, for three reports by Joshua Hammer, *Suicide Mission: A Human Bomb and Her Victim*, April 15; *39 Days in Bethlehem*, May 20; *Code Blue in Jerusalem*, July 1.

The New Yorker: David Remnick, Editor, for *The Man Behind Bin Laden*, by Lawrence Wright, September 16.

The New Yorker: David Remnick, Editor, for *In the Party of God*, a two-part article by Jeffrey Goldberg, Part I, October 14 & 21; Part II, October 28.

Sports Illustrated: Terry McDonell, Managing Editor, for *Totally Juiced*, by Tom Verducci, June 3.

Public Interest

This category recognizes journalism that has the potential to affect national or local policy or lawmaking. It honors investigative reporting or groundbreaking analysis that sheds new light on an issue of public importance.

The Atlantic Monthly: Cullen Murphy, Managing Editor, for *The Fifty-first State?*, by James Fallows, November.

Golf for Women: Susan K. Reed, Editor-in-Chief, for *Ladies Need Not Apply*, by Marcia Chambers, May/June.

Harper's: Lewis H. Lapham, Editor, for *Ex-Con Game*, by Greg Palast, March.

National Review: Richard Lowry, Editor, for two articles by Joel Mowbray, *Catching the Visa Express*, July 1; *Visas for Terrorists*, October 28.

Newsweek: Richard M. Smith, Chairman and Editor-in-Chief; Mark Whitaker, Editor, for *Special Report: The War Crimes of Afghanistan*, by Babak Dehghanpisheh, John Barry and Roy Gutman, August 26.

Texas Monthly: Evan Smith, Editor, for *Death Isn't Fair*, by Michael Hall, December.

Feature Writing

This category recognizes excellence in feature writing. Whether the story is reported narrative or personal reflection, the award honors the stylishness and originality with which the author treats his or her subject.

GQ: Arthur Cooper, Editor-in-Chief, for *The Most Dangerous Beauty*, by Michael Paterniti, September.

Harper's: Lewis H. Lapham, Editor, for *Horseman, Pass By*, by John Jeremiah Sullivan, October.

Men's Journal: Sid Evans, Editor, for *The Survivors*, by Hampton Sides, April.

The New Yorker: David Remnick, Editor, for *The Real Heroes Are Dead*, by James B. Stewart, February 11.

Outside: Hal Espen, Editor, for *Terminal Ice*, by Ian Frazier, October.

Columns and Commentary

This category recognizes excellence in short-form political, social, economic or humorous commentary. The award honors the eloquence, force of argument and succinctness with which the writer presents his or her views.

Fortune: Rik Kirkland, Managing Editor, for three columns by Stanley Bing, *The Shareholders Are Revolting!*, June 24; *Log Off, You Losers!*, November 25; *Phoning It In*, December 9.

The Nation: Katrina vanden Heuvel, Editor, for three columns by Katha Pollitt, *God Changes Everything*, April 1; *Backlash Babies*, May 13; *As Miss World Turns*, December 23.

New York Magazine: Caroline Miller, Editor-in-Chief, for three columns by Michael Wolff, *The Big Fix*, May 13; *Facing the Music*, June 10; *I ♥ Martha*, October 21.

The New Yorker: David Remnick, Editor, for three columns by Hendrik Hertzberg, *Two Little Words*, July 15; *Manifesto*, October 14 & 21; *Too Much Information*, December 9.

Vanity Fair: Graydon Carter, Editor, for three columns by Christopher Hitchens, *Europe, Light and Dark*, July; *Jewish Power, Jewish Peril*, September; *The Maverick Kingdom*, December.

Essays

This category recognizes excellence in essay writing. It honors the eloquence, perspective, fresh thinking and unique voice that an author brings to bear on an issue of social or political significance.

The American Scholar: Anne Fadiman, Editor, for *A Piece of Cotton*, by Anne Fadiman (under the name of Philonoë), Winter.

The Atlantic Monthly: Michael Kelly, Editor; Cullen Murphy, Managing Editor, for *The Next Christianity*, by Philip Jenkins, October.

The New Yorker: David Remnick, Editor, for *Bumping Into Mr. Ravioli*, by Adam Gopnik, September 30.

Self: Lucy S. Danziger, Editor-in-Chief, for *I Gave Up My Breasts to Save My Life*, by Lauren Slater, August.

Vanity Fair: Graydon Carter, Editor, for *On the Frontier of Apocalypse*, by Christopher Hitchens, January.

Reviews and Criticism

This category recognizes excellence in criticism of art, books, movies, television, theater, music, dance, dining, fashion, products and the like. It honors the knowledge, persuasiveness and original voice that the critic brings to his or her reviews.

The Atlantic Monthly: Michael Kelly, Editor, for three reviews by Christopher Hitchens, *The Medals of His Defeats*, April; *The Man of Feeling*, May; *Lightness at Midnight*, September.

The Atlantic Monthly: Michael Kelly, Editor, for three reviews by Caitlin Flanagan, *Leaving It to the Professionals*, March; *What Price Valor?*, June; *Home Alone*, September.

Harper's: Lewis H. Lapham, Editor, for three reviews by Cristina Nehring, *The Vindications*, February; *Last the Night*, July; *The Unbearable Slightness*, November.

The New Yorker: David Remnick, Editor, for three pieces by Louis Menand, *Faith, Hope and Clarity*, September 16; *What Comes Naturally*, November 25; *Cat People*, December 23 & 30.

Vanity Fair: Graydon Carter, Editor, for three articles by James Wolcott, *Terror on the Dotted Line*, January; *U.S. Confidential*, June; *The Penance of Pirates*, October.

Profile Writing

This category recognizes excellence in profile writing. It honors the vividness and perceptiveness with which the writer brings his or her subject to life.

The Atlantic Monthly: Michael Kelly, Editor, for *Tales of the Tyrant*, by Mark Bowden, May.

GQ: Arthur Cooper, Editor-in-Chief, for *Lucky Jim*, by Elizabeth Gilbert, May.

Harper's: Lewis H. Lapham, Editor, for *The Boy Who Loved Transit*, by Jeff Tietz, May.

Outside: Hal Espen, Editor, for *Boy Wonder*, by Daniel Coyle, October.

Sports Illustrated: Terry McDonell, Managing Editor, for *Lying in Wait*, by Gary Smith, April 8.

Single-Topic Issue

This category recognizes magazines that have devoted an issue to an in-depth examination of one topic. It honors the ambition, comprehensiveness and imagination with which a magazine treats its subject.

GQ: Arthur Cooper, Editor-in-Chief, for its special issue *The Male Species*, May.

Popular Science: Scott Mowbray, Editor-in-Chief, for its special issue *Making America Safe*, September.

Scientific American: John Rennie, Editor-in-Chief, for *A Matter of Time*, September.

Technology Review: John Benditt, Editor-in-Chief, for its special issue *Energy*, January/February.

Texas Monthly: Evan Smith, Editor, for *Crime: A Special Issue*, July.

Design

This category recognizes excellence in magazine design. It honors the effectiveness of overall design, artwork, graphics and typography in enhancing a magazine's unique mission and personality.

Details: Daniel Peres, Editor-in-Chief; Rockwell Harwood, Design Director, for March, September, December issues.

Dwell: Karrie Jacobs, Editor-in-Chief (August, October); Allison Arieff, Editor-in-Chief (December); Jeanette Hodge Abbink, Creative Director, for August, October, December issues.

Esquire: David Granger, Editor-in-Chief; John Korpics, Design Director, for May, August, September issues.

Nest: Joseph Holtzman, Editor-in-Chief and Art Director, for Spring, Fall, Winter issues.

Surface: Riley Johndonnell, Editorial Director; Steven Baillie, Creative Director, for September, October/November, December/January issues.

Photography

This category recognizes excellence in magazine photography. It honors the effectiveness of photography, photojournalism and photo illustration in enhancing a magazine's unique mission and personality.

Condé Nast Traveler: Thomas J. Wallace, Editor-in-Chief; Robert Best, Design Director; Kathleen Klech, Photography Director, for September, October, November issues.

Elegant Bride: Deborah S. Moses, Editor-in-Chief and Creative Director; Daniel Chen, Art Director, for Spring, Fall, Winter issues.

GQ: Arthur Cooper, Editor-in-Chief; Fred Woodward, Design Director; Jim Moore, Creative Director; Jennifer Crandall, Director of Photography, for March, September, November issues.

National Geographic: William L. Allen, Editor-in-Chief; Chris Johns, Senior Editor, Illustrations; Kent J. Kobersteen, Senior Editor, Photography, for May, November, December issues.

Vanity Fair: Graydon Carter, Editor; David Harris, Design Director; Susan White, Photography Director, for April, May, November issues.

Fiction

This category recognizes excellence in magazine fiction writing. It honors the quality of a publication's literary selections.

Book: Jerome Kramer, Editor-in-Chief, for *Sorrow Comes in the Night*, by Dan Chaon, January/February; *Wonders*, by Owen King, May/June; *Evening*, by Beth Lordan, November/December.

The Georgia Review: T. R. Hummer, Editor, for *Space*, by Kevin Brockmeier, Summer; *Wings*, by Carrie Brown, Summer; *A Jeweler's Eye for Flaw*, by Christie Hodgen, Summer.

The Georgia Review: T. R. Hummer, Editor, for *The Owl of Minerva*, by Guy Davenport, Summer; *For Those of Us Who Need Such Things*, by Brock Clarke, Fall; *Three Girls*, by Joyce Carol Oates, Fall.

The New Yorker: David Remnick, Editor, for *Baader-Meinhof*, by Don DeLillo, April 1; *The Thing in the Forest*, by A. S. Byatt, June 3; *Jolene: A Life*, by E. L. Doctorow, December 23 & 30.

The New Yorker: David Remnick, Editor, for *The Prior's Room*, by Andrea Lee, May 6; *Fun With Problems*, by Robert Stone, July 15; *Drummond & Son*, by Charles D'Ambrosio, October 7.

General Excellence Online

This category recognizes outstanding magazine Internet sites. It honors the use of Web technology and design to display and build on the core strengths of a site's print counterpart, if any, or to create an entirely original "magazine environment" on the Web.

The Chronicle of Higher Education (www.chronicle.com): Phil Semas, Editor-in Chief

CNET News.com (www.news.com): Jeff Pelline, Editor

National Geographic Online (www.nationalgeographic.com/ngm): Valerie May, Senior Editor, New Media

Slate (www.slate.msn.com): Jacob Weisberg, Editor

Style.com (www.style.com): James Pallot, Editor-in-Chief

1966–2003 National Magazine Award Winners

General Excellence

1973	Business Week
1981	ARTnews
	Audubon
	Business Week
	Glamour
1982	Camera Arts
	Newsweek
	Rocky Mountain Magazine
	Science81
1983	Harper's
	Life
	Louisiana Life
	Science82
1984	The American Lawyer
	House & Garden
	National Geographic
	Outside
1985	American Health
	American Heritage
	Manhattan, inc.
	Time
1986	Discover
	Money
	New England Monthly
	3-2-1 Contact
1987	Common Cause
	Elle
	New England Monthly
	People Weekly
1988	Fortune
	Hippocrates
	Parents
	The Sciences
1989	American Heritage
	Sports Illustrated
	The Sciences
	Vanity Fair
1990	Metropolitan Home
	7 Days
	Sports Illustrated
	Texas Monthly
1991	Condé Nast Traveler
	Glamour
	Interview
	The New Republic
1992	Mirabella
	National Geographic
	The New Republic
	Texas Monthly
1993	American Photo
	The Atlantic Monthly
	Lingua Franca
	Newsweek
1994	Business Week
	Health
	Print
	Wired
1995	Entertainment Weekly
	I.D. Magazine
	Men's Journal
	The New Yorker
1996	Business Week
	Civilization
	Outside
	The Sciences
1997	I.D. Magazine
	Outside
	Vanity Fair
	Wired

1998	DoubleTake
	Outside
	Preservation
	Rolling Stone
1999	Condé Nast Traveler
	Fast Company
	I.D. Magazine
	Vanity Fair
2000	National Geographic
	Nest
	The New Yorker
	Saveur
2001	The American Scholar
	Mother Jones
	The New Yorker
	Teen People
2002	Entertainment Weekly
	National Geographic Adventure
	Newsweek
	Print
	Vibe
2003	Architectural Record
	The Atlantic Monthly
	ESPN The Magazine
	Foreign Policy
	Parenting
	Texas Monthly

Personal Service

1986	Farm Journal
1987	Consumer Reports
1988	Money
1989	Good Housekeeping
1990	Consumer Reports
1991	New York
1992	Creative Classroom
1993	Good Housekeeping

1994	Fortune
1995	SmartMoney
1996	SmartMoney
1997	Glamour
1998	Men's Journal
1999	Good Housekeeping
2000	PC Computing
2001	National Geographic Adventure
2002	National Geographic Adventure
2003	Outside

Leisure Interests (formerly Special Interests)

| 2002 | Vogue |
| 2003 | National Geographic Adventure |

Special Interests

1986	Popular Mechanics
1987	Sports Afield
1988	Condé Nast Traveler
1989	Condé Nast Traveler
1990	Art & Antiques
1991	New York
1992	Sports Afield
1993	Philadelphia
1994	Outside
1995	GQ
1996	Saveur
1997	Smithsonian
1998	Entertainment Weekly
1999	PC Computing
2000	I.D. Magazine
2001	The New Yorker

Reporting

1970	The New Yorker
1971	The Atlantic Monthly
1972	The Atlantic Monthly
1973	New York
1974	The New Yorker
1975	The New Yorker
1976	Audubon
1977	Audubon
1978	The New Yorker
1979	Texas Monthly
1980	Mother Jones
1981	National Journal
1982	The Washingtonian
1983	Institutional Investor
1984	Vanity Fair
1985	Texas Monthly
1986	Rolling Stone
1987	Life
1988	The Washingtonian and Baltimore Magazine
1989	The New Yorker
1990	The New Yorker
1991	The New Yorker
1992	The New Republic
1993	IEEE Spectrum
1994	The New Yorker
1995	The Atlantic Monthly
1996	The New Yorker
1997	Outside
1998	Rolling Stone
1999	Newsweek
2000	Vanity Fair
2001	Esquire
2002	The Atlantic Monthly
2003	The New Yorker

Public Interest

1970	Life
1971	The Nation
1972	Philadelphia
1974	Scientific American
1975	Consumer Reports
1976	Business Week
1977	Philadelphia
1978	Mother Jones
1979	New West
1980	Texas Monthly
1981	Reader's Digest
1982	The Atlantic
1983	Foreign Affairs
1984	The New Yorker
1985	The Washingtonian
1986	Science85
1987	Money
1988	The Atlantic
1989	California
1990	Southern Exposure
1991	Family Circle
1992	Glamour
1993	The Family Therapy Networker
1994	Philadelphia
1995	The New Republic
1996	Texas Monthly
1997	Fortune
1998	The Atlantic Monthly
1999	Time
2000	The New Yorker
2001	Time
2002	The Atlantic Monthly
2003	The Atlantic Monthly

430

1966–2003 National Magazine Award Winners

Feature Writing

1988	The Atlantic
1989	Esquire
1990	The Washingtonian
1991	U.S. News & World Report
1992	Sports Illustrated
1993	The New Yorker
1994	Harper's
1995	GQ
1996	GQ
1997	Sports Illustrated
1998	Harper's
1999	The American Scholar
2000	Sports Illustrated
2001	Rolling Stone
2002	The Atlantic Monthly
2003	Harper's

Columns and Commentary

2002	New York
2003	The Nation

Essays

2000	The Sciences
2001	The New Yorker
2002	The New Yorker
2003	The American Scholar

Reviews and Criticism

2000	Esquire
2001	The New Yorker
2002	Harper's
2003	Vanity Fair

Profile Writing

2000	Sports Illustrated
2001	The New Yorker
2002	The New Yorker
2003	Sports Illustrated

Single-Topic Issue

1979	Progressive Architecture
1980	Scientific American
1981	Business Week
1982	Newsweek
1983	IEEE Spectrum
1984	Esquire
1985	American Heritage
1986	IEEE Spectrum
1987	Bulletin of the Atomic Scientists
1988	Life
1989	Hippocrates
1990	National Geographic
1991	The American Lawyer
1992	Business Week
1993	Newsweek
1994	Health
1995	Discover
1996	Bon Appétit
1997	Scientific American
1998	The Sciences
1999	The Oxford American
2002	Time
2003	Scientific American

Design

1980	Geo
1981	Attenzione
1982	Nautical Quarterly
1983	New York

1984	House & Garden
1985	Forbes
1986	Time
1987	Elle
1988	Life
1989	Rolling Stone
1990	Esquire
1991	Condé Nast Traveler
1992	Vanity Fair
1993	Harper's Bazaar
1994	Allure
1995	Martha Stewart Living
1996	Wired
1997	I.D. Magazine
1998	Entertainment Weekly
1999	ESPN The Magazine
2000	Fast Company
2001	Nest
2002	Details
2003	Details

Photography

1985	Life
1986	Vogue
1987	National Geographic
1988	Rolling Stone
1989	National Geographic
1990	Texas Monthly
1991	National Geographic
1992	National Geographic
1993	Harper's Bazaar
1994	Martha Stewart Living
1995	Rolling Stone
1996	Saveur
1997	National Geographic
1998	W
1999	Martha Stewart Living
2000	Vanity Fair
2001	National Geographic

2002	Vanity Fair
2003	Condé Nast Traveler

Fiction

1978	The New Yorker
1979	The Atlantic Monthly
1980	Antaeus
1981	The North American Review
1982	The New Yorker
1983	The North American Review
1984	Seventeen
1985	Playboy
1986	The Georgia Review
1987	Esquire
1988	The Atlantic
1989	The New Yorker
1990	The New Yorker
1991	Esquire
1992	Story
1993	The New Yorker
1994	Harper's
1995	Story
1996	Harper's
1997	The New Yorker
1998	The New Yorker
1999	Harper's
2000	The New Yorker
2001	Zoetrope: All-Story
2002	The New Yorker
2003	The New Yorker

General Excellence Online

1997	Money
1998	The Sporting News Online
1999	Cigar Aficionado
2000	Business Week Online
2001	U.S. News Online

| 2002 | National Geographic Magazine Online |
| 2003 | Slate |

Best Interactive Design

| 2001 | SmartMoney.com |

Essays & Criticism

1978	Esquire
1979	Life
1980	Natural History
1981	Time
1982	The Atlantic
1983	The American Lawyer
1984	The New Republic
1985	Boston Magazine
1986	The Sciences
1987	Outside
1988	Harper's
1989	Harper's
1990	Vanity Fair
1991	The Sciences
1992	The Nation
1993	The American Lawyer
1994	Harper's
1995	Harper's
1996	The New Yorker
1997	The New Yorker
1998	The New Yorker
1999	The Atlantic Monthly

Single Awards

1966	Look
1967	Life
1968	Newsweek
1969	American Machinist

Specialized Journalism

1970	Philadelphia
1971	Rolling Stone
1972	Architectural Record
1973	Psychology Today
1974	Texas Monthly
1975	Medical Economics
1976	United Mine Workers Journal
1977	Architectural Record
1978	Scientific American
1979	National Journal
1980	IEEE Spectrum

Visual Excellence

1970	Look
1971	Vogue
1972	Esquire
1973	Horizon
1974	Newsweek
1975	Country Journal
	National Lampoon
1976	Horticulture
1977	Rolling Stone
1978	Architectural Digest
1979	Audubon

Fiction and Belles Lettres

1970	Redbook
1971	Esquire
1972	Mademoiselle
1973	The Atlantic Monthly
1974	The New Yorker
1975	Redbook
1976	Essence
1977	Mother Jones

Service to the Individual

1974	Sports Illustrated
1975	Esquire
1976	Modern Medicine
1977	Harper's
1978	Newsweek
1979	The American Journal of Nursing
1980	Saturday Review
1982	Philadelphia
1983	Sunset
1984	New York
1985	The Washingtonian

Special Award

1976	Time
1989	Robert E. Kenyon, Jr.

ASME Board of Directors 2002–2003

The American Society of Magazine Editors (ASME) is a non-profit professional organization for editors of print and online magazines that are edited, published, and sold in the United States.

ASME's mission is to:

- Bring magazine editors together for the exchange of information on matters of mutual interest

- Encourage and reward outstanding and innovative achievement in the creation of magazines and their content

- Disseminate useful information on magazine editing to magazine staff members and others

- Attract young people of talent to magazine editorial work

- Safeguard the First Amendment

- Defend magazines against external pressures

- Acquaint the general public with the work of magazine editors and the special character of magazines as a channel of communication.

ASME was founded in 1963, and currently has more than 900 members nationwide.

Permissions

440